Computer Supported Cooperative Work

For other titles published in this series, go to
http://www.springer.com/series/2861

Saadi Lahlou
Editor

Designing User Friendly Augmented Work Environments

From Meeting Rooms to Digital Collaborative Spaces

 Springer

Editor
Pr Saadi Lahlou
London School of Economics and Political Science, Institute of Social Psychology,
London, UK
CNRS-EHESS, UMR 8177, Centre Edgar Morin, Paris, France
EDF R&D, Laboratory of Design for Cognition, Clamart, France
s.lahlou@lse.ac.uk

ISBN 978-1-4471-2515-0   e-ISBN 978-1-84800-098-8
DOI 10.1007/978-1-84800-098-8
Springer London Dordrecht Heidelberg New York

British Library Cataloguing in Publication Data
A catalogue record for this book is available from the British Library

Printed on acid-free paper

Springer is part of Springer Science+Business Media (www.springer.com)

Foreword

This book aims at capitalizing and transmitting know-how about the design of Augmented Environments (AE) from some of the most prominent laboratories in the field worldwide. The authors belong to the RUFAE network (Research on User-Friendly Augmented Environments, founded in 2002) who meet in research seminars to share experience; Writing this book was perceived as an opportunity to look back over the last few years to sum up important findings; and formalize their approach and experience, which they never had the time or opportunity to do.

Although the authors of this book have very different backgrounds, striking similarities emerge in their approach and design principles: never-endingness, activity-orientedness, continuous design, realism are some of the pillars of this approach; enabling to deal with the complex, heterogeneous, multi-user and multi-purpose constructions which AE designers have to face.

The book illustrates how these principles enabled them to construct robust, efficient, and user-friendly Augmented Environments in spite of the many challenges to make these operational. We hope their experience will help the reader.

Primary audience: Academics, Students and Professionals involved in the CHI, CSCW, Ubicomp, Cooperative Building communities. Computer Scientists interested by end-users and applications, Social Scientists operating in the IT domain, IT & Organization Consultants.

Secondary audience: Developers of office and conferencing applications or middleware, Architects of office buildings, Space Planners, Designers; Facility Managers; IT, furniture & building Business Communities.

Contents

1 Augmented Environments and Design 1
Saadi Lahlou

2 The Stanford Interactive Workspaces Project 31
Brad Johanson, Armando Fox, and Terry Winograd

3 Towards a Global Concept of Collaborative Space 63
Vivian Loftness, Volker Hartkopf, and Azizan Aziz

**4 Designing an Easy-to-use Executive Conference
Room Control System** 87
Maribeth Back, Gene Golovchinsky, Pernilla Qvarfordt,
William van Melle, John Boreczky, Tony Dunnigan,
and Scott Carter

**5 Experimental Reality: Principles for the Design of Augmented
Environments** 113
Saadi Lahlou

**6 Co-design Approaches for Early Phases of Augmented
Environments** 159
François Jégou

7 Ubiquitous Working Environments 191
Carl Gustaf Jansson

**8 Psychological Methods for the Study
of Augmented Environments** 213
Valery N. Nosulenko and Elena S. Samoylenko

**9 Opportunities and Challenges for Augmented
Environments: A Distributed Cognition Perspective** 237
James D. Hollan and Edwin L. Hutchins

**10 The Aachen Media Space: Design Patterns for Augmented
     Work Environments**.. 261
     Jan Borchers

Index... 313

Contributors

Azizan Aziz
Senior Researcher, CBPD Carnegie Mellon University, Pittsburgh, PA, USA
azizan@cmu.edu

Maribeth Back
FX Palo Alto Laboratory, Palo Alto, CA, USA
back@fxpal.com

Jan Borchers
RWTH Aachen University, Aachen, Germany
borchers@cs.rwth-aachen.de

John Boreczky
FX Palo Alto Laboratory, Palo Alto, CA, USA
johnb@fxpal.com

Scott Carter
FX Palo Alto Laboratory, Palo Alto, CA, USA
carter@fxpal.com

Tony Dunnigan
FX Palo Alto Laboratory, Palo Alto, CA, USA
tonyd@fxpal.com

Armando Fox
UC Berkeley, EECS Department, Berkeley, CA, USA
fox@cs.berkeley.edu

Gene Golovchinsky
FX Palo Alto Laboratory, Palo Alto, CA, USA
gene@fxpal.com

Volker Hartkopf
Center for Building Performance and Diagnostics (CBPD), Carnegie Mellon
University, Pittsburgh, PA, USA
hartkopf@cmu.edu

James D. Hollan
University of California, San Diego, Department of Cognitive Science,
Distributed Cognition and Human-Computer Interaction Lab, CA, USA
hollan@cogsci.ucsd.edu

Edwin L. Hutchins
University of California, San Diego, Department of Cognitive Science,
Distributed Cognition and Human-Computer Interaction Lab, CA, USA
hutchins@cogsci.ucsd.edu

Carl Gustaf Jansson
Royal Institute of Technology (KTH), School for Information and Communication
Technology, Stockholm, Sweden
calle@dsv.su.se

François Jégou
Strategic Design Scenarios, Brussels, Belgium and Politecnico di Milano,
DIS Indaco Dept, Italy
francois.jegou@solutioning-design.net

Brad Johanson
Tidebreak, Inc., Palo Alto, CA, USA
bradj@tidebreak.com

Saadi Lahlou
London School of Economics, Institute of Social Psychology, UK
and CNRS-EHESS, UMR 8177, Centre Edgar Morin, Paris, France
and EDF R&D, Laboratory of Design for Cognition, Clamart, France
and Fondation Maison des Sciences de l'Homme/DEVAR/TeCog,
Paris, France
s.lahlou@lse.ac.uk, saadi.lahlou@edf.fr

Vivian Loftness
Professor of Architecture, Carnegie Mellon University, Pittsburgh, PA, USA
loftness@cmu.edu

Valery N. Nosulenko
Institute of Psychology, Russian Academy of Sciences, Moscow, Russia
valery.nosulenlo@gmail.com

Pernilla Qvarfordt
FX Palo Alto Laboratory, Palo Alto, CA, USA
pernilla@fxpal.com

Elena S. Samoylenko
Institute of Psychology, Russian Academy of Sciences, Moscow, Russia

William van Melle
FX Palo Alto Laboratory, Palo Alto, CA, USA
billvm@fxpal.com

Terry Winograd
Stanford University, Stanford, CA, USA
winograd@cs.stanford.edu

Chapter 1
Augmented Environments and Design

Saadi Lahlou

Abstract What are Augmented Environments (AE)? What are the trends? What are the main challenges? After a quick introduction, we summarize each chapter of this book. We also sum up a few ideas that are present throughout all the chapters and constitute the pillars of design for AE.

1.1 What's in This Book?

As we all know, the present trend is to make information and communication technologies (ICT) ubiquitous: they are now not only resident in computers, but also will soon reside in every appliances, piece of furniture, and products.

All objects of the World, and people too, are gradually being connected through the digital network: in the Internet of Things, by Home and Office Automation, and in socio-technical networks. Through chips and connectivity, everyday objects gain some agency which, supposedly, will make life easier for users.

The result of this trend is that we will soon live in "Augmented Environments" (AE), where physical objects of the world are augmented with ICT intelligence. Automatic doors already recognize users, Xerox copiers try to help the office worker fix minor incidents, vehicles are beginning to sense the driver's vigilance, personal computers (PC) become aware of the user's emotional arousal, etc. Soon washing machines will be able to have conversation with users and fellow machines. Cheaper sensors, decreasing cost of computer processing unit (CPU) and memory, progress in robotics, etc. feed the industry drive. Ageing, demand for security, safety, efficiency, reactivity, comfort, and entertainment feed the demand.

Thus, AE are the final result, as seen from the user, of devices and systems developed in the fields of "Ubiquitous Computing," "Disappearing Computer," Computer Supported Collective Work," "Pervasive Computing," "Haptics," "Context-Aware Computing," and, more generally, ICT.

S. Lahlou (✉)
Institute of Social Psychology, London School of Economics and Political Science
e-mail: s.lahlou@lse.ac.uk

S. Lahlou (ed.), *Designing User Friendly Augmented Work Environments: From Meeting Rooms to Digital Collaborative Spaces,* Computer Supported Cooperative Work, DOI 10.1007/978-1-84800-098-8_1, © Springer-Verlag London Limited 2009

Each of these ICT applications already presents human computer interaction (HCI) issues in itself. Now, from the user's viewpoint, these applications do not come separately: they come as a bundle, integrated as resources (and sometimes problems) in the physical environment, in offices, and in homes. They are experienced as AE, where each specific device or service is part of a larger functional whole, which constitutes the user's setting for activity.

The user arrives at a situation with his/her own motives, usually with the intentions of achieving some personal goals. Anything that gets in the way is a hassle; and especially devices that do not readily deliver satisfying results. Nobody wants to spend time in learning how to activate a reluctant system, reading complicated manuals, solving interoperability or format problems, etc. Car drivers no longer need to be skilled mechanics; in the near future, no user will accept the necessity of being a "computer literate" to operate a home or an office. When performing activity, users need to use both the physical and the digital artifacts in a seamless process; which object is augmented and which is not is irrelevant to them. What they desire is fluent and comfortable use.

This brings a series of serious problems to the integration of the systems and devices (in the physical world, in the user's everyday activity), which are unsolved. Designing efficient and comfortable "user-friendly" AE is a multidisciplinary challenge, involving technical issues with respect to infrastructure and technology as well as psychological and social issues. A successful AE is the combination of several layers: building's architecture, technical infrastructure, IT equipment, interior design, network and provider, services, support and maintenance, activity organization, user practice and expertise, and institutional support and control.

The final quality of the AE results from the *integration* of these different layers, which call for different specialists: architects, designers, computer scientists, psychologists, engineers, social scientists, etc. Specific design methods must be applied.

The authors of this book share a deep experience in developing, running, evaluating, and promoting such environments, because they have built and used actual AE, mostly workspaces. They are all members of the RUFAE[1] network, which connects some of the most advanced AE "living laboratories." These labs face many real life issues, from funding to long-term maintenance, and discuss them in a monthly seminar, which takes place in a multiplex videoconference connecting their augmented meeting rooms (Fig 1.1).

The goal of this book is to formalize and share our experience of this topic. The state of the art is not yet mature enough for a text book, even though most of us teach the topic in academic settings.

A considerable part of the material proposed here is new. The book gathers, summarizes, and puts into perspective material that was until now dispersed in often hard-to-access conference proceedings and grey literature.

---

[1] We founded the RUFAE "Research on User-Friendly Augmented Environments" in 2002. Figure 1.1 shows the initial participants.

Fig. 1.1 The Paris meeting of the RUFAE network in July 2003 in the Laboratory of Design for Cognition at EDF R&D. From *left to right*: Saadi Lahlou (EDF R&D), Norbert Streitz (Fraunhofer-IPSI), Jim Hollan (UC San Diego), Jan Borchers (RWTH Aachen), Calle Jansson (Stockholm University and KTH), Volker Hartkopf (Carnegie-Mellon University), Valery Nosulenko (Russian Academy of Science) wearing a subcam, and Terry Winograd (Stanford) in screen capture lower left, participating in videoconference

Our first target is the public of ACM conferences like CHI, CSCW, Ubicomp, and more generally those who are concerned with the application of ICT, at HCII, HFES, for example, and this includes students.

Our secondary target is the professionals (consultancies, corporate clients) involved in the decision process and construction of AE in large organizations. This book is for these professionals and for the students in these professions; it is also for the researchers and consultants who will be involved in the study and evaluation of such environments.

The authors' approach is grounded on actual experience: they have designed, and operated, real augmented workspaces that are in use daily (no vapor-ware here); hereby gathering a unique know-how funded by many grants. They summarize lessons learned over years of actual practice in actual AE, some of which are now "classic places." This encompasses the various aspects of design, maintenance, improvement, and even selling of AE environments.

The chapters go beyond computer science: Architecture, behavioral theories (activity, distributed cognition, cognitive attractors), patterns for knowledge transmission, models of innovation and behavioral control are also encompassed, because this is what designing AE is about. Computer scientists, architects, designers, space planners, facility managers, hardware and software designers, system engineers, service providers, managers, human resources, and end-users may be all, at some point, involved in the design of such environments. For all these stakeholders, who are usually specialized in only one or two layers, the main difficulty is to get hold of the complexity, to understand the perspective of the specialists of other layers, and to keep a coherent vision of the whole system. Special effort has been made to

avoid technical or disciplinary-narrow descriptions, so as to make the book accessible
to this multidisciplinary audience.

Although many aspects of what is discussed in this book are also relevant for
homes and public spaces, this book focuses on workplace applications.

1.2 The Goal and the Challenge: Make it Useful and Usable

AE is the product of the interplay of several layers with the physical environment:
computing (ubiquitous computing), networks (pervasive networks), services, and
data. This produces embedded "ambient intelligence": capacity of sensing, processing,
remembering, and communicating in any place. "Ambient intelligence" is a designer's
perspective. From the user's perspective, it is AE. By the way, we shall see that Ambient
Intelligence may not be always what the user wants, and that *obedience* may often
be preferred to *intelligence*.

Users do not know how refrigerators or TVs work from a technical point of
view; nor will they know how Wifi, RFID, sensors, and robots work. They do not
really want these systems and devices to take too much initiative and power either.
They do not operate these systems, nor cooperate with them: they use them.

Designing good AE is therefore a matter of supporting the user's goals and
activity more than a matter of clever programming. What we need to do is not to
write good code, but to deliver useful and usable environments to users.

1.3 Challenges

AE are by nature open to the network and connected. Because of this nature, a
series of design issues emerge, which make the problem different from the design
of isolated physical artifacts or stand-alone systems. These issues are never-endingness,
openness, heterogeneity, relation with users and socio-technical emergent effects,
and privacy. These issues make Dissemination, Operations, Maintenance, and Evolution
(DOME) become tricky. They also come back to a deeper philosophical problem,
that is the degree to which the AE will be independent of human operation (wizardless
environments, Winograd's "semantic Rubicon" cf. Chap. 2, and the trade-off between
the three levels of behavioral control described by Lahlou in Chap. 5 and in Lahlou,
2008a). This philosophical problem produces immediate design issues.

We describe these issues further. Solutions are proposed in this book: principles
for specifications, for architecture, and for design.

1.3.1 Never-endingness

AE design and management will usually be a daunting task because it is never-ending.
This is quite easy to understand especially for conference rooms: a meeting room

needs connectivity and interoperability with other meeting rooms, often outside the organization. This means that it will have to cope with environments that run new versions of the software; engage in new functionalities, for example, growing resolution or speed of videoconferencing systems, use new releases of your nonfavorite OS, other norms for tags, languages that are not compatible with your own hardware keyboards, etc. These other rooms are hidden behind a maze of fast-evolving security procedures, which are not accommodated by your own communication system; distant participants have different rules, codes, habits, ontology. Multiply the issues that you encounter with continuously updating your own PC by an unknown factor, and you get the idea. Of course, the decisions of change are distributed over vendors and organizations upon which you have no control, but your users want to get connected anyway.

You may decide to keep your environment fixed because it is easier for the maintenance people, but this only isolates you from the rest of the world, and so the augmented room loses its purpose. There are solutions, though: read this book!

1.3.2 Openness

Openness is another face of the never-endingness issue. The AE must be open to incoming visitors who come with their own system and to nomadic users who carry embarked devices and systems that have limited capacity. Jansson provides powerful vision for this in Chap. 7. AE must be tolerant to these challenged users and host them gracefully. Fortunately, the solutions for this aspect of openness are quite similar to those for never-endingness.

But another aspect of openness is to let users enter the AE, whether physically or through the network. This has to do with security and is more complex to deal with because it combines physical and digital solutions. There is also a classic trade-off between security and usability. Too often, AE environments die because they are locked too tightly. For example, some meeting rooms will be physically difficult to access because of cumbersome reservation procedures or impenetrable firewalls.

Some of these issues are addressed by digital authentication processes, and others by organizational rules.

1.3.3 Heterogeneity

There is no such thing as an all-devices-of-a-single-brand AE. Such an environment would soon become obsolete. One cannot expect users to throw away all their legacy equipment for each new release of one of the elements, or when one buys a new subsystem. Therefore, AE must accommodate a diversity of norms, vendors, and communication systems in their current operation protocols and in their updating or repair protocols. Some types of architecture and procurement strategies can help to sort out this issue.

1.3.4   Relation with Users and Socio-technical Emergent Effects

As SMART Technologies' senior engineer Gerald Morrison pointed out in a recent workshop,[2] ownership of the room is one of its most critical features. Without an identified owner, AE die. As Hollan and Hutchins point out in Chap. 9, cognitive systems include both artifacts and humans, and AE can work only if the suitable sets of social and institutional rules, representations, and competence of the users are coherent with the systems' technical specifications and processes. For example, the role of meeting animators or secretaries does change in augmented meeting rooms; fluid cooperation involving AE can take place only if users perform the adapted practices. These practices, rules, and representations are emergent, that is, they do not exist, and are even unimaginable, before the actual AE are there. Take, for example, the rules of netiquette, without which life on the net would be even more difficult. Could we have coined them in 1990, when the Internet was in infancy? This means, as we shall see, that design of AE will have to encompass more than computer systems and devices alone. Back et al. provide insightful and grounded examples of these issues in Chap. 4.

1.3.5   Privacy

AE potentially have the capacity of tracing all events they host. The dangers are the classical privacy threats of being continuously monitored by somebody or something that will use the knowledge gathered on us for its own benefit, and eventually at our own expense. Or that the system simply goes wrong and interferes with our life.

As we demonstrate elsewhere (Lahlou 2008b), ubiquitous activity logging combined with powerful data-mining techniques enables a third party to be aware of past, present, and to some extent, future actions of individuals, with serious threats to privacy. Benefits of AE are clear: as users we can get customized service, relevant offers for goods services, or transactions; as suppliers we can target potential users. We can get continuous assistance by machines or humans: more safety, more security, more comfort and more fluid interface. This is why we should design AE, especially in the workplace, to be respectful of privacy.

---

[2] UbiWORK@Ubicomp: design and evaluation of smart environments in the workplace.(Maribeth Back, Scott Carter, Saadi Lahlou, Kazunori Horikiri, Gerald Morrison, Masatomi Inagaki, organizers.) Ubicomp 2008, Seoul, South Korea, September, 21, 2008.

In private life, experiences show that some degree of benign lie or denial may bring better social experience. The essence of politeness is often in pretending to ignore some facts which we know, and leave the other the possibility of choosing the face s(he) present to us.

So here's the privacy dilemma: good interaction requires disclosing personal data. The problem is that these data may be used later in another context and against our interest. Lahlou (2008b) makes an extensive analysis of the issue and comes out with the "Privacy as Face-Keeping" principle. Using an Asian social construct ("face"), he shows how privacy breach is often a matter of being shown with the wrong face in a given situation. This happens, for example, when data collected in another context surface in an irrelevant manner and compromise the "face" the person is wearing at that moment. Hence comes the idea of tailoring the systems, so that they actively support the user in keeping the face (s)he wants to wear in this given interaction.

But there are also larger scale dangers for culture and organizations: subjects who are aware of being constantly monitored and having their actions traced will tend to behave exactly according to the rules, in what is called "agentic" manner. This produces rigid, bureaucratic, and maladapted operation of the global organization. Every manager or administrative expert knows this basic rule of organizational sociology that there is a gap between what is actual and "prescribed" behavior, and that this gap is necessary. Lucy Suchman provided some spectacular examples even in the apparently rather formalized domain of accounting (Suchman 1983): the nature of activity is rather to reach the goal with the constraint of respecting the rules, than to follow a rigid procedure. No rule can exactly encompass the complexity of reality; there is a need for some free space of initiative when one should have to "adapt" the rules to be more efficient. Besides, expert professionalism and responsibility include precisely the capacity of playing with the rule when necessary. Minute tracing of every step of professional's activity may result in people rigidly applying the procedures without consideration of the goals and results.

To avoid these problems, the European Disappearing Computer Privacy Design Guidelines (Lahlou and Jégou 2003; Lahlou 2008b) should be applied. These guidelines, developed with funding of the European Community in the framework of a research program of "disappearing computing" (DC), are a set of recommendations in this direction, which complement the more classic OECD rules on data protection. The most important is number 4, the "privacy razor." The nine recommendations are given below.

1.3.5.1 Think Before Doing

Evaluate potential system impacts. The very nature of a system or its parts may contrary privacy in their intention. Privacy issues should always be discussed in specifications. Discuss with clients/stakeholders specifications you think are questionable from a privacy standpoint. Designers as humans have freedom of speech and a social responsibility. Be responsible; you may refuse contribution to some systems.

1.3.5.2 Revisit Classic Solutions

Search for existing solutions in the physical world or in old systems for a similar class of problem/service, and understand the way in which new technologies change the effects of classic issues. Most emerging privacy issues (identification, transaction, control, payment, access keys, codes, etc.) have been socially resolved in other "classic" settings. They may not always be reusable, but sometimes transposing these solutions or their mental model may capitalize on experience, minimize surprises, and make systems more familiar to the human users. Location of data or devices (who holds what) in these classic solutions is often a crucial feature for privacy.

1.3.5.3 Openness

Systems should give human users access to what they do, do it, and do nothing else. Help human users construct a valid and simple mental model of what the system does. Goals, ownership, and state of system should be explicit, true, and easily accessible to human users, in a simple format. What the system does especially concerns here the final destination of data gathered by the system.

Each system should display, upon request, the list of variables required from the human user for operation (cf. below, "Privacy razor"). Display of user profile should be a systematic design option. This possibility should be restricted to the user only for his/her own data (protecting data is an obligation, consider encryption).

Beware: excessive verbosity of systems and excessive notice to users without demand provoke bypass and are unrealistic. Openness is a goal and the possibility for the willing user to access his/her data in the system; it does not mean systematic notice.

Open source is a guarantee of transparency.

When "system" is another human user (live, mediated by communication system), disclosure should be symmetrical.

System state should be accessible on demand as display and as data.

1.3.5.4 Privacy Razor

Human user characteristics seen by the system should contain ONLY elements necessary for the explicit goal of the activity performed with the system. No data should be copied without necessity. In case of doubt, remember that further information may be added in the context when needed.

During design, *privacy reduction* consists in examining each of all variables describing user-face, and trying to eliminate as many as possible. Identity is seldom necessary. The best system is the one so lean that nothing more could be taken away. Ideally, Client should "display minimal characteristics," and System should "require minimal characteristics" to operate.

This includes display issues (display needs no copy; prefer displays on the user's devices). Hardware sometimes copies data in cache or buffers: implement erasing procedure.

This is a hard guideline; it imposes a very clear vision of the system's functionalities and is far from current practice. The list of variables should be made in any case, and the choice left to the user for providing nonnecessary data.

When appliances are embedded into larger systems, the privacy razor helps clarify which application gathers data for what. It may be a legitimate design choice to bypass locally the privacy razor rule for better global operation; consider the sensitivity of data at stake.

1.3.5.5 Third-party Guarantee

Using a neutral or trusted third party may open more solutions or lighter design. It may enable entitlement, validation, control, claim, archive, etc. without direct data transfer between system and human user. In case of third-party involvement, give the user choice.

Using simultaneously three keys (human user, system, third party) enables transactions in which each party can impeach the transaction, and future cancellation of entitlement is possible.

Access rights to the services provided by the system may be granted through tokens. Token validation or verification should be possible only with the human user's agreement; avoid direct identification of human user by system.

Third-party guarantee may prove useful to enable recovering from incidents (client claims with lost tokens, local system failure, identity theft issues, etc.), without imposing to collect extra local data capture within the system "in case for such incidents."

1.3.5.6 Make Risky Operations Expensive

No system is one hundred percent privacy safe. Human users should be made aware of which operations are privacy sensitive.

Operations identified as privacy sensitive should be made costly for the system, the human user, and the third party.

This is a general design guideline here also intended to make the operation costly and difficult to be done on a large scale for computer agents. Systematic cost (a few cents or small time delay) or mere obligation of tracing the record of who accessed the data may be a high enough cost to discourage potential abusers.

In some cases this guideline can be dangerous (e.g., access to medical data in emergency situations). Consider exceptions and plan solutions (e.g., third-party control).

1.3.5.7 Avoid Surprise

Human users should be made aware when their activity has an effect on the system. Acknowledgement should be explicit for irreversible major changes. Cancellation should be an option as much as possible, not only in the interface but also in the whole interaction with the system.

This is a general design guideline, but crucial in DC, where user awareness is lower.

System should display a response to human user's action if it has an influence on their state, and display major changes of state. Traces of these acknowledgements should be recorded on system and recordable by user. Be aware of the trade-off between cognitive overflow and awareness; enable customizing default acknowledgements.

Technical and social solutions exist to make default privacy level choices without overloading the user with acknowledgement demands. Consider P3P.

1.3.5.8   Consider Time

Expiry date should be the default option for all data. Expiry delay is often fixed by law. Use common sense. User benefits should be proportionate to risks.

Saving data is often a design choice for reasons not directly relevant to the services provided, for example, security against system crash, cache, resource optimization, or design simplicity. These design issues are legitimate but should be considered separately and resolved in relevant ways.

It makes a big difference to plan oblivion, even in the long (legal) term. Privacy issues may arise from traces of what users did long ago in former social positions.

The DC design case is quite specific: leave long-time record to legal systems. In case of doubt, be on the user's side.

1.3.5.9   Good Privacy is Not Enough

Safety, security, sustainability, equity... are important issues with which trade-offs may have to be considered. These trade-offs should be discussed with stakeholders or their representatives as much as possible.

The designer's point of view is always limited. Most rules are social compromises. Make explicit the trade-offs between privacy and other issues (e.g., reciprocity, emergency access, global security) and trace design choices for further discussion with stakeholders, and for future updates: new technologies may enable a better solution to the trade-off.

Things change. New issues appear. Make sure human users are empowered to feed back and complain by implementing the function in the interface.

These guidelines are complementary of the classic OECD privacy guidelines; they may be incomplete and sometimes difficult to implement; nevertheless they should be reviewed as a checklist early in the design process.

1.3.6   Design Process Issues

Finally, beyond the issues connected with the AE themselves (what are the specifications for good AE) there are technical issues to feed the design process per se. Designing AE needs, as we shall see, specific observation techniques and theories (Hollan and Hutchins); new techniques for involving user participation (Lahlou, Jégou), specific evaluation methods (Nosulenko); tools to support stakeholder decision (Loftness et al.); formats for capitalizing and transmitting knowledge (Borchers). Key theories (activity theory, activity patterns, distributed cognition, affordances, cognitive attractors, etc.) will be presented, and relevant bibliography provided.

1.4 Overview of the Book Chapters

Each chapter highlights some specific aspects of designing AE: failure-resistant and adaptive middleware (Stanford, Chap. 2), flexible infrastructure design (Carnegie-Mellon, Chap. 3), progressive design with users (FX-PAL, Chap. 4), hands-on design (EDF R&D, Chap. 5), quick prototyping and scenario-building (Politecnico di Milano, Chap. 6), ubiquitous collaboration (KTH, Chap. 7), user perception evaluation (Russian Academy of Science, Chap. 8), distributed cognition and digital cognitive ethnography (UC San Diego, Chap. 9), design patterns for functions (Aachen RWTH, Chap. 10).

1.4.1 The Stanford Interactive Workspaces Project

(Brad Johanson, Armando Fox, Terry Winograd, Stanford University)
Terry Winograd's group is one of the most famous and a pioneer in the domain. Many innovations took birth in the mythical iRoom, located in the basement of the Gates Information Sciences Building at Stanford. In this iRoom, many a now prominent manager of the IT industry presented their work as a student or as guest during one of the weekly lab meetings, while a laid back but attentive audience chewed tacos or Asian food. In this chapter, Brad, Armando, and Terry present the philosophy of system design they applied in the augmented meeting room project called "Interactive workspaces." This philosophy is illustrated by the architecture of the iROS infrastructure (Johanson et al. 1993) which has inspired many office and home automation systems since then.

Winograd's team originated the terms fluid (use) and graceful (degradation) in the ICT vocabulary. The system must not stand between the user and use should be as "invisible and effortless" as the use of natural language. These terms characterize the user experience they try to attain; and in contrast, their design approach for the system is robustness, heterogeneity, commercial-off-the-shelf, dynamism, and multiplicities. In other words, the system presents the user an elegant, transparent, and seamless face, precisely because it is built with harsh design assuming that equipments and device are diverse, will continuously fail without warning, use incompatible formats, will have difficulty to communicate, will be switched off or plugged in brutally, etc. Their design philosophy is a realist pessimistic one. It assumes the worse *will* happen and prepares for it. Actually, blind and savage reboot is a preferred solution to solve some issues. Their architecture is designed for failure management, and system crash recovery is part of the specification:

> [iROS] assumes that transient failures will be common in any heterogeneous collection of
> hardware and software components; and wherever possible emphasizes ease of development

or prototyping rather than striving for an optimal but necessarily ephemeral "packaged" solution to a problem.

This is obtained by an original computer architecture that will not be described in detail here because it is done with perfect clarity in their chapter. iROS acts as a meta-operating system ("overface") that integrates, in a seamless way for the user, the underlying "babelian" herd of heterogeneous systems and devices. iROS pioneered several ideas, like the Event Heap, and proved to be remarkably robust. Years after its first implementation, it is still a source of inspiration for programmers and many of its aspects can be directly used in new designs.

The Stanford group's paper focuses on three aspects of their work: interaction design for augmented spaces; robust flexible infrastructure for integration; empirical studies on collaborative work.

The group is well known for seminal work on collaboration systems using huge (vertical or horizontal) large displays and multiple displays. The account given of the history and design strategies of the development of some new classic work ("the interactive mural," which was the world's first high resolution interactive surface) are a vivid example of how a design strategy focusing on the user's tasks instead of on the device itself and "tackling disfluency in the design of the overall user experience" results in clever, robust, and long-lasting architecture surviving the continuous flow of change in the underlying technology. We shall find the same activity-centric philosophy in the Lahlou's and Nosulenko's groups, and in the light and fast design approach developed by Jégou.

User studies led Terry and his group to define some powerful design principles regarding the limits of computing in creating AE. The *boundary principle* is geographic. It "states that ubiquitous computing infrastructure should only allow interaction between devices within the bounds of the local physical space within which a human would assume devices to be collocated" – roughly, that the limits are the physical room. The *Semantic Rubicon* rule is that "users and social conventions take responsibility for actions, and the system infrastructure is responsible for providing a fluid means to execute those actions."

Terry's group approach, just as it accepted mechanical or software failure and instability as given that the system must cope with, is pragmatic regarding evolution:

> there is no such thing as a stable system when we are dealing with rapidly evolving technologies (...) some ability to smoothly and incrementally integrate and migrate to new technology must be provided (...). Consequently our designs focus not on solving "the problem" as we see it today, but on facilitating evolutionary progress into the future.

This principle of managing continuous change is a basic pillar of the design philosophy for AE (cf. supra "never-endingness"). It will appear again and again in the chapters, for example, at architectural level in the Loftness, Hartkopf and Aziz Chap. 3, where flexibility and adaptability of the space are key; in the experimental reality approach where a "mother room" is kept as a continuous testbed for integrating incoming new technology before deploying in the fleet of the company conference rooms; etc.

1.4.2 Towards a Global Concept of Collaborative Space

(Vivian Loftness, Volker Hartkopf, Azizan Aziz, Carnegie Mellon University, Center for Building Performance and Diagnostics)

The Center for Building Performance and Diagnostics (CBPD) is a pioneer team for adaptable workspace and "green" buildings long before these topics became fashionable. The team is a major intellectual reference and active player at international level (and especially in Asia) for green building development. The "Building as Power Plant" (Hartkopf 2001, 2004) originated there, as well as, long before, the concept of "grids and nodes" infrastructure for flexible environments, explained in this chapter. Their Intelligent Workplace (IW) building overlooking the Carnegie Mellon campus is the Mecca of architects interested in advanced flexible buildings to such a point that in order to contain the continuously growing flow of requests for visits, the team had to decide a charge for admission. Just as the iROS computer architecture stays modern and inspiriting years after its creation, the physical architecture of the IW remains as a cutting edge, thanks to some design principles that are described in this chapter. In a world of continuous technological change, it is comforting to see that good design is durable.

This chapter will prove especially useful for stakeholders who decide the installation of AE (e.g., top managers, space planners, facility managers), because it explains why there is no good AE without proper physical infrastructure at building level. Bad infrastructure makes it very difficult to build AE, and flexibility starts at architectural level.

In this chapter, Vivian, Volker, and Azizan first give us a functional vision of buildings and physical environments as enabling production tools and continuously renewable assets. They distinguish seven types of "places" to support collaboration:

1. Leadership places/amenities (LP)
2. Crossroads/circulation places (CP)
3. Service pubs/shared equipment places (SP)
4. Dedicated meeting places (MP)
5. Dedicated project places (PP)
6. Office collaborative places (IP)
7. Digital/electronic collaborative places (EP)

Each place supports different kinds of collaboration and provides different affordances for work. The chapter addresses the issues of the infrastructure layer underlying the computer architecture and the user services: the grids and nodes concept enables a modular and evolutive approach, while considerably limiting costs and user efforts in churn. As a daily user of this concept (the Carnegie-Mellon team designed the infrastructure of our experimental K1 building, described in Chap. 5), we can testify that (almost a decade after construction!) not 1 week passes without the occupants explicitly expressing enthusiast amazement at the comfort and efficiency of their design, as we use its affordances for flexibility. On the other hand, among the many "AE spaces" we visited, it was clear that most limitations of use actually came from the lack of some of the flexible infrastructure design advocated for by the CBPD team. It is now crystal-clear for us that applying the design principles of the CBPD team is a major added value for AE, and this is why this "architectural" chapter comes early in this mostly computer and cognitive science book.

The IW, completed and occupied since 1997, is a 700 m^2 living lab where all types of collaboration places are evaluated in a continuous work-in-progress. The goals are individual productivity and comfort, organizational flexibility, technological adaptability, and environmental sustainability. The grids and nodes concept for modular flexibility illustrates this philosophy. Interestingly, the design issues at physical level are very similar to those for software architecture. The vision developed by Vivian, Volker, and their colleagues are food for thought also for computer scientists. Some design principles are very similar to what was adopted by other teams: for example, while Winograd et al. set a Semantic Rubicon, where some actions have to be taken by the system and others by the user, the Hartkopf team also deliberately puts on individual users (instead of a global automated system) the task of setting their own ambiance parameters, and takes the corresponding design options (operable windows, workstation controls, and HVAC, etc.). In a similar way, the reconfigurable plenum acts as an overface separating a fluid plug-and-play user interface, and technically opens integration logic underneath. Some questions are refreshing for a computed science audience, for example, the issue of "decommissioning" the system and recycling its elements: how would we translate it for data or procedures migration in an AE context?

The notion of flexibility, continuous adaptation to a multi-vendor variety of components with different life-cycles, and failure management is central in the design philosophy:

> To avoid frequent environmental quality failures and long term obsolescence, it is critical to invest in user-based infrastructures that are modular, reconfigurable, and expandable for all key services – ventilation air, thermal conditioning, lighting, data/voice and power networks". (…) "Access in the "open" system and plug-and-play technologies allow for the complete component by component, or system by system change-out of technology, completely recyclable when and where necessary. These concepts also insure that the building is a renewable asset for its investors and will not become a straightjacket that eventually has to be discarded in whole or in part.

The chapter goes one step beyond these design principles and provides tools for AE stakeholders and decision makers by showing the links with work productivity. Good environments have an impact and this can be measured (e.g., West Bend increased productivity by 16% by moving into a new building). The CBPD constructed an online tool that enabled assessment of the potential productivity impact, in terms of ROI of various changes in different types of buildings/organizations, based on evidence from case studies, which are gathered in a worldwide database by continuous survey of the literature and projects. This tool (BIDS), as well as the survey tools and indicators set up by this group in the framework of the Productivity Protocol team at US federal level, will be both a resource to AE project leaders in their interaction with sponsors and a source of inspiration for designers.

Finally, even if this topic seems to be aside from present AE designers' preoccupation, it is interesting to note that this visionary team included this perspective as core in their vision from the start, as early as the 1980s. We may all be inspired to take this aspect into account at design stage immediately; and not wait until it becomes a compulsory aspect, which will have to be installed at higher cost in retrofit.

1.4.3   Designing an Easy-to-Use Executive Conference Room System

(Maribeth Back, Gene Golovchinsky, Pernilla Qvarfordt, William van Melle, John Boreczky, Tony Dunnigan, Scott Carter; Fuji-Xerox Palo Alto Laboratory)

The Fuji-Xerox research team in Palo-Alto is among the most productive groups in the domain. It is unfortunate that many of their works remain covered by industrial secret, and that few researchers are admitted to visit their augmented rooms; they work both on software and hardware. This chapter is more about the design process, and describes how they gradually constructed an Augmented meeting room for their executives, who have the daily issue of working with their colleagues in Japan (where there are also very clever and creative groups, and among other researchers, Kazunori Horikiri and Masatomi Inagaki).

The usable smart environments (USE) project is a quest towards the "no wizards" augmented conference room; the test users are executives, who are by force very demanding users who have no time to lose in interaction with a lousy interface. The USE conference room explores the idea of customizing the interface to the user's needs for smooth and fast operation.

The chapter first describes how the designers analyze the actual work flow of the user, and how the meeting activity is performed. Instead of trying to force the user into some new practice, the design process gradually constructs a custom system that fits the user's needs and makes the various steps easier, yet with very simple "one button" interface. The basic (off the shelf) elements are simple: two large interactive whiteboards, a videoconferencing system, an authentication system (biometrics, RFID), a PDA for control, and a tabletop screen console. How Back's group constructs a comfortable personal smart environment with these simple elements is a lesson of user-oriented design.

The initial idea is to understand the user's activity, and to design a system that will propose the user at every step "just one big button that would do the right thing." The solution is more flexible, but almost as simple as with a tabletop control that proposes the user very simple actions, in a timely and relevant manner. The architecture behind this is a series of web services. We find again here the notion of a simple overface for the user, with an interface based on activity analysis; this overface covers and commands a series of computer services and device commands managing the underlying devices, programs, and databases, which the user does not need to know the detail of.

Step one is an extensive ethnographic observation of the users' activity, here the cluster includes the main user, the executive, and his assistants and collaborators (and some interviews). This produced a taxonomy of different meeting types, situations, and types of supports (often PowerPoint and annotations), which are used to construct the specifications of the system. From these observations emerge the important parts of work of the executive: communication and relationship building. These are the crucial features the system must support, without interrupting the activity flow – being calm technology, as the late xerox chief technologist Mark Wiser called it.

These ethnographic studies are used to construct realistic scenarios, which are tested. Testing shows how much devil is the detail, and that fluid operation means considerable constraints on the form factor and of system response by the AE; for example, if the system is too slow to answer, the user will tend to repeat the command, and mess up (this is in fact a general case in AE). The case of designing the console, which is one of the main interfaces, is reviewed in detail, with the various solutions tested. This exercise is enlightening and gives a pedagogic demonstration of what applying good design principles means in practice. Going into detail of the underlying infrastructure and technical choices shows the rationale of the choice of using Flash as a consequence of design specifications. One may note that if a user-oriented approach had not been applied prior to development, another choice would probably have been made, which would then have been problematic and probably difficult to change.

Finally, the authors provide some insight into the future problems of accommodating mobile users and other directions of their work; they also raise issues about the way the AE system provides acknowledgement to the users' commands; as novice and expert users may have different expectations based on their experience of the system and their trust in it. This question is more general and highlights that not the only AE should accommodate different users, but that the same user will evolve with experience. Activity in AE is a coproduction between the system and the user, but the distribution of who/which does what should not be rigid, but rather flexible to adapt to different situations and users.

1.4.4   Experimental Reality: Principles for the Design of Augmented Environments

(Saadi Lahlou, EDF R&D and CNRS-EHESS)

The AE, described in this chapter, the K1 testbed, is unique by the size of investment and efforts which were put into it. A non-IT company (EDF) created a whole "building of the future" inhabited by real users for the sole purpose of designing efficient workplace to be scaled out in the company. The building itself is a giant *vivarium*, continuously monitored by powerful observation systems and a dedicated design team, the Laboratory of Design for Cognition (LDC). This initiative benefited from know-how of the whole rufae network. Flexible infrastructure was designed by the Carnegie-Mellon team (Hartkopf et al.), interior design by Jégou, and many of its IT systems are derived from other authors in this book, not to mention Valery Nosulenko and Lena Samoylenko being full-time residents during the 3 years it took to set up the observation protocols and analysis techniques.

The testbed houses environments that are used daily for real work by users from the large Clamart EDF R&D facility (staff: 2000), and especially the RAO augmented meeting room (several hundred meetings per year). This flux of natural users contributes to a continuous work-in-progress design process, "augmented reality." We created the concept of "mother room": RAO serves as the permanent work-in-progress testbed pushing the state of the art. When solutions reach a satisfying state they are scaled out in other rooms in the company, but keep on being updated in the mother room for further versions. This solves the never-endingness problem of AE design.

The chapter describes the history of decision making and DOME issues of the AE, including the organizational aspects. It explains the theories and techniques used for design, which originated in this team. "Cognitive attractors" theory accounts for the users being captured by the setting and being continuously sidetracked instead of doing what they intended (e.g., being captured by email). This model is also used in the team's design approach to "frame" the setting to empower users. New digital ethnography tools, the SubCam and the OffSats, enable detailed observation of activity in the information age. SubCams, wearable miniature cameras worn at eye level, are used to follow users in their "phenomenological tunnel" and spot problems in their daily practice, which are then addressed by design. OffSats (ceiling time-lapse cameras) capture the evolution of activity in the long run (months, years) and enable evaluating the long-term impacts of changes.

The chapter describes in some detail with many photos the architecture, flexible furniture, videoconferencing setting, augmented reality interface, and shared collaboration software. It provides a series of design principles: the "zero list" of usability requirements for IC collaborative systems; the three-layered strategy which distributes over three possible layers of mediating structures (technology, representations, institutions) the affordances and support for activity.

This testbed, which has been operational for over 8 years now, is used as a platform to deploy AE in the company, now not only in offices but in other domains (production, clients). We discuss the positive aspects of augmented reality, and the possible limitations to its extension in other settings.

1.4.5 Co-design Approaches for Early Phases of Augmented Environments

(François Jégou, Strategic Design Scenarios and Politecnico di Milano)

Jégou is mostly known for his work in international projects in the sustainability domain with the Politecnico di Milano group. As a member of the initial core of the rufae network, he accepted to deliver what is up to now the first and only written account of the techniques he and his group invented for quick design of product service systems (PSS), with examples of application in the IT domain, which were until now accessible only through hints in the grey literature.

Jégou describes two techniques that address the problem of involving the user in the generation of ideas. As he explains, there are two opposite strategies, each with its own problems. One can integrate users within the development team, but then users have difficulties "entering" the simulations of potential services, because they experience difficulty in understanding the potentialities from technical descriptions alone. Another strategy is to show early prototypes to users at specific phases of project cycle: but convincing prototypes are costly to make, and so designers self-limit to very few solutions.

Jégou describes two techniques. *Scenario co-design* and *Spot-experiment*. Both are quick-and-dirty, efficient, and compatible with tight resource constraints.

In Scenario co-design, the users co-construct general scenarios of potential use with a toolbox. In Spot-Experiment, the focus is on local elements of the future PSS, even though the PSS is yet undefined.

Interestingly, the general framework behind scenarios as used by Jégou is similar to Borcher's design patterns: a vision (how would it be if?), a motivation (what is it for?), a proposition (how could it be implemented).

In scenario co-building, a major point in Jégou's approach is the deliberately "cheap" rendering and open visualizations, in the sense that users can very easily act on the visualization and change it at low cost. An example is using PowerPoint slides where the participants can cut and paste preset elements or a physical mock-up where the elements can be re-assembled. In VideoSketching, users are induced into playing the scenarios as sketches with very minimal instruments (just as kids would play "pretend" with wooden sticks, cardboard boxes or anything they find at hand). This frees the imagination of users on what the form factor of the PSS could be and focuses on the realism of the social interaction. Video is used as a sketch board to trace these scenarios. This "cheap" approach encourages the team to multiply trials as each one is light and fast, and so it is easy to keep a critical distance and stay creative.

François provides many examples of illustrations in real projects. It appears that the general ideas he proposes can be used in many different ways, which the design team adapts to the circumstances.

The techniques provided here are useful because they take into account the real constraints of designers of AE, which is no surprise as the techniques have been partly developed through design experiences for AE. Among the specifics is making a mock up of AE, which makes sense for users.

As François points out:

> the degree of detail to which the product-services system must be operational to get a relevant evaluation from real users is very high. This means an enormous effort of recruiting users, installing the product-services system in real settings, comparing ex-ante and ex-post practice, gathering data with a high quality, processing and analyzing them, to finally obtain information. Moreover, this situation is extremely frustrating to the project team: user feed-back is slow, and arrives at a stage where basic design options are already taken, equipments bought, and emotional investment in solutions made. Therefore deep changes in the functional specifications are not anymore, in fact, acceptable.

Spot Experiments address this problem by testing subsystems of the global AE. The rest of the system is provided as general description of make-believe or by a Wizard-of-Oz. This light and fast approach enables testing some crucial points of the system to be designed without stopping the whole design (subsystems can be tested in parallel).

François also defines in this chapter the notion of "friendly user" (Jégou and Lahlou, 2003), which has been systematically applied in the LDC (cf. Lahlou 2007, and Chap. 5). Friendly users are users that have been selected for their capacity and will to cooperate in a constructive manner in the design process.

This notion is in line with François' and his group's approach: in the first phases of design, when the mock ups are fragile, the proofs for concept are still hesitant, the form factors are undefined, and the rigorous protocols of classic ergonomics are not applicable. More generally, Jégou's approach aims at enabling the trial of a very large array of potential solutions with the users, instead of focusing only on what the engineers imagined. The systems he proposes are most stimulating for the users; at the same time, they enable abandoning some design orientations very early in the process by showing that they would not yield good usability if continued, which saves time and money.

Although these techniques are applicable (and are indeed applied) in many other domains, they prove especially useful for AE because, as we know, technology makes almost anything possible, so what counts is selecting the proper scenarios of use and making them very fluid; rather than piling up lists of functionalities that remain unused.

1.4.6 Ubiquitous Working Environments

(Carl Gustaf Jansson, Royal Institute of Technology – KTH)

Calle Jansson's dynamic group is located in Kista, the Swedish Silicon Valley, but they have always had a large amount of international collaboration, and this openness and connectivity deeply influences the vision and habitus of the members of this group. For example, their i-Lounge augmented room (funded by the Wallenberg Foundation iSpace project) was designed in close cooperation with Terry Winograd's Stanford group and used for distributed seminars; when Calle's doctoral student Hillevi Sundholm stayed for 2 years at the EDF LDC, she set up an "i-coffee" ritual where the members of both labs could chat in van open videoconference channel connecting the two coffee areas on a regular basis. Hence it is no surprise the vision that Calle presents in this chapter goes one step beyond the classic augmented conference rooms and encompasses what is most probably the next step of work environments: a continuous, fluid workspace. This is coherent with the rise of nomadism enabled by ICT (Attali 2009).

Calle first comes back to the roots of the Ubiquitous computing paradigm and shows how the dissolution of computing and sensing power in the context, multiple interaction modalities, and parallelism will produce more human-centered interaction, and some blurring of the frontier between physical and virtual space.

In this framework, Calle's group focuses on creating collaborative environments for mobile scenarios, especially for the learning environments. One of the typical issues of such scenarios is managing how participants and devices enter or leave the system. Design issues focus mainly on the three following aspects: proactive services, self-configuration, and new ways of sharing resources in collaboration. Each aspect raises specific issues: context awareness, personalization, adaptability; discovery of resources, connectivity and synchronization, dynamic configuration; multimodal interface and display property (private/public). The fact that these augmented environments are used by a group of users and not one single person raises an enormous amount of design issues, and traditional HCI solutions must be revisited: for example, how do we share an input device like a mouse?

The chapter then describes the i-Lounge, the augmented room built at KTH. The i-Lounge is both a research environment where new solutions are tested and a work-space for students. It is constructed as a room within a room, and feels cozy because of a rich choice of materials and devices. The room is described in detail and a floor-plan provided, and Calle provides a scenario showing how the room affordances enable both (and simultaneously) group work and individual work. The i-Lounge runs on i-ROS, and the reader will not be surprised to find again here the application of a series of design principles that are also described in other chapters, which are used to combine in a rather transparent way to the user a series of technologies ranging from RFID to sound tracking. The methodology used is then described: scenario work, theoretical analysis, interaction design then prototyping, and user studies.

The chapter also describes other AE projects of the KTH group: *Fasade* (exploring the balance between reactivity and proactivity); Weblabs (education environments); FEEL (context-aware and ad-hoc functionality); ACAS (adaptive and context-aware services).

Finally, the lessons learned through this vast experience are summarized – in a clear and concise manner which makes my comments here superfluous: go and read!

1.4.7 *Psychological Methods for the Study of Augmented Environments*

(Valery N. Nosulenko and Elena S. Samoylenko, Russian Academy of Sciences)

If we want to design a user-friendly AE, producing a pleasant user experience, we need to analyze the subjective user perception of AE. How can we describe the quality of AE? This issue is especially difficult for AE, as quality is the result of an integration of many elements working together in a (more or less) seamless way: to which item can we attribute quality? What framework can we use to analyze interaction in complex environments?

Russian activity theory (RAT) brings a useful new perspective because it focuses on what motives and goals people have when they realize activities in such AE. RAT provides a framework to describe activity in terms of its structure. This focus on user activity provides a clear outline for investigation; RAT is presently gaining considerable momentum in the HCI community these days (e.g., Nardi 1996).

In this chapter we receive a description of RAT "from the horse's mouth," so to say. Valery Nosulenko and his colleague Elena Samoylenko are part of the original team set up by Boris Fedorovich Lomov at the Russian Academy of Science in the 1970s, which developed the Russian engineering psychology, and led its applications in aerospace and other industrial domains. As Lomov's assistant, it was Valery who toured the famous American scientist Don Norman around the labs and theories during his visit to the former USSR in 1979; our personal guess being that this exposure to RAT had some effects on Norman's theories.

In this chapter, we see more of the Russian ideas, namely the perceived quality approach developed by Valery, and partly based on RAT. This methodology has been mitigated with other theoretical influences (distributed cognition, social representations, cognitive attractors) in the last 10 years, especially in the industrial applications at the LDC (EDF R&D, France) where Valery and Lena were full-time senior researchers in charge of the evaluation protocols for several years.

Valery and Lena first present RAT, then the perceived quality methodology, and then illustrate with case studies.

RAT is anthropocentric: it considers activity from the perspective of the subject, where action is always intentional (it is aimed towards a goal, and directed towards objects-of-the-world). The goal is a conscious representation the subject has of the future situation to be reached; a goal is a local means of satisfying one or several more general motives. To reach the goal in the conditions given by the environment, the subject goes through steps ("tasks"); each one having its own aim (subgoal). Execution of some of these tasks might reveal problems and need conscious monitoring of motor and mental actions by the subject, while for some others the routine sequence of automatic actions is sufficient. When actions are automatic and are applied beyond conscious control (e.g., changing gear when driving a car, turning on the cooker, typing a password, etc.), they are called "operations." As we can see, RAT is tricky because the meaning of words may be different from mainstream Western psychology. RAT provides a framework to describe the various elements of activity, whether subjective (goals, etc.) or objective ("objects". In fact, in the philosophical foundations, Rubinstein gave the theory, everything is "objective" and can be scientifically measured, including "internal conditions" representations, evaluations, emotions, etc.) as these have some materiality as physico-chemical structures in the nervous system. But the techniques to measure them in AE context are mostly behavioral or verbal protocols.

Perceived quality approach is an operationalization of RAT, mitigated with communication theories and theory of mental image. The strategy is a fine grained description of activity, using the framework of RAT: elements of activity are isolated and described (goals, motives, aims, actions, operations), and also their subjective evaluation by the individual. Then, statistical techniques are used to characterize the objectively observed elements of activity in parallel with their subjective evaluation. In contrast to classical paradigms of investigation, the perceived quality approach begins with identifying the aspects of the object or system that are valuable for a certain individual in the course of the given activity. The strategy is to elaborate and empirically prove a number of hypothesis concerning those of its parameters that constitute a core of its perceived quality. It assumes that these aspects will be included into their perceived quality, and sets up a measurement system based on them as they appear in open-ended individual evaluations.

To analyze subjective experience, the analysis of verbal data constitutes an important moment in the approach. In a nutshell, this method consists of the following:

1. Obtaining a verbal description of what the user thinks (in very open terms) of performing the activity with the system to be evaluated
2. Extracting from the verbatim individual evaluations (e.g., "this one is faster than the one I have") and finding out all dimensions used for evaluation (e.g., fast/slow, light/heavy, clear/cluttered, etc.)
3. Constructing a database of evaluations where each of them is attributed to a specific point of activity (object, operation, etc.)
4. To make statistical analysis of the database using evaluation dimensions as variables (e.g., verbal portrait giving a profile of an object on all characteristics; comparison of objects, comparison of operations on different objects, etc.)

The *verbatim* are obtained by asking subjects to describe their activity as they perform it, usually by comparing the present situation with another (comparing two or more systems successively for the same activity, or comparing the "new" system with what their usual practice, etc.)

This description of the perceived quality of activity is useful in comparing different systems or versions of the same system with quantitative measures. It also enables discovering which dimensions are relevant for the user.

Moreover, it is important for design. By confronting the evaluations with moments of actual activity and their description by activity theory, we are able to see at what point in the activity a given impression of quality is constructed. For example, we shall discover for which subgoal or operation the artifact produces an impression of clarity or slowness in use. And it will then become obvious what affordances are at stake. The next step is redesigning the system to modify this affordance to better support the local goal. This is where, once again, activity theory brings a crucial contribution to efficient design by uncovering a functional basis to subjective perception.

As a personal note, I should mention that not only is activity theory a powerful design tool, but that we discovered that it solved the problem of "how to analyze video recordings of daily activities." Before using RAT, we were stuck by such trivial problems in digital ethnography as "how do we cut and index the tape into behavioral units." RAT provided us with simple units and criteria to do this division (tasks, operations…) and made our life simpler.

1.4.8 Opportunities and Challenges for Augmented Environments: A Distributed Cognition Perspective

(James D. Hollan and Edwin L. Hutchins, University of California, San Diego)

In AE, functionalities are, unlike in single artifacts, distributed in space on a series of objects and subsystems; also on different subjects especially when there is distant collaboration. This calls for a different theoretical approach.

The theory of distributed cognition is especially relevant for AE. In this chapter, Jim and Ed present this new paradigm, which they created, that is gaining considerable momentum in the scientific community. This chapter also describes cognitive ethnography, the techniques they use to investigate the behavior of subjects, in the wild and especially in AE. Jim and Ed work on varied AE, some in the office setting (and their Distributed Cognition and HCI Laboratory at UCSD has been involved in the development of a series of systems and interfaces for AE) and also in complex socio-technical settings such as plane cockpits or cars. Digital cognitive ethnography has been one core projects of Jim and Ed's laboratory. It capitalizes on new technologies, especially digital recording, and is of great interest for user studies in AE.

Distributed cognition "looks for cognitive processes wherever they may occur and does that looking on the basis of the functional relationships of elements that participate together in the process." In this perspective, the boundaries of the human body are not necessarily relevant: a cognitive process emerge in the interaction of several elements, and the processing of representations, for example, can involve the human mind, physical objects in the environment, and mediating structures such as rules or instruments. For example, Hutchins (1995) shows that an airplane cockpit as a whole (including the pilots) is the unit to be considered for the processing of the aircraft speed.

Ed and Jim highlight similar issues regarding analysis and design as do Valery and Lena (see Nosulenko and Samoylenko, Chap. 8), that is, the distribution of the elements of activity across people, space, and time.

> Cognitive processes may be distributed across the members of a social group. (...). (2) Cognitive processes may be distributed in the sense that the operation of the cognitive system involves coordination between internal and external (material or environmental) structure. (...) Processes may be distributed through time in such a way that the products of earlier events can transform the nature of later events.

This is in the nature of Culture as a large system of psycho-socio-technical behavioral control (see Lahlou, Chap. 5), but naturally it is a problem for designers who want to change the environment of activity and augment it with technology. To observe and analyze the cognitive processes across people, space, and time, not only do we need good theory, but also a special methodological approach and toolbox.

Cognitive ethnography is the science of studying cognitive processes "in the wild," and its main objective, in our context, is to understand everyday activity for "an improved functional specification for the human cognitive system." It is a set of techniques building on the opportunities of digital recording, from video to automatic computer logging of all activities by the user and his/her devices.

Jim and Ed provide five examples:

1. Following the driving activity by installing 10 cameras, and various sensors, in an automobile (and a SubCam on the driver) to design safer driving environments
2. Logging all the "activity trails" in a workstation with screen capture and event logging to create (among other things) better memory aid systems
3. Observing airline cockpits, in the wild and in flight simulators

4. Designing graphic aids for medical conversations between physicians and deaf
   patients
5. Using augmented paper

These examples show how technical progress (e.g., object recognition, new
visualization techniques, touch sensitive tables) can be put on use for both analysis
and design.

Finally, this article shows how, if digital technology is enabling the construction
of new and very complex AE where activity is distributed over space, time, and people
in a way that makes it more and more difficult to observe and design, fortunately
the problem also comes with part of the solution: digital technology enables digital
cognitive ethnography, an approach appropriate for the observation and design
of AE. Distributed cognition is a framework that helps analysts to make sense of
the huge amount of data gathered, and focuses the analysis on functional aspects
instead of individual devices.

1.4.9   The Aachen Media Space: Design Patterns
for Augmented Work Environments

(Jan Borchers, RWTH Aachen University)

In this chapter, Jan Borchers describes and illustrates a capitalization and
transmission technique for recommendations: *Design Patterns*. Design Patterns
capture good solutions installed in real AE. They describe the problem, extract the
principles of the solution and its gist, present them in a compact and easy-to-
understand format with an example. Borcher's patterns are the equivalent for AE
of the famous pattern language architect Christopher Alexander invented for
non-augmented buildings.

Each pattern has a striking name for easy reference, and it includes the following:

- A ranking of how critical this pattern is to solve the problem
- A picture of an implementation example
- The context for installation
- A short problem statement summarizing design tradeoffs
- A more extensive problem description
- The solution: a generic set of instructions
- A diagram
- References

Behind Jan's patterns is an enterprise he started at the end of last century
(Borchers, 2001), the intention to create a language that will enable better communication between users and designers based on a common vocabulary and
references where the relation of functional goals and technical solutions is
explicit.

Jan presents in Chap. 19 patterns of AE, roughly "in the order in which they are
faced when planning an AE."

This chapter has an immediate use for the reader: Jan took the trouble to visit the best Augmented workplaces and discuss them with their creators and managers (in some cases he did not have to go far as he was in charge of the Stanford lab during the sabbatical year Terry spent at Google). Not only do we benefit from the expert eye of one of the prominent specialists, but Jan's approach is especially critical and pragmatic as he was preparing his own Augmented space at the time. These patterns hereby provide some of the best design ideas across the Carnegie-Mellon Intelligent Workplace, the Stanford IRoom, the Stockholm KTH i-Lounge, the Fraunhofer-IPSI Ambiente room, the Paris EDF LDC, and of course Jan's RTWH Aachen Mediaspace. In fact, in the course of the rufae meetings to which all the contributors here adhere, ideas from the FX-PAL augmented rooms (especially the Kumo room), the UCSD DCog-HCI lab, and a few others are also incorporated in these design patterns. As these labs were constructed, they copied the good ideas from one another and suppressed what was problematic. For example, Hartkopf et al. were the architects of the EDF LDC building, where Lahlou also introduced ideas he had copied from Hollan's lab at UCSD; and in turn these ideas were implemented in the Aachen Mediaspace. We all hope that with this book and chapter these ideas will disseminate even more for more user comfort and efficiency.

Experience shows that facility managers are sometimes reluctant to apply new ideas (especially if they seem costly), and that professionals tend to replicate their ordinary routine, for example, for cabling. In this respect, Jan's chapter is again useful because it provides the reader with a format that will enable producing her own patterns, and give them to the various stakeholders involved in the construction of AE, ensuring that the vision is well shared. Too often, one of the stakeholders, because he does not fully understand the vision underlying the Augmented space, will ruin some affordances during the design or installation, for example, by implementing something too rigid in the infrastructure.

This principle of designing for flexibility and continuous change is a fundamental pillar in the approach of all other contributors to this book. "Display" is a movable commodity; network and power must be available anywhere and in a mobile way, etc.

A constant focus of Jan's pattern is on the sensorial aspects of the rooms as lived by the users: light, glare, noise or audio quality, etc. (we could add air quality, as shown by the Loftness et al. studies, the availability of fresh water and coffee, or even the view – refer to the IW and the LDC). Computer scientists should meditate these aspects, as they are not only important for the perceived quality of the space, but also because they have direct implication on what devices are usable or not: for example, Jan recommends LCD screen over plasma, laptops over desktop PCs precisely because of noise aspects.

1.5 The Pillars of AE Design

It is striking to see that, although the groups authoring these chapters are very diverse in origin, discipline, history, and institutional context, a few ideas keep being repeated throughout the various approaches. This is a case of what is called in Biology "evolutionary convergence": organisms with very different origin develop similar solutions to similar problems. For example, the eye of the Octopus is very similar to the eye of Mammals, although these species have traveled a completely different evolution chain. In our case, these design principles include never-endingness, activity-orientedness, continuous design, realism, and considering externalities.

1.5.1   Never-Endingness

A key principle is open adaptability. By this we do not mean that the systems would be like a Swiss army knife, so sophisticated that it can adapt to any situation, but rather that the system is always in a state of an incomplete and never-ending "work-in-progress," which should be designed to incorporate easily, seamlessly – and reversibly – new elements. The problem behind this answer is the fact that AE live in open environments that constantly evolve; and that their nature of communication platforms obliges them to be compatible with distant participants, visitors, etc. who all live their own life, enter the space with their own devices, and protocols. We cannot oblige all these users to convert to the local protocols, and this drags the AE in the general flow of ICT evolution, with the obligation to keep up.

This never-endingness has implications in the hardware and software architectures, for example, as follows:

- Using Commercial Off-the-Shelf elements so as not to be obliged to maintain one's own systems, and naturally benefit from the upgrades
- Adopting a software architecture with independent functional blocks and sub-systems which can easily be changed
- Making some "overface" to present the user one single homogeneous look-and-feel while managing transparently with each subsystem and device with its own protocol
- It also has implications in design, especially by replacing the traditional design cycle with a final deliverable by a design process with continuous upgrade

1.5.2   Activity-orientedness

As devices and systems evolve on a continuous basis and the possible combinatory is endless, and never-ended, the stable target that orients design (and evaluation) is not specifications of the system, but rather understanding the goals of activity. So activity-orientedness is somewhat opposed to "device-orientedness." Activity is the process of reaching goals in the conditions given, and in different conditions, with different affordances (e.g., with the new AE which we are designing) intelligent subjects or groups will change strategy; so "what they do now" is not a good basis for design orientation, but rather "what they want to achieve." Hence the focus on activity and subjects intentions is another pillar of AE design.

This translates into specific attention to the subjects' goals, an introduction of users in the core of the design team to make them participate in an "if/then" creative process rather than simply in the evaluation of prototypes. This also means using new theories and methods that are tailored for these purposes: activity theory, cognitive attractors, distributed cognition, ecological psychology. And also new powerful tools that enable diving into the activity to understand its motives, turning points, the economy of attention, the use of cognitive resources within and beyond the skin boundaries: cognitive ethnography, SubCams, perceived quality, group techniques, and also at scenario-building and prototyping stage.

1.5.3   Continuous Design

Continuous design is a consequence of the never-endingness of the AE systems. We need to invent new institutional, technical, and administrative formats. The idea that design phase would produce a finished product which will then be deployed and maintained in its "constant" operational state is obsolete.

The idea that the system would reach a stable state was of course always a fiction for all complex systems as there is always some evolution. But this evolution was slow, or marginal, or optional. This is not the case any more with AE: evolution is rapid, massive, and compulsory because these systems are entangled with other systems "out there," which undergo continuous and fast change. This Continuous design is probably the most difficult aspect of the new regime, because we have just reorganized our production and organizations in project mode, which is precisely not the good way to deal with continuous processes. By now, most organizations deal with the continuous design issue in some informal way. The existence of "wizards" attached to most operational AE is in fact a way to create this follow up project without admitting it openly. One at least of the teams has institutionalized this continuous design with the "Mother Room" concept of one site being sacrificed to be the continuous realist experiment where new solutions are selected.

1.5.4   Realism

Realism is another pillar of AE design. Realism is both a philosophy and a technique for design. Realism is some sort of active pessimism, which admits as a basic specification that the system will *always* operate in degraded mode, that devices will certainly fail at some point (but in an unpredictable way), that users will use the devices with different intentions than originally thought, that they will misuse and abuse the system, and that there is an unbridgeable gap between what designers imagine and what will actually emerge in real use. Realism is accepting these facts as inevitable, and to design the system in such a way that it can cope in a satisficing if not perfect way. It is also admitting that the openness and the never-endingness mean that the designer has only limited capacity, and therefore that the subsystem should be designed in a way that makes its continuous redesign easy.

As William, the Silent Prince of Orange, phrased: "Need not hope to undertake, need not success to persevere"[3]. Strange as it may seem, we have often experienced in designing AE that one should not stop because a challenge seems difficult on paper. In fact many of the things which seem impossible in theory are feasible in practice, with the help of users.

1.5.5   Considering Externalities

The technical system has limitations and boundaries; activity is a larger framework that involves users, social rules, institutions, etc. A final pillar of AE design is to integrate these external factors both as resources and constraints at the design phase, and consider them potentially in the realm of what can de redesigned, beyond devices and ICT. This means stepping back when constructing the vision and amending it, in order to distribute the affordances and mediating structures over the whole socio-technical system.

Winograd's Semantic Rubicon, which sets a limit to what is the responsibility of users vs. the responsibility of the system, is a perfect illustration; so are the data/lata approach of Lahlou. The design of AE considers the problem space as not limited to the set of devices, and searches for potential "non technical" solutions to some design issues, for example, social, psychological, or even legal solutions. This is, once again, a logical consequence of the open-nature of AE and their strong connection with the rest of the World as an installation for activity (Lahlou, 2008a).

1.6   Conclusion

Although the research groups who contributed the chapters of this book come from rather different disciplines (from architecture to cognitive science, from computer science to social psychology or design), tackling with the same issue of AE produced a similar philosophy. When designing AE, we saw that never-endingness, activity-orientedness, continuous design, realism, and considering externalities are good principles.

Now some final *caveats*. As designers, we often, in our enthusiasm, tend to focus on technology, but the ultimate goal of design is to provide user-friendly environments for people. Mark Weiser, a pioneer of the ubiquitous computing domain, advocated for "calm" technology (Weiser and Brown 1995), that is, one which enables us to focus on what is important while keeping us aware of what is peripheral. We must be careful to create an installation of the World that will not add extra burden on the user by bombarding the subject with demands and cognitive attractors (see Chap. 5).

---

[3]"Point n'est besoin d'espérer pour entreprendre, ni de réussir pour persévérer."

Supporting continuous surveillance is also a potential danger of AE; safeguards must be installed at design stage. The systems we create should at least follow the European Disappearing Computing Privacy Design Guidelines.

In this "Brave New World" we are contributing to build, we must be careful to keep the Humans at the center of the systems we create; one way to do so is to involve users in the design process.

References

Attali J (2009) *Brief history of the future: what the World will be in 100 years*. New York: Arcade Publishing

Borchers J (2001) *A pattern approach to interaction design*. Wiley Series in Software Design Patterns. John Wiley & Sons, Chichester, UK

Hartkopf V (2001) *The building as power-plant*. Center For Building Performance and Diagnostics, Carnegie-Mellon University. Concept Paper. http://www.arc.cmu.edu/bapp/Overview/Concept-Paper.pdf

Hartkopf V (2004) Building as power-plant. BAPP. *Cogeneration and Distributed Generation Journal* 19:2, 60–73

Hutchins E (1995) How a cockpit remembers its speed. *Cognitive Science: A Multidisciplinary Journal* 19, 265–288

Jégou F, Lahlou S (2003) *Design methodology report D1.3*. LDC, EDF. R&D, Dec 2003, p 17

Johanson B, Winograd T, Fox A (1993) Interactive workspaces. *IEEE Computer* 36:4, 99–103

Lahlou S (2007) Human activity modelling for systems design: a trans-disciplinary and empirical approach. In: Harris D (Ed.) *Engineering psychology and cognitive ergonomics, HCII 2007*. Lecture notes in artificial intelligence, vol. 4562. Heidelberg: Springer, pp. 512–521

Lahlou S (2008a) Cognitive technologies, social science and the three-layered leopard skin of change. *Social Science Information* 47:3, 299–332

Lahlou S (2008b) Identity, social status, privacy and face-keeping in digital society. *Social Science Information* 47:3, 227–252

Lahlou S, Jégou F (2003) European disappearing computer privacy design guidelines V1 [EDC-PG 2003]. Ambient *Agoras IST-DC report D15.4*. LDC, EDF R&D, Oct 2003, p 8. www.rufae.net/privacy

Nardi B (1996) *Context and consciousness: activity theory and human-computer interaction*. Cambridge: MIT

Suchman LA (1983) Office procedure as practical action: models of work and system design. *ACM Transactions on Information Systems (TOIS)* 1:4, 320–328

Weiser M, Brown JS (1995) *Designing calm technology*. Xerox Park. http://www.ubiq.com/hypertext/weiser/calmtech/calmtech.htm

Chapter 2
The Stanford Interactive Workspaces Project

Brad Johanson, Armando Fox, and Terry Winograd

Abstract The Stanford Interactive Workspaces project developed a set of technologies for integrating multiple devices in a co-located workspace, based on a few basic principles:

1. The interactions should maximize the potential for "fluency" of the users, reducing as much as possible the need to shift attention from the content of the work to the mechanism.
2. The integration should focus on commodity devices running existing operating systems and applications, so the workspace is not an isolated island. It should provide an "overface" that brings them together, rather than replacing the existing widely used interfaces.
3. The system should be loosely coupled and robust, so that failures and changes of individual elements are gracefully handled and do not disrupt the functioning of the overall workspace.

The project developed a middleware layer named iROS, based on these principles, which employed a mechanism called the Event Heap to provide robustness and dynamic loose coupling between the components. Other developments included PostBrainstorm, a large high-resolution pen-based display to facilitate group activities such as brainstorming, and a number of other tools that extended the iRoom capacities to new devices and interaction modes.

2.1 Introduction

The Stanford Interactive Workspaces Project has created and studied new technologies for integrated multi-person, multi-device collaborative work settings. In addition to our primary testbed, the iRoom, we have deployed a number of interactive workspaces

B. Johanson (✉)
Tidebreak, Inc., Palo Alto, CA
e-mail: bradj@tidebreak.com

S. Lahlou (ed.), *Designing User Friendly Augmented Work Environments: From Meeting Rooms to Digital Collaborative Spaces,* Computer Supported Cooperative Work, DOI 10.1007/978-1-84800-098-8_2, © Springer-Verlag London Limited 2009

at Stanford and at other institutions and evaluated their use in educational settings. The core technologies in these spaces are built around our software infrastructure, iROS, which provides a suite of tools for integration and interaction.

Within the broad field of ubiquitous computing, we have chosen to focus on co-located collaborative work, emphasizing large shared and walk-up displays using touch or pen interaction.

There are three major aspects to our research:

- Interaction design for shared computer-augmented spaces
- Robust flexible infrastructure for integration
- Empirical studies of collaborative work

This section describes our approach to each and highlights some of the results. More detail on the specific projects is presented in the subsequent sections.

2.1.1   Fluid Interaction in Ubiquitous Environments

When a person speaks a language fluently, the use of that language is invisible and effortless. The speaker's attention is on what is being said and on the interaction with other people, not on the language itself. Disfluency, on the other hand, leads to interruption and reflection. "What does that mean?," "How do I say that?," and "Why didn't they understand me?" Everyday interaction with computers is full of disfluencies, even for experts with long experience and deep knowledge of computing. Tremendous improvements can be achieved by tackling disfluency in the design of the overall user experience. Design concerns go beyond a particular interface or interaction device to encompass the setting, the user's background, and interaction with other people.

In a ubiquitous computing environment, computing appears in many forms, including interactive displays, handheld mobile devices, pads, wearables, and computers that watch and listen. Without careful design, this will be a Tower of Babel that requires users to operate in not one but several languages, all at the same time. Also, in an interactive environment, computers are a part of a dynamic that incorporates people and artifacts, with attention being shared among them.

In designing the interactive aspects of iROS, our focus has been on providing an integrated environment that allows the user's attention to remain focused on the work and people, rather than on the mechanics of interaction. We have started with a general kind of use that we call an "open participatory meeting." In this setting, a small group of people (up to a dozen) works together to accomplish a task, usually as part of an ongoing project. People come to the meeting with relevant materials on their laptops or saved on file servers in a variety of formats for different applications that will be used as part of the meeting. During the meeting, there is often a shared focus of attention on a "primary display," with some amount of side work that both draws material from shared displays and brings new material to them. In many cases, a facilitator stands at the primary display and is responsible for overall flow of the activities. Examples of such meetings we have supported and observed include our own project group meetings, student project groups in courses, construction management meetings, brainstorming meetings by design firms, collaborative writing courses, and design project group work in a variety of physical settings, including dedicated project spaces and walk-up group facilities.

Our interaction research has included three main components: the development of interaction techniques especially suited for large wall-based or table-based displays shared by a group; the design of overface capabilities that are used on top of the standard interfaces to provide access and control to information and interfaces in the room as a whole; and support for prototyping interactions involving new tangible interaction devices.

2.1.2 Robust Flexible Infrastructure for Integration

We have identified some key characteristics of practical Ubicomp environments that must be accounted for in any infrastructure designed to support such environments:

Heterogeneity: A variety of different devices will be used in the workspace, chosen for their efficacy in accomplishing specific tasks. In addition to desktop workstations, these include laptops and PDAs with wireless connections used in conjunction with shared displays, as well as physical and tangible technologies specially designed for Ubicomp settings. All these need to interoperate in spite of heterogeneity in software, including legacy applications, as it is infeasible in most cases to write new applications or versions just to take advantage of interactive workspace facilities. One of the main consequences of this heterogeneity is that the software framework must provide cross-platform support. From the HCI perspective, interfaces need to be customized to different sized displays, and possibly different input/output modalities such as speech and voice. The situation is even more complicated, in that interfaces will span multiple devices that come and go dynamically in the space.

Dynamism: Interactive workspaces are dynamic on both short and long time-scales. On short time scales, individual devices are turned on and off, wireless devices enter and exit the space, and pieces of equipment may break down for periods of hours or days. On longer timescales, workspaces will incrementally evolve as devices are introduced to facilitate some specific meeting or design task rather than being coherently designed and instantiated once and for all (this is also conjectured to be true for smart homes (Edwards and Grinter 2001)). The dynamic nature of workspaces means that a software framework must handle applications and devices joining and leaving, while minimizing the impact on other entities in the space.

Transient Failures: For interactive workspaces to become widely deployed, they need to be robust and provide system stability in the face of change and transient failures. They must "just work" without requiring a full-time system administrator. Users will treat the devices in interactive workspaces as appliances that should not fail in unexplainable ways.

Commercial-off-the-shelf (COTS) hardware and software are prone to transient failures and are not designed to be integrated into a heterogeneous environment. Thus, failure needs to be anticipated as a common case, rather than an exception (Kindberg and Fox 2002). All of this means that the software framework must ensure that failures in individual applications and devices are non-catastrophic, and must provide for quick recovery, either automatically or by providing a simple set of recovery steps for the users.

Multiplicities: Finally, unlike a standard PC where a single user and set of input and output devices provide interaction with the machine, an interactive workspace by its nature has multiple users, devices, and applications all simultaneously active. A software framework must allow group interactions and flexible partitioning of devices into sub-groups.

Our central design philosophy for infrastructure is design for integration. There is no such thing as a stable system when we are dealing with rapidly evolving technologies: this was demonstrably true of the Internet as well as of the personal-computer industry, and there is every reason to believe it will be true in ubiquitous computing for the foreseeable future. As a corollary, we cannot expect people to discard their existing systems and workspaces in favor of newer technology: some degree of backwards compatibility must be retained, and some ability to smoothly and incrementally integrate and migrate to new technology must be provided. Today's exotic new hardware and latest-version software are tomorrow's legacy components. Although efforts such as Jini and UPnP (Universal Plug and Play) are attempting to establish universal standards for devices and interaction, we note that even after several years of discussion, the Jini standard for a "printer" device is still in committee, suggesting that it is trickier than expected to establish a standard even for seemingly simple and well-understood devices.

Consequently, our designs focus is not on solving "the problem" as we see it today, but on facilitating evolutionary progress into the future. Rather than investigating systems, application suites, and their use just in our specific space, we decided to investigate software techniques that can be used in differently configured interactive workspaces. Our goal is to provide a framework that serves a role similar to the device-driver model, window-manager system, and look-and-feel guidelines for PCs. In other words, we want to create standard abstraction and application design methodologies that apply to any interactive workspace (Winograd 2001a, b).

Our overall system is called iROS, which stands for Interactive Room Operating System. It embodies "design for integration" at all levels: it leverages as many existing subsystems and protocols as possible (Web protocols, Win32 applications, Java); provides specific facilities for allowing the introduction of new functionality gradually and without breaking compatibility with existing functionality; assumes that transient failures will be common in any heterogeneous collection of hardware and software components; and wherever possible emphasizes ease of development or prototyping rather than striving for an optimal but necessarily ephemeral "packaged" solution to a problem.

iROS is best viewed as a meta-operating system or middleware infrastructure, tying together devices that each have their own low-level operating system. It is a multiple server-based architecture, with each server dedicated to a physically bounded space (typically a room or building). This allows the system to honor the boundary principle (Kindberg and Fox 2002), which states that ubiquitous computing infrastructure should only allow interaction between devices within the bounds of the local physical space within which a human would assume devices to be collocated. For example, a user might assume that all the devices currently in the conference room could interact, but none of them would be assumed to interact with devices back in his office, unless networking were to be explicitly invoked. We have sought to create a software infrastructure that is associated with a specific physical interactive workspace, and that supports the human–computer interaction needs of applications in that space. To that end, the basic components of our software are charged with making this boundary explicit to applications and devices in the interactive space.

Much of our experimentation has been in a specific instantiation of the space, called the iRoom (see Sect. 2.2). Other experiments have been in the iLoft in the Stanford Center for Design Research (Milne and Winograd 2003), the iLounge at the KTH in Sweden (Croné 2002), the Teamspace in the Meyer Library at Stanford, and a variety of other sites.

2.1.3 Applications and Empirical Studies of Collaborative Interaction

Our collaborative technologies have been tested in a variety of modes and settings, ranging from informal observation of our own use of the iRoom to controlled studies of relevant aspects of human perception and the use of particular devices and systems. These studies have some common threads:

- *Emphasize co-location.* There is a long history of research on computer supported cooperative work for distributed access (teleconferencing support). To complement this work, we chose to primarily explore new kinds of support for team meetings in single spaces, taking advantage of the shared physical space for orientation and interaction.
- *Reliance on social conventions.* Many projects have attempted to make an interactive workspace "smart" (usually called an intelligent environment) (Brumitt 2000; Coen 1999). Rather than have the room figure out what a group is doing and react appropriately, we have chosen to focus on providing the affordances necessary for a group to adjust with the environment as they proceed with their task. In other words, we have set our semantic Rubicon (Kindberg and Fox 2002) such that users and social conventions take responsibility for actions, and the system infrastructure is responsible for providing a fluid means to execute those actions.

Some of the experiments are described in more detail below. They have included the following:

- *Construction information workspace.* In our development, we have collaborated with other research groups and practitioners to construct "non-toy" applications in design, education, and engineering. One extended development project in conjunction with the Stanford Center for Integrated Facilities Engineering (CIFE) included studies of users in the construction industry and the design of a construction information workspace (Liston et al. 2001). Studies of users in construction planning meetings without computer augmentation showed that they spent almost half of their time simply locating and displaying information. The goal of the prototype system, combining iROS technologies with 4D CAD (McKinney et al. 1996), was to automate the retrieval and cross-correlation of information so that the bulk of the human effort could be directed to discussion and planning.
- *Collaborative writing.* Students in a series of courses offered by the Stanford Program in Writing and Rhetoric used an iROS installation combining individual laptops, small-group shared plasma displays, and a classroom-shared projection display. They could move writing samples from one to the other and jointly edit and work on them while having discussions.
- *Walk-up collaboration.* In the TeamSpace project (Shih et al. 2004), a simple subset of iROS facilities was provided for casual use by students in a public study space. Studies showed that they were able to easily and quickly master the technologies and adapt them to their group practices.
- *Design project capture and recall.* WorkspaceNavigator (Ju et al. 2004) consists of a suite of tools built on iROS for the capture and review of activity in ongoing design projects. It was deployed in design project spaces in Mechanical Engineering and used over the course of several months. One interface, intended for the design team members, used timelines and visual overviews of the workspace to help index and access both snapshots and online activity records. Another interface, for use in design research, provided visualizations of group activity based on sensors and monitors in the workspace.
- *Remote design team drawing sharing.* An experiment called GroupBoard (Milne and Winograd 2003) studied the effects of shared vs. individual display visibility in the work of tele-distributed design engineering teams.
- *Sharing and communication in tabletop interaction.* We have conducted studies both on the bottom-projected iTable and the top-projected multi-touch Diamond Touch table (Dietz and Leigh 2001), in which users cooperatively perform tasks that involve the organization and arrangement of visual materials. In one experiment on sorting photographs (Grant 2002), behaviors on electronic vs. manual tables were compared. In another (Morris et al. 2004), the tabletop interaction has been augmented by audio in both private and shared modes, leading to different kinds of cooperative behavior.

After giving a brief history of the project, in subsequent sections, we provide details of our attempts to enable fluid interaction as well as the software abstractions that support the required mechanisms. We then describe in more detail some of the empirical studies mentioned earlier.

2.2   History of the Project

2.2.1   Interactive Mural

The initial impetus for the interactive workspaces project in 1999 was the research done jointly with the Stanford Graphics Laboratory on large (white-board sized) high-resolution displays. The graphics group was developing software to display large high-resolution images on tiled displays using multiple projectors (Humphreys 2001; Stone 2001). We designed and built an initial four-projector prototype display, called the Interactive Mural. It was followed by one using eight projectors for a resolution of approximately 4,000 by 1,500 pixels. To support interactive applications, we experimented with several different kinds of pointing devices and their integration into the OpenGL-based display software. Candidate devices included a gyroscopic mouse, an ultrasonic pen, and laser pointer tracking (Chen and Davis 2002; Winograd and Guimbretière 1999). We standardized on the use of an ultrasonic (eBeam) pen (The eBeam System 2000). Several experiments were done on the use of this device to support different interactive techniques, including the FlowMenu (Guimbretière and Winograd 2000) and a multi-pane Geometer's Workbench for interactive mathematics visualization (Guimbretière et al. 2000). As part of a joint interactive art project with the art department, we installed a 10′ × 12′ pressure-sensitive floor in front of the mural. Each of the 120 1′ × 1′ "footsels" returned a binary value based on a pressure threshold. The input was accurate enough to indicate when someone was standing with at least 1 ft within the area.

The final version of the Interactive Mural was installed in the iRoom and used for the development of the PostBrainstorm interface (Guimbretière et al. 2001). Twelve projectors achieve an overall resolution of about 70 dpi over a 6′ diagonal screen. A custom-built mounting system (Fig. 2.1) was used to align the projectors with sub-pixel resolution (Stone 2001). The 9 megapixels provided a whiteboard-like space with approximately the same resolution as a standard 21″ monitor. This allows both fine work at the surface and the ability to stand at a distance to get the overall picture. The mural was powered by a 32 PC rendering cluster and a custom software system called WireGL (Humphreys 2001), which allows it to appear at applications as a single large OpenGL device. It uses an eBeam ultrasonic pen (The eBeam System 2000), augmented with a button that provides two distinct modes (used for drawing and commands).

2.2.2   iRoom Version 1

Although the free-standing first version of the mural was useful for experimenting with interaction techniques, its middle-of-the-lab setting meant that it could not be used practically for long periods of time and offered little integration with other devices, such as workstations, laptops, and PDAs, through which people got their

Fig. 2.1 View behind interactive mural, showing custom mounting hardware and projectors

work done. To enhance utility in studying realistic uses, we began to investigate the design of rooms containing one or more large displays with the ability to integrate portable devices and to create applications integrating the use of multiple devices in the space.

In Summer 1999, we designed and constructed a conference-room-like setting called the Interactive Room, or iRoom. Our initial iRoom was very similar to the second and final version of the iRoom, which is discussed in the next section and appears in Fig. 2.2. It contained three 5′ diagonal SMART Board touch-screens along one wall and a custom-designed bottom-projection table, called the iTable, which uses a projector and mirror under the raised floor to project the image on the table surface. No barrier is used to prevent legs from obstructing the light path, which makes the iTable look more like a standard conference room table. The initial iRoom also had a front-projected full-wall display and a wireless network that enabled laptops in the room to communicate.

In a student project course on "Interactive Workplaces," five student teams wrote applications for the iRoom, including an application to do movie storyboarding, which integrated Adobe Premiere; an image sorter with the ability to scan hand-drawn sketches; and a presentation application, which allowed all three screens to be used as part of a coordinated PowerPoint application. One of the projects also created a directional sound API for the iRoom and installed a 4.1 speaker surround-sound system. With Barehands (Ringel et al. 2001), we also experimented with augmenting the touch-screen interaction on the wall displays so that hand posture (as viewed by a behind-screen camera) could provide an additional input channel.

Fig. 2.2 A view of the interactive room v2 (iRoom). The hi-res mural, visible at far *left*, is mounted in a wall that was used as a passive projection surface in our original iRoom. The orientation of the space was also rotated 90° relative to the original iRoom, requiring compact light-folding optics for the three SMART board rear-projected displays

2.2.3   iRoom Version 2

In Summer of 2000, we rebuilt both the physical environment and the software infrastructure. The 12-projector version of the Interactive Mural (Sect. 2.1) was integrated as the front of the iRoom. This required a reconfiguration of the entire workspace. During the remodel, we introduced more compact light-folding optics for the projectors on the SMART Boards, and did a better job of running the over one-half mile of cables for the room. Based on a plan arrived at with the help of designers from IDEO, a developer lab adjacent to the room was added along with a sign-in area that holds mobile devices and a dedicated machine that can be used for room control. The room itself, with the interactive mural, can be seen in Fig. 2.2.

Most of the hardware in the room is standard commercial equipment, the major exceptions being the interactive mural and the iTable (the physical table, not the projected computer display). All displays other than the interactive mural are driven by standard Windows 2000 PCs. The room also has 802.11b wireless support for laptops and hand-helds.

For experiments with telecollaboration (Virtual Auditorium (Chen, 2001)) and meeting capture (WorkspaceNavigator (Ju et al., 2004)), there are three video cameras, one above each board, plus others with a general room view.

Additional devices such as the wireless receiver for iStuff devices and the barcode scanner for RedBoard have also been deployed in the room.

From the time it was completed in 2001, we have been using the iRoom as an everyday workspace for our own research groups, for a number of collaborations with application development groups, for courses and student projects, and for structured experiments.

2.2.4 The Proliferation of Interactive Workspaces

Since the building of iRoom v2, interactive workspaces technology has been deployed at many more locations around the Stanford campus including a prototype construction trailer setup at CIFE, a future classroom prototype at the Stanford Learning Lab, a classroom used for joint critiquing in the Program on Writing and Rhetoric, and a number of classroom spaces in a new Stanford building for innovation in education, Wallenberg Hall. We have deployed interactive workspaces with the WorkspaceNavigator system in two project-based engineering design courses, in which each project team has a dedicated project space in the engineering building. The TeamSpace system (Shih et al. 2004), a portable, robust iROS installation, has been tested in a common access area of the undergraduate library and is being deployed to a number of other settings. It is based in part on joint work with the Hewlett-Packard Laboratories on a "meeting machine" (Barton 2003).

Beginning in 2001, we collaborated in the iSpaces Project with research groups at KTH in Stockholm under the sponsorship of the Wallenberg Global Learning Network. During the subsequent 3 years, we cooperated on a number of projects, including installing iROS-based workspaces at several locations in Sweden and jointly conducting usability studies. We have provided open source versions of our software to the research community and it has been deployed in a number of additional sites in Sweden, Switzerland, Finland, and the US. The iROS system is available as open source for download and installation with Windows 2000 and Mac OS X installers for both servers and clients (iROS Meta-Operating System 2001). A startup company, Tidebreak (Tidebreak, Inc.), has been created to create commercial versions of iROS-like software.

2.3 Details of Fluid Interaction

2.3.1 Interaction with Shared Displays

The initial motivation for the iRoom was to take advantage of interaction with large high-resolution displays, such as the Interactive Mural (Guimbretière 2002; Guimbretière et al. 2000; Winograd and Guimbretière 1999). Through a series of prototypes, we have explored means for interacting directly with a wall-mounted display (rather than controlling it remotely from a laptop or other machine). The attention of a presenter or facilitator in a meeting is focused on the contents of the board and on the other participants. Any use of a keyboard is a distraction, and so we have designed methods for direct interaction with a pen-like device and with direct touch on the board. The primary experiment in this area was the PostBrainstorm system, which used a large high-resolution (9 megapixel) display to facilitate design brainstorming sessions (Guimbretière 2002). It was tested in actual use by a team of professional designers from IDEO and introduced a number of interaction innovations, including menu selection (FlowMenu (Guimbretière et al. 2005; Guimbretière and Winograd 2000)), spatial information management (ZoomScape (Guimbretière et al. 2001)), and integration of handwriting, sketching, and 3D manipulation using a pen as the only input device.

Using a bottom-projected table (see Fig. 2.3), we developed an experimental interface for organizing images, such as photographs, and experimented with different visualizations and affordances for common actions, such as creating piles and browsing collections (Grant 2002). In other experiments, using a DiamondTouch (Dietz and Leigh 2001) table, a top-projected display with a touch-sensitive surface, which accepts simultaneous input from up to four people, we have explored a number of issues about the tradeoffs between shared and private information (Morris et al. 2004).

Although most of our work has focused on co-located collaboration, one experiment has explored the potentials for tele-presentation of lectures using technologies that provide a high degree of presence with relatively low bandwidth and computation. The Stanford Video Auditorium (Chen 2001) (see Fig. 2.9) allows an instructor to

Fig. 2.3 The iTable, a bottom projected table used to experiment with table top UIs

see dozens of students on a tiled wall-sized display and establish eye contact with any student, with telephone-quality audio and SD (Standard Definition) television-quality video.

2.3.2   Overface

In providing software for an open interactive environment, we faced a fundamental tradeoff in interaction design. On the one hand, we are committed to accepting the diversity of devices, operating systems, and legacy applications that people bring to the space. On the other hand, we need to keep the interface simple, or people will not use it. Spaces such as the iRoom are intended to be used inter-mittently by people with little explicit training, who are engaged in a variety of interactions with other people during the meeting. This is very different from a "heads-down" desktop application that receives long training and full attention focus for many hours at a span.

The overface needs to be uniform across devices and provide several core functions from any of the devices in the room, including PDAs, laptops, and any of the wall-mounted or table-top displays:

- Moving information of all kinds from anywhere onto any of the display surfaces
- Controlling applications running on any of the display surfaces, from any device
- Controlling the environment (lights, projectors, display sources, etc.)

A number of other projects have proposed mechanisms for information mobility (Bolt 1980; Rekimoto 1997; Streitz et al. 1999; Ullmer et al. 1998) and for portability of control (Myers 2001). As part of our iROS environment (Ponnekanti et al. 2003), we have developed a suite of related applications, including Multibrowse, the room applet, PointRight, and InterfaceCrafter, which are described further in Sect. 4.2.

2.3.3   Post Desktop Devices

A key aspect of emerging ubiquitous computing environments is the variety of input devices and modalities that work together. In an interactive workspace, it can be confusing to have physical input devices associated with specific machines. We are all accustomed to thinking of output devices, such as printers, as networked resources accessible from any machine, and this should apply to inputs as well. In addition to the pen-based and touch-based interfaces described in the previous sections, we have experimented with a variety of physical and tangible devices.

To facilitate prototyping of these interactions, we developed a protocol and set of sample devices, such as sliders, orientation sensors, audio output, and even a stuffed "iDog" as part of a project called iStuff (Ballagas 2003). These devices can post events on a shared Event Heap (see Sect. 4) for any program to use, and can therefore be easily adapted to different functions. The iStuff infrastructure is a first step towards general human-centered interaction architecture (Winograd 2001a, b), in which the architecture is centered around people and the physical devices they encounter, instead of being tied to the implementation of processes, drivers, and the like. iStuff devices were tested in a number of experimental projects, including iPong (a multi-screen version of the original Pong video game), iClub (an interactive disco application), and a collection of simple one-button devices that could be associated with arbitrary actions through a web-form interface. For example, a push on a particular button can bring up a set of pre-designated applications on multiple devices in the room to set up a meeting context.

In our experiments with sketch-based brainstorming, we discovered that designers wanted to be able to draw sketches independently and then "post" them when finished to a digital group surface. In an initial experiment, we gave each of them a tablet computer (Vadem Clio) on which they could enter drawings directly. They found that compared to their standard sketching practices with pens and pencils on paper, the feel of drawing on the tablet was highly disagreeable. We decided instead to make it easy to bring hand-sketched material to the shared surface, getting rid of the interaction overhead of standard flatbed scanners. To enter visual material of any kind (including snapshots and physical objects), the material is placed on the table, and a pair of retro-reflective L-shaped crop marks is positioned to indicate the cropping boundaries. A command to our FlowScan software causes the ceiling-mounted digital camera to take a picture and transmit a JPEG image to the indicated display. Compared to ordinary scanning, the resolution is low (100 dpi) and there is no control of contrast, color, etc. However, the intended use for bringing materials into a meeting is well served and the simplicity of the interface makes it much more usable than one that requires distracting interactions.

In addition to the optical scanner, we have introduced other devices such as a bar code scanner to implement a system for personal information in shared spaces, similar to IBM's BlueBoard (Russell and Gossweiler 2001). When the barcode scanner posts an event due to a user scanning a personal barcode, the application checks a table of codes registered to individual iRoom users, and if there is a match, it posts a portal to the user's personal information space on one of the large electronic white-boards. In work with iROS in the iLounge at KTH, Swedish researchers developed Magic Bowl, a tangible user interface for controlling the interactive workspace (Croné 2004). The Magic Bowl makes it possible to quickly start the interactive workspace with a personalized configuration, using tangible RFID-based tokens to represent different configurations associated with particular groups and users.

2.4 Details of Software Infrastructure

2.4.1 Sharing Resources: iROS Meta-Operating System

For any real world system to support the modalities and characteristics described in the beginning of this chapter, systems infrastructure and human interface issues must be looked at together – the two are inextricably tied. The system infrastructure and API need to reflect the way that applications written on top of it will be used.

Fig. 2.4 iROS component structure

Figure 2.4 shows how the major iROS components fit together. The only component common to all iROS programs is the Event Heap, which is the underlying communication infrastructure for applications within an interactive workspace.

2.4.1.1 Event Heap

Given the heterogeneity in interactive workspaces and the likelihood of failure in individual devices and applications, it is important that the underlying coordination mechanism decouple applications from one another as much as possible. This encourages applications to be written to be less dependent on one another, thereby making the overall system less brittle and more stable. The Event Heap coordination infrastructure for iROS (Johanson et al. 2003; Johanson and Fox 2004; Johanson et al. 2003) expands on the tuplespace model (Carriero and Gelernter 1989) to provide inter-application coordination. The basic operations are put, which posts an event, and get, which queries for the existence of an event based on a template that specifies required fields and constraints on their values. Event subscription is also provided, which allows for publish/subscribe semantics: clients can receive a callback when events matching a particular template are posted to the Event Heap. Various libraries and other software components allow Event Heap clients to be written in Java, C/C++, Visual Basic, Perl, Python, and other languages; servlets allow Web-based clients to post events to the Event Heap as well. The Event Heap itself is written in Java and currently implemented as a centralized server process; elsewhere we have discussed why there appears to be limited benefit to a distributed implementation (Johanson and Fox 2004). Initial versions of the Event Heap were built on top of TSpaces (Wyckoff et al., 1998), but we have moved to our own code base for better performance and cross platform support.

Event Heap semantics differ from the original tuplespace semantics in a few important ways. First, every tuple (unordered set of attribute-value pairs) carries a required type field as one of the attribute-value pairs; the presence and interpretation of any remaining attributes are application-specific and determined by the type. Second, events from the same source are sequenced, so that applications can get and handle events one at a time in submission order, much as they would with an event queue. All applications see the same ordering of events from a particular source, but there is no guaranteed ordering of events from different sources. Third, there is built-in support for routing or receiving events from specific clients, applications, devices, people or groups, via event attributes that are automatically filled in by the Event Heap client libraries rather than having to be explicitly set by the client application. Finally, events automatically expire and are removed from the Event Heap after their expiration time has passed; expiration times are set by the entity posting the event.

In keeping with the Boundary Principle (Kindberg and Fox 2002), a single Event Heap is the locus of interaction for a single ubiquitous computing environment, and a service or device can participate in that environment if and only if it can communicate with that environment's Event Heap. In keeping with the Volatility Principle (Kindberg and Fox 2002), automatic event expiration sidesteps the resource-reclamation problems that might arise if intended event recipients are crashed, hung, etc.; combining expiration with announce-listen beacons for stateful services allows any component of an interactive workspace, including the Event Heap itself, to be recovered by simply restarting it. Of course, there is no guarantee that restarting something will fix the problem, but given frequent transient bugs in off-the-shelf applications, restarting to deal with resource issues such as memory leaks, temporary network failures, etc. can be surprisingly effective, and our design ensures that it is safe to try (Fox and Patterson 2003). All these are discussed in greater depth in Johanson et al. (2003) and Johanson and Fox (2002).

2.4.1.2   The DataHeap

The Event Heap is designed for the exchange of small control messages and by design its contents do not survive crashes. We need a separate facility for persistent state storage and large objects. The DataHeap allows naming and storage of data by attribute-value pairs, including the representation of the format of the data (e.g., GIF vs. JPEG image). When a client requests data and indicates which formats it can consume, the DataHeap automatically transforms the data to the suitable format, if possible. This makes integration of the new media types into existing applications modular when adapters can be provided (Fig. 2.5).

2.4.1.3   The iROS Manager

The iROS Manager user interface provides several functions including selectively restarting groups of applications. One of the iROS Manager components facilitates software packaging and distribution for iSpace applications and works with an iSpace Dependability Manager to keep an iSpace running even when some of the component applications fail. iROS Manager encapsulates dependency information among iSpace applications, which results in "single-click" installation for administrators and "near-zero administration" for dealing with the day-to-day operational issues that inevitably arise in installations of many heterogeneous components.

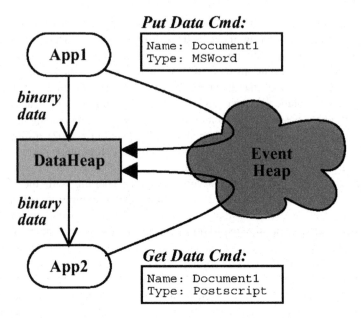

Fig. 2.5 The DataHeap

2.4.1.4 iROS Design Principles

Some common principles run throughout the iROS system:

Decoupling to make system more flexible: Applications do not communicate directly with one another, but use indirection through the Event Heap, which improves fault isolation. iROS systems decouple applications referentially: Rather than routing events based on unique identities of devices, processes, or sockets, they use attributes for posting and retrieval (as in Adjie-Winoto 1999). In addition, the Event Heap and DataHeap also decouple applications temporally: programs need not be running at the same time to communicate. Applications that transiently fail can retrieve nonexpired events they missed while they were down.

Application ensembles: Applications written in the iROS system are not a special-platform monolithic system (as in Gaia OS (Cerqueira 2001) or BEACH (Tandler 2003)), but are bound together into a dynamically changing ensemble as users launch and use them. The Event Heap facilitates this by allowing applications with common event types to coordinate, regardless of the machine on which they are running. Using the DataHeap, applications that use different formats can exchange data.

Modular restartability: In our design, failure is treated as a common case, so when something breaks it can simply be restarted. Clients automatically reconnect when started, so the Event Heap server, interface manager, and DataHeap server can all be restarted in a room full of running devices and applications without interfering with their function. The net result of this is that any subset of machines in the workspace can be restarted in any order. Any important state that might be lost during this process is either stored in persistent form in the DataHeap or is beaconed as soft-state, which is regenerated as clients come back up.

Simplicity: Rather than trying to provide a large API that handles many different situations, we provide simple APIs with minimal client-side overhead. Wherever possible, we rely on existing technologies like the Web, as HTML serves as a baseline presentation to an UI layer. This makes the code base small for impoverished devices (our current Java JAR library for all of the iROS core functionality is less than 200KB), and also simplifies the task of porting the client interface to new devices. This simplicity comes at the expense of more sophisticated functionality, such as atomic transactions, total ordering, etc. Our experience suggests that these features should be provided at a higher level for those applications that need them, but that many of the smaller and simpler (yet very useful) applications and behaviors we and our collaborators have built so far have not required them.

2.4.2 Supporting Overface: Common End-User Tools

Each of the iROS installations has had its own specific interfaces and applications. Within these, there is a small common core of facilities.

2.4.2.1 Multibrowse

Multibrowse (Johanson et al. 2001) allows users to flexibly move and open web content and application documents across the devices in a workspace. For web pages, there is an Internet Explorer plug-in that submits web page display requests and a daemon program that displays the appropriate web page on the requested device upon reception of the requests. For application files, the daemon can use the DataHeap or other shared server to copy the file to the target device and then send commands to open it. We have experimented with a variety of tools for specifying the destination of a MultiBrowse, including drop-down lists and room maps. See the discussion of InterfaceCrafter below for more detail.

2.4.2.2 PointRight

When we began conducting meetings in the prototype iRoom, it became clear that users wanted mixed control of the large displays. At some moments, a person standing at the display needs to control it directly, using touch, pen, etc. At other moments, a person sitting elsewhere in the room wants to perform an operation on that display, which may be as simple as bringing a window to the front or typing a

URL into a browser. The flow is disrupted by asking the person at the board to do it or by getting up and walking to the board. A number of previous systems have dealt with multi-user control of a shared device, often providing sophisticated floor-control mechanisms to manage conflicts. In keeping with our "keep it simple" philosophy, we created a mechanism called PointRight (Johanson et al. 2002), which provides the key functionality without being intrusive. PointRight provides an intuitive model for moving control among displays in an interactive workspace and has proven to be one of the most useful iROS applications.

With PointRight, any machine's pointing device can become a "super pointer," whose field of operation includes all of the display surfaces in the room, as well as the machine it is on. Rather than requiring configuration by the user, we take advantage of the spatial visibility of the room. When a device runs PointRight, the edges of its screen are associated with the edges of other displays. The user simply continues moving the cursor off the edge of the local screen, and it moves onto one of the other screens. The keyboard is mapped to whatever screen the cursor is currently on, providing full application control. The system tracks projector on/off state, machine-display connections, and controllable machines through the posting of events to the Event Heap by the room controller system and PointRight clients. A beaconing mechanism that takes advantage of the automatic expiration of events from the Event Heap insures that machines that go down or are removed from the workspace are also removed from the list of valid control targets.

The PointRight mechanism does not do anything special about simultaneous access. Pointer input is simply fed into the target machine's event queue as absolute cursor positioning events. This means that when two users are moving the pointer on the same screen, the effect is the same as it would be for two absolute physical pointing devices attached to the machine driving that screen. In normal Windows operation, a ghost cursor appears for each user as the system time interleaves the cursor display. Although this would be problematic in a distributed setting, we have found that it causes little problem in a physical shared setting, where people directly see the effects of their actions and can negotiate with others for control in the rare cases when that is necessary. In addition to laptops that are brought to meetings, the iRoom has a dedicated wireless keyboard and mouse running PointRight, which can be used as a general keyboard and pointer interaction device for all of the surfaces.

2.4.2.3 Room Controller

One obvious advantage of working in a room-based environment is that people share a common model of where devices are positioned, which they can use as a convenient way of identifying them. Our "room controller" (see Fig. 2.6) uses a small map of the room to indicate the lights, projectors, and display surfaces. These can be controlled by simple toggles and menus associated with the objects in the map. The room controller can be used to switch video inputs to projectors as well as to turn lights and projectors on or off.

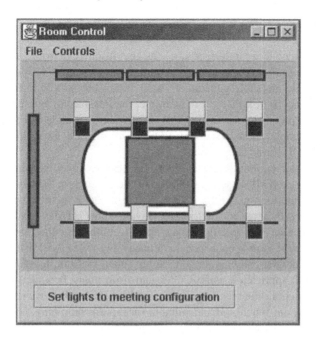

Fig. 2.6 Java swing room control UI generated by interface crafter. The *dark grey rectangles* are surfaces onto which information can be dragged. The *light grey/black rectangles* are light switches corresponding to the array of track lights on the ceiling

Initial versions of this controller were built as standard GUI applications, which could run only on some systems. We broadened their availability to a wider range of devices by providing them as web pages (using forms) and as web applets (using Java). Our later research generalized the process further with InterfaceCrafter (see Sect. 2.4.3.1), which provides for automated generation of interfaces for any set of services, on any device that can support one of a variety of interface languages (Java Swing, HTML, WABA, etc.).

In addition to providing environment control, the same interface serves as a convenient way of moving information onto displays. The user drags an information object (URL or file icon) onto the appropriate region in the map to indicate the display on which it should appear. The MultiBrowse mechanism (Johanson et al. 2001) is used in conjunction with the DataHeap to initiate an application on the target device that displays the indicated object. The room control system stores the geometric arrangement of screens and lights in the room in a configuration file.

2.4.3   Supporting Postdesktop: Interface Development Tools

In addition to the standard facilities, we want to be able to provide end-user interaction mechanisms that are not specific to the devices in the room. We have developed several tools to provide for the mapping from input modalities to effective action.

2.4.3.1   InterfaceCrafter

Rather than hardcode an interface such as the Room Controller for a specific device, InterfaceCrafter (Ponnekanti et al. 2001) provides a way to specify the room geometry and automatically generate a visual controller tailored to the controlling device (e.g., a laptop or a PDA). For example, the interface of Fig. 2.6 is provided to any device supporting a Java Swing UI. If an interface is requested for a standard web browser, for example, a laptop without iROS client software, a simplified controller using only HTML forms is provided instead.

InterfaceCrafter exploits beacon events for service advertisement: a service's beacon contains an XML-based description of the methods callable in that service, and separate "interface generators" can represent those methods in appropriate human interfaces in a variety of formats (Java Swing, HTML, VoiceXML, etc.). Generators can be service-specific, device-specific, both, or neither; InterfaceCrafter attempts to select the most-specific generator in any given scenario. We have developed tools that can automatically create generic but functional InterfaceCrafter beacons from any Win32 application using COM, and from many Java applications using method introspection; the resulting automatically generated user interfaces are not elegant, but they are functional and suitable for rapid prototyping, and they can be replaced by more customized versions as needed.

2.4.3.2   iStuff and PatchPanel

The iStuff (Ballagas 2003) project includes a toolkit of physical devices and a flexible software infrastructure to simplify the prototyping of novel interaction techniques. The toolkit leverages the iROS infrastructure by adding fields to the protocols that are specific to device input and coordination. The toolkit allows developers to rapidly integrate inexpensive "generic" physical interactors such as buttons and dials into applications. We have experimented with a variety of simple wireless devices, as shown in Fig. 2.7.

The PatchPanel (Ballagas et al. 2004) simplifies the dynamic mapping of devices to iSpace behaviors, enabling them to be composed into more sophisticated or even multimodal controllers, and to be programmed to trigger "macro" sequences of actions. It takes advantage of the spatial decoupling provided by the EH. Specifically, as all events must pass through the EH on their way from a sender to one or more receivers, we can intercept those events and rewrite them, copy them for logging, etc. The PatchPanel subscribes to all EH events, allowing users to set up rules indicating how new events should be created in response to events observed being placed into the Event Heap. It supports simple translations, such as changing the event type and copying across field contents, as well as more complex stateful filtering operations, such as creating a new event with average values over several primitive events. Although each device can only output (or input) a fixed repertoire of events, PatchPanel translation can be used to connect the 33 devices to existing behaviors or to combine devices to create multimodal UI's.

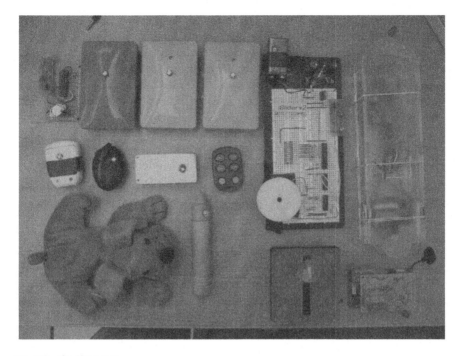

Fig. 2.7 iStuff devices

2.5   Applications and Empirical Studies

Space does not allow for details of all of the experiments, so we will present some notable examples and results.

2.5.1   CIFE Suite: Example of Dynamic Application Coordination

In addition to manual control, we use the Event Heap to link applications for cross-application control. Through submission of events to the Event Heap, interface actions within one application can trigger actions within another running on any of the machines in the workspace. This has been employed in a suite of applications developed by The Center for Integrated Facility Engineering (CIFE) (Liston et al. 2001) for use in construction management meetings. The software provides a set of viewers that run on the various displays in the workspace:

• A construction site map displayed on the iTable, which allows the selection of various view points in the construction site and then emits an appropriate view change event.

Users can click on regions of the map to control the point-of-view (POV) of 3D CAD models of the construction site being displayed by other applications in the workspace. As maps are relatively orientation independent, users can interact with the map regardless of where they are sitting at the table.

- A "4D" viewer that shows a time-sequence 3D model of projected state of the construction site for any date during construction. It responds to events that change the view, select objects and zones, and change the date for the current model view.
- A web based viewer that displays tables of construction plan information. This viewer also emits zone and date selection events when table information is selected and listens for the same events to highlight information in the table.

All the applications are essentially standalone, and communicate through the Event Heap. The 4D viewer was originally designed for use on a single PC and was modified to use the Event Heap by adding around 100 lines of code. As the viewers use common event types, the various components of the suite retain their ability to coordinate while being displayed on any screen in a workspace. As the components are loosely coupled, the absence or disappearance of an event source or event sink does not affect any of the application components currently in use. The overall effect for the user is that clicking on an element in any one of the applications produces a corresponding change in the other applications running in the workspace.

2.5.2 PostBrainstorm

The PostBrainstorm interface on the interactive mural provides a high-resolution display with the ability to intermix direct marking, control of images and 3D renderings, and arbitrary desktop applications. The details are given in other papers (Guimbretière 2002; Guimbretière et al. 2001; Guimbretière and Winograd 2000) and will only be briefly described here. The key design goal was to provide "fluid interaction," which does not require focused attention of the user, who is typically focused on person-to-person interactions in a meeting. This goal led to the development of several new mechanisms:

- *FlowMenu.* A contextual pop-up menu system that combines the choice of an action with parameter specification in a single pen stroke. This makes it possible to avoid interface modes, in which the first part of an action leaves the system in an altered state, which affects the interpretation of subsequent actions. Modes lead to confusion and errors for a user who is not paying full attention (see Raskin (2000) for discussion). Because the menu is radial rather than linear, multilevel operations can be learned as a single motion path or gesture, and so an experienced user does not even need to look at the menu to select an action (Guimbretière et al. 2005).
- *ZoomScape.* A configurable "warping" of the screen space so that the visible scale of an object is implicitly controlled by where it is moved. The object retains its geometry while being scaled as a whole. In our default configuration,

the top quarter of the screen is a reduction area, in which objects are one-quarter size. An object can be moved out of the primary attention area and reduced all in one pen stroke, with a smooth size transition as it goes through a boundary area. This provides a simple mechanism for screen real-estate management without requiring explicit commands to change size, iconify, etc.

- *Typed* drag-*and*-*drop*. Handwriting on the screen is recognized by a background process, retaining the digital ink and annotating it with the interpreted characters. Through FlowMenu commands, a sheet of writing can be specified to have a desired semantic (e.g., the name and value of a property to be associated with an object) and then dragged onto the target object to have the intended effect. This provides a crossover between simple board interaction (hand drawn text) and application-specific GUI interactions.

The overall system was tested in actual use by several groups of industrial designers from two local design firms (IDEO and SpeckDesign). Their overall evaluation of the facility was quite positive (Guimbretière 2002) and provided us with a number of specific areas for improvement.

In addition to experimenting with these facilities on the high-resolution interactive mural, we have ported them to standard Windows systems, and have made use of them on the SmartBoard screens.

2.5.3 Workspace Navigator

The WorkspaceNavigator is a suite of iROS-based tools to support the capture, recall, and reuse of material and ideas generated by a group doing semi-structured work in an interactive workspace. Our focus is on the capture of digital information, including screenshots, files, and URLs. This automatically captured information can be augmented by user-supplied annotations both during and after a session. All the information is stored as a sequence of time slices, integrated by an overview image of the physical space at the time of the capture. The overview image provides spatial cues for accessing the captured information, and is treated as an image map with links to the other information captured during that time slice. We have conducted two user studies of the WorkspaceNavigator tools and found that capturing coordinated slices of digital information is useful for recall and summarization activities, and that coordinating access through the visual metaphor of the overview image is understandable and effective (Ionescu et al. 2002; Ju et al. 2004) (Fig. 2.8).

2.5.4 Virtual Auditorium

The Virtual Auditorium (Chen 2001) is a system for teleconferenced remote teaching, with a central instructor node and up to a few dozen student nodes at other locations.

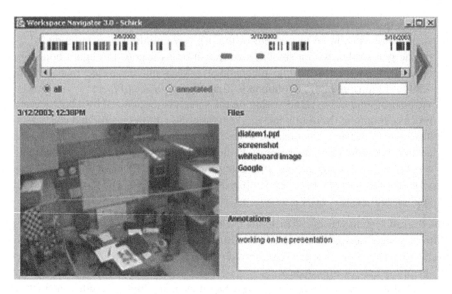

Fig. 2.8 Snapshot-based browser for workspace navigator

Fig. 2.9 Virtual auditorium display wall

The instructor node in the initial prototype uses the three large wall-display computers in the iRoom, the interactive table, and the cameras mounted above the wall displays. Student nodes are workstations with simple video cameras. All nodes are connected by high-speed computer networks.

The conceptual usage model of the Virtual Auditorium is that all participants can be seen and heard with minimal latency at all times. The instructor can see the remote students on the display wall at a roughly life size, shown in a grid of positions as in Fig. 2.9.

The instructor can alter the seating arrangement by dragging a student's video to any empty seat using PointRight. Each of the three sections of the display wall has a speaker, enabling the instructor to locate the general direction of the speaking student from the location of the loudspeaker. Each student's instantaneous audio volume is displayed next to his name to enhance the visual signal of lip movement; thus, allowing the instructor to easily locate the speaking student.

The design was particularly optimized to deal with issues of eye contact, which remains one of the key problems in remote video applications. In situations with more than a pair of communicating speakers, eye contact is a fundamental cue as to where a speaker's attention and communication is directed. In a teleconferencing system, gazing at the picture of the recipient does not generally cause the recipient to see an image of the speaker looking at him or her (which would require looking into the camera, instead). Also, with a single camera, every recipient sees the same view, eliminating the cue of who is being addressed. In the Virtual Auditorium, the instructor can establish eye contact with any one student, a group of students, or the entire class using a technique called directed gaze, which functions in part by placing the video feed of the active student directly beneath one of the three video cameras and sending that feed only to the active student.

2.5.5   Teamspace

A typical Stanford undergraduate student spends only 15–18 hours a week in the classroom. Far more time is spent in technology spaces such as those in libraries and residences, where learning, research, and course project collaboration take place, primarily using student-owned laptops. Teamspace packages key iRoom functionality in a simple "zero-configuration" download for students and a near-zero-administration server installation designed for "walk-up" use by small student groups. Open casual public workspaces such as Teamspace require security and access control that does not require pre-registration and yet prevents unwanted incursion or snooping. The key element is physical co-location: people who are in the space should have access, while those who are not currently there should not. We address this through line-of-sight login and session expiration. A person wishing to log in to Teamspace must enter a server-generated password that appears on the group display, thereby restricting login to people who can physically see the group display. Once a session ends or times out, users who wish to continue must login again with a new password to continue the session. These simple mechanisms combined with social protocols appear sufficient for adequate access control.

We conducted user studies on 50 undergraduate students representing a wide range of technical and nontechnical majors. Details are in Shih et al. (2004). In one study, groups were arbitrarily formed and given a specific group task. We found that users tended to work relatively independently, collaborating at the beginning to divide the work and at the end to compile the work. During these moments of collaboration, they tended to multibrowse documents to the shared display (but generally not from the shared display to their own screens), with a single individual using PointRight to control the main display. Often, the choice of this individual was determined by pointer contention early in the session. In the second study, existing student teams working on real group projects used Teamspace for their collaboration. These participants, sharing a common external purpose and already familiar with one another, were more apt not only to collaborate on the project at hand but also to learn the Teamspace technology. They tended to multibrowse throughout the session both to the public screen and to one another's laptops, and felt more comfortable vying for the group screen pointer, resulting in increased collaboration on the group display and more frequent switching between private and public workspaces.

2.6 Future Directions

2.6.1 Interaction

Much of the initial work emphasized wall-mounted touch-screen displays. We have more recently been incorporating table-based displays, including ones that are able to handle multiple touches and distinguish users, and have added audio modalities. We are exploring the ways in which the boundaries between shared and private information and activity in cooperative tasks are affected by the choice of technologies.

Also, we have begun an investigation from a theoretical perspective of how users move information and control in an interactive environment (Winograd and Lee 2004). We are exploring a variety of mechanisms from selected existing real-world and research systems and have built an experimental platform in Java that we call the iWall, for experimenting with alternative ways to move objects across multiple displays. Our research interests lie in the area of fluency: which methods of moving data do users find easier, simpler, or more natural than others, and why?

The cognitive theories most generally applied to HCI deal with task-related measures (speed, error, etc.). In an interactive environment, we need situation-related measures, such as the degree to which computer use interferes with other activities. This can be across people (my action interferes with yours) or within task (e.g., having to figure out how to move a visual image interferes with my work in using it, or in explaining it to you). Some modes of interaction may be significantly better or worse in this dimension, and we want to understand what determines a user's fluency, or lack thereof, with an interface.

2.6.2 Infrastructure

While our system tries to minimize the amount of time required to integrate a device into an interactive workspace, there is still overhead in configuring room geometries and specifying which servers to use. We plan to make it simpler to create and extend a workspace and to move portable devices between them. Users should only have to plug in a device or bring it into a physical space in order for it to become a part of the corresponding software infrastructure. User configuration should be simple and prompted by the space – for example, the user might be requested to specify where in the room the device is located. The logical extension of this is to allow ad hoc interactive workspaces to form wherever a group of devices are gathered. A group of laptop computers brought together by field engineers could, for example, automatically be used as an iRoom-to-go.

So far, we have focused primarily on co-located collaboration. As we continue, we want to support project teams in remotely located interlinked workspaces, facilitating coordination between desired applications while insuring that workspace-specific events remain in the appropriate location. For example, sending an event to turn on all lights should have effects only in the environment where it was generated. One of the design decisions in the Event Heap was to assume workspaces with fixed infrastructure, with the Event Heap server running on a permanent machine in the workspace. Given the ubiquity of laptops and other portable devices, however, it is quite possible to create ad hoc interactive workspaces.

2.7 Final Words

As with all systems being built in relatively new domains, and particularly with systems that involve user interaction, it is difficult to come up with a quantitative measure of success. We have had a number of experimental uses, including the following:

- Design brainstorming sessions by professional designers
- Implementation of class projects built on the iROS system
- Training sessions for secondary school principals
- Construction management experiments
- Group interactions in several Stanford courses, including Latin, English, Japanese, and Archaeology
- Project groups from an interaction design course
- Casual team use in a public space
- and, of course, our own weekly group meetings.

The overall results have been positive, with many suggestions for further development and improvement. We have provided open source versions of our software to the research community and it has been deployed in a number of institutions. The iROS system is available for download and installation on Windows 2000 and Mac OS X for both servers and clients. A company, Tidebreak, Inc., has also been formed to commercialize the technology.

Comments from developers who have appreciated how easy it is to develop applications with our framework are also encouraging. Finally, the adoption and spread of our technology to other research groups (discussed earlier in the chapter) also suggests that our system is meeting the needs of the growing community of developers for interactive workspaces.

Acknowledgments The work described here owes a great deal to many people, both at Stanford and at our partner institutions. In addition to all of our excellent students, we want to especially thank Pat Hanrahan, Maureen Stone, John Barton, Carl Gustaf Jansson, Bjorn Pehrson, and Brian Luehrs. The research was supported by grants from Hewlett-Packard, IBM, Intel, Mitsubishi Electronics Research Lab, the Stanford Learning Lab, and most substantially by the Wallenberg Global Learning Network.

iSpaces Systems Glossary

eBeam is a commercially available ultrasonic pen input device (from Luidia, Inc.), which is used for the Interactive Mural and for other surfaces in the iRoom.

Event Heap is a piece of software that is the basic system "glue" that enables ease of integration, ease of development, and robustness.

FlowMenu is an integrated interface mechanism for menu selection and parameter entry, designed for use on large direct-contact boards such as the Interactive Mural.

FlowScan is a system using iROS that allows user of the iRoom to enter pictures into the information space through an overhead camera with minimal interaction.

Interactive Mural is a large high-resolution wall-mounted display, of which several versions were developed in our research.

InterfaceCrafter is a general mechanism for producing interfaces based on service descriptions that are tailored to the devices on which the interface is to be used.

iRoom is the prototype room in the Computer Science Department at Stanford, in which we have done our primary experiments in interactive workspaces.

iROS is the umbrella term for the iRoom Operating System – the software that integrates all parts of our interactive workspaces.

iStuff is a collection of wireless input/output devices using the Event Heap to communicate easily with programs of all kinds.

iTable is a table with a bottom-projected computer display, used for experiments with interaction on horizontal surfaces.

iWall is an infrastructure that supports display and movement of information on multiple screens for experimenting with different affordances.

MultiBrowse is an iROS application that allows any computer in a workspace to bring up materials on another computer by remote control.

Overface is a general term for the collection of interaction mechanisms that we provide on top of the regular interfaces to the devices in the workspace.

PatchPanel is a software component for integrating actions of devices that use the Event Heap.

PointRight is an iROS application that lets any of the displays in a room be controlled from any laptop or pointing device.

PostBrainstorm is an application of the Interactive Mural with a number of innovative interaction mechanisms designed to facilitate graphical brainstorming.

Redboard is a distributed access system that makes it easy for a person or group to bring into a workspace environment materials from their online files and to transmit materials to others.

SmartBoard is a commercial touch-screen device for large displays (from Smart Technologies), which is used on many of our experimental display surfaces.

SmartPresenter is an iROS application that allows lecture presenters to make flexible use of multiple screens.

TeamSpace is a simplified version of iROS with a minimal equipment configuration, intended for walk-up use.

Virtual Auditorium is a system for remote education that uses interactive workspace mechanisms for the instructor node, allowing management of eye contact and attention.

WorkspaceNavigator is a collection of multi-modal capture & viewer components that can be reused and deployed to reflect the needs of a variety of instructional situations.

ZoomScape is a mechanism for managing the size and position of materials on a large screen, enabling its use as for activities such as brainstorming.

References

Adjie-Winoto W et al (1999) The design and implementation of an intentional naming system. Oper. Syst. Rev. (USA), Operating Systems Review 33: 186–201

Andersson H et al (2003) iSecurity. CSD 2003 Class report. Swedish Royal Institute of Technology (KTH) and Stanford University, 76. http://www.tslab.ssvl.kth.se/csd/projects/0316/final_report.pdf

Ballagas R et al (2003) iStuff: a physical user interface toolkit for ubiquitous computing environments. In CHI 2003: Human Factors in computing systems. Fort Lauderdale, FL, USA: Association for Computing Machinery, pp. 537–544

Ballagas R, Szybalski A, Fox A. (2004) The PatchPanel: enabling control-flow interoperability in Ubicomp environments. In Second IEEE International Conference on Pervasive Computing and Communications (PerCom 2004). Orlando, FL, USA: IEEE, pp. 241–252

Barton JJ et al (2003) The MeetingMachine: interactive workspace support for nomadic users. In Fifth IEEE Workshop on Mobile Computing Systems and Applications, 2003. Monterey, CA, USA: Los Alamitos, CA, USA: IEEE Computer Society, p. 2–12

Bolt RA (1980) Put-that-there: voice and gesture at the graphics interface. In SIGGRAPH 1980 Seventh Annual Conference on Computer Graphics and Interactive Techniques, 1980. Seattle, WA, USA, pp. 262–270

Brumitt B et al (2000) EasyLiving: technologies for intelligent environments. In Handheld and Ubiquitous Computing Second International Symposium HUC 2000. Bristol, UK: Berlin, Germany: Springer, pp 12–29

Carriero N, Gelernter D (1989) Linda in context (parallel programming). Communications of the ACM 32(4): 444–458

Cerqueira R et al (2001) Gaia: a development infrastructure for active spaces. In Ubitools Workshop at Ubicomp 2001. Atlanta, GA

Chen M (2001) Design of a virtual auditorium. In Ninth ACM International Conference on Multimedia. Ottawa, Canada: ACM: New York, NY, USA, pp. 19–28

Chen XC, Davis J (2002) LumiPoint: multi-user laser-based interaction on large tiled displays. Displays 22(1): 205–211

Coen MH et al (1999) Meeting the computational needs of intelligent environments: the metaglue system. In MANSE99: First International Workshop Managing Interactions in Smart Environments. Dublin, Ireland, pp. 201–212

Croné M (2002) Persistence in interactive workspaces. In Collaboration with Interactive Walls and Tables Workshop at UbiComp 2002. Goteborg, Sweden

Croné M et al (2004) Magic bowl: a tangible user interface for configuration of interactive environments. In Sixth International Conference on the Design of Cooperative Systems. French Riviera, France

Dietz P, Leigh D (2001) DiamondTouch: a multi-user touch technology. In UIST'01: ACM Symposium on User Interface Software and Technology. Orlando, FL, USA: New York, NY, USA: ACM, pp. 219–26

Edwards WK, Grinter R (2001) At home with ubiquitous computing: seven challenges. In Ubicomp 2001. Atlanta, GA, USA, pp. 256–272

Fox A, Patterson DA-SU (2003) Self-repairing computers. Scientific American, 288(6): 54–61

Grant K et al (2002) Beyond the shoe box: foundations for flexibly organizing photographs on a computer. Digital Libraries Report, 2002–45. 2002, Stanford, CA: Stanford University

Guimbretière F (2002) Fluid interaction for high resolution wall-size displays. Ph.D. Dissertation, Computer Science. Stanford, CA, USA: Stanford University, 140

Guimbretière F, Winograd T (2000) FlowMenu: combining command, text, and data entry. UIST (User Interface Software and Technology): Proceedings of the ACM Symposium, pp. 213–216

Guimbretière F, Winograd T, Wei SX (2000) The geometer's workbench: an experiment in interacting with a large, hgh resolution display. Interactivity Lab Technical Report, Stanford, CA, USA: Stanford University, 7. http://graphics.stanford.edu/~francois/Papers/UIST2000/geometerworkbench.pdf

Guimbretière F, Stone M, Winograd T (2001) Fluid Interaction with High-resolution Wall-Size Displays. UIST (User Interface Software and Technology): Proceedings of the ACM Symposium, pp. 21–30

Guimbretière F, Martin A, Winograd T (2005) Benefits of merging command selection and direct manipulation. ACM Trans. Comput.–Hum. Interact, ACM, New York, NY, USA, 12(3): 460–476. http://doi.acm.org/10.1145/1096737.1096742

Humphreys G et al (2001) WireGL: a scalable graphics system for clusters. Proceedings of the ACM SIGGRAPH Conference on Computer Graphics, pp. 129–140

Ionescu A, Stone M, Winograd T (2002) WorkspaceNavigator: capture, recall and reuse using spatial cues in an interactive workspace. Technical Report, TR2002–04. Stanford, CA, USA: Stanford University, 8. http://www.stanford.edu/~arna/persist/wkspcNav-286.pdf Verified: 11/2002)

iROS Meta-Operating System (2001–2004) Interactive workspaces group, Stanford University: Stanford, CA. http://iros.sourceforge.net

Johanson B (2003) Application coordination infrastructure for ubiquitous computing rooms. Ph.D. Dissertation, Electrical Engineering. Stanford, CA, USA: Stanford University, 231

Johanson B, Fox A (2002) The Event Heap: a coordination infrastructure for interactive workspaces. In Fourth IEEE Workshop on Mobile Computing Systems and Applications. Callicoon, NY, USA: Los Alamitos, CA, USA: IEEE Comput. Soc, 2002, pp. 83–93

Johanson B, Fox A (2004) Extending tuplespaces for coordination in interactive workspaces. Journal of Systems and Software 69(3):243–266

Johanson B et al (2001) Multibrowsing: moving web content across multiple displays. In Ubicomp 2001. Atlanta, GA, USA, pp. 256–272

Johanson B et al (2002) PointRight: experience with flexible input redirection in interactive workspaces. In ACM Symposium on User Interface Software and Technology (UIST-2002). Paris, France, pp. 227–234

Johanson B, Winograd T, Fox A (2003) Interactive workspaces. Computer, 36(4): 99–101

Ju W, Ionescu A, Neeley L, Winograd T (2004) Where the wild things work: capturing shared physical design workspaces. CSCW '04: Proceedings of the 2004 ACM conference on Computer supported cooperative work. Chicago, IL, USA, pp. 533–541. http://doi.acm.org/10.1145/1031607.1031696

Kindberg T, Fox A (2002) System software for ubiquitous computing, In IEEE Pervasive Computing, pp. 70–81

Liston K, Fischer M, Winograd T (2001) Focused sharing of information for multi-disciplinary decision making by project teams. ITcon, 6: 69–81

McKinney K et al (1996) Interactive 4D-CAD. In Third Congress on Computing in Civil Engineering. Anaheim, CA, USA, pp. 383–389

Milne A, Winograd T (2003) The iLoft project: a technologically advanced collaborative design workspace as research instrument. In 14th Annual International Conference on Engineering Design (ICED'03). Stockholm, Sweden

Morris MR, Morris D, Winograd T (2004) Individual audio channels with single display groupware: effects on communication and task strategy. In Conference on Computer-Supported Cooperative Work. Chicago, IL, USA, pp. 242–251

Myers B (2001) Using handhelds and PCs together. In Communications of the ACM, pp. 34–41

Ponnekanti S et al (2001) ICrafter: a service framework for ubiquitous computing environments. UBICOMP 2001, Atlanta, Georgia, USA

Ponnekanti S et al (2003) Portability, extensibility and robustness in iROS. In First IEEE International Conference on Pervasive Computing and Communications (PerCom 2003). Dallas-Fort Worth, Texas, USA: IEEE, pp. 11–19

Raskin J (2000) The humane interface: new directions for designing interactive systems. Reading, MA: Addison Wesley. XIX, 233

Rekimoto J (1997) Pick-and-drop: a direct manipulation technique for multiple computer environments. In Tenth Annual Symposium on User Interface Software and Technology, 1997. Banff Alta. Canada: New York, NY, USA: ACM, pp. 31–39

Ringel M et al (2001) Barehands: implement-free interaction with a wall mounted display. In CHI '01 extended abstracts on Human factors in computer systems. Seattle, Washington: ACM, pp. 367–368

Russell D, Gossweiler R (2001) On the design of personal & communal large information scale appliances. In Ubicomp 2001. Atlanta, GA, USA, pp. 354–361

Shih CC et al (2004) Teamspace: a simple, low-cost and self-sufficient workspace for small-group collaborative computing. In Submitted to the Conference on Computer-Supported Cooperative Work. Chicago, IL, USA

Stone MC (2001) Color and brightness appearance issues in tiled displays. IEEE Computer Graphics and Applications, 21(5): 58–66

Streitz N et al (1999) i-LAND: an interactive landscape for creativity and innovation. In ACM Conference on Human Factors in Computing Systems (CHI'99). Pittsburgh, PA, USA: ACM, New York, NY, USA, pp. 120–127

Tandler P (2003) The BEACH application model and software framework for synchronous collaboration in ubiquitous computing environments. To appear in Journal of Systems and Software (Special Issue on Application Models and Programming Tools for Ubiquitous Computing)

The eBeam System (2000) Foster City, CA: Luidia, Inc. http://www.luidia.com/

Tidebreak, Inc. http://www.tidebreak.com

Ullmer B, Ishii H, Glas D (1998) mediaBlocks: physical containers, transports, and controls for online media. In SIGGRAPH 98: 25th International Conference on Computer Graphics and Interactive Techniques. Orlando, FL, USA: New York, NY, USA: ACM, 1998, pp. 379–386

Winograd T (2001a) Architectures for context. Human-Computer Interaction, 16(2/4), pp. 401–419

Winograd T (2001b) Interaction Spaces for 21st Century Computing, In Carroll J (Ed.) HCI in the New Millennium, Addison Wesley

Winograd T, Guimbretière F (1999) Visual instruments for an interactive mural. In CHI '99 extended abstracts on Human factors in computer systems. Pittsburgh, PA, USA: ACM, pp. 234–235

Winograd T, Lee B (2004) Cognitive factors in multi-device interaction. In HCI Consortium. Winter Park, CO, USA

Wyckoff P et al (1998) T spaces. IBM Systems Journal 37(3): 454–74

Chapter 3
Towards a Global Concept of Collaborative Space

Volker Hartkopf, Vivian Loftness, and Azizan Aziz

Abstract Both distraction-free and interactive officing strategies will be required for a number of different key work places: the Individual Place, Project Place, Meeting Place, Social Place, and the Electronic Place. Mobility and flexibility in furniture, lighting, thermal, and networking will have significant opportunities for innovation, with the Project Place the most innovative and unknown of these work environments.

Providing "layers of ownership" in Project Places is critical to ensuring collaboration, immersion, and creativity. The combination of nonterritorial offices, or hoteling, with dispersed teaming and conference spaces is "not good enough" to ensure collaboration, immersion, and creativity. We contend that not only are these environments inadequate for individual work due to distractions and dispersion of needed references, they are ineffective for collective work.

For effective individual work, there will be growing emphasis on "owned" workstations, however small, and on multiple work environments for both the "road warrior" and the multidisciplinary innovator.

For successful collaborative work, the most innovative "layer of ownership" will be of project places, collaboratively owned physical places dedicated to a project for a critical period of time to ensure project deliverables. Successful project places support critical functions that individual workplaces or conventional meeting spaces cannot support. The opportunities and dynamics in innovative officing, however, are entirely dependent on flexible infrastructures - a new era in intelligent workplace design.

3.1 Smart Interior Systems to Support Augmented Work Environments

Workplaces are changing to respond to technological and organizational challenges, as well as the globalization of business, engineering, design, and manufacturing processes. Increasingly, interactive multimedia and web-based technologies create

V. Loftness (✉)
Carnegie Mellon University, PA, USA
e-mail: loftness@cmu.edu

S. Lahlou (ed.), *Designing User Friendly Augmented Work Environments: From Meeting Rooms to Digital Collaborative Spaces,* Computer Supported Cooperative Work, DOI 10.1007/978-1-84800-098-8_3, © Springer-Verlag London Limited 2009

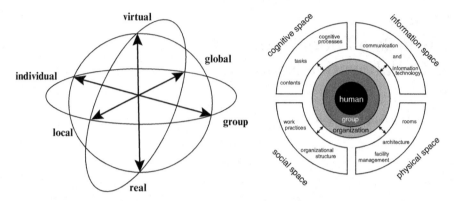

Fig. 3.1 The built environments has to respond to ever changing organizational and technological circumstances (Streitz et al. 1998)

the possibility to work within ever changing teams, both locally and globally. This requires that built environments must be responsive to ever changing organizational and rapidly evolving technological circumstances. Increasingly, people during the course of the single day work within continua of local/global, individual/group, and real/virtual circumstances (Fig 3.1).

In this perspective, the Center for Building Performance and Diagnostics at CMU constructed a test-bed in 1997 to research:

- Organizational innovations for the advanced workplace
- Innovations in information technology
- Innovative enclosure, HVAC, power, voice, data networking, and interior systems
- Products for thermal, air, visual, acoustic, connectivity, and spatial quality
- Demonstrations of products' performance in an integrated setting
- Training in material, component, and systems choices and their integration for performance
- Hands-on training in instrumentation and metrics for evaluating performance and occupancy comfort, and
- Development of CAD packages for design, simulation, and management

This test-bed, the Robert L. Preger Intelligent Workplace™, is a living laboratory with the design philosophy and principles presented in Section 4. and the relationship of workspace to productivity presented in Sect. 6. and our vision of the relation of architecture and infrastructure to augmented environments is presented in Sect. 5. First, however, the following section presents the seven "places" for collaborative work and their relation to various types of collaboration.

3.2 Places for Collaborative Work

While the values of the various levels of collaboration are being explored, the physical spaces that will support each level of collaboration should also be evaluated. Building on earlier work by the CMU Center for Building Performance and Dr. Thomas Moran of Xerox PARC, at least seven types of collaborative places may be instrumental to the next generation of collaborative work.

3.2.1 Seven Types of Collaborative Places

1. Leadership places/amenities (LP)
   (Showcase/leadership places; Food service places; Recreation/health places; Childcare places, Event places, Atrium/courtyard places)
2. Crossroads/circulation places (CP)
   (Stairway landings/elevator lobbies; Hallways/niches, Reception Areas; Landmark areas/meeting points)
3. Service pubs/shared equipment places (SP)
   (Copy/printer/scanner shared equipment areas (CAT); Kitchen areas with indoor/outdoor lunch spaces (KIT))
4. Dedicated meeting places (MP)
   (Informal meeting spaces, various scales; Formal meeting rooms, various scales)
5. Dedicated project places (PP)
   (Dedicated project rooms, various scales)
6. In-office collaborative places (IP)
   (Shared offices with meeting space; Individual offices with meeting space within; Individual offices with meeting space between)
7. Digital/electronic collaborative places (EP)
   (E-mail, Video teleconference, Web servers/b-boards/common apps; Media-spaces)

The most obvious collaborative spaces are dedicated meeting rooms, but they may not be the most successful spaces, given the range of collaborative exchange needed in organizations. Figure 3.2 indicates a preliminary assessment of the types of collaboration that might be supported in the range of collaborative space types (Loftness et al. 2002).

3.2.2 Types of Place and Affordances for Work Activities

The social networking that is enabled in building wide amenity or leadership spaces (LP) is invaluable in building long-term relationships between individuals from

	Amenity Spaces LP	Circulation CP	Shared Equipment SP	Dedicated Room/Mtg Spaces MP & PP	Individual-Office IP	Digital Space EP
Social Networking & Inculturation	✳ ✳	✳	✳ ✳			
Knowledge Transfer Info Exchange Training		✳	✳ ✳	✳ ✳	✳ ✳	✳
Coordinated Work Task Sequencing Material Sharing			✳	✳ ✳ (mtg.rm.)	✳ ✳	✳ ✳
Ideation & Creative Development Incubation Emerging Established	✳			✳ ✳ ✳ (project rm)	✳ ✳	

Fig. 3.2 Preliminary assessment of the types of collaboration that might be supported in the range of collaborative space type

different disciplines with different tasks. Cafeterias and coffee bars, health clubs, recreation areas, and childcare are not only great equalizers but also strong "collegiality" builders that can contribute to both multidisciplinary multiagency collaboration and longer retention rates. Three other space types may also increase social networking, but probably with less reliable interactions – showcase/leadership spaces shared by the entire organization for hosting customers and clients; holiday and celebratory events in event places such as atria and "all hands" spaces; and outdoor spaces and activities that offer "fresh-air" breaks. These spaces may also play a major role in providing the inspiration that contributes to the "ideation" and in providing information exchange between work groups if displays are continuously kept up-to-date and information rich.

Similarly, circulation areas and crossroads are the most prevalent location for social networking and some level of information transfer. They are integral with our natural movements in a working day, instead of destinations that require commitment to (and the appearance of time off). Elevator lobbies and reception areas, the hallways outside the restrooms and meeting rooms, are the most common "crossroads" for employees to dialogue. Many organizations have begun to add open stairs that connect two or three floors (beyond the dual fire stairs that meet code) to reintroduce a "crossroads" where people can stop to exchange information. With the introduction of landmarks and distributed amenities such as mail boxes, espresso bars, bulletin boards and white boards, as well as outside seating in relation to these natural circulation paths, crossroads are an important design contribution for collaboration (Loftness et al. 2002).

During a typical workday, members of engineering and design teams migrate from individual place (which could be their own dedicated office, a shared office, or a free address system assigned by need) to meeting places, project places, and social places, as desired and/or required.

The individual place should be available at the discretion of the team member to work on project deliverables requiring concentration, attention, and creativity. Individual work places, must have acoustic privacy and offer a range of visual privacy choices to enable such work, in addition to thermal comfort, air quality, spatial/ergonomic comfort, and a view to the outside. The ubiquitous cubicle, prevalent in the United States, does not offer those necessities, especially when the company has adopted a policy of high-density workplace settings with less than 8 m^2 per individual. In such an environment, neither acoustic nor visual privacy can be achieved. The well designed mix of individual and collaborative workplaces are critical to social networking, knowledge transfer, coordinated work and creative development.

3.3   The Robert L. Preger Intelligent Workplace™: The Living Laboratory

The Robert L. Preger Intelligent Workplace™ (IW) (Fig 3.3) is the result of an unprecedented collaboration between the Center for Building Performance and Diagnostics, a National Science Foundation Industry/University Cooperative Research Center, and its supporting industry and governmental members, organized in the Advanced Building Systems Integration Consortium (ABSIC). The 700 m^2 IW is a living laboratory of office environments and innovations.

Fig. 3.3   The Intelligent Workplace™, a rooftop extension of Margaret Morrison Hall at Carnegie Mellon University

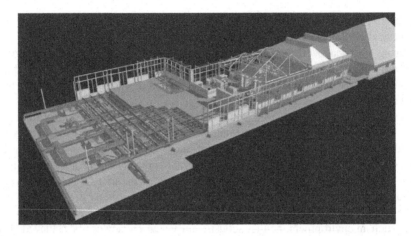

Fig. 3.4 Peel – away view of the IW illustrates the integration of all the building systems and subsystems

Completed and occupied in 1997, the IW is a rooftop extension of Margaret Morrison Carnegie Hall on the Carnegie Mellon campus.

The IW enables the interchangeability and side-by-side demonstrations of innovations in HVAC, enclosure, interior, and telecommunication components and assemblies. Most importantly, as a "lived-in" occupied office, research, and educational environment, the IW provides a testing ground to assess the performance of new products in an integrated, occupied setting (Fig. 3.4).

3.3.1 Goals

1. *Individual productivity and comfort*: The demonstration of advances in individual comfort and productivity requires that both interior system and engineering infrastructures are "plug and play" to ensure that furniture and space reconfigurations for individual productivity and creativity are immediately matched by technology and environment reconfigurations for comfort, health, and corresponding productivity.

2. *Organizational flexibility*: The demonstration of advances in organizational flexibility requires that the community of workplaces be reconfigurable on both annual and daily levels to ensure "organizational re-engineering" for collaboration supporting regrouping and sharing for organizational productivity, creativity, and innovation.

3. *Technological adaptability*: The demonstration of advances in technological adaptability requires that vertical and horizontal pathways for connectivity are accessible and open and that both interior systems and engineering infrastructures

support changing technological demands for horizontal and vertical work surface, lighting, acoustics, thermal conditioning, and ergonomics.

4. *Environmental sustainability*: The demonstration of advances in environmental sustainability requires that both energy and materials are used effectively over a building's life cycle. Concepts, such as system efficacy, user controls, micro-zoning for flex-time, just-in-time delivery of infrastructures, environmentally sustainable and healthy materials, and natural conditioning, should all be demonstrated and comparably measured to standard practice.

3.3.2 Systems Integration for Performance

While the Intelligent Workplace demonstrates a number of advances and innovations in material, components, and assemblies for thermal, visual, acoustic, air quality, and spatial performance, the overall effectiveness of these components and assemblies depends on how well they are integrated, and how they address overriding concerns about resource management, health, as well as individual and organizational effectiveness.

The IW is not envisioned as a onetime "show-and-tell" demonstration project, but rather as a dynamic environment for the teaching and evaluation of how integrated building components, systems, and assemblies affect building performance. In-house post-occupancy research is critical to validating predicted performance through simulation, and to assessing the performance in the integrated setting. The IW also provides the platform to explore broad environmental and ecological issues such as recyclability of building products and assemblies and long-term resource management. As a test bed of new ideas and as a demonstration center for successful innovations, combined with innovative officing concepts and portable diagnostics, the IW is a unique living laboratory of office environments.

The IW is conceived as a modular system, the units of which can be stacked or reconfigured to adapt to the needs of multiple office settings, such as urban areas or office campuses. The inherent rules of this system – enabling decisions such as building configuration, size of work neighborhoods, cabling and wiring dynamics, and the ratio of shared services and collaborative workspaces to workstations – ensures its application on a wider scale.

3.3.3 Reduced Waste in Construction

The IW project exemplifies how design and engineering decisionmaking, as well as material selection, can result in 70–90% reduction of emissions and waste during production of the materials used for the exterior wall, floor, and roof, compared to a conventional building (Fig. 3.5). This includes the reduction of NO_x by 90%, SO_2 by 70%, and CO_2 by 80%. The project also revealed the additional savings potential

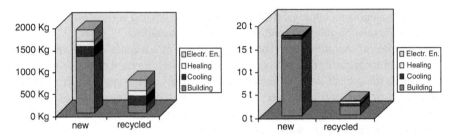

Fig. 3.5 The IW utilizes recycled primary materials in the aluminum facade system (left) and the steel structure (right) resulting in reduced emissions in material production.

when selecting recycled aluminum and steel rather than virgin materials. Here the avoided emissions ranges were similarly pronounced.

In addition, there was no on-site waste during most of the construction phase (steel structure and facade erection as well as interior fit-out), because of the IW's modular design and its off-site fabrication, with complete recycling capacity of all by-products. This also resulted in a reduced potential for injury and significant time savings during construction, which ultimately leads to capital savings.

3.3.4 Reduced Waste in Operation

The IW is conditioned for six or more months through "natural" energies alone-passive and active solar heating, cooling, daylighting, and ventilation-during dayligh hours.

In addition to the resource savings of operating a building, there is significant potential to reduce material waste through the management of material and subsystem obsolescence. Demonstrated in the IW, the reconfigurable/relocatable interior systems, with modular interfaces to the envelope, structure HVAC, lighting, communication, power systems, enable organizational as well as technological change on demand.

This dual concept of just-in-time organizational change and technological change assures that the building is meeting flexibility and adaptability requirements without redundancy or waste. Access in the "open" system to plug-and-play technologies allow for the complete component-by-component or system-by-system change-out of technology with complete recyclability when and where necessary. These concepts also insure that the building is a renewable asset for its investors and will not become a "straightjacket" that eventually has to be discarded in whole or in part. These concepts also insure that all changed-out components or systems are fully recyclable, since composite materials are avoided, and systems are demountable. For instance, the IW enclosure and structural elements are pinned or bolted and made from recycled aluminum and steel.

The integrated, modular, and demountable systems reflect the fact that buildings are made from components that have different life cycles. The envelope as a system should have a life of 50–100 years, with a possibility of exchanging glazing materials, photovoltaic elements, and other components, when superior performance becomes economically feasible. The structural system should have a life of 100 years, and when becoming obsolete at a particular site should become redeployable elsewhere (a column is a column, a truss is a truss). Interior systems may have considerably less "life expectancy," with computing systems that might have a useful life of 2–3 years. Demountable systems, however, can be recycled completely.

In summary, the four waste-management and environmental benefits of the IW are the following:

1. Materials, components, and systems are designed to require a fraction of the energies during their production and assembly and produce a fraction of the emissions of comparable systems.
2. Due to prefabrication and modular design, waste is eliminated, During the construction phase.
3. During the operational phase, design innovation supports organizational and technological changes-on-demand to manage obsolescence. This is enabled through relocatable infrastructures: HVAC, lighting, power, communication. and interior systems. The fact that major building components and systems have different life cycles is accounted for through the use of the modular, plug and play systems. This allows for easy change-out and advancement of technology as the need or opportunity arise.
4. The design anticipates a complete decommissioning of the building and its constituent parts. The "long life systems," such as structure and envelope, can be redeployed elsewhere. Or, as in all other cases, the materials of nonunified components of subsystems can be completely recycled.

3.4 New Design Approaches to Absorb Change and Avoid Obsolescence: Flexible Grid, Flexible Density, Flexible Closure Systems

To avoid frequent environmental quality failures and long term obsolescence, it is critical to invest in user-based infrastructures that are modular, reconfigurable, and expandable for all key services – ventilation air, thermal conditioning, lighting, data/voice, and power networks. The dynamic reconfigurations of space and technology typical in buildings today cannot be accommodated through the existing service infrastructures – neither the "blanket systems" for uniform open-plan configurations nor the idiosyncratic systems for unique configurations. Instead, what is needed are flexible infrastructures capable of changing both location and density of services.

Flexible Grid-Flexible Density-Flexible Closure Systems are a constellation of building subsystems that permit each individual to set the location and density of HVAC, lighting, telecommunications, and furniture, and the level of workspace enclosure (Loftness et al. 1995). These services can be provided by separate ambient and task systems where users set task requirement and the central system responds with the appropriate ambient conditions, or they can be fully relocatable, expandable task/ambient systems.

3.4.1 The Concept of Grids and Nodes: Ensuring Seven Basic Needs for Each Individual

Access to all of the basic needs for a healthy, productive workplace – air, temperature control, daylight and view, electric light control, privacy and working quiet, network access and ergonomic furniture – can only be provided by a shift away from blanket and centrally controlled infrastructures to the concept of grids and nodes (Fig. 3.6). The "grids" establish the overall level of capacitance available to support the working group or neighborhood (fresh air, cooling, power, and network capacitance). Then, the "nodes" or user interfaces must be flexible in terms of location, density, and type of service offered.

These grids and nodes should not be dealt with in isolation but as compatible assemblies and in some cases integrated systems. "Plug-and-play" technologies developed in other markets (unlike the building industry) assume distributed capability, user preferences in customization, and the ability for end users to help themselves if systems are not meeting requirements. This also reflects the introduction of home and car functionality in the office, something clearly affordable today, though not often seen in the workplace.

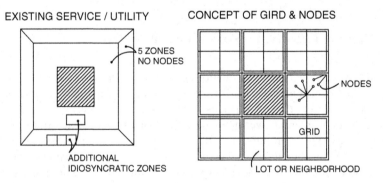

Fig. 3.6 Conventional large zone approaches to thermal conditioning and lighting are incapable of delivering adequate environmental quality to accommodate the dynamics of technology, workstation density, and teaming concepts (Loftness et al. 1996)

3.4.2 *Flexible Infrastructures Begin with Accessible and Expandable Vertical Service*

First, the central capacities of power, data, phone, cooling, and ventilation must be reexamined. In many buildings, the central capacity and backup is inadequate in the following:

- Central power capacity and reliability
- Data/voice capacity and ease of reliability
- Central chiller capacity and the ability to increase zone densities
- Central ventilation capacity independent control from thermal conditioning
- Riser space and easy access for modification

One way to ensure that these central capacities and vertical distribution capacities will be adequate over time is to clearly label allowable floor densities. Moreover, there should be a significant shift towards distributed systems to support local control by organizational units with differing equipment and occupant densities, or with different work schedules, ensuring appropriate technical and environmental service without excessive costs.

3.4.3 *Flexible Infrastructures Require Collaborative Horizontal Plenum Design and Relocatable "Nodes" of Service*

Advanced buildings today demonstrate that floor-based servicing may more effectively support the dynamic workplace (Fig. 3.7). As networking, ventilation, and thermal conditioning needs to be delivered to each workstation, services at floor level or at desktop offer a greater ease of reconfiguration than ceiling-based systems. In addition, floor-based systems such as electrical and telecommunication cabling and terminal units/outlets can be continuously updated to meet changing needs. Today, a number of industry partnerships are forming to offer collaborative solutions to flexible infrastructures – raised floors, data/voice, power, thermal conditioning, and ventilation. With these modular, floor-based services, the ceiling can become more playful and elegant – as a light and acoustic diffuser – defining working groups and work neighborhoods as well as rediscovering the crafted ceilings of landmark buildings.

3.4.4 *Flexible Infrastructures can Support Reconfigurable Workstations and Workgroups*

Once the appropriate modular, relocatable infrastructures are provided, the continuous recreation of workstations and workgroups can finally be achieved with the assurance

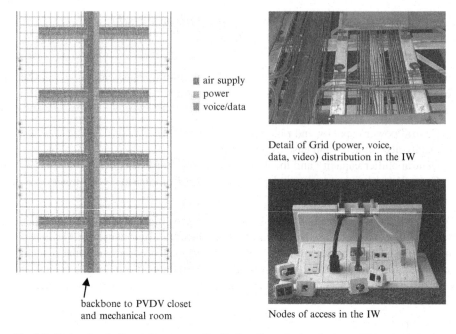

air supply
power
voice/data

Detail of Grid (power, voice,
data, video) distribution in the IW

backbone to PVDV closet
and mechanical room

Nodes of access in the IW

Fig. 3.7 Rational underfloor infrastructure distribution allows for just-in-time additions and changes to support the dynamic workplace

of thermal comfort, lighting quality, air quality, and connectivity. It is critical, however, to design the furniture/wall system to support rapid changes between open and closed layouts, between individual and teaming spaces, as well as rapid changes in occupant density, equipment density, and infrastructure/service to match these configurations. While the grid of service and the number of nodes will determine the maximum densities on a floor, the ability to continuously rethink the organization should be fully supported by modular, reconfigurable desks, storage, walls, doors, and ceiling components.

We need to move beyond embedded fixed technologies in buildings to flexible and adaptable end-user technologies. Both the next generation of new buildings and the revaluing of existing buildings must explore the attributes of micro-zoning and user modifiable systems – through neighborhood service grids and individual, user-responsive nodes – to support the dramatic changes in technologies and organizations. The manufacturers of building components and subsystems will have to develop products that are compatible in open architectural systems, user-modifiable, expandable and relocatable through modularity, and support multiple vendor plug-in capability. Justifications for user-based systems are growing, from measurable productivity to measurable reductions in operating and renovation costs, to significant increases in building longevity with life cycle investment values. The development of life cycle costing techniques should fully recognize buildings as enabling environments and continuously renewable assets.

3.5   Impact of Environment on Productivity

3.5.1   Literature

The impact of the work environment on individual productivity has been shown in numerous studies to be of major economic importance. For instance, during a typical workday, 5 minutes of lost time equate to 1% loss of productive time. Programmers, engineers, writers, designers, and many other creative professionals require up to 30 minutes to get back to the creative moment, once their flow of thought is interrupted. One interruption can equates to 6% of productive time lost per day.

A simple calculation is as follows: Assume 500 office workers to be housed in a new facility. At 20 m² gross per person, the facility would be 10,000 m² in area. Assuming $1,000 m⁻² of construction cost, the necessary investment would be $10 million. The average salary, including fringe benefits, in our example, can be conservatively estimated to amount to $100,000 per person per year. Therefore, the total salary outlay per year would be $50 million. A 5% productivity increase through appropriate building design and interior building systems provisions would equate to $2.5 million in savings per year. Even assuming that the investment for a more 'productive' building would have to be increased by 50% the payback period would be only 2 years.

At the same time, the negative impact of inappropriate building decisions could result in an equivalent productivity loss - a 10% span from +5% to −5%. Performance increases and performance degradations are the most important factors that should govern building investment decisions.

3.5.2   BIDS™

The CBPD has developed a web-based Building Investment Decision Support Tool (BIDS™), to support an interactive assessment of the relationship of building design, engineering, and investment decisions to the major dimensions of productivity. These include absenteeism, cost of churn (cost of moving employees and making the appropriate spatial, environmental, and technical accomodations), productivity impacts (where measurable), energy cost savings, employee attraction and retention, and user satisfaction.

The BIDS tool also illustrates the fact that many decisions which lead to measurably improved performance do not necessarily increase first costs if the systems are appropriately integrated.

Three case studies in BIDS™ include the Penn Center West Soffer building in Pittsburgh, Pennsylvania; the Owens Corning Headquarters in Toledo, Ohio; and the West Bend Mutual Insurance Company of West Bend, Wisconsin. These environments have become indispensable to the companies competitive capacity to manage change through their flexible infrastructures in raised floor plenums. For instance, the measured productivity increase of West Bend after moving into their new building was 16%, with 2% linked to task air thermal control. (Kroner 1992). They provide examples of enlightened thinking on the part of the chief executive officers and their teams.

3.5.3   Collaborative Work Settings

In addition to providing settings for productive individual work, buildings need to provide opportunities for impromptu and planned collaborative work. Such collaborative work takes place by chance through social encounters- while waiting for a copying job to be finished, a fax to be received or sent, or a cup of coffee to be brewed (Fig. 3.8).

Therefore, it is beneficial to create places for serendipity, especially since so much work is conducted with only the computer screen as interface. It is important for coworkers to have a chance to encounter each other and discuss their work in ways that are not planned and not scheduled. This is especially true for highly creative groups.

Project places (PP) support short-to-medium term teamwork dedicated spaces. Such project places encourage the build-up of the collective knowledge through the storing of the relevant material, exhibiting intermediate results and physical artifacts, providing places for group discussions, group work, as well as for intermittent individual work between group sessions. Such project places also benefit from advanced electronic equipment for the development and storage and retrieval of ideas, concepts, and designs (Fig. 3.9).

Meeting places (MP) allow only for short-term group interaction and must be left in the condition that they were entered, thereby serving only short-term purposes. This typically does not enable the best results for teamwork, because the collective understanding does not have a place to evolve continuously.

The electronic place (EP), ideally, allows for seamless transitions between the individual place, project place, meeting place, and social place (Fig. 3.10). As computing and multimedia systems become increasingly ubiquitous and mobile and are capable of global connectivity, the physical environment needs to be adaptable to

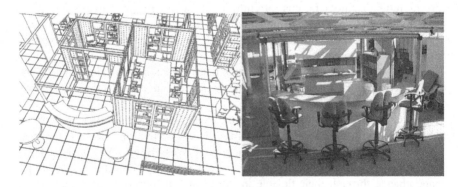

Fig. 3.8 Information exchange and team-building occurs most effectively over common technology devices at social places

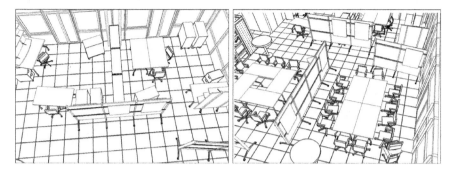

Fig. 3.9 Differently equipped and configured project places accommodate different types of project needs

Steelcase "Leadership Community"   IPSI/Wilkhahn "Interactable" workstations

Fig. 3.10 Various electronic technologies allow for seamless transitions between places for enhanced collaborative work

allow effective use of these rapidly evolving technologies. In addition, the technologies themselves must move from being interface design oriented to truly functioning as interactive systems.

On this basis, we can envision work environments that allow the seamless migration from individual to group, from local to global work, and from real to virtual contexts. Environments could be developed to provide substantially the same interior systems and technological contexts to enable the globally connected engineering and design team members to encounter familiar work environments, no matter where they work, in Stuttgart, Germany; Detroit; Michigan; or Shanghai, China.

3.5.4 Experimental Settings in the Intelligent Workplace

The CBPD currently uses 300 m² of the IW for project, meeting, social, and electronic collaboration (Fig. 3.11). This environment is to serve the Center's creative project work, as well as establish the feasibility of the overall concept.

The following illustrations and diagrams depict individual components of this environment, as well as showing three-dimensional images of the overall space and its places.

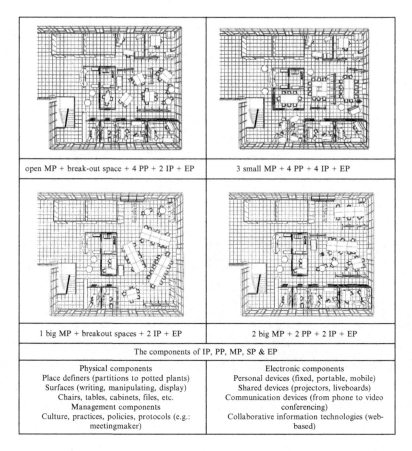

open MP + break-out space + 4 PP + 2 IP + EP	3 small MP + 4 PP + 4 IP + EP
1 big MP + breakout spaces + 2 IP + EP	2 big MP + 2 PP + 2 IP + EP

The components of IP, PP, MP, SP & EP	
Physical components	Electronic components
Place definers (partitions to potted plants)	Personal devices (fixed, portable, mobile)
Surfaces (writing, manipulating, display)	Shared devices (projectors, liveboards)
Chairs, tables, cabinets, files, etc.	Communication devices (from phone to video
Management components	conferencing)
Culture, practices, policies, protocols (e.g.:	Collaborative information technologies (web-
meetingmaker)	based)

Fig. 3.11 Flexible plug-and-play infrastructures at the IW allow for just-in-time reorganization of the space to accommodate various configurations of IP, PP, MP, SP, and EP

The illustrations show the plug-and-play and kit-of-parts oriented approaches that allow for organizational flexibility and technological adaptability, while serving individual needs and conserving nonrenewable resources.

3.6 The Role of Real Estate and Facilities in Individual and Organizational Effectiveness

3.6.1 Goals and Objectives

The US GSA Productivity Protocol at the Center for Building Performance and Diagnostics at Carnegie Mellon University, was established to develop the methods for critical research to definitively demonstrate the role of real estate and facilities in individual and organizational effectiveness.

The Productivity Protocol Development team has developed building evaluation protocols linking environmental, technical, and spatial quality to individual and organizational effectiveness.

In order to identify the performance/financial data sets of real interest to the federal sector, the team defined five goals:

1. More effective organizational performance
2. Greater collaboration and social integration
3. More effective individual work
4. Greater health of worker
5. More effective resource use – energy and materials throughout the lifecycle.

The Productivity Protocol research efforts, through the support of the US General Services Administration, has established data on key building attributes, key productivity/effectiveness indices, and proven techniques and measures of productivity or performance. Research scenarios of critical importance to federal real estate decision-making were prioritized to establish the role of real estate and facilities in individual and organizational effectiveness.

The Productivity Protocol team has been working collaboratively in multiple workshops. Each workshop builds on materials assembled by the team members and their expertise to further the definition of all four major task areas:

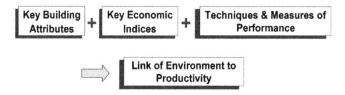

The widespread interest in productivity studies has illuminated the paucity of sustained research GSA efforts linking the role of real estate and facilities to individual and organizational effectiveness. Indeed, the prevailing management belief is that "place" is insignificant compared to management practices, remuneration, and individual motivation/commitment to organizational goals. The building community has funded so little research in this area in the last 25 years that there are few proofs to counter this prevailing belief. The GSA effort was launched to identify key building attributes that impact individual comfort, health, and productivity and the cost benefit indices that could substantiate "productive" directions for design decision-making in the workplace.

3.6.2 Key Building Attributes

The Productivity Protocol team identified over 80 building attributes that potentially had significant impact on individual and organizational productivity/effectiveness.

The team then debated the availability of data for these attributes for portfolio-wide, building before and after, and workgroup before and after studies. The team also debated the significance of the attributes to present decision-making and the magnitude of the potential impact. These efforts reduced the key attributes into the 20 key scenarios for study, grouped into the following:

- Spatial/Ergonomics for the individual
- Spatial/Ergonomics for the group
- Environment for the individual
- Environment for the group
- Technology for the individual
- Technology for the group
- Resource effectiveness

3.6.3   Key Economic Indices

The Productivity Protocol team identified over 45 Productivity/Cost-Benefit Indices that could be significant for federal studies. The team then debated the availability of this data from a range of federal agencies for portfolio wide, building before and after, and workgroup before and after studies. They also debated the significance of the cost-benefit measures to present decision-making and the magnitude of the potential impact. In the mean time, more detailed study of the economic variables and baseline costs/employee has been undertaken in collaboration with the Building Investment Decision Support Tool (BIDS™). These efforts reduced the key economic indices to the 25 and defined key scenarios for study, which relate to the following:

- More effective organizational performance/internal processes cost-benefit indices
- Greater collaboration and social integration cost-benefit indices
- More effective individual work cost-benefit indices
- Greater health of worker cost-benefit indices
- More effective resource use – energy and churn/materials cost benefit indices

3.6.4   Techniques and Measures of Productivity/Performance

A number of the proposed productivity studies rely on existing building attribute data sets and existing/in-hand measures of productivity/performance. In addition, there is a need to identify a range of field techniques and measures that could be used in federal productivity studies. The development of new techniques and measures, including the application of measures developed in other disciplines (such as medicine), was advanced. The Productivity Protocol team documented the range of field measurement techniques, including international approaches and methods. The collected techniques include the following:

- Satisfaction and performance questionnaires
- Performance ratings/scales
- Individual performance testing
- Health testing
- Environmental factors testing
- Business benchmarks

At the same time, the Productivity Protocol team developed a number of web-based techniques to collect critical data related to federal facility use, for which there seem to be no standards. The advantage of web-based data collection is the speed and quantity of response that is possible, provided that the on-line surveys are easy to use and meaningful to the individuals and the organizations administering them. These Productivity Protocol efforts include on-line data acquisition surveys such as the following:

- How Do You Spend Your Time?
- Occupant Satisfaction Survey
- Environmental Control Survey
- What Work Tools Do You Use?

  - Individual WorkTools
  - Group/Team WorkTools
  - Copy Area WorkTools
  - Kitchen Area WorkTools

For example, the results of the "How Do You Spend Your Time?" survey provide insights as to how individuals think they use their time:

- Identifying the range of tasks undertaken in a typical week in relation to a variety of job descriptions, which is critical to understanding and developing productivity test materials (such as simple and complex task tests).
- Identifying the percent of time at tasks that need freedom from distraction, which is critical to decisions about the levels of spatial, visual, and acoustic privacy; as well as the percent of time at tasks that create distraction.
- Identifying the percent of time spent in planned and unplanned meetings, as well as the numbers involved in those meetings, which is critical to the mix of spaces.
- Identifying the percent of time spent on tasks that require work materials and ergonomic conditions to support those materials.
- Identifying the percent of time spent on "full-life" tasks that could be resolved through building wide amenities or building locations in mixed-use communities.

The results from the suite of surveys support the design/specification of the following spatial and organizational goals:

- Which description of collaboration is most important to organizational success? Exchanging information and training, innovation, social networking, and coordinating tasks.

- What type of spaces will induce the greatest collaboration?
  Circulation spaces, dedicated project rooms, in-office meeting spaces, digital spaces, shared equipment spaces, meeting rooms, and building amenity spaces.
- How can the value of collaboration to financial goals be measured?
  Employee attraction/retention, customer base/satisfaction, organizational profit, quality for price, innovations/patents, time to market.
- What major research studies would help you convince clients to invest in collaborative spaces? (open question)
- What types of collaboration space enable you to collaborate both formally and spontaneously?

These questions are central to determining the percentage of floor area dedicated to teaming and the nature of the collaboration spaces, from guest chairs in individual offices to dedicated project spaces.

3.6.5   National Environmental Assessment Toolkit: NEAT

With GSA support, a National Environmental Assessment Toolkit - NEAT, was developed at the CBPD to assess the performance of projects in-situ and with the direct involvement of the occupants, thereby developing detailed "portraits" of buildings. This tool is useful in pre- and post-rehabilitation projects, as well as in comparing user assessment and quantifiable performance characteristics of different work environments/facilities before and after a move.

The application NEAT continues with direct support from the General Services Administration in the before and after field evaluation of over 29 federal facilities nationwide. The NEAT toolkit combines portable instrumentation with questionnaires and expert walkthrough to create robust baseline assessments of thermal, visual, acoustic, and air quality in the workplace. The CBPD team has developed data collection techniques, GIS based data records, and innovative data analysis tools from scatterplots to create environmental "EKGs" for buildings linked to the quality of building systems and facilities management. This toolkit and the GSA field studies are central to building the business case for high performance buildings, and linking indoor environmental quality to facility management costs, health, and productivity.

3.7   Other Current Projects

3.7.1   Intelligent Workplace Energy Supply System: IWESS

The Robert L. Preger Intelligent Workplace as a living laboratory (always adapted and improved) allows the successive integration of innovative components and systems. The Intelligent Workplace Energy Supply System - IWESS is currently such a work in progress, with an emphasis on energy effectiveness through systems integration. IWESS is an integrated set of components that uses solar thermal energy bio-fuels to provide power, cooling, heating, and ventilation for Carnegie Mellon's Intelligent Workplace. Graduate students and faculty in the School of Architecture's Center for Building Performance and Diagnostics have been involved with selecting, installing, testing, and evaluating these components and with integrating their operation with in the IW and with the campus power, steam, and chilled water grids. The objective of IWESS is to provide a healthy, productive, and comfortable environment for the occupants of the IW and to reduce the primary energy requirements for operating the space by a factor of two. The knowledge gained in this IWESS effort will improve the design of equipment, of systems, and of their operation, to reduce the energy consumed by buildings, currently 40% of the total consumption of primary energy in the US.

3.7.2 Information Technology Enabled Sustainability Testbed: ITEST

In addition to IWESS, the IW is a test-bed for advanced integrated sensing, actuating, and control systems: ITEST. The goal of ITEST is to integrate "state of the art" IT systems with sensing, actuating, and controls technologies to enable effective performance of systems to achieve sustainability in building operations. As a test-bed for ITEST, the IW offers an appropriate laboratory for testing systems' performance and occupant comfort. The IW offers a dynamic and flexible platform for integrating natural conditioning, high performance flexible infrastructures for active conditioning, and advanced energy systems. The CBPD has assembled a team of federal and industry partners to create a rich test environment.

3.7.3 The Building as Power Plant: BAPP

The 10 years of research in the IW has provided significant opportunities to study, develop, and apply energy saving techniques, while simultaneously improving indoor environmental conditions to ensure the circumstance for superior human health, comfort, and productivity. As buildings in the United States consume 70% of electricity and 40% of all primary energy for heating, cooling, ventilation and lighting, it is imperative that paths to a sustainable future be created, especially in the light of the fact that major emerging economies, including China and India, are rapidly urbanizing with enormous environmental and energy consequences.

A second, larger living laboratory in development, the Building as Power Plant - BAPP. The BAPP is designed to integrate advanced energy-effective building technologies (ascending strategies) with innovative distributed energy generation systems (cascading strategies), such that all of the building's energy needs for heating, cooling, ventilating, and lighting are met on-site. Furthermore, the BAPP will generate more energy on-site than is brought to it in the form of non - renewable resources.

A next generation "Intelligent Workplace," the built success of the 50,000 ft^2 BAPP, will be a demonstration of zero carbon/net energy performance as well as user comfort, health and satisfaction, organizational flexibility and technological adaptability as an academic, office and research lab building. Through a series of workshops with leading professionals from around the world, the Center has written design guidelines and developed engineering innovations for BAPP, and successfully written legislation towards a multi-university National Testbed effort.

This paper has provided an introduction to the design, engineering, and systems integration concepts which are the foundation to creating environments that can meet important human, organizational, economic, and environmental goals.

Tomorrow's work environments must maximize the value of three key resources:

- Human attention to perform concentrated and creative work.
- Organizational responsiveness to remain competitive.
- Renewable resources to protect the environment and to provide opportunities for those who succeed us.

Acknowledgments The Advanced Building Systems Integration Consortium (ABSIC), supporting the CBPD, is a university-industry-government partnership established in July 1988 at Carnegie Mellon University. ABSIC conducts research, development, and demonstrations for the purpose of increasing the satisfaction, health, well-being, and productivity of occupants, of enabling organizational change, and technological adaptability while improving cost, energy, and environmental effectiveness. ABSIC has been created for the advancement of the building industry in pursuing the technologies and the settings needed for high-performance work environments.

Recognizing the significance of the work of CBPD and its industrial sponsors, The National Science Foundation designated the CBPD as an Industry/University Cooperative Research Center, the first center that focused on the building industry.

A portion of this paper draws from the results of several workshops with Dr. Thomas Moran who spent a sabbatical at CMU from Xerox PARC. He was assisted by Dr. Jayakrishna Shankavaram, who was a researcher at CBPD before joining a consulting firm in Washington DC. The authors offered a seminar in the fall of 2000 on the subject of Design of Integrated Systems that resulted in a group submission by Tracy Yu, Edith Lau, and Young Joon Miki. Some of the images are from that class. We all gratefully acknowledge the long-term financial and professional support of ABSIC.

References

Becker F, Joroff M, Sims W. Teamspace strategies: creating and managing environments to support high-performance teamwork. International Development Research Council: Atlanta, 1998

Cooper A. The inmates are running the asylum. Sams Publishing: NJ, 1999

Covi L, Olson J, Rocco E. A room of your own: what do we learn about support of teamwork from assessing teams in dedicated project rooms? from In Cooperative Buildings: Integrating Information, Organization and Architecture: First International Workshop. Cooperative Buildings Workshop: Darmstadt, 1998

Duffy F. The new office. Coran Octopus Limited: London, 1997

Elder J, Rubin A. Building for people: behavioral research approaches and directions. National Bureau of Standards, 1980

Hartkopf V. Whole building performance in the international arena, IFMA Conference. Philadelphia, PA, March, 1992

Hartkopf V, Loftness V, Drake P, Dubin F, Mill P, Ziga G. Designing the office of the future: the Japanese approach to tomorrows workplace. Wiley: New York, 1991

Hartkopf V, Loftness V, Aziz A, Shankavaram J, Lee S. The GSA adaptable workplace laboratory. Cooperative Buildings: Integrating Information, Organization and Architecture. Springer: Heidelberg, pp 12–28, October 1999

Konomi S, Müller-Tomfelde C, Streitz NA. Passage: physical transportation of digital information in cooperative buildings. In: Streitz NA, Siegel J, Hartkopf V, Konomi S (eds) Cooperative Buildings: Integrating Information, Organization and Architecture, Lecture Notes in Computer Science 1670. Springer: Heidelberg, pp 45–54, Pittsburgh, US, October 1999

Kroner W. The west bend mutual study, Ashrae workshop on indoor environment and productivity 1992. The Center for Architectural Research, Rensselaer Polytechnic Institute: Baltimore, March 1992

Loftness V, Hartkopf W, Mahdavi A, Lee S, Aziz A, Shankavaram J, Tu KJ, Mathew P. Flexible grid - Flexible density – Flexible closure – the intelligent workplace. USACERL Contract DACA88–93-D-0004, Phase I, January 1995

Loftness V, Hartkopf V, Mahdavi A, Shankavaram J. Flexible infrastructures for environmental quality, productivity and energy effectiveness in the office of the future. International Facility Management Association (IFMA) - Intellibuild'96 Anaheim, CA, 17–20 June 1996

Loftness V, Aziz A, Mondazzi M, Moustapha H, Yoon H. Collaborative work settings US General Services Administration, April 2002

Ruck N (ed). Building design and human performance. Van Nostrand Reinhold: New York, 1989

Streitz NA, Geißler J, Holmer T. Roomware for cooperative buildings: integrated design of architectural spaces and information spaces. cooperative buildings: integrating information, organization and architecture Springer: Heidelberg, pp 4–21, February 1998

Chapter 4
Designing an Easy-to-use Executive Conference Room Control System

Maribeth Back, Gene Golovchinsky, Pernilla Qvarfordt, William van Melle, John Boreczky, Tony Dunnigan, and Scott Carter

Abstract The Usable Smart Environment project (USE) aims at designing easy-to-use, highly functional, next-generation conference rooms. Our first design prototype focuses on creating a "no wizards" room for an American executive; that is, a room the executive could walk into and use by himself, without help from a technologist. A key idea in the USE framework is that customization is one of the best ways to create a smooth user experience. As the system needs to fit both with the personal leadership style of the executive and the corporation's meeting culture, we began the design process by exploring the work flow in and around meetings attended by the executive.

Based on our work flow analysis and the scenarios we developed from it, USE developed a flexible, extensible architecture specifically designed to enhance ease of use in smart environment technologies. The architecture allows customization and personalization of smart environments for particular people and groups, types of work, and specific physical spaces. The first USE room was designed for FXPAL's executive "Ian" and installed in Niji, a small executive conference room at FXPAL.

The room Niji currently contains two large interactive whiteboards for projection of presentation material, for annotations using a digital whiteboard, or for teleconferencing; a Tandberg teleconferencing system; an RFID authentication plus biometric identification system; printing via network; a PDA-based simple controller, and a tabletop touch-screen console. The console is used for the USE room control interface, which controls and switches between all of the equipment mentioned earlier.

M. Back (✉)
FX Palo Alto Laboratory, Palo Alto, CA, USA
e-mail: back@fxpal.com

S. Lahlou (ed.), *Designing User Friendly Augmented Work Environments: From Meeting Rooms to Digital Collaborative Spaces,* Computer Supported Cooperative Work, DOI 10.1007/978-1-84800-098-8_4, © Springer-Verlag London Limited 2009

4.1 Introduction

As conference rooms add functionality, they often lose usability. A standard conference room is often quite literally crammed full of equipment: multiple displays, teleconferencing systems, meeting capture systems, and room controls (light, sound, screens, projectors) (Foote et al. 2004; Fox et al. 2000; Streitz et al. 1998). In one of the conference rooms at FXPAL, for example, there are four computers, three projectors, and a videoconferencing system, along with three SmartBoards (interactive whiteboards). Each of these items is controlled via its own unique interface (often a remote with dozens of small buttons) and none of these devices are interconnected (except at second hand, via the net). Using this room often requires the help of a technology expert – a "wizard" – who specializes in conference room systems.

The goal of the Usable Smart Environments (USE) project is to allow a user to make use of all this technology without having to pay any special attention to it. We based our design on observations, workflow studies and use scenarios for the executive's use of the room, and concluded that what was really needed was one big button that would "do the right thing" at any given point. That proved to be both impractical and undesired; however, extending the simplicity of this idea led us to a workable solution. In this chapter, we detail the discovery and design process for the USE ConsoleUI (a tabletop touchscreen kiosk) and its underlying system, which is our solution to the room and data control problem.

The USE control software has a number of web services that manage a collection of devices and applications that populate a meeting room. The control system that sits on top of these web services is designed to allow the user to select devices (e.g., video conference) or applications (e.g., whiteboard) as appropriate during a meeting. The software is controlled in the room through a console. The design goal of the console UI was an easy-to-use user interface that enables contextually appropriate interaction with the functions of the room. As is often the case, apparent simplicity often means enormous care and much work has been implemented "behind the scenes" to enable ease of use and a wizard-free conference room.

The current system allows customization and personalization of smart environments for particular people and groups, types of work, and specific physical spaces. The system architecture consists of a database of devices with attributes, rooms, and meetings that implements a prototype-instance inheritance mechanism through which contextual information (e.g., IP addresses, application settings, phone numbers for teleconferencing systems, etc.) can be associated with specific devices for specific users, rooms, and meetings.

4.2 Needfinding: An Executive's Workflow

As our goal was to fully understand an executive's use of meeting rooms, our approach was to investigate not only what happens during a meeting but also the general work process of an executive and how he and his staff prepared for the different types of meetings he attended. In particular, we explored the meeting practices of an executive of a research laboratory with 50 employees in Silicon Valley, which is a subsidiary to a Japanese international company. We made direct observations, over a 2 month period, of the executive's activities before, during, and after meetings, and tracked and analyzed the paper-based and computer-based scheduling and document handling systems involved. We also conducted interviews based on our observations with the executive, Ian, and with his support staff: an administrative assistant, Erica, and a Japanese market researcher, Mari, who also serves as Ian's personal assistant during travels to Japan.

4.2.1 Types of Meetings Within the Company

Ian participates in a variety of types of meetings during a week: face-to-face informal meetings (sometimes including lunches and dinners), formal or semi-formal meetings with explicit or implicit agendas, video conferences, and occasionally offsite meetings. About 70% of the meetings are face-to-face informal meetings; 10–20% of the meetings are face-to-face formal or semi-formal meetings. Ian also frequently attends video conferences. When a video conference cannot deliver the appropriate level of personal contact, Ian goes to Japan to meet with executives and managers in the parent company; this happens a few times a year. The least common type of meetings is offsite meetings. In the past, Ian has taken his management team for off-site meetings every year or two.

Still, the large majority of the meetings take place at the company's facilities. Ian has space for meetings in his office, although this space does not have any projection surface for sharing digital content. Adjacent to Ian's office is the conference room Niji. This room is used when Ian meets with a larger group of people, more than five or six, or if anyone in the meeting needs to use the projector for presentations or demonstrations. We identified this room as the space in which to develop our system.

Before the USE project began, Niji had an analog whiteboard, a data projector/ screen for laptop hookup capability, a network connection, and a telephone conferencing system (audio only).

4.2.2 The Most Common Meeting: Informal Face-to-Face

Ian meets with researchers, consultants, and managers in his office for informal face-to-face meetings. These meetings often have a stated purpose, such as discussion about the researchers' projects, or reviewing a presentation for a Japanese executive visiting the company. Some attendees bring their laptops to show a presentation or to make a demonstration. To get connected, many use the wireless internet connection while others plug in their computer to wired connections available for this purpose.

However, as the word is out in the company that Ian likes to get a copy of the presentation on paper to take notes, many choose to give the presentation from paper rather than from their laptops. Ian does not keep the annotations he makes on the printouts of the presentations; instead he gives them back to the presenter as a form of feedback.

The preparation for the face to face meeting mainly falls on Ian's assistant, Erica. She books the meeting and informs the attendee about the stated purpose. Depending on the purpose of the meeting, the attendee prepares supporting documents. After the meeting, the task of the attendee is to implement eventual action items discussed.

4.2.3   The Recurring Semiformal Meeting

Ian attends a number of more or less formal meetings during a week. The degree of formality shifts slightly between the meetings. For example, the Tuesday morning staff meeting which all employees are expected to attend has a predefined agenda that is followed throughout the meeting. This meeting is held in Kumo, a larger conference room across the hall. Other meetings have a more informal procedure that has developed over the years. As these meetings have an implicit agenda rather than a predefined one, we call them semiformal. These semiformal meetings often have a few more attendees, and so they are often held in the conference room Niji rather than Ian's office.

4.2.4   Video Conferences

Ian increasingly attends video conference meetings. Nearly all of his video conferences are with Japan, usually with executives at the Japanese parent company. Ian has two options for video conferencing: either he can use the one-person Tandberg video conference system on his desk or a larger system set up in a dedicated room near his office. Ian rarely uses any other documents than his handwritten notes during video conferences, although he thinks it would be nice to have supporting documents, such as emails and PowerPoint, in the meeting.

When the meeting has more than one attendee on Ian's side, another room, Yuki, is used. This room also uses a Tandberg video conference system in addition to an in-house system for sharing and annotating PowerPoint slides in distributed meetings. This system allows the people in the remote locations to see the slides in real time. When Ian needs to use this system, it is set up by a member of the support staff. Ian rarely has any documents prepared for these meetings. If PowerPoint or other documents are shared, other meeting attendees on his side or on the Japanese side provide them. Usually the documents have been shared between the meeting participants before the meeting starts; however, the shared version may not be the version used in the meeting.

4.3   Observations

In this section, we detail and discuss our observations from the executive study.

4.3.1   Lack of Technological Support for Everyday Tasks

One of the most salient observations from this interview study is Ian's lack of technological support for his everyday tasks. Ian mainly uses the computer to read his email; the rest of his work is captured in the notes he makes in his calendar. The low use of technology can be explained by two factors; personal preferences and the essential nature of a CEO's work.

Over the years, Ian has developed methods and techniques to get his work done, which reflect his personal management style. Part of his style is to externalize his ideas as lists on paper, either in his calendar or from his notepad. The calendar provides him with a quick overview of important issues. It easily opens flat to the current week; it is lightweight and Ian can easily take it with him to meetings. A few notes on the pages remind Ian of the issues at hand. The characteristics of the calendar let Ian focus on what needs to be focused on in the meeting: both the issues that need to be solved or communicated, and the attendees of the meeting.

The technological tools that Ian uses reflect two essential parts of a CEO's work: communication and relationship building. This is particularly true in meetings. Besides the important information sharing and decision-making functions, the meetings are also an arena for building and maintaining relations with people critical for the success of the company. It is through communication and relationship building that the CEO conducts his leadership. The three computer-based tools that Ian uses, email, PowerPoint, and video conferencing, all play important roles in communication and relation building.

The technological tools Ian uses today support his way of working. However, the question is how to make the technology useful for him, so that he will use it. The key issues seem to be not only whether the new technology continues to support Ian's work practice, but whether the technology can provide a tangible benefit for Ian's work process as well as the work process of his support staff. In addition, the technology must not intrude on the most important aspect of the meeting as a place for creating and maintaining relations. Technology introduced in the meeting room should be as unobtrusive as possible, melting into the background, yet easily accessible to allow spontaneous use by the attendees without interrupting workflow, that is, it should feel as though it is part of the basic infrastructure of the room (Star 1999).

4.3.2   The Persistence of Notes and Products

The meetings produce different kinds of products, with varying degrees of persistence and reusability. Some are notes in the attendees' personal notebooks or calendars. The meeting can also have more formal products, such as minutes.

A third kind of product is annotations to presentations given during the meeting. In the setting we studied, the number of products was limited. The semiformal meeting produced the most, although generally only one product came out of the meeting: the minutes. On occasion, meetings were followed up by email communication. There is a relation between the kind of meetings and the kind of products produced during the meeting. The semiformal meeting tends to produce formal products, while the informal meeting produces annotations on presentation printouts (if any products are produced at all). Production of personal notes can occur in any kind of meeting.

The long-term usefulness of the products and the notes in the everyday work of the CEO varies. The (physical, paper-based) minutes, for example, are kept on file, but are rarely accessed. The reason might be that ongoing activities and future events require more attention than decisions about past activities and events. This fact is also reflected in how the CEO refers back to the notes in his calendar. These notes are often used – and more are created – during an activity or during the planning of an event. After the event is past or the activity completed, the notes are no longer used. The lifespan of the notes is thus limited to the life span of the activity they support.

A meeting product not discussed is notes on the whiteboards in the meeting room. Whiteboard notes are the most uncommon type of product for Ian (though not for his employees). When we interviewed the CEO's administrative assistant, we noticed that Ian did have some notes on his whiteboard. Upon inquiry, however, it turned out these were about 3 months old and were not produced by the CEO. The main reason the notes were still there had less to do with their long-term usefulness and more to do with the fact that the whiteboard had not been in use since the notes were written down. As the whiteboard has doors covering it, the notes could stay on the white-board without negatively influencing the overall appearance of the CEO's room.

PowerPoint presentations, when used within the company, are living documents. Although care is taken by the researchers to prepare them, notes and comments get added to them during the meetings with Ian and changes are made to the presentation in the meeting. Most of the presentations given to Ian are work in progress, such as research updates, presentation of research ideas, and drafts of high profile presentations to executives of the parent company. Similarly, Ian's presentations are often works in progress as a step for preparing his Japan trips. The work in progress character of the presentation affects the sharing of the material. In particular, Ian's presentations are confidential. He does not like people to get their hands on unfinished material, as he may still be working on what to present and how to present particular issues. For the researchers, the presentations generally do not have the same level of confidentiality.

4.3.3   Discussion: The Successful Introduction of Technology

From the execution and work process of the CEO's meetings, we can draw several conclusions:

- The workflow this CEO has developed over the years includes very little technological support. When technology is needed, the primary users of it are his support staff.
- The meetings have few products. The semiformal meetings produce more products than other meeting types. These products mainly get archived to a location only known by the CEO's administrative assistant. Some of the products are returned to the original producer with added annotations.
- PowerPoint presentations are ubiquitous. They not only are shared from a computer, but very often communicated as printouts. The presenter most often has lower status in the organization than the person receiving the presentation. For example, researchers and managers present to Ian, while Ian presents to the executives he reports to in Japan.
- Presentation and material shown and discussed during a meeting may be confidential. Copies of confidential materials are disposed of after the meeting.

Introducing new technology to support the meeting culture of the CEO is challenging, in particular as the meeting culture has evolved without any significant amount of technology. This section summarizes in our view the most important factors for a successful introduction of new technology in the meeting room.

- The technology needs to fit with the current work practice. Although some changes to the current practice are probably needed, these changes should be as minimal as possible and should fit into the current work practice as seamlessly as possible (Weiser 1991). Any changes that are perceived as unnecessary or as added work compared to the current work practice may cause the user not to use the new technology.
- The technology needs to be perceived as lightweight. Ian uses lightweight tools today: pencil, eraser, and paper. These tools are easy and quick to use and provide a tangible result of the actions taken. The new technology should share these characteristics. There should be no need for figuring out how to use the technology, and the results of the user's actions should be immediately visible. In a meeting, there is no time for figuring out how the technology works. In addition, the user risks losing face by showing a lack of understanding of the technology in the meeting, making adoption less likely (Preece et al. 2002). Therefore, preserving meeting flow is both technically and personally important.
- The technology should work in the background so that people in the meeting can focus on the participants of the meeting and not on the technology. For example, there should be no need for troubleshooting presentations. The technology should also be immediately accessible in the same way a whiteboard is immediately accessible when walking into a conference room.
- The technology needs to be developed with a holistic approach where the focus is not only on what is going on in the meeting room, but also on the activities preceding and following the meeting. Extra work the user needs to do while creating or transferring the presentation to a meeting room may influence how often he or she uses the available technology.

4.4   Use Case Scenarios: Implications for Design Implementation

Based on the findings from the aforementioned workflow study, we developed six use case scenarios for a USE conference room that fits into the work flow of the executive. This section gives examples of one of the scenarios and our exploration of different solutions to the scenarios and some implications of the design of the user interfaces and the system architecture.

4.4.1   Scenarios and Roles: Task-level Definition, Transition Points

The example scenario describes how the CEO, Ian, prepares and gives a presentation for his staff. Although we created several scenarios to match the workflow task discoveries, we describe only one here due to space constraints. This scenario was uncommon, only occurring around six to seven times a year, but it highlights the constraints of designing for Ian and the different aspects of his work process that the USE system we were designing needed to support.

In developing the scenarios, we first wrote a rich description to match with the current work process, in order to introduce changes only where it was technologically necessary. We then broke down the scenarios in table format. The first (Table 4.1) describes each step of the process and different design alternatives. The second table (Table 4.2) describes the order in which actions needed to be performed, and the responsibilities of the users and the system.

4.4.1.1   Scenario 1: Before the Meeting

Ian needs to have a meeting debriefing six lab members about a presentation he is to give to the CEO of the parent company. Ian wants to have input on the presentation before he finalizes it.

Ian asks Erica to schedule the meeting. He tells her who he wants to attend and what the purpose of the meeting is. Erica schedules the meeting into Niji, as there will be more than six people in the meeting and Ian wants to show slides. When Erica reserves Niji, she records the time and date of the meeting, and a title of the meeting.

To prepare his draft, Ian asks Erica to print out several older presentations, which each have some of the content he would like to show. He uses these as well as blank sheets of paper to design his presentation. He also meets with a few people in his office to gather ideas again on paper, by hand. In addition, he asks some researchers to send him their slides on a particular topic.

Erica authors the presentation in PowerPoint from the sheets of paper and prints Ian gives her. When she is done, she prints the presentation and gives it to Ian to check over.

Table 4.1 Read down each of the four columns in this table to walk through the first four alternatives in the "Ian presents" scenario

Alternative 1	Alternative 2	Alternative 3	Alternative 4
PDA: When Ian is ready to head to Niji, Erica gives him a PDA set up for the kind of meeting Ian is going to	*No PDA*: Ian goes without PDA to Niji, where he will use in-room devices		
			When Ian comes to the room, he walks up to a sign-in device attached to the wall beside the door and identifies himself
Ian walks into the room where the rest of the attendees are already seated. He puts down his papers [and the PDA] and greets everyone			
Ian identifies himself to the system			
System fires up and one of the screens shows the first slide of his presentation. The other screen is set to whiteboard mode			
Ian starts up the meeting with a few short announcements. When ready to present…			
…he takes the PDA and presses the start button		…he launches presentation from a device in the room and presses the start button	
The presentation is shown on one of the displays. The other display is set in whiteboard mode (already done in [2])			
Ian proceeds through the presentation slides using…			
…the PDA	…a device on the table	…same device that launched presentation	
The presentation comes to an end, Ian and the attendees have a discussion about it, and actions items are assigned			
Ian leaves and takes the PDA with him. When Ian leaves the room, his presentation disappears from the screens. Ian returns the PDA to Erica			Ian prepares to leave the room and signs out/exits the presentation so that the presentation and the controls for it are not accessible to the meeting attendees
Some of the other attendees linger in the conference room and continue the discussion.			
After Ian left/signed out, both screens became digital whiteboards			

Table 4.2 This table describes order of actions and who is responsible for each action.

	Presenter (Ian)	Admin (Erica)	System
1	Sets meeting	Schedules meeting in outlook; creates a new meeting for presenting PowerPoint with USE	Creates the meeting object; sets owner (Ian), date
2	Creates presentation sketch	Creates PowerPoint presentation	
3	Specifies changes	Makes changes to presentation	
4	Approves final copy	Uploads to system; configures primary display to be PowerPoint and other display to be blank	Associates presentation with meeting; records meeting configuration
5	Enters room; swipes card or uses biometric ID to start meeting (or carries PDA, which room notices)		Authenticates Ian, loads configuration for meeting, pre-loads PowerPoint presentation onto primary display; blanks second display; switches console interface to PowerPoint control mode
6	Advances through slides		Advances through slides
7	Advances past last slide of presentation (the black screen)		Returns console to its main menu (Whiteboard, Teleconference, PowerPoint, End)
8	Presses "End" button		Clears displays; resets room to its default state
9		Checks that room has been reset; if not, presses "End" button on the console	Clears displays; resets room to its default state
10			Clears displays and resets room if steps 8 or 9 have not been performed, the meeting time has elapsed, and no other room activity

This cycle repeats a few times, until Ian is satisfied with the content of the presentation. Erica prints a final version for him to mull over the day before the meeting. These tasks can be performed also by Mari, the other assistant; however, the process is basically the same. Erica uploads the presentation so that it is accessible from the equipment in the conference room.

4.4.1.2   Scenario 1: Day of the Meeting

Ian tells Erica in the morning that he wants some changes to the presentation before the meeting. She makes them and uploads it again. In addition, she also prints out a final clean copy on paper for Ian to take into the meeting.

Up to this point, we did not envision any major changes to the work processes when introducing the USE system. But when Ian enters the room, we envisioned four different alternatives for the sign-in process. The main difference between these first four alternatives is which devices are used for signing in. Alternative 1 uses a contextual aware PDA, Alternative 4 uses a specific console at the door. Alternatives 2 and 3 use a device inside the room close to the executive's chair: a console or a tablet PC. Table 4.1 illustrates the differences in a unified manner.

4.4.1.3   Roles for Scenario 1

Next we worked out the actions of, and the causal relationships between, the various roles (*Presenter* (Ian), *Admin* (Erica), and *System*) required to fulfill the scenario in which Ian presents. The roles and the order of events are summarized in tables. Table 4.2 shows the roles for Scenario 1. This table should be read left to right, top to bottom to understand the causal relationships.

4.4.2   Lessons Learned: The Scenarios

One central technology from the user's point of view in these scenarios is the device to control the conference room. This device needs to be connected to the rest of the system so that it can send commands to the technology installed in the room. It also needs to be aware of the system's status so that it can inform the user of it. The connections must be fast and reliable. For example, when the user shows a presentation, the slide control must be instantaneous in order to give appropriate feedback to the user; if the slide does not change immediately, the user will most likely hit the "forward" button repeatedly, confusing the system (and the user). It is essential that the user interface (UI) of the control device communicate to the user clearly and immediately the complex settings of the room: a glanceable, immediately updated state display. In the next section, we discuss in detail the iterative design of the console.

The UI does not rely on a particular form factor or type of device. The UI is designed in such a way that it can be accessed and easily used on a wide range of devices such as PDA, touch screens in the room, personal laptops, or cell phones. For the room Niji, we use a touch screen tablet PC as a tabletop kiosk, dedicated to the Console UI.

The conference room envisioned in these scenarios includes several separate technologies accessible through a single UI. To accomplish this, we designed a conference room control system that can connect with authentication equipment, projectors, video conference equipment, and whiteboard applications. This system acts like a mediator between the adaptable UI on the device in the room and the technologies such as video conference equipment installed in the room. In addition to supporting the capabilities during an ongoing meeting, the system also needs to support the preparations and the activities following up the meeting.

The USE system uses card readers and/or fingerprint readers to allow Ian to sign in securely. When Ian signs in, a successful authentication starts a number of processes, adapts the UI on the device, starts appropriate applications, etc. Ease of use and good feedback in the authentication process are essential. One important issue with the authentication is that it must succeed every time for high profile users, such as Ian, the CEO. For these people, failure is often unacceptable; for example, the CEO could lose face if failure with authentication occurred in the presence of others. For this reason, we chose RFID authentication over biometrics, such as fingerprint readers; the successful read rate on off-the-shelf fingerprint readers is much lower than RFID card readers, often requiring multiple tries.

As the room includes video conference equipment, the system needs to be able to deal with the capabilities of the remote partner in a video conference. The simplest scenario is that the remote room uses a similar installation as our conference room, with the same kind of control system architecture. In that case, the system can communicate with the remote room to launch applications. Also, if the system regularly connects to a particular remote location, a profile of that remote location can be set.

4.5   Designing the Console: Requirements of the Executive

The current interface to the USE system is a standalone application known as the ConsoleUI. A few key ideas guided its design, based on the needfinding and use scenarios noted earlier. Most importantly, we wanted to let the user focus on the communication tasks at hand in the meeting, and specifically avoided approaches that exposed any procedural issues involving technology control (Ponnekanti 2001). On the technical side, we wanted to make sure that the pace of the user's interaction matched with the response times of devices in the room, in order to reduce frustration and the perception that "this thing isn't working." Finally, we wanted the interface to be flexible and extensible to accommodate changes in system capabilities.

Our first design is for a user who is generally interested in the goals of a meeting rather than the engineering of a conference room's systems. For example, a phrase like "I want to call Tom" means much more to most users than "I want to switch my video source from the presentation computer to the video conferencing system and initiate a video conferencing call via an ISDN line ...." In its simplest form, the USE Console UI presents only potential end results to the user, for example: "call Tom," or "present my PowerPoint file." This form of the UI is intended to insulate the user from the complex processes that are necessary to carry out their requests. By presenting all options in a manner in which the user is comfortable, our hope is that the user will come to trust the system; this will allow them to focus on their tasks, not on using the UI.

This trust allows the USE console to overcome one of the USE system's perpetual HCI problems: latency. Some of the devices in the room take a few seconds to react to user input. As these devices can be affected by any number of factors (e.g., heat and network congestion), the duration of these delays can be very difficult to predict. As a consequence, the USE ConsoleUI deliberately slows the user interaction down. This is accomplished by slowing down any animations or transitions in the UI. Even objects like animated buttons have slower than normal animation cycles.

Finally, conference rooms are constantly evolving. Because of this, the USE system is designed to be open-ended, allowing integration of new applications and equipments that might come into a conference room. This meant that we needed a highly adaptable UI. We accomplished this by keeping the ConsoleUI almost purely devoted to interface logic – the actual code for controlling devices in the room is distributed throughout a number of web service applications. All control elements within the UI can be automatically configured, within some range of possible configurations.

4.5.1   Contextually Aware UI: A One Button Interface?

It took extensive user studies and several meetings, but the basic UI that we needed to develop became pretty clear. We needed one big button that always did the right thing at any given time. We came to think of it as a contextually aware "next" button: "Next, I want to see some slides." "Next, I want to place a conference call." Our initial design came quite close to the one-button goal. The user's activities were heavily scripted via a configuration UI. The configuration UI allows the user to add presentations or set up a videoconference ahead of time. In this early version, it also determined the order in which the events occurred. When the user completed a task, they pressed the done button and were presented with the next task. If a task was completed naturally, the next task would be presented automatically. While this UI was certainly simple, it did not allow for much flexibility. The flexibility that it did allow took several steps to achieve. One feature from this design that did survive into the final design is the division of the screen into two distinct areas that reflect the two displays in the prototype conference room. After several iterations, we finally arrived at the design that became our first working prototype (Fig. 4.1–4.3). This design stayed fairly faithful to the one-button esthetic, but did provide a great deal more flexibility.

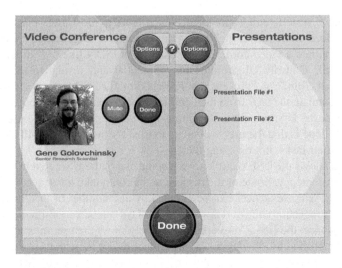

Fig. 4.1 First working interface: running a video conference on the *left screen* and viewing a presentation list on the *right screen*

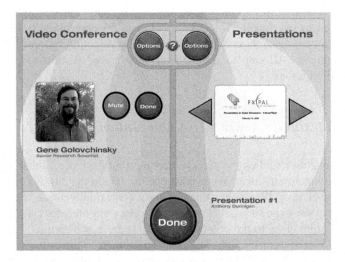

Fig. 4.2 First working interface: (running a video conference on the *left screen* and a presentation on the *right screen*) after selecting presentation #1 from the right screen in Fig 4.1

This new design incorporated option buttons, one per side, which allowed the user to select specific tasks (Fig. 4.3). This change offered the user a great deal of freedom without adding much complexity. Our initial prototype functioned quite well, but testing did reveal one flaw in our design logic. To switch between displaying two presentations, the user needed to perform three actions and visit three screens. This was an unacceptably complex interaction within the "One Button for one task" paradigm.

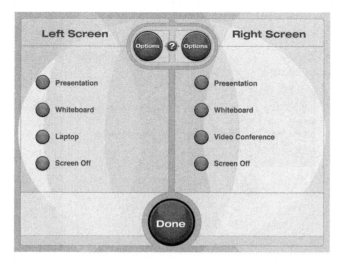

Fig. 4.3 First working interface: viewing option lists on both screens

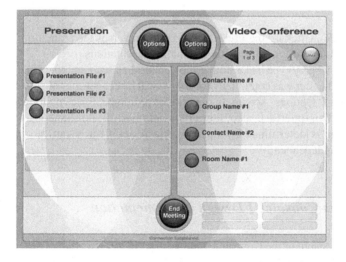

Fig. 4.4 Current solution: viewing a list of loaded presentations on the *left screen* and the video conference "address book" on the *right screen*

Our quick solution to the problem was to add more buttons to each screen. This solved the "three clicks" problem, but at the expense of clutter and ease of use. These new buttons were just too small to select on our touch screen. Our current solution is a compromise. Switching between presentations requires two clicks, but a bridging animation makes the operation "feel" seamless. From the "Presentation Options Screen" (Fig. 4.4), the user selects a presentation. The graphics that embody the selected presentation's "button" transform into the presentation's controls

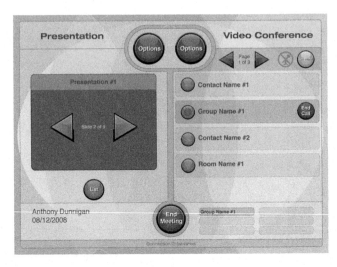

Fig. 4.5 Current solution: running a presentation on the *left screen* and a video conference on the *right screen*

(Fig. 4.5, left). Clicking the green "List" button reverses the animation, presenting the user with the original list of the available presentations.

Our original prototype had a similar problem dealing with multiple videoconference selections. The user was continually forced to switch between the "Video Conference" screen and its "Options" screen. In our current prototype, this is no longer necessary (Fig. 4.5). This interface also supports a number of simultaneous connections (the number is determined by device capabilities). Each can be initiated and terminated independently.

4.5.2   The ConsoleUI Design Implementation

The current design of the Console UI allows for the manipulation of several physical devices from one touch screen. Currently, the interface is an Adobe Flash MX graphical interface that communicates with other components of the system via messages passed through a web service (the ConsoleService). The UI communicates with the ConsoleService via an XML socket. The socket communication is bi-directional and asynchronous: either end may initiate an exchange of messages, but user interaction is not automatically blocked during these exchanges.

The XML messages sent to the user interface describe the setup of the room, the devices and applications available, and objects available to those devices and applications. For example, PowerPoint is one application running on a particular display, and its objects are the set of PowerPoint files assigned for the current meeting. Another example is a video conference device with contact objects that specify who can be called and which ISDN number or IP address to use. The interface sends command messages to the ConsoleService; the ConsoleService in turn forwards them to the RoomControl service, where commands are executed. Commands include selecting a particular device or application, and manipulating them by advancing slides, making calls, etc. as appropriate to each device or application.

After the ConsoleUI initializes, users can invoke actions by pressing various buttons on the touch screen. All actions are asynchronous and have the following logic: the user requests an action via button-press; the request is passed to the ConsoleService; the ConsoleService responds with a "working" message and queues the request for processing by the RoomControl; the ConsoleUI displays a waiting state (in the button) – most of the interface is still live at that point, though some selected options may be disabled; the ConsoleService receives a response from the RoomControl (error, or success with further details), and sends a "completed" message to the ConsoleUI; and the ConsoleUI updates its state (either by displaying an error or by making some change in visible state).

We chose to use Flash, as this application is very good at presenting and animating graphics. The ConsoleUI relies on custom graphics and animations to impart important information to the user. UIs are fairly easy to design and iterate in Flash, whereas they require sophisticated and time-consuming development in conventional user interfaces. Many platforms support Flash, allowing one UI to be deployed on many dissimilar devices. With little or no alterations, the ConsoleUI can be run from a laptop computer (PC or MAC), a tablet PC, or a handheld mobile device. This is another feature of the ConsoleUI that has proven very valuable during the development of the USE system. It is often helpful to control the USE system from within the Flash development environment.

Flash also makes it possible to exchange XML over a socket connection, which makes it possible for a Flash program to act as a peer for another program, such as a web service. While it may be possible to implement a Web Service client directly in Flash, we required bi-directional communication among the services in our system. We found it easier to have a WebService front end to mediate communication with the rest of the system, leaving the complexity of SOAP/WSDL communication to .NET. We are now exploring the possibility of embedding Flash and a COM component in a .NET Windows form.

Because different conference rooms can have different capabilities, and even different culturally determined decor, we have set up the ConsoleUI application so that it can be auto-configured, within some range of possible configurations. This includes room capabilities, the user's preferred language, UI colors, on-screen messages, and all labels. So, for example, one conference room might have two display computers, and another conference room might have three. Similarly, a user might choose one set of colors for a ConsoleUI running in a corporate boardroom in the USA, and an entirely different set of colors for the same UI running in the conference room of a small design firm in Japan. Configuration information is passed to the ConsoleUI from the ConsoleService in an initialization message, which gets it in turn from the user's preferences, the room's preferences, and the entries made in the Configuration UI.

4.5.3   Lessons Learned: ConsoleUI Design

It was surprisingly easy to develop this UI in Flash. Much of this surprise was due to a lack of documentation concerning Flash's ability to pass data via an open socket, especially XML data. Once we were able to write the necessary code, Flash proved to be quite stable, sending and receiving hundreds of thousands of messages in one particular test.

For the Flash to have a predictable partner to communicate with, a web service was created in C# that contained a built-in socket communication module that sent and received data. In our method, Flash connects to this web service; after that, data flows both ways. There was some trial and error involved in getting clean messages into and out of Flash. Again, once the proper method was discovered, Flash proved very stable.

Our choice of a Slate tablet PC to host the ConsoleUI is one we will change. The limited video capabilities of the tablet have sometimes interfered with the UI's animation effects. This poses a real problem, as so much important information is contained in those animations. When they move at the wrong speed or stutter, their meaning becomes corrupted. It also looks bad, which lessens a user's confidence in the system. We are now testing a touch screen driven by a more capable PC that should solve this and other performance problems.

4.6   System Architecture

The USE system consists of several components: a configuration repository, one or more orchestration components (for each physical space that needs to be controlled), an optional user console for each space, and (for each physical space) one or more devices to be controlled. Figure 4.6 shows a diagram of one instantiation of this architecture. It should be understood that more than one serial device and more than one TCP/IP device can be controlled simultaneously; similarly, more than two applications can be run on each display machine.

4.6.1   Component Configuration

The USE system coordinates multiple devices based on a given configuration to put each device into an appropriate state for the specific task. The user can exercise control over the system by selecting task-oriented actions; the system performs the required device orchestration.

Unlike canned room control environments that are designed to work with specific sets of devices, this architecture supports dynamic plug-and-play capability: devices can be swapped out without rebooting the system or affecting existing configuration scripts.

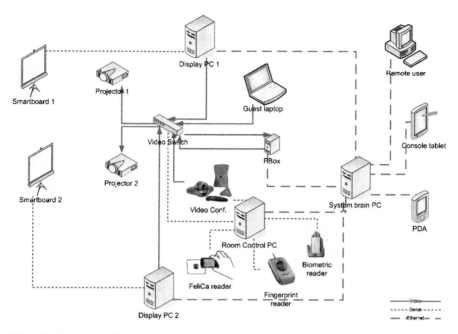

Fig. 4.6 Devices and their connections

New devices can be introduced without requiring any code changes in the existing orchestration framework.

Although all components of the system can run on the same computer, typically the components are distributed among several machines, some of which may be co-located, while others may be remote. Communication among components is mediated by web services calls, although other communication mechanisms such as RPC may also be used. Figure 4.6 illustrates the architecture , which consists of a configuration repository, a room control PC, and two Display PCs. The Display PCs have their displays projected onto Smartboard electronic whiteboards through overhead projectors. The video switch controls the routing of displays, including guest laptops that can be plugged into a VGA cable in the room. The system may be controlled through any number of devices shown on the right.

4.6.2 Devices and Device States

The configuration repository manages a database of devices, device states, rooms, users, meetings, and configurations. Each room contains one or more devices, and each meeting involves the use of a configuration that orchestrates the use of some subset of the room's devices. Each object (Device, DeviceState, Room, Meeting, etc.)

has a unique ID, and zero or more named attributes. A configuration orchestrates devices by collecting a set of DeviceStates, each of which represents some device in a particular context. For example, a room may contain two identical projectors. The database would contain one Device object that characterizes the type of projector, and a meeting configuration would contain two DeviceState objects, one for each of the projectors. The attributes of each DeviceState would specify how the particular projector should be connected to the system, including how it is connected to the video switch device, and what serial port should be used to control it.

4.6.3   Meetings

Prior to starting a meeting, the meeting owner configures it by selecting the applications and devices that will be used, and by specifying which documents and video contacts (if any) will be used during the meeting.

When the system is started, the orchestration component requests from the configuration repository the configuration appropriate to the space being controlled, the time of day, and (optionally) the person making the request. The information returned by the repository is translated into a configuration for the meeting. The configuration consists of a collection of DeviceState objects that describe how each device and application that participates in the meeting should be configured. This allows the system to put the devices into known states, regardless of their earlier state. Thus, manual operation of devices (such as switching video sources or changing projector settings, for example) during gaps between meetings will not affect system behavior during a scheduled meeting.

4.6.4   Applications

Devices controlled by the framework include serially-controlled devices such as projectors, video switchers, and some video conference devices, and network-controlled devices such as other computers, some video conference devices, etc. From the perspective of the orchestration architecture, applications (e.g., PowerPoint) that run on computers in the space being controlled also constitute devices to be orchestrated. Applications are controlled by a Controller component that receives input from the orchestration engine and selects the corresponding application for display. Multiple applications can be run simultaneously on each display machine; the system places no restrictions of what kinds of applications can be run in this manner.

Each application can receive commands through the Controller component. There are three classes of application in the system: built-in applications, opaque applications, and applications with some automated control. The whiteboard application is an example of a system-specific application. It can be controlled on a fine-grained level by injecting custom messages into its message queue. An opaque application (such as a web browser) can be opened, closed, hidden, or displayed, but cannot be controlled in any custom way by the system. Finally, the third kind of application is one that has a published API for controlling its execution. PowerPoint, for example, has a COM API for advancing slides and performing other remote control actions. A special IDevice is created for controlling PowerPoint programmatically. This allows users of the system to use a console user interface to drive a presentation on a public display without physically interacting with the computer that controls the display. Thus remote users can present to local audiences.

4.6.5   Interaction

The system's use of scripts allows much of the interaction with the system for control purposes to be reduced to a few simple selections, or to be entirely unnecessary.

One class of interactions involves logging into the system. This can be accomplished through an RFID (FeliCa) badge, through a fingerprint or other biometric reader, or by typing the user ID and password into a trusted application. A successful swipe of a thumb or an RFID is sufficient to open a document or an electronic whiteboard application on one screen and to initiate a teleconference call on another. In each example, the user focuses on the task – sketching, presenting, and communicating – rather than on the mechanics of controlling devices or figuring out which remote control to use.

Once a person is logged in, he does not need to use remote controls or buttons on the various devices to control the room. Most of the device state is configured automatically; the few cases where some input is required (e.g., choosing which contact to call to establish a videoconference) is accomplished with a single selection on a touchscreen console used to control the room. The system automatically takes care of switching the projector to video mode, determining the appropriate way to initiate the connection, and connecting to the remote site. This avoids one of the pitfalls of unorchestrated spaces in which some devices can be left in unknown states, making it difficult to know what needs to be done to accomplish the desired task.

4.6.6   Component Structure

The system can be decomposed into a stack of components, as shown in Fig. 4.7. Starting from the bottom, the system contains databases for storing configurations and authentication information. These databases are wrapped by abstraction layers that manage database access and make the rest of the system independent from the particular choice of databases. In addition, the persistence layer makes it possible to manipulate database records as first class objects, further isolating persistent storage details from the system. The Generic Objects layer represents the

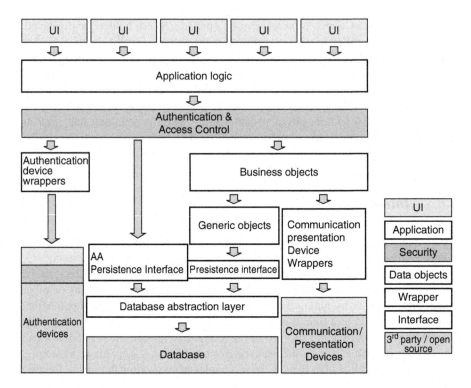

Fig. 4.7 Architecture stack

schema of the objects stored in the database. The Business Objects layer contains objects that directly control the various devices and applications that make up an instance of the system.

Authentication and access control is performed by the security component. This consists of authenticating users who want to sign in, generating session tokens for signed-in users, distributing these session tokens to other components of the system, and validating session tokens on request. This component maintains user accounts, but will use Windows Domain authentication to authenticate users, unless the login credentials do not correspond to a Windows domain login. Thus the authentication component allows both domain users and remote users to use the system. In addition, trusted authentication devices are used to generate authentication requests. This hardware includes RFID and biometric readers.

The application logic layer corresponds to the network of distributed components that deliver the appropriate configuration information to the right room at the right time, and orchestrate the meetings. Finally, multiple user interfaces (such as the meeting console, the configuration editor, scheduler, etc.) allow users to create, modify, and use the information stored in the system.

4.7 Related Work

The USE system bears some similarities with other systems for managing devices in smart environments, including Patch Panel (Ballagas et al. 2004), Metaglue (Coen et al. 1999), Gaia (Román et al. 2002), and Aura (Sousa and Garlan 2002). Unlike Patch Panel, we are concerned with integrating complex existing devices such as video switchers, video conferencing systems, and applications rather than "primitives" such as joysticks and buttons. We do not require applications to be designed specifically for our system, as is done in Metaglue and Gaia.

The system is designed to be predictable and controllable by the user, rather than autonomous, as are other systems (Coen et al. 1999; Román et al. 2002; Sousa and Garlan 2002). This means that there is a clear relationship between users' actions and system responses in our system than in autonomous ones. We focus on short-term meeting support rather than on long-running tasks that may be moved from one location to another (Sousa and Garlan 2002). Our task focus means that the system behaves quite differently from Hanssens et al. (2002) or Sousa and Garlan (2002): if a projector is turned off, the USE system turns it on, whereas Hanssens et al. (2002) will re-route the display to another projector. While this adaptive routing may be useful in a room with many redundant displays, it is not a useful solution in most cases.

We also distinguish our work from presentation management systems such as Epic (Rui and Liu 2004). Epic is designed to orchestrate the presentation of slides on multiple screens in the course of a presentation. The system described here, on the other hand, orchestrates multiple applications and devices.

4.8 Looking to the Future

New technologies like sensor networks, tangible interaction devices, virtual environments, and an array of mobile devices will have an impact on meetings and meeting rooms. In particular, we plan to focus on two new areas as we extend the USE system.

4.8.1 Mobile Interaction

Increasingly distributed work processes along with the ubiquity of mobile devices provide motivation and means for mobile meeting support. But what does it mean to be in a meeting while mobile? Mobile users face higher demands on their attention and thus it may be difficult for them to maintain the level of awareness necessary to follow a meeting in real time (Oulasvirta et al. 2005). By the same token, it can be difficult for non-mobile participants to understand the disposition of a mobile user (Cheverst et al. 1999). However, systems should not merely make allowances for mobile participants but also allow them to contribute in ways non-mobile participants are not able to. Should we create a section of the room-based UI for enabling mobile clients?

We see design and development possibilities rooted in the following questions: How do people who are mobile contribute to a meeting? How can they interact seamlessly with other mobile users as well as participants in augmented environments? How can systems support mobile meeting participants who may be distributing their attention across multiple activities? What is the right level of awareness to convey between mobile participants and those in augmented environments? How can a system support activities unique to mobile users, such as data capture in the field?

4.8.2 Sensing

To support fluid communication and promote rapid recovery from conversational breakdowns in a meeting, it is necessary to convey a rich representation of the participants' context. To achieve this, the system must be able to collect and convey a wide spectrum of information (Marshall and Bly 2005), while still providing mechanisms for participants to reveal and potentially alter sensing policies (Lederer et al. 2004). Furthermore, a system may need to resolve conflicting policies between meeting sites and participants.

Interesting aspects of sensing for smart meeting environments include: In what ways can information sensed implicitly about meeting participants be used to augment awareness or in some other way support participants in situ? What are the appropriate interfaces or mechanisms to access captured information? What is the right information to capture and how should it be modeled? What straightforward methods can be employed to regulate privacy settings on sensed data? And, how do all these ideas inform the design of the next USE system?

4.9   Conclusion

We have found that the USE system as designed has allowed not only Ian, the principal user, but also multiple users with varying degrees of technical skill to control our conference room. In each case, the limited number of options the UI provides was sufficient for their needs. This has led us to believe that our design approach, initially targeted to one specific user type, might be extensible to most users.

We have noted some focus issues: users seem not to, and probably should not, lavish any more attention on the ConsoleUI than is necessary to accomplish their goals. We have observed users pressing a button in the UI and then looking at the appropriate room display almost immediately. Because of this behavior, much of the feedback that the UI provides to users is ignored. A solution to this problem might involve incorporating environmental cues into the USE system.

Lighting cues or subtle graphical overlays on the displays in the room might provide the necessary feedback. At a minimum, users must trust that their command was sent and is being executed. They must also know when a command has been completed or has failed. Our current UI provides all of this information, as well as some visual cues as to the amount of time a command will take to complete; however, often this information is missed by the user.

Our next interface will certainly be more customizable, but our initial prototypes have indicated a definite range for that customizability. Our understanding and the basis for our design iterations will be further enhanced by design reviews, use studies, and the extension of the USE system into a larger conference room with more users and different, less constrained requirements.

Acknowledgments We thank our colleagues at FXPAL for supporting the USE project and tolerating the constant flux of our conference rooms. Special thanks to our informants and to John Doherty, Jonathan Cohen, Paul MacEvoy, and Gerry Filby, who provided various technical underpinnings for the USE system.

References

Ballagas R, Szybalski A, Fox A (2004) *Patch Panel: Enabling Control-Flow Interoperability in Ubicomp Environments*. In Paper presented at the PerCom 2004 Second IEEE International Conference on Pervasive Computing and Communications, Orlando, Florida, USA, March 2004, http://media.informatik.rwth-aachen.de/materials/publications/ballagas2004a.pdf

Cheverst K, Blair GS, Davies N, Friday A (1999) The support of mobile-awareness in collaborative groupware. *Personal and Ubiquitous Computing 3*(1/2), 33–42

Coen M, Phillips B, Warshawsky N, Weisman L, Peters S, Finin P (1999) *Meeting the Computational Needs of Intelligent Environments: The Metaglue System*. In Proceedings of the 1st International Workshop on Managing Interactions in Smart Environments (MANSE'99), Dublin, Ireland. 1999 pp. 201–212.

Foote J, Liu Q, Kimber D, Chiu P, Zhao F (2004) *Reach Through the Screen: A New Metaphor for Remote Collaboration*. In Proceedings of the PCM 2004 Fifth Pacific Rim Conference on Multimedia, Tokyo, Japan

Fox A, Johanson B, Hanrahan P, Winograd T (2000) Integrating information appliances into an interactive space. *IEEE Computer Graphics and Applications 20*(3), 54–65

Hanssens N, Kulkarni A, Tuchida R, Horton T (2002) Building agent-based intelligent workspaces. *International Conference on Internet Computing* 675–681

Lederer S, Hong J, Dey AK, Landay JA (2004) Personal privacy through understanding and action: Five pitfalls for designers. *Personal and Ubiquitous Computing 8*(6), 440–454

Marshall CC, Bly S (2005) *Saving and Using Encountered Information: Implications for Electronic Periodicals*. In Paper presented at the Conference of Human Factors in Computing Systems, 2–7 April 2005, New York

Oulasvirta A, Tamminen S, Roto V, Kuorelahti J (2005) *Interaction in 4-second bursts: The fragmented nature of attentional resources in mobile HCI*. In Proceedings of SIGCHI Conference on Human Factors in Computing Systems, New York: ACM Press, pp. 919–928

Ponnekanti S, Lee B, Fox A, Hanrahan P, Winograd T (2001) *Crafter: A Service Framework for Ubiquitous Computing Environments*. In Ubicomp, Atlanta, Georgia pp 56–75

Preece J, Rogers Y, Sharp H (2002) *Interaction Design: Beyond Human-Computer Interaction*. New York: Wiley

Román M, Hess CK, Cerqueira R, Ranganathan A, Campbell RH, Nahrstedt K (2002) Gaia: a middleware platform for active spaces. *Mobile Computing and Communications Review* 6(4), 65–67

Rui Y, Liu Z (2004) ARTiFACIAL: Automated reverse turing test using FACIAL features. *Multimedia Systems 9*(6), 493–502

Sousa JP, Garlan D (2002) *Aura: an architectural framework for user mobility in ubiquitous computing environments*. Software Architecture: System Design, Development and Maintenance, IFIP 17th World Computer Congress – TC2 Stream/3rd IEEE/IFIP Conference on Software Architecture (WICSA3), August 25–30 2002, Montréal, QC, Canada, 224, 29–43

Star SL (1999) The ethnography of infrastructure. *American Behavioral Scientist 43*(3), 377–391

Streitz N, Geisler J, Holmer T (1998) Roomware for Cooperative Buildings: Integrated Design of Architectural Spaces and Information Spaces. *Lecture Notes in Computer Science 1370*, 4–21

Weiser M (1991) The computer for the 21st century. *Scientific American 265*(3), 94–104

Chapter 5
Experimental Reality: Principles for the Design of Augmented Environments

Saadi Lahlou

Abstract The Laboratory of Design for Cognition at EDF R&D (LDC) is a living laboratory, which we created to develop Augmented Environment (AE) for collaborative work, more specifically "cognitive work" (white collars, engineers, office workers). It is a corporate laboratory in a large industry, where natural activity of real users is observed in a continuous manner in various spaces (project space, meeting room, lounge, etc.) The RAO room, an augmented meeting room, is used daily for "normal" meetings; it is also the "mother room" of all augmented meeting rooms in the company, where new systems, services, and devices are tested. The LDC has gathered a unique set of data on the use of AE, and developed various observation and design techniques, described in this chapter. LDC uses novel techniques of digital ethnography, some of which were invented there (SubCam, offsat) and some of which were developed elsewhere and adapted (360° video, WebDiver, etc.). At LDC, some new theories have also been developed to explain behavior and guide innovation: cognitive attractors, experimental reality, and the triple-determination framework.

5.1 Context: The Digitization of Work and Its Impacts

As work is being digitized, redesigning office environments becomes an efficiency challenge for those organizations who rely heavily on "white collar" performance: administration, media, and research; more generally, office work is a significant contribution to the production process of every organization. In fact, in most organizations, there is a general trend of automation of "white collar" work (Lansdale 1990; Malone 1983, 1996).

For example, at Electricité de France (EDF), one of the world's largest energy production and distribution companies, more than half of EDF employees are "cognitive workers" (or "knowledge workers": Kidd 1994), who spend their workday in offices interacting with computers, information systems, and other people.

S. Lahlou (✉)
Laboratory of Design for Cognition , EDF R&D, Clamart , France
e-mail: saadi.lahlou@edf.fr, s.lahlou@lse.ac.uk

S. Lahlou (ed.), *Designing User Friendly Augmented Work Environments: From Meeting Rooms to Digital Collaborative Spaces,* Computer Supported Cooperative Work,
DOI 10.1007/978-1-84800-098-8_5, © Springer-Verlag London Limited 2009

While organizations are interested in more efficient and productive environments and focus on systems and their costs, users are under strong pressure. More than the 1940s' administrators studied by Herb Simon (1997), they tend to adopt bounded rationality because they are short of time and attention, and will therefore discard new systems if they fail to "satisfice" at first use.[1] They simply could not afford otherwise, considering the current work rhythms and pressure. This is visible in the demands of the executive studied by Back et al. (Chap. 4). Users will tend to focus on their own activity, and pay little effort in operations that are useful at collective level but bring themselves little added value. New systems should then integrate graciously into existing environments, institutions, procedures; avoid creating more problems than they solve and in general not add overhead to users. Dissemination, Operations, Maintenance, and Evolution ("DOME") of these systems are part of the design problem and of the costs (Lahlou 2005, 2007a) – we cannot afford considering that we create isolated artefacts.

In this context, how can we design environments that will produce good and sustainable practice at collective level? This chapter describes our efforts in tackling these issues in the real industrial context of a non-IT industry in the last decade, which led us to set up a novel design process: "experimental reality."

Section 2 will provide corporate reasons why industry needs specific design efforts for Augmented Environments. Section 3 will explicit our design strategy: experimental reality. Section 4 describes two instruments we use in the design process: a tool, the SubCam, and a model, cognitive attractors. Section 5, "the triple determination framework," explains why AE design must go beyond mere ICT implementation and include also training and institutional change. Section 6 details our experimental reality process and the AE testbed we constructed, the K1 building, its content and layout, digital ethnography observation techniques. Section 7 zooms on the RAO augmented meeting room, its installation, and some of the AE systems we installed in it.

5.2   Why Design-specific Environments for Cognitive Workers?

At LDC we study activity in the workplace, with emphasis on information and communication technology (ICT) and collaborative work. Based on workplace studies, LDC helps EDF R&D Division design more comfortable and efficient environments for cognitive workers. LDC research staff includes psychologists,

---

[1] *Satisficing* is one of the "crucial alterations" that depart Simon's *bounded rationality* model from the classic rational actor model: "While economic man supposedly maximizes – selects the best alternative from among all those available to him – his cousin, the administrator, satisfices – looks for a course of action that is satisfactory or "good enough." (...) Administrators (and everyone else, for that matter) take into account just a few of the factors of the situation regarded as most relevant and crucial. In particular, they deal with one or few problems at a time, because the limits of attention simply do not permit everything to be attended to at once" (Simon 1997, p. 119).

Fig. 5.1 The K1 project space seen from an OffSat in the ceiling grid. Notice the glass box enclave on the *right*

cognitive scientists, ergonomists, computer scientists, engineers. LDC uses an experimental building dedicated to naturalistic work observation, the K1, as a living laboratory where new environments are developed in a continuous design process with the help of the users themselves, in realistic conditions (Fig. 5.1).

Setting up an ICT design laboratory is not a natural move for an electricity company. The decision was the result of a series of surveys on the use of information in the workplace (Fischler and Lahlou 1995; Lahlou and Fischler 1996; Autissier et al. 1997; Lahlou 1998; Lahlou et al. 1999; Autissier and Lahlou 1999) and a natural effect of the conclusion that the digitization of all work processes needed to be addressed with specific tools. Indeed, digitization of work brings some new issues. Most users agree that ICT led to enormous progress and change to such an extent that they sometimes can hardly describe what they did "before," when there were no PCs and email. They also express some dissatisfaction, mainly about the increased volume of information and "lack of time."

In this section, we trace back how the decision to study and deploy AE in this large company emerged. This section may seem a bit off topic; it is not. Augmented work environments are expensive; they imply some painful decisions (hiring wizards or specialized maintenance personnel, adapting firewall procedures, buying unfamiliar equipment etc.); therefore, the issue of their necessity and return on investment (ROI) is at the heart of decision-making and determines the budget envelopes. So "selling" the AE to the organization is a primary aspect of their design.

Starting in the 1980s, surveys showed that new digital communication channels add to the previous paper and oral media without much substitution (Moatty 1994), but it is difficult to measure the volume and the content of the circulating information. Information is not reducible to its size in bytes or the number of printed pages (which, by the way, explode). Acknowledgment of individual problems due to excess of information came along with digitization. Lea (1987) described the "information shock syndrome" of some information system users; "information overload" (Hiltz and Turoff 1985) is a widespread term, and various forms of the phenomenon are repeatedly described in various places: "communication overflow" (Ljundberg 1996), "information fatigue syndrome" (Lewis 1996), "infoglut," etc.

In the mid-1990s, the French Association for Cognitive Research mandated a subgroup to study the problem, and came out with a comprehensive description adding organizational aspects to the classical individual symptoms under the name of cognitive overflow syndrome ("COS"). The syndrome combines the following:

- *A growing production of information:* as measured by media volume (paper, disks, etc.), message flow, and cost of information systems
- *Individual stress:* subjects complain to be overloaded by "useless" information; complaints focus on the "lack of time" and delay in the processing of "real work"
- *Organizational incapacity to point at a specific cause:* overflow seems to come from many sources. From the field, the problem appears systemic, without cure, and no specific entity is in charge of it
- *Loss of meaning:* individuals cannot make sense of information and tend to fall back in short term, local, information processing concerning their own duty, with little care about the overall effect (Lahlou et al. 1997)

COS is an organizational problem with individual symptoms. As industrial production is the result of labor division and coordination, group efficiency is impaired by its members' hampering. Individuals complain they do not have time to carry their "real work"; there are also effects at aggregate level: reactive rather than proactive units, loss of control over large projects, and a growing distance between reports and reality.

In 1999, a survey of a representative sample of 501 white collars, following several years of qualitative research, enabled us to quantify the COS. These results are especially interesting since at the time of survey (1999), only 63% of respondents declared of receiving more than six emails per day.

Table 5.1 shows some of the results of this survey, which are coherent with field observations (Fischler and Lahlou 1995; Lahlou and Fischler 1999). Other results from the same survey show that cognitive workers indeed are far from having full control over their activity:

• 67% declared having a "to-do" list, including in most cases one to five items.
• 17% had more than 20 items on their list.
• The oldest task on the list is in most cases (74%) from 1–6 months overdue, although this task is considered important (64%).

Obviously the work context seems to get in the way of "getting the job done" rather than helping. This points at the need for redesigning more supportive AE.

To go beyond user's subjective declarations, we tested the actual destiny of the information through the same telephone survey with three messages: "which had been sent recently [to the respondent] by the top management." The first was a massive

Table 5.1 Some results of the "Use of Information" survey (Fischler and Lahlou 2000): percent of white collars agreeing with a series of COS symptoms (telephone survey on 501 white collars, drawn at random in the telephone list, representative of the R&D Division)

Do you agree with the following statements?	Totally agree	Slightly agree	Slightly disagree	Disagree	Don't know
We have too much administrative work	23	41	25	11	1
I am overloaded	11	39	37	11	1
I dream of a tidy office	16	25	33	26	
My colleagues are overloaded	20	49	22	4	5
I spend a lot of time in tasks of sorting and filing which could be done by someone less qualified	10	21	40	30	1
I lose an incredible time fixing details	23	40	28	10	
I am continuously interrupted in my work	21	41	30	9	
My successor will easily find his (her) way in my archive	22	47	23	6	1
I would need more time	22	43	26	8	1
I often stay late at the office, or work at home in the evening	28	34	17	19	1
I often cannot find a document although I know it is somewhere in my files	11	27	37	5	
Sometimes I delay a decision because I can't find time to read the case	11	37	38	14	1
I cannot manage to do what I had planned to do during the day	18	44	31	7	1
Sometimes I come home exhausted but wondering what I have been doing today	19	31	32	18	
I have the feeling I process what's urgent before what's important	25	44.5	23.6	6	1
Sometimes I wonder whether I did receive a document I am told about	9	30	37	24	0
Sometimes I forget tasks or commitments	5	21	45	29	0

corporate emailing operation targeting *all* employees: 31% did not even recall receiving it, less than 2 weeks after it was sent.

The second was about "the safety survey of the Division," 21% declared recalling reception of this message (5% "perhaps"). Eighteen individual respondents even reported having responded or filled and/or sent a form to the department in charge. Which is embarrassing because no such mail about a safety survey had in fact been sent: this question was asked as a bias control item.

Answers about this inexistent message may sound funny, but the results of questions about the third (real) message were not. Let us remind readers that the survey was done during the second half of December 1999, where the W2K bug was a major preoccupation worldwide; the Corporate IT Division had sent *everyone*, a few days before the survey, a special warning asking each user to backup and close their workstations on a specific day for preventive maintenance operations against this potential W2K bug: 49.7% did not recall having received the message (6% "perhaps"). The survey then included precise investigation on those respondents recalling this specific email. We started by clarifying which mail was considered, giving the exact header and date. "Did you receive this message and keep it?" Eighty-eight respondents said yes, and 164 no. Out of the 88 who said yes, 29 people were indeed able to find, on request of the interviewer, the dates given for preventive maintenance operations (6% of the total sample!); 20 subjects said they had in fact erased the document, 25 searched but did not find, 14 said they found it but that it contained no date. Fortunately, the company had no problem with the W2K bug, and the results of the survey would have been quite different in the production division where the rules are almost military, rather than in this R&D back office setting. Still, these results were worrying. In parallel to this survey, we conducted a benchmark study on 17 large companies in many sectors (bank, agro-food, transports, telecom, etc.): their situation regarding COS was similar (Autissier and Lahlou 1999). We can see here that COS can produce delay in decision or reaction, loss in information, inadequate representations, and finally that some critical information may not be processed by its destinators. In other industries, some organizational catastrophes have been attributed precisely to this kind of problem; one of the most prominent is the explosion of a NASA space shuttle.

The conclusion is that the COS is not simply a matter of user comfort, but a menace for the organization. Therefore, investing in a specific design effort to create appropriate environments for digitized work is not a waste. Although this conclusion was quickly adopted at the executive level in the mid-1990s (and triggered a multi-million investment in the creation of LDC), for a while many people still regarded LDC suspiciously as a place where mad engineers played with expensive and futuristic gadgets, because ICT was not in the core business of the company ("why don't we just buy solutions outside?"). It took almost 6 years, until the lesson was fully understood, before the ICT solutions designed by LDC started to scale out in the company.

A lesson to learn here is that many users fear that the new ICT systems will bring them more stress, overheads, and work pressure. Sponsors are aware of potential costs. Their fears, alas, are grounded in actual experience of poorly designed ICT systems. Therefore, the first implementations of AE should indeed address painful issues for the users and bring clear added value. Once this added value is perceived in daily operations, the users' attitude changes and they become more open and receptive.

To anticipate results presented later in this chapter, our experience shows that not only is redesigning work environment for digital work a way to prevent the risks of organizational catastrophe, but it is also a way to make cognitive workers more comfortable, and a way to save money and pollution. The use of the sole augmented RAO meeting room for videoconferencing saves over \$50,000 per month in transportation[2] and the reduction of over 9 tons of CO_2 emission. Not to mention the fact that our survey showed that using videoconferencing enables the reduction of the delay to find a date for a meeting (between two people) of about 50% – and more for a multi-party meetings: it is much easier to find a 1 h slot in a packed schedule than to find the 3 h needed for a 1 h meeting plus 2 h of transport.

5.3 Design Strategy

The issues in cognitive work are many, and as I outlined in Chap. 1 of this book, designing for it is a never-ending problem, which continuously develops as technology changes, as users become more demanding, as new uses appear, etc. We have limited resources. We try to find the best cost/use ratio functional targets for new implementation, and also avoid introducing excessive overheads or problems with the new system. Our final goal is to set up sustainable administrative ecosystems, where the systems we launch should grow and survive with support from their users, with a minimum need for "top-down" organizational pressure.

Our strategy for the first aspect ("find where it hurts and what has an easy cure") is simple: we follow the subjects in their actual daily practice, spot every occasion where there is a problem or discomfort. Then we try to solve it by addressing the three dimensions of the environment (physical, institutional, cognitive) either by designing appropriate physical or digital systems, changing the organization rules, or providing new representations to help the subjects in framing the situation properly. Among these possible directions, we choose the best efficiency/cost ratio with pragmatic opportunism. Often, we have to act upon at least two of those three levels simultaneously. How do we do this in practice? Section 4 will describe our capture instruments and techniques (SubCam, etc.). Nosulenko and Samoylenko, in Chap. 8, describe some of the evaluation techniques we use.

For the second aspect (easy and harmless implementation), we have gradually set up a series of requirements for our systems, which we familiarly call the "zeroes" list:

- Zero training
- Zero configuration, Zero impact on user workstation
- Zero user maintenance
- Zero complication

---

[2]This includes direct transport costs plus valuation of "improductive" time lost in transportation.

- Zero payment
- Immediate benefit for individual end-user
- High security and privacy

5.3.1   Zero Training

Zero training means that the user should be able to get a first successful use of the system immediately, without having to read a manual. When the user first comes to the system, she is usually pushed by the immediate need of using it, not by the desire of learning how the system works. Most of the time, users have "no time to learn" anyway.

The way we address this apparently strong zero condition is by building on preexisting cognitive skills and representations in the user; and by providing strong contextual guidance from the context (interface, fellow users, or institutional procedures). For example, one can assume that the average user in the company will know how to use an internet browser, the company's choice of desktop suite (e.g., Open Office), etc. We design the system so that the interface logics follow these pre-existing skills, representations, and mental models. Now this is true only for the minimal use; for more sophisticated functions, the user may have to learn (through online contextual help, colleagues, hotline, etc.), but at least this first successful experience will give the user a good image of the system and motivate her to learn the more sophisticated functions.

5.3.2   Zero Configuration, Zero Impact on User Workstation

Configuration, as Jansson notes in his Chap. 7, is a major obstacle to fluid use.

Users have "no time to instal" new software on their devices, and often they simply do not even have the administrative rights or the necessary skills. We try to provide services in such a way that users do not have to modify their own devices. In the current state of the art, this can be obtained either by providing the proper interface on-site (e.g., with a touch screen in the room like the one described by Back et al. in their Chap. 4, or with augmented tokens like the ServiceTags described infra in Sect. 6.5) or through web services, for example. In some cases, when forced (e.g., Gridboard, cf. Sect. 6.5), we use some Active-X or java applets, which are more or less transparent to users.

5.3.3   Zero User Maintenance

Expecting that the users can do some maintenance is simply "not manageable" and this is true for hardware as well as for software. There should be a specific dedicated workforce and online help. Systems that need frequent maintenance, for example, which have batteries, are usually a problem: failure always happens during use, of course. All occasions for maintenance must be listed when they occur during the test phase, and specific solutions found. Often, some changes in form factor do help minimize maintenance or failure. For example, the less moving pieces, the less apparent cables, the best. Any apparent possibility for customizing the system by users may lead some users to change the parameters and then make the whole system behave in an unexpected way to the next user.

5.3.4 Zero Complication

Of course, this is a general guideline. Two clicks maximum to get the action done, and a trivial graphic user interface (GUI) are preferable, refer to your favorite HCI gurus. The way we get there is to carefully observe activity and do *activity-based design*. Complicated interface usually occurs when the system has to propose many choices to the user. It may be better to identify the possibilities of action a user is likely to take in a given situation, then propose one command artifact for each, rather than have one single interface that leads to all possible actions. For example, our DumbleTag system proposes a credit-card style tag for each possible action (which the user puts on the desk antenna to perform an action) instead of a screen interface, which would mean lists and choices. One possibility of AE is precisely to use physical objects as commands (cf. the iStuff principle where ordinary objects can each be used as a one-action button). This makes it easier and unambiguous to operate the system.

5.3.5 Zero Payment

"Not on my budget". Many services have a cost that must be charged somewhere. We suggest that all costs be on the server side, and that payment should not constitute some operation for the user, especially prior to use. If one had to log into the telephone system for charging purposes before dialing a number, using telephones would be cumbersome. We proceed by charging automatically the entity "in charge," for example, the department who owns the room, or who employs the users; or some central corporate support.

5.3.6 Immediate Benefit for Individual End-User

"And God bless you if it's good for the group". The user's real motives are usually individualistic. Of course, in an organization, many services have some collective utility aspect, but it is very difficult to get the users make the efforts to fulfill these.

Therefore, when these collective functions need to be performed, they should
be transparent to the user, or the user should see some immediate personal positive
feedback. This is true of many workflows that are aimed at creating some collective
database or collect user data. In such cases, the possibility of getting personal
feedback on the information input asked to the user will help data collection.
For example, statistics on her own use of the system or some immediately useful
calculation. When we collect a user's identity or pictures to enter into the meeting
room database (which will be used to display his photo, the meeting interface, and
signal which is present, and also give access to the conference room), we want to do
this in such a way that, when the user logs in at the entrance of the meeting room,
he gets a customized physical token in return, which he will be able to use in the
meting, for example, for indexing moments of interest in the recording, or to signal
the system he wants to take a speech turn.

5.3.7 High Security and Privacy

AE systems must be compliant with corporate rules. This constraint is strong: no
IT manager will accept a system that compromises security policy. Alas, security
(and privacy) usually go in opposite way to usability. This is precisely why they
must be taken into account early enough at architectural level.[3] Otherwise, as they
will have to be added anyway, chances are they will add cumbersome procedures
in the interface.

This zero list may appear impossible to comply with. Experience shows that it
is actually feasible, and often easier in AE than in pure ICT environments, because
the material aspects provide new, multimodal, affordances for interface. Also,
physical tokens can solve a large number of security issues, as physical presence in
the space usually means that the user has already satisfied to a series of access
controls.

Our design strategy is to follow the user's actual practice; then try pragmatically
to erase obstacles or cognitive costs on her activity track. This is activity-based
design (cf. Chap. 1). We proceed progressively and with the collaboration of users,
as the next sections will show.

5.4 The SubCam and Cognitive Attractors

This section shows how we proceed in practice to spot the main issues in solving
and understanding the nature of the user's activity.

---

[3]Cf. Chap. 1 and Lahlou (2008b) for the way we recommend tackling privacy issues.

5.4.1 The SubCam

Following the subject's activity from his/her own perspective is a good way to understand the actual problems, which often occur in "details." We need a recording technique that introduces minimal bias while providing fine-grained details and especially pointing at where the subject focuses her attention. After trying most classic techniques (participant observation, interview, videotaping, shadowing, etc.), we found that they either do not give enough detail or produce too much bias. So we specified and constructed a new tool, the "SubCam" (Fig. 5.2): a miniature video camera with a wide-angle and directional microphone worn on a pair of glasses (Lahlou 1999), or other form factors depending on the activity (e.g., attached to a helmet for industrial activity, on a bandana for kids, etc.). We hand this wearable tool to the subject and simply ask her to perform the activity. In some cases, we ask the subject to talk out loud, especially when problems are encountered. The researcher does not need to be present. The subject is left alone and simply gives the subfilms to the researchers at the end of the day. The protocols are described in detail in Lahlou (2006).

This protocol provides the design team with a continuous record of the "phenomenological tunnel" lived by the subject. It provides *situated* recording of what the subject sees, hears, and does. It also provides more. First, this enables to understand where the subject focuses his/her attention. Then, variations in the breathing or voice tone (hearable on the sound track) give indications about emotions.

But, most importantly, a lot of the subject's intentions and subjective interpretations are accessible through self-confrontation of the subjects with their subfilms. Watching the subtapes and discussing them with the subjects, designers, engineers and other stakeholders is a crucial part of the process; because what we are interested in is the *goals* of the subjects, and how they *subjectively* judge the quality of the environment

Fig. 5.2 Two versions of the SubCam: office work (*left*), plant version (*right*)

in supporting them to reach these goals. Confronted with their subfilms, subjects, because they are put back in the same activity track they actually lived, exhibit an amazing capacity to remember and describe their intentions, emotions, reasoning, and hereby provide us with the elements necessary to make a good activity analysis (goals, motives, intentions, evaluation, etc.).

The current version of the SubCam has high resolution ("HD") and enables reading the documents the subjects hold in their hands or read on their PC screen. The SubCam is a merciless observation tool, it enables monitoring the activity in its multimodal dimensions in detail. For example, when a subject works, she may use *simultaneously*, her PC, her fixed and mobile phone, paper, colleagues, etc. The SubCam alone enables recording all these dimensions, which is easier than having to record each device separately.

Discussion with the subjects is crucial to understanding the issues in depth. Actions that may appear strange at first sight are often explained by the far reaching consequences they may have in the global organization or past experience of the subject. Situations may be more complex than visible because every detail is connected to many issues in the full life-cycle of the system. For example, often we refused to implement some nice features because they could cause nasty maintenance problems or would be too integrated with others and therefore make it impossible to have a "plan B" in case of failure. Users know these issues and can illustrate them with actual examples to designers and system engineers; therefore, the SubCam debrief sessions are extremely useful for specification. Also, watching the subject's SubCam films helps designers get a first person experience of the activity they are designing, and also some empathy with the problems the subjects encounter as they progress in their activity through their own phenomenological tunnel. This "entheasy" (neologism expressing this state of "sharing the vision of action" we had to forge in order to describe this very special and unprecedented feeling of being a passenger in someone else's head: Lahlou 2006) is a strong experience for designers, and certainly helps them to have a more realistic approach (Fig. 5.3).

With SubCam data, not only do we get a realistic account of what subjects do and the capacity to quantify, for example, the time lost in inadequate operations, but also we can spot in an almost trivial manner all the points where improvement and redesign is necessary (or wished). The design choices then become arbitrating which issues can be solved with existing technology at reasonable DOME cost. When the current state of Commercial-Off-The-Shelf technology is not mature enough for robust implementation, we usually delay or abandon, and address an easier issue.

We then proceed to some quick prototyping, change the environment with the prototypes (or some "Wizard of Oz" mock-ups), and ask subjects to use the environment again; watch their subtapes with them for evaluation, and reiterate until we reach some satisfying state. The number of such iterations is unpredictable. This is, by the way, a problem for design planning. Sometimes we need 20 or more iterations to reach a fluid interaction. On the other hand, as the evaluation procedure is informal and much lighter than classic ergonomic studies, one iteration can be very fast and cheap, and so the problem of being unable to plan the exact number of iterations is not so dramatic.

Fig. 5.3   A frame extracted from a SubCam film

At LDC, we collected hundreds of hours of the natural activity of (volunteer) office workers, using the SubCam. These records show that users, unlike what is predicted by classic psychological theories, often *do not do what they intended*, even when they could have. They continuously get sidetracked in unplanned activities. This is consistent with Table 5.1, where 62% declared fully or rather agree that they cannot manage to do what they had planned for the day. Some sidetracks are forced by usability issues, when the subject cannot manage to operate the system as planned. For example, in a simple action of sending an email with a PDA, we measured how interface issues produced a final sequence quite different from what the subject said he was going to operate before starting the task, and as a result, unplanned operations took 58% of the some 8 min total (Lahlou et al. 2002). The analysis of this single sequence, by comparing what the subject said what he intended to do and what he actually did enabled us to spot nine unplanned operations that pinpoint interface issues.

But interface issues are not the only sidetracking points. Subjects are captured by interrupting colleagues (on the phone...), by the context (fixing the copier...), by activities planned by others (meetings...), or even by themselves through sidetracking routines (answering email, clearing their desk from "small" or "urgent" tasks...). Any disruption in a planned task (e.g., not reaching immediately the person one tries to get in contact with) may result in pausing current task and opening a new, potentially disruptive, activity path, and this is one more reason to design AE for fluid and seamless interaction. In the course of this new path, the original activity track may be lost. As a result, subjects often do not manage to do what they had planned for themselves in their day (cf. the survey results supra in Table 5.1).

The underlying reason is that people are not simply deciding what they do individually; they are entangled in a whole environment that guides and constrains their activity. The guidance is on three levels: affordances of the physical world, social rules, internal representations and learned routines which automatically provide interpretation of the context and trigger behavior in an almost unconscious manner. Our design effort against COS aims at controlling these effects, and giving back the user more decision on her own activity. AE should be empowering for the users and not force them into following some rigid workflow.

The next section will describe in more detail the model of "cognitive attractors" (Lahlou 2000), which helps us in understanding human behavior, and also in designing environments that support humans as they perform their activity.

5.4.2 Cognitive Attractors

The cognitive attractor theory (Lahlou 2000; Lahlou et al. 2009) describes how subjects are led into a specific activity path by a combination of patterns in the context ("data") and matching representations in their mind ("lata"). In conjunction, data and lata produce an automatic *interpretation* of the context. Interpretation should be understood here both in the sense of understanding (meaning) and of playing (like a musician would interpret a piece). Cognitive attractor theory predicts that if a critical mass of data and matching lata are present, the drive for the corresponding *activity* spontaneously emerges. What is amazing is that the process of interpretation emerges automatically, beyond the subject's will: "it just happens," just like a Gestalt imposes a pattern to perception when a sufficient portion of the pattern is present (Fig. 5.4).

A trivial example is the coffee discussion. A couple of colleagues chatting next to the coffee-machine are an attractor for "coffee discussion." Such an attractor is so strong that some other colleague who comes by during a pause in his (say, report writing) activity, with the sole intention of taking a coffee and going back to his office, has few chances to escape it and will probably stay and chat for a few minutes, although a debrief will show that this was *not* his intention in the first place. This subject escaped from the initial attractor "report writing" and got caught in the "coffee discussion" attractor.

Fig. 5.4 This set of elements is "naturally" interpreted as a single triangular pattern

Another, less trivial, example is email. The fact that email is a cognitive attractor has major impacts on office life. When a subject is in front of his email box, the mental and physical framework becomes "doing email" activity, which means looking at the mails and answering them. So, when a subject finds himself with hands on the keyboard and the email messaging system open, chances are that he will automatically interpret the situation as "doing email" activity: checking new ones and processing all emails that are easily processable. It is like a bicycle rider who gets the wheel locked in the tramway's track, and starts following that track. The problem with the "doing email" attractor is that there are many cases when the subject gets exposed to this situation, especially if the mailbox windows is always open on the desktop screen, or if the subject is prompted by some popup when a new mail comes in. Two nasty effects appear. The first is email capture: every time the subject gets into the email attraction situation (hands on keyboard, mailbox open), he will tend to process emails until something stops him (e.g., external interruption, or one email too difficult to process). The second is less obvious but maybe worse. Often, an email contains some demand, for example, information processing or action. This action can usually be performed in many ways, for example, calling the email sender on the phone for discussion, consulting colleagues, or acting on some real-world object. More often than not, the best way to solve a problem in collaboration is to have face-to-face or at least vocal interaction. But as the subject is caught into this attractor of "email processing," there is a tunneling effect. The modalities of output for the action he will use will be within this email processing activity: the subject will tend to consider output in the form of text processing only, and input as well. Instead of calling or meeting face-to-face the sender or others for discussion, which would allow wide communication bandwidth, the subject will tend to spend hours writing a complex message and copy others for action; hereby contributing to a snowballing effect where email finally unduly absorbs an enormous part of the workflow. This forces complex issues into the low bandwidth and poor textual representation format and contributes to information overload, among other things.

These behaviors are not systematic or compulsory, but obviously some situations *attract* us into performing a specific type of activity, which indeed produces some kind of benefit. Salutations, putting things into order, checking incoming information are of this kind. Social prompts are almost impossible to avoid answering; for example, interruptions or jokes call for a response. A close-up look at users' video tapes suggests that a substantial part of our everyday activity is composed by following the paths of these stereotyped attractors. This does not mean that subjects do not display original and creative behaviors, they do indeed. Most of the time though, creation is in a new assembly of existing segments, just like a new text can be composed by assembling pre-existing words, expressions, or sentences.

Attractors are a different notion from stimuli. For example, they may need to be disambiguated, they do not exist independently of the observer's frame of mind, they may be ignored and have no automatic implication on the subject's behavior. Any given setting may contain many different attractors for the subject. The issue is *which* attractor will be seized by the subject. It is a matter of competition between attractors.

5.4.2.1 Data in the Environment and Lata in the Mind

Attractors are a combination of *data* (located in the environment) and *lata* (located in the observer). The combination of both may form patterns that trigger activities. Therefore, presence of the relevant data in the environment will change the probability of occurrence of a given activity. By affording a specific activity track, data will favor this track over another possible activity. By evoking the associated lata, data may induce motivation for an activity in subjects among participants who were initially without this motivation. Space is too scarce here for a full description of the cognitive attractor theory and its psychological basis, which are described in more detail in Lahlou (2000, 2005). Let us simply note that subjects are continuously confronted with a large numbers of attractors in their context. An attractor acts like a script that feeds-forward the action.

As long as the activity is fluid, with continuous coupling with the environment and adequate system response, chances are that the subject will continue on the same track. But if some obstacle or failure occurs, there may be a re-computation of "what to do" and some locally stronger attractor may take over. For example, in the course of some activity, Robert needs to send an e-mail to someone. He opens his mailbox to do so and sees a just-arrived message from his big boss. Chances are he will open the message, and get sidetracked.

Cognitive attractors are not simply distractors capturing subjects: they are at the very basis of the efficiency of human behavior. An attractor is a routine procedure, and following it is a way of doing something in an efficient and proved way, while liberating attentional resources, like any routine. It also makes the world predictable for others and hence makes cooperation possible as each participant will act as expected (if they all follow the same attractor), each one performing his local role in the play.

5.4.2.2 Tuning Attractors

The strength of attractors is a combination of three factors: pregnance (attraction of attention), value (attraction of desire), and cost to be completed (attraction of effort). As designers, we can address the system at the level of data, by modifying affordances or pregnance; at the level of lata in creating or disseminating new interpretations of the situation or raising motivation; at the level of coupling by changing the costs of coupling with the system. We must also remember that the relation between the user and the system is immersed in a social space of institutional rules, and that other people can – and do indeed – intervene in one's activity. Therefore, many control mechanisms are in fact at the social level, either because they prompt the subject into doing something, guide or help him, or inhibit or prevent the subject from choosing some specific behavioral tracks that would be physically possible, and psychologically imaginable, but are not socially acceptable. "Other people" can be a resource for our design of AE as well as physical objects or mental representations.

Attractors are complex patterns and difficult to investigate because each pattern
is distributed over the external context and within the mind of the subjects. In practice,
we explore attractors through a trial and error process, which is de facto already a
design process. What we need is not a complete model of each attractor, but rather
to find a way to frame the attractor for better user comfort in an activity. Just as in
economics for the notion of Utility, there is no absolute scale, but rather the possibility
of evaluating marginal differences between two situations (one being preferred by
users). This is enough for practical purposes. Incidentally, in this exploration
procedure, we learn more about the deep nature of the attractor itself, but this is not
always the case and sometimes we find a better design solution before understanding
why this design was better.

Our design therefore aims at guiding users into efficient behavior, by offering
specific affordances along their activity path. The idea is not to design artifacts
and devices, but rather to understand activity and functions, and *then* design into
the environment a set of affordances which will keep the subjects on the best
practice tracks.

Ideally, the best practice track should have, at every step, a lower cognitive cost
than other possibilities, thereby inclining the subjects to naturally follow the easiest
slope. This includes the first adoption phase when subjects are lured into choosing
our new system instead of their previous one. Of course, we hardly ever succeed
completely. But if a good practice activity track is kept at low cognitive cost, for
example by erasing the spots of high cost on the way, spreading good practice is
easier, and social control may become a strong enough safeguard to keep good
practice dominant. Specific to our approach is doing this at social level, and
considering environments as a whole.

In an experiment conducted in individual offices in 1998 and 1999, we changed
the arrangement of the furniture and displays and created new affordances for
collaboration (by making it easy and inviting for a pair of people to sit together in
front of a better quality computer screen). Before, the main occupant of the workstation was mostly working on a stand-alone basis. We left a time-lapse camera
on the ceiling above the workplace ("offsat": Lahlou 1999, cf. infra Sect. 6.4) for
9 months and observed change. The speeded up films showed a dramatic increase
of collaborative sessions with two or three individuals, facing the screen, in contrast
with the previous period where work was more solitary. During a presentation of
these results, the managers of this group expressed surprise: they had tried for years
to obtain this result (collaboration) but never succeeded. Interestingly, this behavior
had occurred spontaneously after our office refurbishment, simply because the new
setting offered good affordances for collaboration. This affordance was not planned
by us, but it produced effects anyway. The new behavior, documented 2 months
after installation of the new setting, remained stable (Lahlou 2008c).

The fact that changing instruments will change practices and vice-versa has
been known and documented for a long time (Bödker 1996; Engeström 1990, 1993;
Engeström and Middleton 1996). Our experience shows that providing new
affordances can spontaneously produce new behaviors, in a smoother and more
effective manner than managerial pressure. This grounds our strategy of social change:

"don't try to change the people, simply change the context." This strategy has some advantages: context is persistent, and can "talk" to the users any time they will use it, which a teacher cannot. Also, there are fewer power and social issues in interacting with the context; therefore, it provokes less resistance among users.

5.5   The Triple Determination Framework ("Installation" Theory)

The subject is part, as a worker and as a social being, of a larger ecosystem than the local technical system being designed. As we saw with cognitive attractors, this coupling between the subject and the setting tends to determine the subject's behavior far beyond what classic psychological theories describe. This systemic view has much in common with the one developed by Hutchins and Hollan in distributed cognition (see Chap. 9), and also with the Russian approach of the engineering psychology school (see Nosulenko and Samoylenko, Chap. 8). It implies that to design new work environments, we must actually design a whole new system, encompassing the three levels of guidance: the physical artifacts and ICT, the subjects' cognitive models, and the institutional rules of practice.

The World can be considered as a cultural "installation" (Lahlou 2008a), which guides subjects into their activity track, at three levels: physical, mental, institutional. The physical level refers to material artifacts; it provides *affordances* (Gibson 1967): which activities can be supported by the objects. For example, chairs afford sitting; screens afford collaborative viewing; etc. This is the first level that determines what is physically possible to do.

Humans have mental representations of what is feasible in a given situation. These representations provide possible interpretations and enable the elaboration of plans or decision-making. With this second level of determination, people can interpret affordances into support for their activities. Objects may be interpreted as "connotation for activity" (Uexküll 1956).

Representations and the objects they represent follow a co-evolution process: representations are constructed by the practice people have of objects. Conversely, objects are made after the pattern of their representation: chairs are made to look like chairs; firemen are trained to behave as firemen; email software are built after the representation of email. And this is the reason why representations match with objects. So if we want new ICT systems to be usable and sustainable, we also have to work on their representations among users and designers.

At a social level, the co-evolution of objects and representations is monitored by domain-local communities of interest (users, providers, administrators, etc.) who set the patterns of objects, the rules of practice, etc. Because these stakeholders know the field, objects, representations, and rules are adapted to behaviors. These stakeholders create "institutions," which are both sets of rules to be applied to keep order and cooperation, and communities of interest aware that they play in the same game.

Knowing how to use the affordances is not always sufficient to execute adequate behavior. Not all that is feasible is socially acceptable. Some people might do wrong and provoke (by ignorance, personal interest) negative externalities for themselves or others. Institutions are a social answer: they create and enforce rules to control these potential misuses or abuses; they set common conventions that enable cooperation (e.g., people should all drive on the same side of the road; they should use "netiquette" in their digital communication, etc.). Many of these rules are already contained in the mental representations, which are by nature normative. But institutions bring a physical control layer to these norms. They enforce them with special personnel. Also, every loyal member of the community tends to serve as a rule-enforcer and bring back mavericks or ignorants on track. Often these rules are made formal and explicit (regulations, laws, etc.), but they may stay informal rules of good practice, tricks of the trade, or traditions. As these rules are the result of compromise between local interests, they vary from place to place. The co-evolution between artifacts and representations is done under continuous monitoring and control of stakeholder communities, which use institutions as social and economics tools to safeguard their interests.

The resources and constraints provided at these three levels guide our social life and make it possible and fluid. Subjects rely on them simultaneously and alternatively. They are compatible and somewhat redundant, which makes this triple-determination system pretty robust and stable. This triple determination framework explains how we behave at a given moment in time.

Evolving towards a stable and sustainable state of the system therefore means making changes at three levels: physical (technical system ICT framework, from digital networks to software and business models); representational (the ideas people have of what "using AE" means); institutional (rules of good practice accepted and enforced).

So the limits of what is to be designed are not bounded to the technical system of devices and software. When Winograd talks about setting a "semantic Rubicon" as a design principle for AE, one could interpret this in a strict sense and conclude that the designer should draw limits to what the system is supposed to do. But tracing such a limit is also a choice of what the subjects and institutions must learn to do on the other side of the Rubicon. These changes to be implemented on the other side of the Rubicon are also a matter of (organizational) design and training, and part of the system design itself. So, if the computer systems should not take initiatives beyond the Rubicon, this does not mean that the designer should not. That is what interaction design is about; the Russian psychology of engineering has long recognized this issue, and they talk about "activity design" (Lomov 1977), referring to a process where redesign of the global system includes all the aspects of the system, from building new machines to setting up new training programs for the operators.

Take a simple example: meeting room access. Access, especially if the doors are usually locked, is a matter of technology (biometrics etc.) but primarily is an organizational matter of access rights management. Depending upon who (users, management, secretaries, facility managers) is entitled to make reservations or grant access, and on what basis (permanent, or based on participation in meetings), the specifications of the technical system which is supposed to unlock the door for authorized users will be quite different. For example, if the local "owner" of the meeting room (e.g., the Department owning the corridor) wants to have control over the use of the room (and therefore not allow online reservation), this will make any multisite reservation procedure difficult because nobody can get an instant and reliable global vision of which rooms are available for multi-site videoconferencing. The same type of issue comes with digital meeting support specifications: how far should the convener, or the animator, have priority access on resources over other participants? What is traceable in the meeting? Who is allowed to access the records of the meeting? These issues are not technical, they are political. Different groups may take different options; OK: but should the system support all options?

These simple issues of "who will be allowed to use the system," "who will grant access (and suppress it)," and "with what procedures"; "who will help novice users," "who will maintain and repair," "who will pay for operations, consumables, telecom" etc. must be made clear, because they will have a major impact on design. Experience shows that settling these issues is a matter of time and negotiation and that rarely "obvious" answers are "obvious" for all stakeholders.

In the present state of the art, designing a wizardless self-service room where systems are robust and integrated enough to leave the room unlocked is very difficult. We know many augmented meeting rooms which did not survive because they were designed on the base of providing nice features but did not address these simple daily operation issues. It may be, often, simpler to act upon external non-ICT constraints (e.g., making sure one secretary has the responsibility for giving the key of the room or the access codes, or for enrolling users in the biometric system) than to implement complex ICT functions. These supposedly make the system autonomous, but in fact often end up in awfully complicated procedures because of the multiplicity of cases to handle. Keep in mind that these systems must be designed for evolution anyway: functionalities for which we do not yet have robust solutions should *not* be implemented but rather provided by a separate, old fashioned human resource until robust ICT solutions are available. A single, minor failure in an AE will jeopardize the whole system because users will get a bad experience, which may cast a halo effect on the whole service. This three-layered approach (solve the issues with the layer that makes it easier) is a great resource for AE, and designers should cross the technical Rubicon more often.

As an example of our three-layered strategy, access rights management to the K1 testbed has two levels: access from the outside of the building to the lounge (the lounge acts as an airlock to the project space) is granted by the general R&D facility management upon request made by the testbed manager (Olivier Nadiras), because of the safety regulations of the facility, while internal access from the lounge to the project space is granted by Olivier and/or the head of LDC (Saadi) who control the K1 testbed local information system. This is why there is a specific biometric enroll-ment totem in the lounge, where those members of the lab who are entitled to recruit new users can empower access tags with habilitation tokens. The totem also enables automatic activation of the badges of people participating in meetings in RAO to cross the automatic door from RAO to the lounge during their presence in K1.

It took a long time to set up this procedure which ensures compatibility with facility security, protection of the project space, and still easy circulation between the RAO room and the lounge (strategic because toilets and public coffee machine are in the lounge: the devil is in the detail).

Another case is the new role for "conveners" in augmented meetings. It is socially implicit that the local organizer finds himself in charge of all the issues regarding access to the meeting room; during videoconferences it extends to digital spaces, and this often causes many problems when the convener is also the meeting animator (Lahlou 2007a). We therefore try to find a social solution for this by constructing the role of "convener" in the room reservation system. Then, in the case of technical issues, while the convener solves the problems with the distant sites and local wizards, the meeting animator can still concentrate on the content rather than on technical trivialities.

Finally, an example on the issue of mental models: the mental model underlying the use of Gridboard is: "we are all in front of the same screen, each with our own mouse and keyboard." We need all participants, especially the new ones, to be aware of this. In version 2008 of Gridboard, when accessing the Gridboard URL, a small animation is launched showing the Gridboard machine coming from cyberspace and sticking its window onto the users' desktop. Also desktop contour is specific to visualize that *this* is a window into another distant machine (Fig. 5.5).

As we see here, AE designers must be prepared to go beyond ICT issues, and cross the technological Rubicon. The environment often serves as an "external" memory or as a local plan, or "mediating structures"[4] (Hutchins 1987), through its affordances. Architecture, organization and management rules, individual training are part of the picture and must be considered as parameters in design.

Fig. 5.5 The Gridboard login animation ("reaching a distant shared desktop") frames the user mental model

---

[4] "Mediation refers to a particular mode of organizing behavior with respect to some task by achieving coordination with a mediating structure that is not itself inherent in the domain of the task. That is, in a mediated performance, the actor does not simply coordinate with the task environment, instead, the actor coordinates with something else as well, something that provides structure that can be used to shape the actor's behavior (...) Language, cultural knowledge, mental models, arithmetic procedures, and rules of logic are all mediating structures too. So are traffic lights, supermarket layouts, and the contexts we arrange for each other's behaviors. Mediating structures can be embodied in artifacts, in ideas, in systems of social interaction, or in all of these at once" (Hutchins 1987).

5.6 Experimental Reality and Design

We apply a pragmatic design process, which we call "experimental reality." The underlying vision is as follows: designing AE is a progressive task, because new functionalities emerge as the users get acquainted with the new system, and the number of elements involved (devices, users, institutions) is so high that one can hardly model what is actually going to fit beforehand. So we need to test the new AE in real environments (real users, real tasks), which will provide a good reality test. On the other hand, proper observation, evaluation, and design needs to be done in a lab. So we made a lab big enough to encapsulate real situations, and constructed an institutional framework that filled this lab with real users in a cooperative mood.

We built a specific building, the K1 (Fig. 5.6), where we implement and test AE with real users. Users are volunteers who work in the AE, and use them on an everyday basis. The AE are monitored by a multidisciplinary team of designers, engineers, and cognitive scientists aided by powerful observation tools. A specific highly skilled task force (at least two system engineers, designers) maintains systems in operation and installs modifications. The team as a group, with the help of the users, decides what modifications should be made, based on the problems encountered by users and their wishes. We observe the users in detail in their daily activities, with the SubCam and other instruments, and analyze activity and the perceived quality of the AE. When the systems or functions installed in the K1 testbed have reached a satisfying state, we scale them out in the company.

The K1 is a 400 m² (4,000 ft²) user laboratory (described further in this section); but it also has a virtual part which is used by volunteers who do not inhabit the physical building and are distributed in the company and sister labs outside of the company. The K1 AE are a continuous work-in-progress; sometimes, when a sub-system reaches maturity, this stable version is disseminated in the company, but we keep working on the future versions in the K1. This is especially true for the RAO room, which is the "mother room" of all other augmented meeting rooms in the company. This organization enables dealing with the never-endingness of the

Fig. 5.6 The laboratory of design for cognition K1 building: CAD view and outside view

design process. The RAO room is where new systems and artifacts are tested, in a realistic manner, as it is actually connected with the rest of the company's information system, and used for real meetings. For example, in 2007, 210 videoconferences took place in the K1, often with distant sites outside the company. Participants in such meetings are a natural flow of potential testers for our new systems.

Why do users come into the lab? Because it offers better comfort and functionalities that they cannot get elsewhere. Why do they trust us? Because we are part of the company, share their culture, and are bound by strict professional and privacy rules. Why are they in cooperative mode? Because they know that our work does indeed bring *them* individual benefits in their daily activity. In fact, it took a long time to create this situation and trust came gradually, as useful and user-friendly systems designed in the K1 started to disseminate in the company. Also, the work process we apply is not a "project mode" where we use the users as testers to design new systems, but rather accompanying them in their activity and try to solve the issues with them in a cooperative mode; a process in which they can freely benefit from our own resources to solve their individual problems.

5.6.1 The K1: A Flexible Infrastructure

The K1 is a 1950s' building which was completely cleaned out: we kept only some of the architectural envelope; The K1 was retrofitted according to plans made by the Carnegie-Mellon architecture department: we applied the design principles of the CBPD for flexibility (cf. the Loftness et al., Chap. 2). Everything in the building is flexible, from the wiring to walls and furniture. We installed the raised floors systems described by Loftness et al. in Chap. 2 and Borchers in Chap. 10 (Fig. 5.7), the ceiling grid described by Borchers in pattern no. 5 in Chap. 10, etc. We have moveable furniture (cf. furniture section, further down) and even moveable "flying walls" (Figs. 5.8 and 5.9) designed by François Jégou.

Fig. 5.7 The infrastructure of K1 Building: raised floors. *Left*: a user moves a tile with a suction grip. *Right*: the "highway" of network cables as they originate from a control room and run to underfloor distribution boxes in various areas of the building, where local cables with a loose end can be plugged

Fig. 5.8 Users moving a "flying wall"

Fig. 5.9 Reconfiguration of the K1 project space by its occupants between December 2000 (*left*) and March 2001 (*right*)

The walls are self-standing because they are thick and curved, and mounted on a layer that enables the users to slide them and assemble them in a few seconds, without any equipment (unlike the so-called "moveable partitions" installed in many office buildings, which actually never move). The walls also are sound-proof and covered on one side with studio-quality absorbing fabric, of a light grey color, which also provides low-contrast background for videoconferencing.

5.6.2   *The Architectural Charrette*

All this flexibility is extremely handy on a daily basis, and almost everyday users open the floor, change the installation, and rearrange the furniture. By the way, this shows that provided good affordances, users indeed do often change the setting. But this is possible only if the infrastructure is planned beforehand. Devil is in the detail. For example, when one wants to move walls, it is necessary that lighting controls are also moveable, and that there is an easy way to change the ventilation outlets (a meeting room needs more ventilation). In our case, all controls are wireless (presence sensors in the ceiling grid, plus handheld remote controls). The HVAC system is unusual: fresh air comes pressurized in the plenum underneath the raised floor (which is about 40 cm high). Some of the floor tiles are ventilation grids (they are full of small holes); there are return air ducts in the ceiling: the clean air flows naturally from floor to ceiling slowly and silently, clearing away the dust and producing a cleaner atmosphere. When we want to have more ventilation somewhere, moving the tile grids takes a matter of minutes and the users do it themselves.

Therefore, constructing an AE starts at architectural stage. A good envelope (with operable windows, easy access, etc.) and infrastructure must be planned beforehand, and this involves more stakeholders than computer system administrators only. In that respect, most interesting to note is that the CMU team organized an "architectural charrette" crash workshop for the K1, including all stakeholders at the very onset of the design process. There were two intense days which were completely recorded with 35 participants: architects, future users, facility managers, lawyers, administrators, specialists of the future construction team (electricity, HVAC, etc.), IT and security, designers, and members of supplying industries or potential subcontractors (lighting, automation and controls, security etc.).

Design hypotheses were sketched on the fly and introduced in a CAD representation of the building in real time for discussion. Decisions were traced and stakeholders were therefore committed. Having all stakeholders assembled enabled them to discover many potential issues, and to solve them on the spot, which enabled the construction to be done very fast. The workshop took place on 27 and 28 March 2000, and produced a detailed specifications document (Hartkopf et al. 2000). At that time the building was installed with classic office partition inside, on two levels. Following this charrette, everything except the outside walls was destroyed and the new infrastructure installed. The K1 in its new form was finished, fully operational including ICT systems and inhabited when inaugurated 9 months later, on 20 December 2000. While the construction team retrofitted the building and installed the infrastructure, the ICT team was preparing the internal systems in parallel, which were tested separately and finally assembled on the spot in 2 weeks.

Without this previous discussion of all stakeholders, such short and quick turnaround for the overall installation would have been impossible; because with the usual procedure, one discovers problems as the construction goes, and they are more difficult and longer to solve as they were not planned.

The ICT infrastructure is also designed to be modular, and assembles off-the-shelf components with web-services, in a spirit similar to that described by other authors of this book.

5.6.3 *Multiple Spaces*

The K1 building includes several functional spaces, which all serve as testbed. The main space K is a 25 × 12 m² platform, we call the project space (Fig. 5.10 and 5.11). This project space is a mixture of open space and enclaves. We now know that open

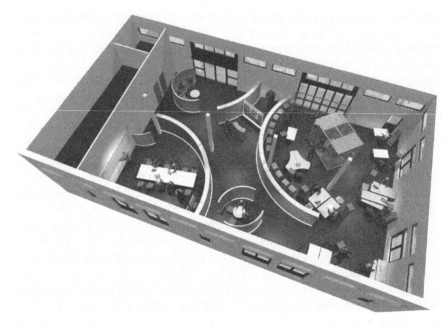

Fig. 5.10 The K1 project space (floorplan as in December 2000)

Fig. 5.11 A view from the K1 project space. Notice one of the movable glass-box enclaves, next to one of the users

space is only good for some types of activities (when participants need awareness of what others do); individual work requires closed and sound isolated spaces, whereas meetings need dedicated meeting rooms with large displays and a variable number of tables and seats.

The project space currently includes two small fully closed enclaves (at one point we had three of these, and only one in the beginning, as depicted on the floorplan on Fig. 5.10). These enclaves made by Burkhardt-Leitner Constructiv are glass boxes (3×3 m^2 and 3×2 m^2); they are soundproof and mounted on wheels; each can serve as a videoconference room for small groups.

The project space is partitioned with moveable "flying walls" (Fig. 5.8). It also contains an augmented meeting room of variable surface (usually about 60 m^2), the RAO room (see Sect. 6.5).

Next to the project space and on the same level, a 5×20 m^2 lounge with a nice view (Fig. 5.12) including a small work area for visiting nomadic workers (with meeting and videoconferencing capability) and toilets.

Adjacent to the project space, and on the same ground floor, two more technical rooms: one for electricity, one for servicing the conference room and next to it, which contains the backstage equipment of RAO, including the beamers. There is also a kitchen.

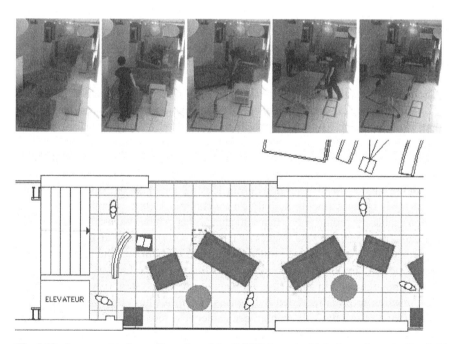

Fig. 5.12 An example of reconfiguration of the GATEP from the "default configuration" to "table group work + pause area." The operation takes less than 5 min, and is effortless since all furniture is on wheels. Notice the markings on the floor for the default configuration which helps users reset the environment at the end of the meeting

On the first floor, there is a relaxation room with a special bed, a space dedicated to data and video analysis and editing, a computer room.

The building is designed to be a comfortable workplace with amenities to test AE. Any kind of environment from the classic one-person closed office to Augmented open spaces can be installed in a matter of hours or days. This is true as well for the ICT infrastructure: all types of networks are available from fiber to wireless, including powerline, infrared, RFID, different types of radio, etc. We also have several types of biometric and geolocation systems, and access to the large EDF R&D computer infrastructure with virtually unlimited computing power and storage (massive clusters, BlueGene supercomputer, etc.).

5.6.4 Digital Ethnography

K1 is a *vivarium* designed for human observation. We use classic ethnographic and ergonomic techniques (observation, interviews, videos, etc.) and some we invented for continuous detailed record with minimal burden on the subjects and researcher.

5.6.4.1 Observation Systems

Anything happening in the meeting room is recordable. Inhabitants are volunteers, who are sometimes asked to wear SubCams (cf. Sect. 4.1 supra) and other systems for lifelogging (Gemmell et al. 2002) ranging from the Microsoft Research SenseCam (Hodges et al. 2006) to the Portapres (ambulatory blood pressure recorder) or having their workstations screens recorded, for example, with Camtasia.

The lab was designed as an observation box: over 25 video cameras ("OffSats") run 24/7 in the lab. A ceiling grid enables fixing cameras anywhere at any angle; the ceiling is high enough to get good coverage. The Offsat (short for Office Satellite: Lahlou 1998) is a time lapse camera situated above a workspace. It has no moving part and can stay for long periods of time (in the K1, the older of these OffSats have been operating continuously for over 8 years, and yield a spectacular accelerated movie of the building history, starting during construction in 2000). Automatic movement analysis enables tracing activity zones (Lahlou 1998); automatic movement detection enables recording only when something is happening. We use Axis NetEye® server cameras, which send the images on a remote securized hard disk.

Spaces within the K1 (not the toilet and relaxation room, nor the inside of glass enclaves though) are under continuous observation by these OffSats, connected to an automatic archival and automated movement analysis system (Fig. 5.13).

The meeting room is recorded by a series of OffSats but also by several video cameras (we also use the videoconference cameras as recording sources); the large displays of the RAO room are directly recorded; this includes the videoconference displays. Films from RAO are recorded on a single digital recorder, and so by one single gesture (putting the "record" ServiceTag on the room's reader) everything is recorded (Fig. 5.14).

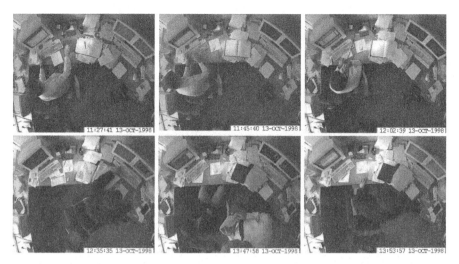

Fig. 5.13 A series of OffSat image, showing the activity in an office

Fig. 5.14 Example of automatic recording of a meeting in RAO. Here, a videoconference of the rufae group. Tico Ballagas, then in Borcher's Aachen group (*top left*) presents a PowerPoint presentation which all participants follow in the rufae labs on both sides of the Atlantic. The PowerPoint is viewed on the right screen of the RAO room, and is record on *lower right* of this image. The two other views (*top right, bottom left*) are views of the RAO room, one from the back, one from the front. This kind of recording enables us to analyze in detail every part of the meeting, and more specifically issues with the ICT and AE systems (cf. Lahlou 2007b)

Fig. 5.15 The Point Grey high resolution "Ladybug" 360° panoramic video camera (*on top*) to which our colleague Antoine Cordelois added a panoramic sound capture system (array of 5 microphones below)

Fig. 5.16 A frame from our portable 360° panoramic video camera: here a seminar with LDC members in the UCSD DCog-HCI laboratory of Jim Hollan and Ed Hutchins

We also have a 360° panoramic video camera, which enables capturing complex scenes in one single take and take any perspective for analysis. This camera is handy because it is light and portable, although very high resolution, and can be transported to capture meetings in any room (Figs. 5.15 and 5.16).

We use several systems for video analysis, but the most useful is WebDiver, developed by the Stanford CISL (Pea et al. 2008), which enables collaborative analysis of videos by searching, visualizing, annotating, and editing in a shared manner all of the videos.

In order not to get drowned in the data we apply the "retro-sampling" strategy. This consists in recording everything, with automatic gross indexation by timestamp and automatic logs (e.g., meeting agendas from the room reservation system, incoming participants, etc.). Then, when we know what we look for (for example, the detailed history of a specific process or incident), we locate in time the relevant moments by a fast cueing of offsat images based on the gross indexing, and proceed to close analysis of the activity by confronting users with the films at normal speed (Lahlou et al. 2002, 2009).

Our observation techniques are potentially invasive. Respecting users' privacy is a basic requirement. Of course, users are aware of the observation; they sign an informed consent as they enter the building. We apply very strict privacy enhancing rules. Users have control over their data, including the right to erase them without giving any reason. For example, users go away with their SubCam data and watch them before giving them to us for analysis, if they wish (if they do not, we destroy the data in their presence, no questions asked). See Lahlou (2006) for a detailed account of our SubCam protocols. The subjects' interest and face are a crucial asset of the lab, more important to us than any data set. Any incident would destroy the whole project, as all is based on trust; we are therefore extremely careful, and the subjects as well as the research group are quite aware of the risks and the necessary precautions.

Of course, data capture should bring no overhead to users, and this is why most of our data capture is automatic.

5.6.4.2 Enrolling Users

The final quality of what is designed is deeply dependant upon how much clever input users actually put in.

The key of success is *active* user collaboration. Putting users in the loop is not enough; they must be involved in a constructive way – beyond simply reacting to propositions of designers. The expertise in the goals, the knowledge of how the company *really* works, and the actual limits of its flexibility lay in the users. So a critical feature of our process is to *spark users into creative mode.*

Not all users are creative, not all users can envision what technology could bring them. More often than not, when they are asked about their needs and wants, their answer is a not-very-imaginative modification of the present process (e.g., faster, cheaper, etc.). This is because it takes time and trust for them to dare give their opinion and wishes, or simply tell the truth about their practices, which are often in contravention with the company rules. To get there, one positive aspect of experimental reality is that we actually deliver operational service. This makes relations with users that are direct, pragmatic, and focused on actual issues. We often find ourselves trying to solve issues in cooperation with users: for example, helping organizing nomadic videoconferencing, inserting exotic new subsystems etc. Discussing specifications and possible improvements is easier with someone whom you have helped a few days before organizing a hazardous satellite connection for a live collaborative session with engineers on the field in some jungle on the other side of the globe!

Another risky choice we made was to enroll the board of executives of the Division as a test user group (an option similar to the Fuji–Xerox approach described in Chap. 4). This is challenging because executives often have tough requirements, which push the system to its limits; it is useful because we get better support when we need the collaboration of other entities inside the group to realize some environments; it helps disseminating the technology because it has some prestigious managerial aura; it is of course dangerous because system failures have big consequences.

So the nature of users involved in the process is far from neutral. There is nothing such as "normal" users. We suggest to choose "friendly users" (see Chap. 1 and Jégou's Chap. 6) in the first phases of design, and gradually extend the scope to less cooperative users.

5.6.5   The RAO Augmented Meeting Room: A "Mother of Rooms"

The RAO (Réunion Assistée par Ordinateur) room is a flexible space where users can arrange the physical and digital setting in a matter of minutes, according to their needs. Technically, its main features are flexible furniture, multimedia connectivity to other spaces, and physical interface ("Augmented Reality": Ishii and Ullmer 1997). Functionally, RAO is both an observation lab and the "mother room" of augmented rooms at EDF.[5] It is continuously in a beta version, and when upgrading is considered stable, the solutions are transferred into other rooms. This enables us to address the never-endingness of AE design.

5.6.5.1   Flexible and Mobile Furniture

What users enjoy first in the RAO room is simply its quality as a room in terms of lighting, acoustic, and thermal ambiance. RAO has large operable windows, at two levels in order to avoid glare. Walls and ceiling have advanced acoustic treatment. Whatever the quality of the ICT layer, if the physical infrastructure is poor, the result will be mediocre. Conference rooms without daylight meetings are usually less productive: humans are animals who need clean air, good light, and enjoy a nice view - and leg-space (Fig. 5.17).

The electric lighting has "sunlight" quality with appropriate wavelength. The ventilation is intense but silent, thanks to the laminar flux. The ceiling is high (4.5 m). RAO is comfortable, and has comfortable amenities (access lounge with excellent espresso machine, nice toilets, etc.). It also always seems to be the appropriate size, as we adapt the furniture to the number of participants and the type of meetings (Fig. 5.18).

The rounded walls give a nice cozy feeling, and the furniture, although stackable and on wheels, is heavy and of excellent quality.

We use a dozen stackable chairs of various models, seven folding tables on wheels designed by Wilkhahn, foldable tables and various prototypes of smaller wheeled furniture, two dozen chairs "0.03" designed by Vitra (some visible on Fig. 5.19), stools by Stokke and Wilkhahn; these chairs have no wheels, unlike the ergonomic chairs used in the project space, in order to take less floor footprint around the tables.

---

[5]Films presenting the RAO room are available at www.tecog.org.

Fig. 5.17 Well lit screens enable use of the RAO room in daylight

Fig. 5.18 *Left*: a small videoconference between two sites in the RAO room in 2003. Notice the control screen and keyboard in the *left corner*. The window at the time still had classic Venetian blinds which we later replaced with "white screen" blinds. *Right*: a more classic creativity meeting of the "Ambient Agoras" project group

Lighting is automatic with ceiling-based presence sensors; intensity is variable and can be overridden by manual remote controls, like the windows' blinds. The blinds (as in the lounge) are designed to serve also as projection screens when needed, and have their inner face white. In the lounge where the windows are not operable, a second internal layer of sliding glass transforms the windows (each bay is 4×2.5 m^2) into huge whiteboards. In general, every glass window can be turned

Fig. 5.19 Stackable chairs and foldable tables and tablets stored on the edge of RAO

into a whiteboard, as whiteboard markers erase well on glass, but it is more convenient to have a plane white background, which we get by sliding opaque white
blinders between the two layers of double glazing.

A vast choice of sensing devices can then be used to transform these into
electronic whiteboards (we use e-Beam or Mimio, and also the Wiimote system
designed by Johnny Lee at CMU). We also have a choice of classic white boards
and repositionable paper boards (3 M Post-it Self-Stick Easel Wall Pads).

Old fashioned technology is a good plan B in case if things fail or some users
simply do not dare using the AE. In our experience, having these classical systems
available makes users at ease, and they will be more willing to try the new devices
in real situations because they know they have a plan B, so they do not fear messing
up the meeting or make a fool of themselves. Anyway, having a plan B, a plan C,
and sometimes D is necessary because one cannot afford failure, for example, in a
multiplex videoconferencing where important negotiations with top executives take
place. It is because our AE systems enable such important meetings to take place
in good conditions that they finally gain trust in the organization. Nevertheless,
bugs and failures are always possible, especially when distant sites who may have
a low mastery of technology are involved. Plan B is necessary to avoid users having
a bad experience which would be a counter-reference.

The 4 m base giant display "TabEc" (Tableau-Ecran) is served by two strong
beamers in back projection, which enables operating the display with full daylight.
This system is cheap and easily scalable (this glass panel cost about 4,000 at a time
when this kind of glass was still produced in very low quantities), and we benefit of
continuous upgrade of the quality of beamers. The COTS elements are compatible

with the standard procurement procedures of the company, and therefore scaling out was easy. A system of plain backlighting (four ordinary strong projectors with translucent screening directed at the screen from the back) transform at the flick of switch the TabEc into a large electronic whiteboard. It must be noted here, though, that we now almost never use the electronic panel capability of these screens, as users are not much used to it. Also, the electronic pens tended to have battery failure in the worst moments, which stressed the users. Finally, automatic handwriting recognition and pen entry into usual software is not always trivial in the current state of the art. We are waiting until COTS elements will reach 100% reliability to reintroduce this feature for lay users. We currently rather give the users easy capability of annotating the screen with remote mouse, keyboard, or pens and tablets, which they can use from their seat. These devices have longer battery autonomy; periodic maintenance is enough to ensure they are always operational, and every lay user knows how to operate them without hesitation.

Figure 5.18 shows views of RAO in operation with small groups, but the room can comfortably house up to 20 people, and less comfortably up to 40 when walls are pushed back. Over this number, the distance the screen is too small for all to see comfortably the small print.

Flexible furniture enables configurating RAO for very different uses, for example, creative meeting, presentation, etc. Figure 5.20 shows how with folding tables and tablets the meeting room can be changed in a few minutes by the users themselves. Figure 5.21 illustrates setting the room from default to decision meeting configuration.

Not for one second did we regret the initial investment cost in high end furniture, which has now been stacked thousands of times and still looks good. If you go for moveable furniture, cheap stuff is not a good choice. Users tend to sit on tables, stack up chairs the wrong way, drop remote controls and, in general, exhibit an amazing creativity using the items in the room in ways which were not forecasted by

Fig. 5.20 The RAO room in collocated discussion (*left*) and collocated presentation (*right*). Notice the folded tablets (*stacked near window on left image*), and the folding tables (*stored folded on right corner in right image*)

Fig. 5.21 The RAO meeting room. The two pictures where taken at 1 min interval. (*Left*) Room in default state, (*Right*) room after the users rolled in and unfolded the tables, and set up the screens and digital work environment by putting the appropriate RFID tags on the reader. Notice the power outlet that was pulled out of one of the floor traps

their makers. The same goes with electronic equipment. This is one reason why we custom-made sturdy big one-button or two-button oversized remote controls.

Mobility is also needed for electronic equipment, thanks to wireless and battery autonomy. Large electric equipment (e.g., large screens) often need to be moved (e.g., from meeting room to lounge, etc.) small distances. We made them moveable by adding an Uninterrupted Power Supply (UPS) to their rolling stand and plugging the equipment to the UPS on a continuous basis (the UPS is plugged to a fixed power outlet and is unplugged when we move the equipment on its rolling stand). Stands are usually large and sturdy enough as they should support heavy equipment anyway. Because equipment usually only needs to be rolled from one place with a power plug to another place with a plug, taking less than 20 min, this trick is enough. For example, our "video trolley" is a (Polycom Polyspan) videoconference camera and microphone, with a screen, connected to a wireless hub – all this equipments being plugged to an UPS with 30 mn autonomy: we can roll the video trolley around the lab to make a "videoconference guided tour" of the lab, or conveniently roll along the distant participants as we go to the coffee area during pauses. In the worst case, such a trolley, securely connected to the internet in controlled bypass of company firewalls under wizard supervision, could be used as a Plan D to "roll into the meeting" a distant participant who can communicate only by Skype videoconferencing.

We currently do these transports by human hand and foot, but in the future autonomous mobile equipment will probably move by itself, and dock in for power when needed, like the lab's robot vacuum cleaner ("Roomba") does when it comes back from its nightly operations.

5.6.5.2   Physical Interface: ServiceTags

Some of the physical interface are incorporated in the walls or in column, for example, RFID antennas, biometric access controls, motion sensors, toilet seat cleaner, etc. (there are no light switches in the toilets or in the kitchen, e.g., which is both easier and cleaner).

We make a massive use of large screen displays for display and also for "system response" (the system tells the user what it is doing, acknowledges orders, etc.). One of the issues we had in the beginning was timing. For example, powerline technology, voice recognition, or pattern identification may be slow in responding. As the user does not know what happens, he repeats the order, and this repetition actually messes up the system. We are very careful now to give the user some feedback on what the system is doing. Graphic or text display (sometimes as simple as a flashing diode) is a better choice than vocal because it is less intrusive.

In some cases though, we need vocal: when the RAO room reminds the last occupants to clean up the room before leaving, when the building welcomes visitors and directs their attention to the displays. Voice tends to have a much stronger emotional impact on the user, both ways: when it works well the user gets a warm feeling, but when it talks in an irrelevant way the users get annoyed. Using voice is like giving a personality to the AE, and the user then reacts in a human-to-human rather than in a cold human-to-machine way. This effect tends to fade when the users know the system well; they will then tend to override the system and give a quick series of orders, rather than having a conversation-like rhythm as first users do. In a way, a double command system seems an interesting option: vocal for beginners, then gesture, remote control or keyboard shortcuts for expert users.

The AE interface that met most success so far is the ServiceTags. Each tag is a physical item that represents an operation (e.g., "switch on the beamer") or a sequence of actions ("switch on the video projector, turn on the videoconferencing software and connect us to the iLounge at KTH"). We were not the first to apply this interface principle: Joan Mattsson (2007), when he was troubadouring[6] in the K1, demonstrated us his iBowl system, which does exactly what is described in the second example: the iStuff approach (Ballagas et al. 2003). We created a series of credit card format (or smaller) RFID tags: each tag is an operation (e.g., "set up a videoconference with the Chatou island EDF R&D site/room XX," record everything in the meeting room," display the current traffic density roadmap in the Paris area" – good to know before you take your car at the end of a meeting, "display the bus schedule from the facility to Paris center," "display on the main screen the screen of the PC that is connected to black VGA cable," "open a Gridboard Mediaspace," "open my DumbleTag virtual machine," etc.).

Each ServiceTag has an icon on it, and the command is explained in natural language. To execute the command, the users simply put the tag on a table antenna (in some executive rooms with beautiful tables, the antenna is hidden under the table and the active area materialized by a circle). When the ServiceTag is taken

---

[6]Rufae lab members can "troubadour" from one lab to another: visitors pay their transport but are lodged and fed by the hosting lab for as long as they stay; in return, the troubadour must leave "something" to the host lab, usually by installing his own system locally. This helps dissemination between member labs.

Fig. 5.22 RFID ServiceTags on a reader (*on the left notice the 1 coin for scale*)

off the antenna, the command is reversed or terminated. The reader can execute as many commands as tags can be piled on the antenna (Fig. 5.22); there are cards in meeting rooms, and users can have their own for personalized commands or authentication, for example, some users have been granted a virtual clone (VMWare) of their workstation, called "DumbleTags," which they can access as a webservice from any machine connected to the company's network (which is handy because they can go around with their hands in their pockets and still have access to their workstation anywhere). The DumbleTag enables them to access their machine in a second on the meeting room display by putting their tag on the antenna. They can then, for example, do their PowerPoint presentation from their own virtual machine.

ServiceTags are nice to hold and fun to use, the users experience the famous "delightful surprise" effect when they use them and fear not failure. On the DOME side, the tags proved robust, batteryless, easy to trace, replace, securized, and cheap. There is no moving part, and the users have no possibility of messing up the system; in fact they have much less than before as we can now let the users control the rooms without granting them access to any hardware (buttons, cables, etc., which are always a cause of problem). The whole system can be maintained at a distance (the central wizards can log the users operations, see the problems, command, or reboot remotely). The system is cheaply scalable and open to modifications.

Of course, this does not solve the classic problems of local hardware failure or infrastructure, but a specific "maintenance" tag enables the local users or secretaries to check whether the system is OK. For example, the day before an important meeting, one can just run the "test" ServiceTag and verify that all controls are green. As RFID tokens are rewriteable, the system enables participants in a meeting to add some resources, credits, or links by putting their personal tags on the antenna.

5.6.5.3   Multimedia Connectivity: Videoconferencing, Gridboard

Videoconferencing

One of the main function of RAO is videoconferencing capability. In RAO IP started videoconferencing at EDF. There are many issues in videoconferencing, which we discuss in detail elsewhere (Lahlou 2007a).

To make a long story short, good videoconferencing needs at least two large screens, one for displaying the participants, one for displaying the contents presented and discussed (e.g., text processor, PowerPoint, etc.). The videoconference must have good sound, and the shared screen must have high resolution (Fig. 5.23). The lighting and sound quality crucially depend upon the physical settings. For example, image depends upon the contrast rather than lighting. A room with white walls will never produce a good image, whatever the lighting; a grey or mid-colored background is better. Rooms with strong ventilation noise will always be more problematic. Also, room layout must be different in videoconferencing: long conference tables with the video camera at the one end are the worst possible setting: the main protagonists (high status) usually sit at the wrong end and visibility is bad for everyone.

There are many sophisticated solutions available for videoconferencing. We focused on cheap and scalable ones that can be installed to augment any meeting room into a videoconference room, and also be usable in many different situations (one-to-many conference, distributed discussion with many small groups, etc.).

Fig. 5.23 A videoconference in the RAO room: the *left screen* is the videoconference screen, the *right* the shared Gridboard

Once again, we tried to keep it simple. The ServiceTags enable connecting to any known room in a matter of 2 or 3 s. For multiple open meetings, we direct all rooms towards one of the multiplex star nodes, each one going independently there. Say: "let's all go to the Kubrick room" – which means both a videoconference node and shared Gridboard workspace (cf. infra): each end user puts the Kubrick ServiceTag on their antennas and they all meet in the multiplex videoconference node.

Shared Workspace: Gridboard

For meetings, one cannot expect to train all participants beforehand. We must check that there is no initial cost barrier in the learning curve for novice users and adapt the system accordingly. The system must respect the "zero" list on the client side: zero training, zero configuration, etc. Unless these requirements are met, when a new participant tries to connect in a meeting, something will usually get into the way.

A good cognitive design will rely on what users already know and provide obvious affordances and systems, which respond accordingly to implicit expectations. This is easier to do when the subjects already share a common socket of competences. All the designer has to do is program the interaction using these implicits.

Let us illustrate this with the case of our digital collaborative space, "Gridboard." From the user's side, it follows the attractor of "being together in front of the same machine and sharing the mouse and the keyboard with the usual interface." Instead of being physically in front of the machine, participants all see it live on their own screen, while being in audio contact by audioconference or videoconference. Figure 5.5 showed how we prompt this mental model into the user.

Technically, we provide a URL. The user, with his browser, goes to this URL and opens a window which *is* the shared screen: inside the window *is* a standard, complete, Microsoft Windows desktop. This shared desktop behaves *exactly* as users expect, because *it is actually* a (virtual) Microsoft Windows desktop, containing the standard Microsoft Office suite and other classic software (Lotus Notes, SAP, etc.) used in the company. All users simultaneously access the same machine, they share the mouse and keyboard (using their own, and resolving conflicts by voice: "Don't use the mouse, I'm writing!").

This interface is "simple" because every user already knows how to use such a desktop (Macintosh users can also share it, but it is still a Windows interface for them). Experience shows that incoming first-time users use the system fluently within seconds, simply because this is not a "new" environment to them.

Of course, we also have ServiceTags pointing to these URLs, but not every PC in the company has a tag reader antenna, so usually people use their browser to type in the URL, click the link in their favorites.

As usual, simplicity on the user's side is paid by some complexity at the programming level. It took us about 2 years to strip down the initial interfaces we had made until we reached something really simple. The files exchange issues and the access rights managements were not so trivial, and the user feedback was precious. There are still screen real-estate issues if the system is used with only one screen.

The environments we now deploy inside the company always use twin screen systems, one for presentation and minutes and the other for videoconferencing.

It is worthy to note that we trained two dozen users only, and have now over 3,000 regular users who were recruited and trained by viral diffusion only. Let us see how we framed the viral diffusion. There is one single URL to access all Gridboards (the ones dedicated to a specific group, the ones shared by departments on the basis of reservation, etc.). On this page are some "sandbox" Gridboards, which are free access with a constant, easy to remember password. So anyone who knows the password can open a shared Gridboard space, for example, to hold a meeting.

Here is how viral diffusion takes place. When one participant in a group knows a good solution to a group problem and can demonstrate its validity on the spot, often the group will adopt the solution (which would not be the case if the same solution was proposed by an outsider or not in a "need" context). Provided that the solution works, the proposer will gain social value in doing this viral contamination because she brought a good solution. And all participants in the group, if they can learn during this first exposure how to use the system, will probably be diffusers later when they find themselves in a situation of being "the one who can bring the solution."

We liberally give out the passwords for sandboxes, therefore empowering all our users to contaminate other users by giving them, in turn, access to the resource.

Of course, at some point, users who use these sandboxes on a regular basis encounter the problem of finding the sandbox occupied by somebody else when they want to use it for a meeting. In such cases, they may decide to click the buy-in button to get their own personal space.

5.7 Conclusion: Design Process vs. Design Project

We described the nature of the problem that makes AE design necessary and specific: digitization of work; we showed how in one specific company this idea led to the creation of a dedicated user Laboratory of Design for Cognition.

We made explicit our design strategy, *experimental reality*, which encapsulates a continuous hands-on design process, with a multidisciplinary team enrolling users to test AE in real work conditions. This approach is based on the use of digital ethnography (especially the SubCam) to spot the problems users encounter in their daily activity.

In practice, we constructed a whole Augmented Building where users work, the K1, fully armed for continuous observation. This building contains various types of workspaces, the most prominent being the RAO augmented meeting room.

RAO is a "mother room" for other augmented rooms in the company: when solutions in RAO reach a satisfying level of usability, they are disseminated, preferably by viral diffusion. This solves the never-endingness issue of AE design, and enables inclusion, in a realistic way, of the DOME aspects of innovation. Our approach enabled us to spark users into creative mode and quickly develop a large number of innovations and robust AE.

We described some of the features of RAO, and more specifically the use of physical artifacts as command interface (ServiceTags), and the Gridboard collaborative desktop which meet the "zero" list of requirements we think is necessary for fluid and sustainable AE systems. Our design approach has specific characteristics, which come from the specific context of its birth; it is quite different from current classic "project" management of design issues; still we believe it can be transferred into other settings.

We found experimental reality has many advantages in our specific context. It enables us to deal with never-endingness to adapt COTS systems to the specifics of the corporation. The initial investment is substantial (a few million euros) but the ROI is good. Also, having a mother room concentrates demand and helps capitalizing know-how.

However, there are a series of limits and unsolved issues. This approach needs a visionary sponsor, at least in the first years, because it does not fit with the dominant project approach. It is very difficult to know beforehand how long it will take to solve a problem; the detailed timing is unclear: this makes it very difficult to "sell" a given project with deliverables. Also, the lab is profitable because it enables us to deal simultaneously with many issues and aspects of AE (meetings, workflows, nomadic use, security, etc.). Setting up the whole installation for one single project would be overkill.

Another issue is the multidisciplinary work and continuous work-in-progress. This makes it difficult for each local specialist to describe his own added value in the process. Especially for ergonomists: their input is directly used in new versioning, but there is hardly a trace of a "clean" user study, as we try to solve the issues rather than document them, which saves time and resources but fails to provide the academic papers needed for our career.

Finally, it took a long time to build a good reputation and users' trust. This was possible because the laboratory was built and directed by an insider, but it is quite infrequent that non-ICT companies dare making such a research lab on issues that they consider are not part of their core business. We must thank EDF R&D for its courage and vision, which partly comes from the fact that this company always had a deep investment in basic research (the R&D staff is over 2,000 people) and long-term vision due to its very long investment cycle (about half a century for power plants, even more for the distribution networks).

We do not know how far subcontracting this kind of experimental reality is possible, as academic or business considerations tend to focus the lab members on showing their sponsors or peers that they do "clean" work, rather than focus them on producing results in a process, which is sometimes quick and dirty. Also, the trust of participants was partly based on the fact that they knew we were insiders bound to company rules, which may not be the case with external teams.

Still, we believe the concept of the mother room and experimental reality can be transplanted, with some adaptation. In fact over the last year, LDC has been involved in adapting the technique for a similar large scale initiative, developing AE in production power plants.

Acknowledgments   The LDC was funded mainly by EDF R&D Division's IT Program; also by the European IST/Disappearing Computer Initiative "Ambient Agoras" contract IST-2000–25134; the Foundation Maison des Sciences de l'Homme (Paris); CNRS collaboration funding with UMR 8177 (EHESS – CNRS, Centre Edgar Morin).
The RUFAE network brought crucial input.
Many researchers and administrators contributed to this large project over the years (apologies for any omissions): Margarita Anastassova, Stéphane Andrieux, Patrick Andujar, Houssem Assadi, David Autissier, Maurice Aymard, Azizan Aziz, Paul Bach-y-Rita, Maribeth Back, Tico Ballagas, Yves Bamberger, Vladimir Barabanchikov, Valerie Beaudouin, André Beillard, Sylvain Bellan, Jean-Yves Berthou, Béatrice Bianchini-Burlot, Nicolas Bielski, Guillaume Billon, Marie-Joëlle Blosseville, René Boillot, Jan Borchers, Clément Boré, Francesca Botta, Pierre Bouchet, François Boulot, Claude Bouquet, Françoise Boutin, Jean-Marc Boutin, Mathilde Boutin, Guy Boy, Philippe Brajeul, Maryse Brinvilliers, Xavier Carcelle, Marie-Thérèse Cerf, Jean-Paul Chabard, Abel Chaibi, Anne-Marie Chemali, Vitaly Chemilis, Milton Chen, Nadia Cheniour, Aaron Cicourel, Brigitte Corde, Antoine Cordelois, Laurent Coudert, Catherine Dassieux, Agnès de Cicco, Lucinda de Cicco, Jean-Paul Delhomel, Yves Denayrolles, Gaetan Derousseaux, Pierre Destang, Catherine Devic, Yves Dherbecourt, Salvator Di Benedetto, Alain d'Iribarne, Evelyne Donnadieux, Sylviane Duchene, Clément-Marc Falinower, Anne-Laure Fayard, Christian Felter, Jaqueline Feuilloy, George Fieldman, Geneviève Filippi, Claude Fischler, Olivier Fergon, Siegfried Frey, Pascal Froment, Colombine Gardair, Vincent Gayrard, Maria Geka, Laure Gioara, Sara Girardi, Jean-Louis Goblet, Charles Godon, Michel Gondran, Pascal Guillermin, Yann Guyonvarc'h, Pierre-Marie Guyonvarc'h, Patricia Guyot, Philippe Guyot, Jean-François Hamelin, Volker Hartkopf, Pascal Henriot, Jean-Marc Herodin, Steve Hodges, Jim Hollan, Kazunori Horikiri, Do Huyhn, Ciro Ibello, Calle Jansson, François Jégou, Raphaëlle Jeune, Pierre Johannet, Nikos Kalampalikis, David Kirsh, Marc Langheinrich, Sophie Le Bellu, Benoît Le Blanc, Anne Le Mouel, Patricia Lecoq, Xavier Lemesle, Tanguy Lemoing, Charles Lenay, Sanna Leppämäki, Nicolas Lesbats, Joëlle Liberman, Christian Licoppe, Vivian Loftness, Eric Lorentz, Jean-Luc Lory, Caroline Luzi, Patrick MacLeod, Yutaka Matsuo, Johann Mattsson, Olaf Maxant, Eric Mathieu, Yves Mayadoux, Roland Melkior, David Menga, Sandro Meneghello, Isabelle Mialon, Martial Monfort, Patrick Morilhat, Patricia Morin-Pagane, Thierry Moreau, Serge Moscovici, Olivier Nadiras, Thierry Nguessan, Pierre Nguyen, Saeko Nomura, Valery Nosulenko, Nicolas Nova, Elisabeth Obe-Guy, Pascal Obry, Joseph Orlinski, Thierry Paturle, Roy Pea, François Peccoud, Régis Petit, Christian Pradelou, Thorsten Prante, Alain Prodhomme, Florence Raud, Christian Raux, Rouzbeh Rezakhanlou, Sophie Richardot, Anne Rocha, Carsten Röcker, Patrick Rojewski, Jean-Yves Romanetti, Joe Rosen, Dan Russell, Jean-Michel Saas, Bertrand Sacepe, Gerard Said, Lena Samoylenko, Bernard Scherrer, Edouard Sikierski, Frédéric Silvi, Luc Simonet, Frank Sonder, Ron Stanonik, Richard Stenzel, Norbert Streitz, Hillevi Sundholm, François-Xavier Testard-Vaillant, Howard Taylor, Arnaud Tarrago, Lidia Tralli, Jean-Louis Vaudescal, Pierre-Louis Viollet, Jean-Louis Vuldy, Françoise Waeckel, Patricia Welinski, Lynn Wilcox, Terry Winograd.
Finally, users and volunteer testers brought precious input; space is too short here to list them, but we thank them gratefully.

References

Autissier D, Lahlou S (1999) *La surcharge informationnelle et la gestion de l'information. Enquête auprès de 17 grandes entreprises françaises.* Clamart: EDF R&D. HN51 99/008. Août 1999, p. 66
Autissier D, Melkior R, Lahlou S (1997) *Analyse de l'activité quotidienne de 6 chefs de groupes à la DER.* Clamart: EDF/DER/MMC. Service AGT

Ballagas R, Ringel M, Stone M, Borchers J (2003) iStuff: a physical user interface toolkit for ubiquitous computing environments. In *Proceedings of the SIGCHI Conference on Human Factors in Computing Systems* (Ft. Lauderdale, Florida, USA, April 05–10, 2003). CHI '03, New York: ACM

Bödker S (1996) Applying activity theory to video analysis: how to make sense of video data in human-computer interaction. In Nardi BA (Ed) *Context and Consciousness: Activity Theory and Human-Computer Interaction.* Cambridge: MIT, pp. 147–174

Engeström Y (1990). *Learning, working and imaging: twelve studies in activity theory.* Helsinki: Orienta-Konsultit

Engeström Y (1993) *Interactive expertise.* Helsinki: University of Helsinki

Engeström Y, Middleton D (1996) *Cognition and communication at work.* Cambridge: Cambridge University Press

Fischler C, Lahlou S (1995) *Dossiers, piles d'attente et corbeilles: la digestion quotidienne de l'information dans les bureaux.* EDF/DER. HN5195017

Fischler C, Lahlou S (2000) *La consommation et la gestion d'information dans les bureaux: enquête quantitative.* EDF R&D, Jan. 2000, p. 32

Gemmell J, Bell G, Lueder R, Drucker S, Wong C (2002) MyLifeBits: Fulfilling the Memex vision. In *Proceedings of ACM multimedia'02,* December 1–6, 2002, Juan-les-Pins

Gibson JJ (1967) Notes on affordances. In Reed E, Jones R (Eds) *Reasons for realism. Selected Essays of James J. Gibson.* London: Lawrence Erlbaum Associates, 1982, pp. 401–418

Hartkopf V, Loftness V, Aziz A (2000) *Implémentation des locaux expérimentaux du Laboratoire de Design Cognitif dans un bâtiment existant sur le campus d'EDF à Clamart* (K1). Analyse du besoin, spécifications fonctionnelles et solutions techniques. Conclusions de l'atelier des 28–29 mars 2000. EDF R&D/LDC. April 2000, p. 45

Hiltz SR, Turoff M (1985) Structuring computer-mediated communication systems to avoid information overload. *Communications of the ACM* 28:7, 680–689

Hodges S, Williams L, Berry E, Izadi S, Srinivasan J, Butler A, Smyth G, Kapur N, Wood K (2006) SenseCam: A retrospective memory aid. In *Proceedings Ubicomp 2006,* pp. 117–193

Hutchins E (1987) *Metaphors for Interface Design.* University of California, San Diego. Institute for Cognitive Science. Report no ICS-8703, Apr. 1987, p. 40. Paper presented at NATO-sponsored workshop on Multimodal Dialogues Including Voice, Venaco, Corsica, France, September 1986

Ishii H, Ullmer B (1997) Tangible bits: towards seamless interfaces between people, bits and atoms. In *Proceedings of CHI'97,* pp. 234–241

Kidd A (1994) The marks are on the knowledge workers. In *Proceedings of CHI'94 Conference on Human Factors in Computing Systems,* New York: ACM, pp. 186–191

Lahlou S (1994) *L'utilisation de l'information dans l'entreprise: quelques réflexions théoriques et une analyse lexicale.* EDF-DER. HN-5194055

Lahlou S (1996) *Representations and the social co-ordination of action.* 3rd International Conference on Social Representations, Aix-en Provence, 9/1996. & EDF/DER HN-5196020

Lahlou S (1998) *Le diable est détail. Le syndrome de saturation cognitive.* EDF- Direction des Etudes et Recherches, HN-51/98/020

Lahlou S (1999) Observing Cognitive Work in Offices. In Streitz N, Siegel J, Hartkopf V, Konomi S (Eds). *Cooperative Buildings. Integrating Information, Organizations and Architecture.* Heidelberg: Springer, Lecture Notes in Computer Science, 1670. pp. 150–163

Lahlou S (2000) Attracteurs cognitifs et travail de bureau. *Intellectica* 2000/1, 30, 75–113

Lahlou S (2005) Cognitive attractors and activity-based design: augmented meeting rooms. Human Computer Interaction International. 22–27 July. 2005, Las Vegas, NA, USA. Volume 1 - *Engineering Psychology, Health and Computer System Design*

Lahlou S (2006) L'activité du point de vue de l'acteur et la question de l'intersubjectivité: huit années d'expériences avec des caméras miniaturisées fixées au front des acteurs (SubCam). *Communications,* 80, 209–234

Lahlou S (2007a) L'activité de réunion à distance. *Réseaux,* 25:44, 59–101

Lahlou S (2007b) Human activity modeling for systems design: a trans-disciplinary and empirical approach. Harris D (Ed) *Engineering Psychology and Cognitive Ergonomics,*

HCII 2007, Lectures Notes in Artificial Intelligence, 4562. Berlin-Heidelberg: Springer, 2007, pp. 512–521

Lahlou S (2008a) Cognitive technologies, Social Science and the Three-Layered Leopard Skin of Change. *Social Science Information*, 47:3, 299–332

Lahlou S (2008b) Identity, social status, privacy and face-keeping in digital society. *Social Science Information*, 47:3, 227–252

Lahlou S (2008c) Supporting collaboration with augmented environments: design and dissemination issues. In Dillenbourg P, Huang J, Cherubini M (Eds) *Interactive Furniture Supporting Collaborative Work/Learning*. Berlin: Springer, pp. 75–93

Lahlou S, Fischler C (1996) Comment gérer et digérer les informations: le traitement de l'information par le bureau. *Sciences Humaines*, 65, 42–45

Lahlou S, Fischler C (1999) Le traitement de l'information par le bureau. In Charles Lenay et Véronique Havelange: Mémoires de la technique et techniques de la mémoire. *Technologies, Idéologies, Pratiques*. ERES. 1999, pp. 109–127

Lahlou S, Nosulenko V, Samoylenko E (2002) Un cadre méthodologique pour le design des environnements augmentés. *Social Science Information*, 41:4, 471–530

Lahlou S, Lenay C, Gueniffey Y, Zacklad M (1997) Le C.O.S. In Compte-rendu de la 152ème réunion du CA de l'ARC, du 2/10/1997. *Bulletin de l'Association pour la Recherche Cognitive*, no 42, Nov. 1997, p. 39

Lahlou S, Kirsh D, Rebotier T, Reeves C, Remy M (1999) *Experimental study of the effect of interruption on office work. Experiments 1 & 2: types of interruptions & recovery devices.* UCSD http://interruptions.net/literature/Lahlou-Unpublished02-2.htm

Lahlou S, Nosulenko V, Samoylenko E (2009) *La numérisation du travail. théories, méthodes, expériences.* Paris: Lavoisier, collection EDF R&D (in press)

Lansdale MW (1990) On the role of memory in personal information management. In Falzon P (Ed) *Cognitive Ergonomics: Understanding, Learning and Designing Human-Computer Interaction*. London: Academic Press, pp. 39–50

Lea G (1987) *Non-users of information services*. Audit Report. Graham Lea & Partners Ltd

Lewis D (1996) *Dying for information? An investigation into the effects of information overload in the UK and Worldwide*. London, UK: Reuters Business Information

Ljundberg F (1996) *An initial exploration of communication overflow*. The 2nd International Conference on the Design of Cooperative Systems (COOP'96), Sophia Antipolis, France. Edited by the COOP group, INRIA, France, pp. 19–36

Lomov BF (1977) O putyakh postroeniya teorii inzhenernoj psikhologii na osnove sistemnogo podkhoda (Perspectives of a conception of engineering psychology in a systemic approach). In Lomov BF, Rubakhin VF, Venda VF (Eds) Inzhenernaya psikhologiya (Engineering Psychology), Moscow: Nauka, pp. 31–54

Malone T (1996) New technologies transforming business organization, efficiency, for the 21st century. *The MIT Report*. 1996, p. 3–4

Malone TW (1983) How do people organize their desks? Implications for the design of office information systems, *ACM Transactions on Office Information Systems*, 1:1, 99–112

Mattsson J (2007) *Pointing, placing, touching – physical manipulation and coordination techniques for interactive meeting spaces*. Ph D Thesis, KTH

Mintzberg H (1996) Une journée avec un dirigeant. *Revue française de gestion*, nov.-déc. 1996, pp. 106–114

Moatty F (1994) Comment les salariés reçoivent-ils leurs instructions de travail? Canaux de communication et formalisation des organisations. *Dossiers du Centre d'Etude de l'Emploi*, 2

Pea R, Lindgren R, Rosen J (2008) Cognitive technologies for establishing, sharing and comparing perspectives on video over computer networks. *Social Science Information*, 47:3, 353–370

Simon HA (1997) *Administrative behavior*, 4th edition. New York: The Free Press

von Uexküll J (1956) *Mondes animaux et monde humain*. Followed by *Théorie de la signification*. Paris: Médiations, Gonthier

Chapter 6
Co-design Approaches for Early Phases of Augmented Environments

François Jégou

Abstract This chapter focuses on the early phases in the development processes of new product-service systems and particularly on the possibility of actively involving users in view of generating a concept. It describes the main hurdles to both the project team and user research and suggests methodological approaches devised by the author.

In particular the chapter describes two tools called: "Scenario co-design" and "Spot Experiment," respectively, featuring examples of how these tools can be used in the field of augmented environments.

6.1 Introduction

This first part will discuss the main difficulties of user-centred approaches in early concept generation phases of the project.

The importance and efficiency of user-centred approaches is commonly admitted especially when considering complex product-service systems and breakthrough innovation (Grandjean and Kroemer 1999; Garrett 2002; Norman 2004). Current practice tends to involve users especially in the preparation and in the validation phases. Before the project starts, user research investigation and, in particular, ethnographic-like observations inform the project, to give a realistic picture of current user practices and to identify key problems. In the final stages of the project's development, user testing in real environments enables researchers to fine-tune prototypes before substantial investments are made in production and the actual launch of the product.

Between these phases, early concept generation is more of an internal creative process, and the sole prerogative of the project team. User involvement appears to

F. Jégou (✉)
Strategic Design Scenarios, Brussels, Belgium
e-mail: francois.jegou@solutioning-design.net

S. Lahlou (ed.), *Designing User Friendly Augmented Work Environments: From Meeting Rooms to Digital Collaborative Spaces,* Computer Supported Cooperative Work, DOI 10.1007/978-1-84800-098-8_6, © Springer-Verlag London Limited 2009

be too expensive and time consuming. The generation of ideas is a process described as holistic (involving all dimensions of a problem at the same time), iterative (jumping back and forth from theory to practice, concept to implementation…) and somewhat irrational (ideas appear in an uncontrolled way). Relationships and communication between users, researchers and designers is a typical bottleneck in the design process. A user-centred approach with strict observation protocols, representative samples, fine grained analysis, etc is incompatible with fluid creativity and needs to be adapted.

The participation of users in concept generation phases could be schematically approached from two different angles, but both present difficulties: either users are integrated directly in the project team and are asked to take part in the concept generation work and to co-design the future product-service system through the production of sketches and early simulation material from the very beginning of the project process; or the classic project process is adapted to create a specific moment of interaction with external users. Instead of sketches and early simulation material, more finalised prototypes are developed early in the project process in order to get feedback and input from the users.

In the first mode, the difficulty lies in making the user "enter" the simulation. In terms of the project process, it means introducing users at an early stage, when ideas and concepts are normally expressed with the help of technical tools addressing only trained professionals. The project team generates sketches, diagrams and schemes to elaborate the project internally, and it is very difficult to get users to interact with this type of material.

In the second mode, the difficulty lies in producing convincing and operational prototypes early on. With regard to the project process, it means anticipating later phases and generating realistic and functional output based only on the first tentative ideas. User participation is easy, but spiraling costs in early prototyping tend to narrow exploration and reduce the number of alternatives that can be envisioned.

The methodological approaches developed hereinafter propose possible compromises between the difficulties of these two alternatives.

The first approach called "Scenario Co-design" focuses on developing new tools for early simulation, compatible both with the involvement of users and the required flexibility of early project phases. These simulation tools facilitate the projection of users in scenarios and, also, enable them to modify the scenarios themselves and actively take part in their definition. The output of this process is said to be a "Scenario co-design" based on a co-production between the users and the project team.

The second approach called "Spot Experiment" proposes techniques of "rapid prototyping" for product-service systems based on the development of "focused working models." Users are involved in very light but realistic experimentations that focus on one aspect of the product-service system. Several of these quick "Spot experimentations" are made during the concept generation phase so that the project team's creative process is "immersed" in user behaviour and user reactions. The resulting tentative ideas integrate the results of these "Spot Experiments" and would appear to be closer to user concerns.

6.2 Scenario Co-design

This section describes a mix of methodological approaches to build, visualize and assess scenarios of product-service systems involving users in a co-design process.

6.2.1 Definition and Purpose: What is Scenario Co-design?

What is meant by scenario? The word scenario covers many different notions all referring to "a synthetic description of an event or series of actions and events." Derived from the meaning of 'scene'as used in theatre and cinema, it is also "an account or synopsis of a projected course of action, events or situations. Scenario development is used in policy planning, organizational development and, generally, when organizations wish to test strategies against uncertain future developments" (Wikipedia). Back in the 1950s, Herman Kahn, from the Rand Corporation, was one of the first to use scenarios as "the description of possible alternative futures that aim to stimulate concrete actions in the present in order to control and orient what will effectively be the future" (Kahn and Mann 1957). More recently Michel Godet, who also has a background in future research, states that "a scenario is the description of a future situation together with a series of events leading from the ground situation to the future situation" (Godet 1985).

Within this definition of scenarios as backcasting tools, a first distinction should be made in terms of scale: "policy orienting scenarios (POS)" address possible evolutions of macro-systems through the combination of different policy instruments whilst "design orienting scenarios (DOS)" address feasible and acceptable solutions at a project scale that is manageable by a group of stakeholders (Manzini and Jégou 2004).

In the field of project development, the notion of "scenario" still covers a wide spectrum, from user research (where the term "scenarios" is used to designate behavioral patterns observed among users) to project management (where scenarios amount to "options," a term designating alternative project strategies).

It should be understood that the term "scenario" in this context features both a hypothetical dimension (unlike the description of current situations commonly used for the purpose of ethnographic research) and a projective dimension (unlike the effective development process of the project they anticipate).

These scenarios are consistently built around the three following components:

1. A vision (a reply to the question: "how would it be if...?")
2. A motivation (a reply to the question "what is it for?")
3. A proposition (a reply to the question: "how can it be implemented.")

And they often appear as narrative forms describing interactions between users and a system of products and services within a given context.

In the field of product-services system innovation, scenarios are commonly used in the early phases of the project to frame and guide the development process.

Scenarios belong to the design toolbox: they are used by the project team to present leading visions of what they intend to develop (Halen et al. 2005). Most of the time scenarios are meant as internal tools to facilitate strategic conversation within the project team and decision-making processes when it comes to project management between stakeholders.

Users are sometimes involved in these early orientation phases through classical user research investigation (i.e., interviews, focus groups etc) to assess the potential interest raised by these scenarios and/or to define conditions of acceptability. But the participation of users is required only to the extent that they express their perception of scenarios developed and illustrated by the project team. They can hardly change them, make them evolve or even suggest alternatives.

The "Scenario co-design" approach marks an evolution, away from this current situation, and towards a stronger involvement and interaction with the user in the project orientation phase. The level of interaction and co-design obtained is such, that the resulting scenario is no longer the single vision of the project team but emerges instead from the conversation between the project team and the users. In that sense, the scenario has been co-designed.

6.2.2   Purpose of Scenario Co-design

Involving real users in the early orientation phases of product-service systems raises several questions.

6.2.2.1   Enabling a Controlled Projection of the User in the Scenario

As discussed in the introduction, involvement of users is easy when the proposed augmented environment is developed at the level of a prototype: users are simply asked to behave and perform activities as they would have done in the real world. They are observed throughout the process and/or interviewed about it afterwards.

On the contrary, when faced with simulations at an early stage – such as the one used in co-design scenarios – user involvement is a more difficult process to control. Two key problems arise.

On the one hand, the simulation may be very "puzzling" and attractive, such that users are more involved with the form of the scenario than with its content.

The world of ICT often proposes visions of new environments produced as TV commercials.[1] In project jargon, these kinds of visualisations are called "renderings."

---

[1] The series of clips "Vision of the Future" (Marzano 1996) produced by Philips Design is a good example of these communication oriented scenario visions.

They intend to picture the project in the most realistic way, as if they would already be available in the market and integrated in daily life. Confronted with this kind of scenario visualisation, users are seduced and tend to lose their critical capabilities. They are "trapped" in the visualisation in the same way that consumers are trapped in commercials. The atmosphere, the characters, the story, etc., take over their judgement. They feel as if they are "in" the scenario. The projection mechanism works too well and users tend to react (positively or negatively) more on the form of the visualisation than on its content. More precisely, they assess the situation as it is presented to them and are unable to focus on whether the proposed new product-service system is or is not able to generate such a situation. The use of such an attractive simulation tends to seduce users but inhibit their critical judgment. Therefore it is of little interest for a co-design process.

On the other hand, the simulation may be so "dry" and descriptive that users will not feel at all involved in the scenario. Most representation tools used in the early phases of project development such as sketches, technical drawings, blue printing, etc. are technical tools requiring professional capabilities and training. Faced with such simulations, users have trouble reading the simulation and understanding the new product-service system on offer. Even when they overcome the technicality of the visual language used, they understand the scenario but don't genuinely feel involved in it. They look at it from a distance and tend to assess it from a rational standpoint. In other words, they do not "project" themselves in the situation described by the scenario. They are not stimulated to imagine what the experience of the new product-service system could mean for them in their daily life and they simply react externally.

The use of such "dry" visualisations does not induce user reaction, beyond their external point of view. They are not involved and therefore the value for a co-design process is also very low.

In order to support co-design processes in early project phases as efficiently as possible, we developed a range of simulation forms between the two extreme situations that were just described. They enable a "controlled projection" of users into the proposed scenario, in the sense that they balance *simulative* and *descriptive* dimensions. They simulate the proposed environment in a realistic and accessible way so that users are able to imagine themselves as if they were experiencing it. They look at it from the perspective of their current daily life. But, at the same time, users are not completely "absorbed" by the simulation and are able to keep a certain critical distance, to consider each aspect of the project, to measure its capacity to produce the expected benefits and to express its acceptability in their daily life. The key to such a "controlled projection" is to introduce, in a realistic scenario, some element of a planned system, when, in fact, its form factor and architecture are still unclear.

VideoSketching enables users to "project" themselves in the scenario and share their feelings, perceptions and reactions as if they really experienced these events in their daily lives. However, these visualisations are not *too* involving, and they enable users to "control" their projection in the scenario, to keep their

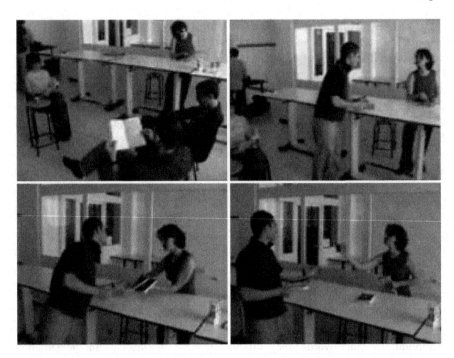

Fig. 6.1 VideoSketching covers a range of techniques used to produce a sketch using video. This example shows snap shots of a 20 s movie where desk interaction is a visualisation for an augmented library scenario. The project team uses a digital camera and available furniture, i.e., the most basic stage props for the scenery. The resulting clip is obtained very quickly, with no further editing and is equivalent, with regards to drafting a service interaction, as a pencil sketch is to drafting a product

critical judgement and express a more rational point of view. Figure 6.1[2] and 6.2[3] describes VideoSketching as a tool that is adapted for co-design with users to produce scenario visualisation.

6.2.2.2   Enabling Scenario Co-design by Users

There is more to Scenario Co-design than the simple assessment of a scenario through user research methods or even creative brainstorming. Users must be enabled not only to criticise the scenario but to reshape it and suggest alternatives. And they

---

[2]M.U.S. Multiservice Urban Space/Visualisation-in-progress, Industrial Design workshop hold by F. Jégou, Politecnico di Milano, 12–16 May 2001.

[3]LDC-EDF/DALT, Digital Bridge social scenario, Paris 2000.

Fig. 6.2 VideoSketching may be more or less elaborate. Simple VideoSketches are obtained by videotaping participants to a brainstorming session and miming ideas to each other. The scenery can also be more elaborate, using a particular stage and accessories. The above example shows a snap shot from a series of short clips presenting a scenario for the use of a digital window connection between two remote working places. The film is made using two rooms, and users act out the scene. The digital window artefact is simulated with screens and beamers between the two rooms, and the characters are asked to improvise a dialogue in this setting. When producing a VideoSketch, the project team improvises mock-ups, directs non-actors in their real environment and holds the camera as well. The result is a sort of "mixed reality," half-way between a fully controlled fiction and a video-observation of real users: the objective is not so much to create the best illustration of the scenario, but rather to "let it happen" as it would probably happen in reality. This rough/realistic style of the movie facilitates projection into the scenario

must be able to do it independently (without the mediation of the project team or any visualisation facilitator) using their own language or using available scenario simulation forms that they are able to manipulate and reformulate.

6.2.2.3   Why is the (Relative) Autonomy of the User in Scenario-Building a Key Difference Between Simple Assessment and Co-design?

In classical user research investigation, scenario material is used as a stimulus. Users are supposed to react to scenarios. They are able to express what they like and don't like, their fears and expectations. In case of "projective" approaches, users are even asked to explore wishes and dreams, but these are often limited to problem-setting and project orientations.

More advanced approaches which bring together the users and the project team in a creative brainstorming session help merge user inputs and idea generation

(Evans et al. 2002). They speed up the interaction process. Compared to previous approaches, they also reduce potential distortions between user research and the creative phases. Direct exchanges between users and the project team help to reconnect the project activity to reality and sometimes to stimulate creative dynamics in the group. But the output remains in the hands of the project team. The exchange process is enhanced but remains the same: user reactions are interpreted by the project team and the resulting scenario is more concrete but still a project team scenario.

The co-design process, as it is intended here, begins when users are able to overcome this intermediation and react by "directly" generating the scenario. They can react intuitively as they do when they experience a real situation in life and operate functional or semantic reorganisation within the scenario, without having to rely on an explicit exchange with the project team.

6.2.3 Enabling Users to Take Part in Scenario Building

6.2.3.1 What are the Concrete Difficulties to Give Users Access to Scenario Building?

In order to enable such a co-design of the scenario, users should have access to and manipulate easily the form in which the scenario is presented. The difficulty is to enable users with no particular visualisation skills (in terms of sketching an idea, performing a scene, choosing an emblematic image, etc.) to act on elaborate visualisations in a limited period of time (generally the time of a short workshop, a focus group or an interview).

There is a trade-off[4] between simulation and flexibility of the visualisation used to support the co-design process towards what can be called an *open visualisation*.

A visualisation can be open in two ways:

1. Either because the visualisations have been designed in an appropriate way, so as to leave a possibility of action by the users: i.e., they can build their own story-board selecting among pre-existing strips and reorganising them, they can modify existing visualisations or define new ones by assembling prefabricated modules from a library of visual elements, etc…
2. Or because a professional "visualiser" is available to edit the visualisation following users' indications. Any classical visualisation form coming from the project

---

[4] It is to be noted that a certain antagonism exists in term of visualization between facilitating the projection of users into a scenario and giving them access to the modification of the same scenario: in order to make users "feel" the proposed environment and somewhat experience it, the related visualization must be quite elaborate and convincing. Such visualization generally requires professional skill to be produced and, consequently, is not easily changeable by the users.

world may be used as soon as it can be edited in real time: i.e., sketch, story-boarding, act-in, etc.

The figure above shows a presentation of early scenarios for the use of an "Interaction room" at EDF headquarter[5] in Paris. The use of Powerpoint allows the project team to immediately adapt the scenarios according to user feedback, simply by moving, adding or deleting icons on the slides.

Figures 6.3–6.7 present different examples of *open visualisation* in relation to product-service systems to support the co-design process. Their common character-istic is to enable users to directly act on the visualisation either because they are able to modify it alone or because a third person is able to change them in quasi real time according to their directions.

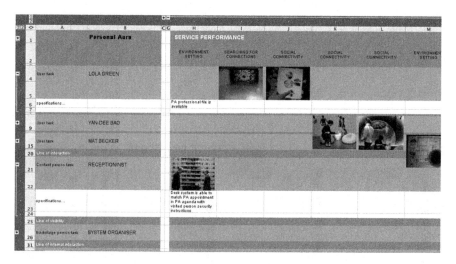

Fig. 6.3 The chart above shows the Interaction Story-Board (Sangiorgi 2005) for the "Personal Aura," a system of communicating personal agents embedded in a PDA and acting as information broker between users and their environment. A 250 s VideoSketch has been produced to show the arrival and registration procedure of a visitor at the entrance desk of a company. This movie is then split horizontally in a succession of ServiceActions, presenting each time different functionalities of the Personal Aura. Vertically, the chart differentiates the stakeholders involved: the receptionist, the system organiser etc and describes for each ServiceAction the context of interaction, the tools needed, the interaction rules and the required competences and information supplied to each actor. This systematic matrix analysis covers in some detail the specifications of Personal Aura services and what each stakeholder must do in order to implement them

---

[5] Interaction room project, EDF headquarters, Paris Wagram, 2001.

Fig. 6.4 When co-designing environments, a rough scale model provides a more open visualisation than a computer 3D animation. It allows users to interact more freely with the visualisation: they can browse through the model as they choose, jump from overview to details. They are also able to modify the model themselves. The image above shows early co-design processes in a new R&D.comm. augmented workspace and distant meeting rooms at EDF's R&D division in Paris, inviting future users to physically cut and paste the model by moving elements (walls, furniture etc) on the mock-up, thereby appropriating the result to a greater extent

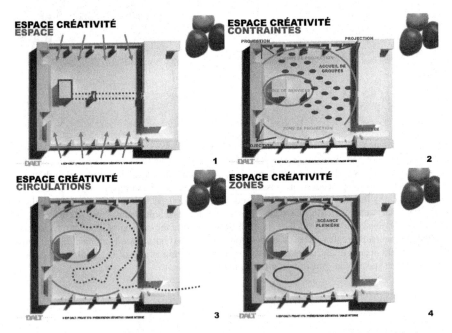

Fig. 6.5 Common presentation software (i.e., Powerpoint, Keynotes etc) allowing quick changes and last minute editing provide support to develop open visualisations. Users intuitively drag and drop elements of the presentation without specific skills and training

Fig. 6.6 Specific tools have been developed to facilitate user participation in the co-design of solutions. *Story-boarding* is a simple approach to get users to produce their own scenarios. In the figure above, a user reviews different functionalities of a service printed on paper cards. He selects and organises them in a coherent sequence integrated in his daily life (Jégou and Liberman 2003). The *Story-Board* is used to help users invent their own stories, interpret the meaning of the services they use and progressively frame the service specifications

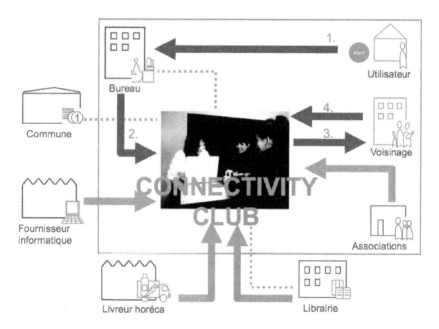

Fig. 6.7 A *SystemMap* is a tool designed to represent interactions between different stakeholders involved in a complex product-service system. The figure above shows interactions between different stakeholders involved in a neighbourhood tele-cottage for distant work. The tool provides a prefabricated library of icons and arrows with a syntax of graphic rules that any participant to the project is able to manipulate to produce the equivalent of a technical drawing of the service (Jégon, Manzini and Meroni 2004; Jégon and Joore 2004)

6.2.4 Description and Application of Scenario Co-design: How to Make it?

Scenario Co-design can be achieved with different methodological approaches using different *open visualisation* techniques and different modes of interaction with users. This part will describe an example of infrastructure to support scenario co-design and the next part will discuss the mix of methodological approaches according to various project contexts.

The situation of scenario co-design presented here was part of a series of four co-design sessions held at Strategic Design Scenarios laboratory in Brussels in September 2002.[6] They belong to the first series of scenario co-design sessions prepared for the Sustainable Everyday exhibition for 'Triennale di Milano'. The purpose was to explore acceptance of a range of local and arguably more sustainable household services, beginning with how they might be incorporated in the daily lives of users and going on to reshape and co-design these services.

Users were invited for three-hour sessions for two consecutives days. The space was organised into two isolated rooms with a video network between them (see Fig. 6.8). In the larger room the user and a facilitator sat on the same table in front of a large screen where the scenarios were presented. In the second room, a member of the project team stood as the provider of the services and controlled the scenario displayed on the large screen.[7] The provider and the user could communicate through the internal video network controlled by the facilitator who could interrupt it. All the interactions were recorded by different cameras for each session.

The scenario was presented through an Animated Story-board visualisation that evolved through the different sessions of discussion.[8] Users first took part in warming exercises exploring their current daily household practices and the related critical points in terms of sustainability. In a second part, they worked at integrating the different services in their respective daily life, whilst taking into account all their personal expectations expressed in the first part. Finally in the last part, they reshaped and modified the different services in a direct dialogue with the "provider." This dialogue was videotaped. The resulting clip showed the interaction between the user and the provider and offers a perfect visualisation of how the scenario evolved.

---

[6] Strategic Design Scenarios and Égérie Research, "Sustainable Everyday, Scenarios of urban life" exhibition preparation work, Brussels, 2002.

[7] This setting is based on the so-called "Wizard of Oz" trick: a member of the design team, hidden, pretends to be the future provider of the system and answers accordingly to the user concerns. The user believes that he/she can interact with the system.

[8] It is to be noted that a co-design session differs in its aim form a user research evaluation. The purpose is not to assess a determinate scenario but to make it evolve. Therefore the visual material presented to the four successive users is not the same. Thanks to the flexibility of the Animated Story-Board technique, it is adapted by the project team between each session and the following user benefits from previous user interaction.

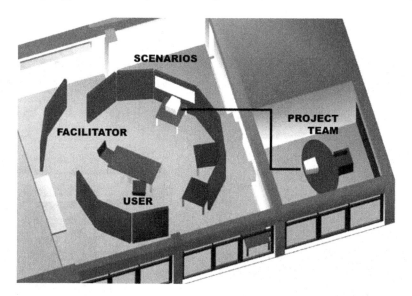

Fig. 6.8 Configuration of the space and video equipments for a co-design process at Strategic Design Scenarios laboratories in Brussels: an interviewer facilites and manages the interaction between a guest user and the project team. A scenario created by the project team is projected onto a screen for the user. The project team, based in a remote location, is available to discuss the scenario through an internal video channel. The facilitator may interrupt the video channel to exclude temporarily the project team and interview the user more freely. In the meantime, the project team integrates the user's reactions in real time in order to improve the scenario. The multiple loops of interaction between the user, the project team and the interviewer help quickly reshape and improve the scenario

Post-editing the clip allows to reintegrate both the user and the provider, recorded on a blue-key in the scenario visualisation. The final movie is a typical example of scenario co-design (see Fig. 6.9) as an evolution of the initial project team scenario, adapted and performed by a user (Fig. 6.10).

6.2.5   How to Use It?

The setting as presented in the previous example shows one of the many possible hybrid techniques to support Scenario Co-design. Other combinations could be preferred depending on the nature of the users involved, the context of interaction or the time and budget available for the co-design process. The following part will discuss the visualisation modes of the scenarios and the type of interaction with the users according to these criteria.

Fig. 6.9 The different pictures show views of the co-design process described in Fig. 6.8 between the project team (*top left*), an interviewer and a guest user (*bottom left*). The interaction between the user and the project team discussing the scenario is videotaped and post-edited to appear super-imposed on the scenario visualisation (*right top and bottom*). This process yields another mixed reality, integrating scenario fiction and real user reactions to produce a mock-up of the service in discussion

In order to structure the various hybrid techniques of Scenario Co-design, two major dimensions have to be considered.

The first dimension relates to the order in which the new product-service system and the related scenario of interaction with the user are generated. It can be characterised by the following alternative.[9] The project team starts with a new system of products and services and tries to understand how the user will react to it and capture it in a user scenario. It answers the question: "which new situation may emerge from the introduction of a specific innovation?". Or the project team starts to imagine a new scenario showing user behaviour and derives from it the

[9]It is to be noted that this dimension corresponds in macro-scenario approach to the two opposite attitudes of back-casting and fore-casting: either the scenario is proposed as a goal to be obtained (and the project team works on understanding what the changes to be implemented are in order to lead to this future situation) or the scenario is proposed as a result to be investigated (and the project team works on an exploration of the potential consequences of the changes implemented).

Fig. 6.10 The scenario co-design approach described in Figs. 6.8 and 6.9 has been adapted on-line to allow distant confrontations. In this case, users from Chicago, Brussels, Milan and Hong-Kong were able to co-design scenarios, locally manipulating images to create a story-board and interacting on-line with the design team. This "light" setting is valuable to the scenario-building process, because it confronts different cultural contexts and requirements

new system of products and services that would enable this behaviour. It answers the question: "Which innovative solution may enable this new situation."

The second dimension relates to when the involvement of the users is scheduled in the project development process. It can be characterised by the following alternative. The new product-service system and the related scenario of interaction are used at the input stage to stimulate and collect user feedback. This is a typical user research process, which asks the question: "how will users react to this innovation?". Or user involvement is the starting point for the generation of a new product-service system and its related scenario of interaction. This is a typical feature of user-centred approaches that ask the question: "what kind of innovation can be inferred from observing spontaneous user behaviour?".

The combination of these two dimensions produces different processes of interaction between the project team and users as well as different ways of using scenarios to induce or deduce the specifications of a new project-service system. Three examples of such processes are proposed hereinafter to conclude this first section on Scenario Co-design.

6.2.5.1 Project Impro

Users directly perform their product-service ideas and generate a visualisation of the related scenario with the support of the project team.

The process is similar to theatre improvisation. Participants to a creative session, either users or project team, perform their ideas, intentions and perceptions using their own miming capabilities and some accessories at hand. The resulting visualisation may be recorded by a camera: participating users are simultaneously *performing* a situation (using a product, experiencing a service etc) and *commenting* on it by talking out loud.

Figure 6.11 shows a snap shot of VideoSketching focusing on questions of privacy in the management of personal medical data. Two designers generate ideas on a patient-owned medical file and perform themselves the resulting interaction between the patient and the doctor. During a half-day creative workshop,[10]

Fig. 6.11 Example of "Project Impro." Two members of a project team present their ideas on new privacy enhancing management of personal medical data during a half-day creative workshop. Through VideoSketching techniques, they explore the potential consequences of their new product-service on the patient-doctor relationship. For instance, through the sequences, new counter-intuitive ideas emerge with a view to protecting patient privacy without hindering the doctor's activity: the user holds her medical data on a usb-key; the doctor asks for the data he wants to access; he consults it on a temporary print; results of new medical investigations are erased from the hospital computer after they are uploaded to the patient's key

---

[10] VideoSketching creative session animated by F. Jégou, "Social business Innovation" workshop coordinated by S. Maschi, Interaction Design Institute Ivrea, January 2003.

they re-edited four versions of the same scenario visualisation, recording new parts and changing others as they would have done sketching a product with a pencil (sequences 1, 2, 3, and 4). The resulting visualisation gives an accurate idea of what the interaction between the patient and the doctor should look like in the final setting of the service. Regarding the definition of the precise specifications of the service, this process allows the project team to debug the new service very quickly: i.e., visualising the scenes they just acted out, they could figure out when patient information was inappropriately disclosed or unprotected. They were also able to notice cumbersome protection procedures that could potentially disturb the medical work. In short, the successive iterations of the VideoSketching help to fine tune a reasonable privacy protection system between the patient and his doctor.

6.2.5.2   Semi-directed Scenes

Users, supported by the project team, interact and deduce the specifications of the related product-service system.

The process is similar to experimental movies/theatre where a story is drafted, a scenery is built and actors are left on their own to perform the scene, beginning with their own reactions. The project team behaves with users as a film director who would only partially direct the actors: The resulting visualisation falls somewhere in between the initial intention of the project team and what the users intuitively made of it. Figure 6.12 shows an example of the semi-directed scene process presenting an application of video-streaming in real time to facilitate different participation modes to distant meetings.[11] A group of users are involved in a meeting.

Fig. 6.12 Example of a scenario co-design process using "Semi-directed Scenes." Real users in their working environment are asked to perform a scene showing how video-streaming in real time and a phone can allow remote participants to intercede in their meeting. The resulting visualisation lies somewhere in between a performed fiction and the observation of intuitive user reactions

---

[11] Videostreaming ClipScape, LDC-EDF/DALT, Paris, 2001.

A remote participant is following the meeting by phone and intercedes in the course of the discussion. The two scenes are taking place in two different working environments. Only a real phone connects the participants. Two cameras are used simultaneously and all the scenes are performed in chronological order. No post-editing of the video is made. The first shots of each scene are just assembled as they happen in front of the camera. The resulting visualisation shows some of the qualities of a *reportage*, combining what happened on the spot with the point of view of the observer. Project-wise and compared to the first "Project Impro" approach, "Semi-directed Scenes" can steer the interaction more precisely and focus on critical points. The resulting movie sequences clearly evidenced certain problems inherent to remote meetings. For instance the "disappearance" of remote participants: the users who attended the physical meeting and were seated around the table tended to discuss amongst themselves and regularly forgot to interact with remote participants in the simulation made for the film, as it happens in real distant meetings.

6.2.5.3 Composition of Modular Elements

The project team imagines a scenario of interaction, visualises it, and observes how users react and modify the scenario to deduce the specifications of the related product-service system.

The process is close to an experimentation with users where the environment proposed to them would not be a real one but a visualisation. They review different scenes ("bits-of-life") showing different functionalities of a service. They select and reorganise the scenes according to their own interest. Figure 6.13 shows the core part of an exhibition that confronts the visitor with various daily life scenarios (grocery shopping, house keeping, mobility, leisure etc), promising in terms of sustainability.[12] At the end of the exhibition, an interactive installation enabled the visitors to "cut & paste" into the various services proposed, to comment and build their own ideal scenario. Data was collected through the duration of the exhibition, and the project team was able to reshape and fine tune the various initial services. Visitors of such exhibitions can be identified from a marketing point of view as potential "early adopters" of these advanced sustainable solutions. The analysis of the many stories constructed by the participating visitors gives a general indication of which services are more appreciated, which functionalities should be introduced in the market first, under what conditions, what the possible synergies between the solutions are, etc.

---

[12]"Sustainable Everyday, Scenarios of urban life" exhibition, F. Jégou, E. Manzini and A. Nandi. Parc d'Aventures Scientifiques et Sociales, Framerie (Belgium) 2004.

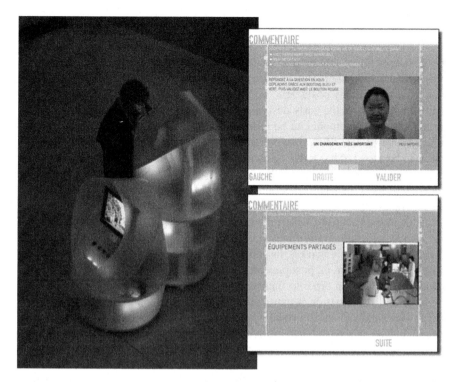

Fig. 6.13 Example of co-design using the "Composition of modular elements" approach. Different scenarios based on new daily urban ways of living (arguably more sustainable) were suggested to visitors of the Sustainable Everyday exhibition in Brussels. Interactive installations (*left*) proposed an interview process (*right, top and bottom*) allowing users to cut and paste into the various daily services and build their own personal scenario. From all the data gathered during the exhibition, the project team was able to tailor the sustainable services to the needs and expectations of visitors

6.3 Spot Experiments

This second part describes a type of quick experimentation with users called "Spot Experiments" and used for early design investigations and approaches of complex product-services systems in augmented environments.

Throughout the text, the presentation of "Spot Experiments" will be illustrated by a European research project called "Ambient Agoras," which explores the possibility of assembling a collective memory of a working environment based on short video-messages.[13]

---

[13] Ambiant Agoras, Dynamic Information Clouds in a Hybrid World, Disappearing Computers.

6.3.1 Definition and Purpose: What are Spot Experiments?

The development of augmented environments relies on user-centred approaches and participative design. But experience shows that, in practice, this philosophy often encounters many obstacles.

Involving users in the early design phases seems feasible on paper. However, in practice, user-involvement can be a time consuming and expensive process if one wants to perform real-life tests with real users. This means that the product-services system to be assessed has to be useable enough for the user to test it. This is usually impossible to achieve at a reasonable cost and within a short time frame. Either the product will have the right functionalities but the wrong form factor, or it will be a non-functional mock-up.

The degree of detail to which the product-services system must be operational to get a relevant evaluation from real users is very high. This requires an enormous effort in terms of recruiting users, installing the product-services system in real settings, comparing ex-ante and ex-post practices, gathering high quality data and processing and analyzing them in order to finally obtain information.

Moreover, this situation is extremely frustrating to the project team: user feedback is slow, and arrives at a stage where basic design options are already chosen, equipments are purchased, and emotional investment in solutions has been made. Therefore profound changes in the functional specifications are, in fact, unacceptable.

There is a need for a less intensive user-involvement process, with a fast return. In other words, can we design a quick-and-messy way of involving the user in design, but not *too* messy?

"Spot Experiments" are a light and quick way to co-elaborate complex product-services systems in the early stages of the development of augmented environments. They are useful for "debugging" a concept and can also be eye-openers in the exploration of new product-services systems.

They are based on a series of short experiments with real users, investigating sub-systems of the targeted product-service.

In this definition, "short experiments with real users" means the observation of users reacting to a new proposed artefact or context for a short period of time, and "sub-systems of the targeted product-service" means simpler products and/or services that either are an integral part of the complete product-services system or simply relate to its functionality.

6.3.2 What are Spot Experiments Used For?

This section will develop three typical situations where Spot Experiments can be a useful support for the project team:

1. Hazardous and unknown contexts where the project team has no experience in a given field and is not representative of potential users;

2. Practice-demanding innovations where the value for the user is not immediately apparent and user benefits can only be perceived after the entire system of products and services has been implemented;
3. Highly integrated product-service systems where a tiny imperfection in the prototype may radically change user perception of the whole system.

6.3.2.1 Hazardous and Unknown Contexts

Any design project is, by definition, an anticipation of a future product-service. The project team has an experience of existing products and services and, from that starting point, is able to imagine new ones.

In research activity relating to augmented product-service systems, the project team often formulates hypotheses in areas or situations where they have no personal experience (and neither does anyone else).

Often, the project team is not even representative of those who are foreseen as the potential users of the final product-service system.

Confronted with situations where it is inexperienced and is not representative of potential users, the project team has to make additional experiments, try specific aspects of the project or observe how users behave in related situations.

For instance, in the case of the "Ambient Agoras" we focused on the use of video to record/exchange short memories of a place and, from these, we attempted to gradually construct an interactive history of the building. The investigations conducted in the office building would address the following questions: what kind of short video recording would one make of his/her current work for others to use?, what are the differences between situations such as team activities or personal desk activities?, what new services could be layered upon this architecture?, etc. The project team had no clue about the potential and limits of using video messages in this context. Six Spot Experiments (Fig. 6.14) enabled the team to "play" with video messages, to see how users tend to react to them in working situations and to gather the minimum personal experience in order to "feel" intuitively this unknown context, to generate ideas and avoid traps in the further development of the project.

6.3.2.2 Practice-demanding Innovations

Designing complex product-service systems requires specific approaches compared to the classical product design process.

The first major change is due to the very nature of a service that must be experienced at real scale in order to be assessed. A user might react at an early stage in the design (prototype, working model, even rendering or sketch) of a new *product* whereas he/she will have more difficulties to project him/herself into the abstract nature of a *service*. Different processes ("story-boarding," "act-in" approaches, etc.) are commonly used to represent a service but they hardly simulate the "experience" the user may have if the service is actually implemented. When it comes to services,

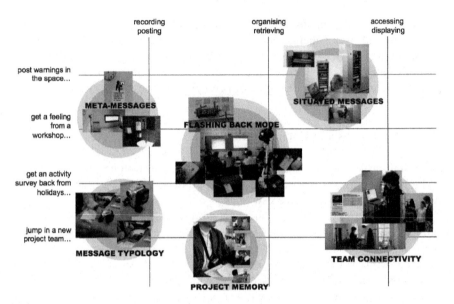

Fig. 6.14 This scheme illustrates one of the applications of "SpotExperiments." Six different short experiments were conducted in relation to the investigation of an augmented office workspace. The aim is to address the problem of the flow of information within a work team, such as recording/posting, organising/retrieving or accessing/displaying (*horizontally*) in different contexts: in the team work environment, in a meeting, when someone is absent or newly arrived (*vertically*). Each SpotExperiment investigates a very specific idea such as a solution to retrieve information discussed in a meeting that some could not attend or a service for posting local information in the collective work environment... The different results allow the project team to steer towards the final definition of the product-service system, avoiding traps and dead-ends and essentially accelerating the project process

a utility is the result of a co-production between the user and the product-service system ("servuction"). It is more difficult to appreciate the exact impact of the product-service system without having actually been involved in some trial of it.

In the case of the "Ambient Agoras" the aim of the research project was to create "a memory of a building." In this case it is trivial that in order to assess the potential interest of making this memory available requires that first, the team working in this building let numerous tracks sediment for a long period of time. Only then can one experience its benefits.

The second major change in the product-service design process relates to the complexity of most product-service systems that we are accustomed to use in our everyday lives. Their very systemic nature doesn't allow a simulation of one individual part: all components of the system relate to each other and need to be implemented before one can appreciate the synergy produced and the resulting benefits.

In the case of the "Ambient Agoras" again it seems obvious that the benefits of recorded memories will only emerge if recording facilities are available in enough places in the building, covering a significant part of the activities that are going on.

Meeting rooms, personal work spaces, social areas etc must be equipped to assess, for example, how this new system will affect current work and recording patterns.

A full-scale experiment to determine whether or not it could be interesting for a building to keep a diffused memory of all activities that take place in it would require an implementation over time and in the entire building, which is not conceivable given the economical constraints and limited time frames of the research project. Some of the Spot Experiments were implemented at a sub-system level (i.e., a personal cabinet used by all employees of the building to store and sort documents). A history of user behavior patterns has been artificially generated (i.e., actively collecting video comments, either recommendations or criticisms, form current users). Then the same users have been asked to explore this collective memory to improve their current practice. Through this process the project team quickly gains insight into how and under what conditions self-recorded user experiences might be useful for the collective and effective use of a working environment.

6.3.2.3   Highly Integrated Product-service Systems

On top of previous considerations on the nature of complex product-service systems, the characteristic of interaction with ICT and augmented environments requires a level of perfection in the prototyping hardly compatible with early stages of research processes. Whereas interior designers, for example, commonly present a project showing simple 3D drawings with some sample materials, thereby obtaining a rather satisfactory level of simulation to the eyes of the average population of users, the simulation of interaction with ICT environments requires more elaborate simulations such as an operational mock-up. On top of it, the experimentation of these mock-ups might be significantly disturbed by tiny imperfections in their realisation such as delays in system response, some missing feature in the interface or simply the availability of only one modality of interaction. The problem comes from the difficulty for users to imagine the new system because they are often not familiar with technologies and because the experience of the new system is much more than even a complete description can offer. While anyone can, more or less, reconstruct a representation of what a new kitchen will look like based on a floor plan, a list of equipment and furniture samples, it is difficult for a normal user to imagine what an augmented conference room will be like based on a floor plan and a list of functionalities.

Users are also accustomed to electronic products and software that provide many more functionalities and options than they will ever be able to use. Therefore what looks like an acceptable ICT mock-up tends to produce a "disillusion effect." The product seems poor and unenjoyable, and induces uncontrollable reactions and perceptions from the user.

In the case of the "Ambient Agoras" research project, many potential applications of the building's collective memory were interfering with key aspects of work activities (i.e., appointments, personal notes, agenda etc) that are considered highly important. Therefore users will never positively rate a mock-up device that is not perceived to be as reliable as their current tools. Evaluating even a very good prototype is very difficult in this type of situation. The Spot Experiment approach makes it possible to "try" new features without "stressing" users. For instance, a video-message system was proposed instead of a collective paper agenda, and it was used by a small team to coordinate between employees and external consultants. Users were invited to leave only video-messages, and a person was appointed to watch the video-message system and take notes in case of failure. The participants to the experiment where relaxed and could "play" with video-messages with no risk of missing any information.

6.3.3   Description and Application of Spot Experiments

Prototyping is the core of user-oriented design, and is part of most modern design techniques. Most of the time "quick prototyping" is done at the early stages (Snyder 2003) in order to get a good idea of the form factor early in the design process. Unfortunately, it is very difficult to obtain quick prototypes of complex product-service systems in augmented environments because, as we just have explained, their benefits arise from the systemic combination of many services.

In order to overcome a series of difficulties in the early phases of the co-elaboration of a complex product-service system listed above, the "Spot Experiment" approach proposes to dissociate in some way the experimentations or trials with users from the product-service system design per say.

This somewhat counterintuitive approach has one main advantage. Indeed, it allows a quick and light investigation that is suitable in the early stages of research. Intensive prototyping is not required to make a draft assessment of ideas.

A quick and targeted experiment often reveals if a path is worth pursuing. Bad orientations are quite easy to recognize when confronted with users and less time is wasted in investigating dead ends.

In order to further describe the "SpotX" approach, two aspects must be considered:

1. How to choose the experimentation that brings relevant information to the project under focus whilst keeping a light approach?
2. How to involve users in a collaborative and constructive approach?

6.3.4   Cases Examples

6.3.4.1   Easy Prototyping

Whereas some solutions are too complex and cannot be prototyped by part and whereas product-services have to be implemented completely in order to be acceptable for users, "Spot Experiments" only model functional "sub-systems" from the interaction point of view. Subsystems are "smaller services" covering "side functionalities" that need to be as close as possible to the focused core product-service, whilst they are sufficiently "stand-alone" and can be isolated for testing.

Most of the time, the experimentation will be done with a "Wizard-of-Oz"-type prototyping, which means that a remote and real person hidden behind a foam-core form factor will simulate the product-service system and "deliver" the service by interacting with the user.

But even if experiments with users are quick and require little preparation, they remain a time-consuming and costly process and should be kept to a minimum, especially at this early stage of the research process where the options are many and the allocated time and budget effort is often low compared to the following steps of the project development.

When approaching a complex product-service system the project team has to choose between various possible experiments, implementing different "sub-systems" relating to this problem or idea. For e.g., in the "Ambient Agoras" research project, many experiments with video messages could investigate the potential of exchanging video content within a social group. From these many possibilities, the project team will choose the most appropriate to inform the project and at the same time the easiest to implement. There are trade-offs in finding the "easy prototype," the least intensive Spot Experiment that will still bring valuable information and experience to the project team (Fig. 6.15).

These trade-offs may somewhat mislead the project development, and the analysis of Spot Experiments needs to be framed in a strict observation protocol that always distinguishes between these three levels of results:

1. What do we learn from the experiment?
2. Does this experiment appear to be representative of the product-service targeted by the research?
3. If so, what lessons, learned from the experiment, can be applied to the product-service that is targeted?

6.3.4.2 Friendly Users

The idea of a "friendly user" is reciprocal to the concept of "user friendly": Whereas the latter indicates product-services that are "friendly" to the user, i.e., easy to use, simple to understand, allowing errors and multiple approaches, the former indicates users that are "friendly" to the products (or the project) in the sense that they are positive about the initial idea, they are looking for solutions rather than problems, they empathise with potential obstacles and focus on what is working, to let it emerge and expand.

Friendly users (see Fig. 6.16) will have a second attempt if things don't work, call the project team when they feel something is going wrong, suggest solutions, and in general "think positive" regarding the test and the system rather than give up. Friendly users may not be friendly to the prototypes, however they are expected to

Fig. 6.15 The particular setting above shows an example of a SpotExperiment investigating the potential social use of a "video scale memory." This particular setting has been chosen for both its relevance to the general goal of the research (How would people react if events from their recent past were recorded on video using this scale memory?) and at the same time for the relative ease with which it could be implemented: participants to the meeting are asked to write down the time at which each interesting event took place during the meeting. Then the project team reports all the sequences marked in parallel by the different participants on the video tape. This simple 2 h experiment clearly shows that key moments are identified by all or part of the group, and it suggests possible applications in automatic editing of a shared video summary of the meeting. SpotExperiments belong to the category of so-called "easy prototyping." Framed in a strict observation protocol, they enable researchers to quickly jump from ideas to trials and to build an impressionistic investigation of a "need area"

bring a lot of (constructive) criticism, therefore they are friendly to the project team and will try to help where they can.

6.3.4.3 Who are These "Friendly Users"?

First and foremost they can be found within the project team itself. Their very position of project developers gives them an obvious positive approach and, to some extent and under certain conditions of experimentation, their involvement in the project doesn't influence their reactions and behaviour too much. They can split into users and observers, or a single designer can carry out self-observation

Auto-investigation   **Close collaborator**

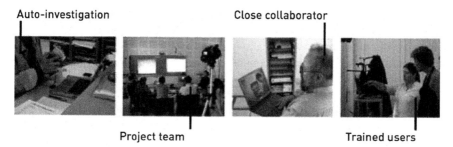

Project team   **Trained users**

Fig. 6.16 The figure shows various categories of users involved in the Ambient Agoras project development and the various degrees of proximity to the research process. They are so-called "friendly users" in the sense that their behaviors tend to overcome the current imperfections of the project and point at the positive aspects to encourage further development

processes. Their availability, their focus on the goals and their creativity are strong advantages for a quick and efficient investigation process.

Other users (outside of the project team) may be preferred in certain experiments, either because of their background, their skills, age etc or due to the time available, the duration of the experiment or anything else the members of the project team may not cope with. In this case, a training period is necessary to shape them into "friendly users." This process, of course, is not typical of what researchers are after in user experimentation: "friendly users" are not "neutral," they know the project, they are kept informed about its progress, they follow the project team from the beginning of the research and have to feel as if they were a part of it.

Naturally, friendly users are not objective, they are biased towards the project, they tend to be technology fans. This is not a problem. They are not considered to be a representative sample of the end users, they are used to debug the concepts and give "voice" (Hirschman 1970) and external feedback.

6.3.5 How to Use it ?

6.3.5.1 Investigation of "Need Areas"

The design approach considered here is far from a classical "problem setting/problem solving" process. No clear goals are set a priori. The research focuses on a category of problems, a "need area." It considers a mix of promising solutions and available technologies, and proposes to investigate possible connections between the two. The research brief is formulated as such, between intention and intuition: e.g., in the case of the Ambient Agoras research project, "How to build a collective memory of the work space recording short movie-clips ?"; "Could video-message technology enhance socialisation and exchanges within workplaces?"

This starting point is often far beyond the identification of potential problems or solutions. The "need area" is circumscribed by a selection of expected results: what would be appreciable when considering this category of problems or another?

Initial visions (see Fig. 6.17 and 6.18) are based on existing critical situations everyone may have experienced in his/her life and the suggestion of a solution that may solve the problem. A visualisation is associated with the vision in order to present it in a synthetic and highly communicative way and facilitate exchanges and collaborations within project teams. The visualisation is based on a picture of a remarkable context-of-use (Manzini et al. 2004) to which a comment from a potential user is added to characterize a solution. The impression produced by this visualisation is that the solution already exists, stimulating the research team to imagine what kind of new artefact, service, application, etc. would be necessary to produce it. In other words, it is as if this image were the last box of a story-board stripe, showing the result of a sequence of actions that still need to be invented.

6.3.5.2 A "Reticular" Approach

Compared to typical project processes based on "trial and error improvement loops" the approach described here is more exploratory. The project team investigates the "need area" as explorers used to approach a new piece of land: progression is partially intuitive and often sinuous, stopping when a problem occurs, going back and forth and in parallel until the area is perceived as "covered."

In the course of project development, creative solutions often uncover unknown obstacles and a deeper investigation then triggers new creative solutions until the design investigation seems to sufficiently "cover" the "need area": solutions and investigation then seem to "reticulate" that is to say that certain user problems and listed solutions begin to make sense together. The project team is able (or seems to be) to direct its efforts in the targeted field and to formulate articulated product-service systems that feature both identified objectives and promising benefits.

Fig. 6.17 Through continuous observation and work around "cognitive saturation in augmented office work," the project team formulated a series of initial visions and selected some of them as a starting point for the Ambient Agoras investigation: a service to facilitate the retrieval of objects in a collective environment (*slide 19*), a support to get on overview of what happens in the office after one is away for a few days (*slide 20*), a shared agenda to find the most appropriate moments to call people without disturbing them (*slide 21*), etc

NARRATIVES
EPISODE 19

Ambient Agoras

I come back after a week off. I would like to get a quick picture of the activity during my absence (who was there ? worked on what ? with who ? during how many time ?...through P.A. interactions) in order to visualise the new context before interacting.

    ABIENT AGORA /NARRATIVES/FIRST COLLECTION OF EPISODES /INTERNAL USE/ 16 FEB. 2001

2

Fig. 6.18 Example of vision used to stimulate users for the "memory of the building" interface in the case of the "Ambient Agoras" research project. Imagine a person has been out of her office for a couple of days. When she/he comes back, she/he would like to know "what has been going on during his/her absence?". The visualisation above suggests how traces of situated activity could be made available to users as digital labels/pointers to projects, meetings, conversations, etc. physically located where they took place. When proposed and discussed with users, these applied visions facilitate concept debugging or scenario exploration

In the Ambient Agoras research project (see Fig. 6.19), the concept of the AmbientVideo "emerged" from the field under focus. Careful observation of user reactions in the Spot Experiments combined with the explored ideas "reticulate" at a certain moment for the project team: the interface of a video recording system should follow the metaphor of a lighting system (Fig. 6.20). The users could interact with the video as they interact with the light and maintain the same social patterns (i.e., flipping a switch on the wall at the entrance of each room; developing a typology of ambient cameras which mirrors the typology of lighting: spot recorder as spot light for specific activities, ambient 360° videos as ambient lighting providing a general atmosphere, etc.).

6.4   Conclusion

This text presented two different tools to be applied at the early stage of design phases that focus on complex product-service systems in augmented environments.

The Scenario co-design approach allows a "controlled projection" of the users (immersed in the experience of the new proposal whilst keeping their critical

Fig. 6.19 The above scheme subsequently reconstructs one of the particular processes of the Ambient Agoras research project. "Dynamic information clouds in a hybrid world," the starting point of the Ambient Agoras, generates a series of initial visions "nice to be" in a working environment. These visions (*on the left*) were pictured as "bits-of-life" (i.e., "I would like to know what happen in this meeting I couldn't attend"; "I would like to see this meeting from the point of view of the finance manager"; etc.). They lead to the idea of "capturing" moments and events with original video recording and trigger the exploration of this idea with a series of spot experiments (*in the middle* and Fig. 6.15) investigating different key contexts (i.e., team meetings) and key issues (i.e. possible applications of video recording). The results of these experiments finally lead, in particular, to use the metaphor of lighting to develop the interaction model of an AmbientVideo system (see also Fig. 6.20)

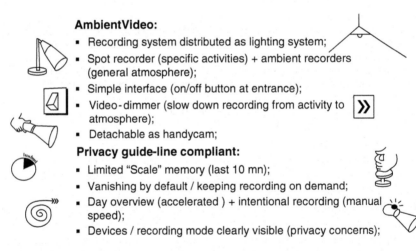

AmbientVideo:

- Recording system distributed as lighting system;
- Spot recorder (specific activities) + ambient recorders (general atmosphere);
- Simple interface (on/off button at entrance);
- Video-dimmer (slow down recording from activity to atmosphere);
- Detachable as handycam;

Privacy guide-line compliant:

- Limited "Scale" memory (last 10 mn);
- Vanishing by default / keeping recording on demand;
- Day overview (accelerated) + intentional recording (manual speed);
- Devices / recording mode clearly visible (privacy concerns);

Fig. 6.20 This figure shows the main specifications of the AmbientVideo product-service system that emerges from the Ambient Agoras investigation: the setting of a video recording system in offices and the modes of interaction with it are reminiscent of the way the lighting system is set and used: wide angle cameras are like ambient light covering an entire room; focused cameras are like spot lights that concentrate on a particular work space; there are switches on the wall to turn the video on and off as one does upon entering or exiting the room; etc. This solution is not borne out of a problem-solving process but should be perceived instead as a sort of "reticulation" where consistent problems and promising solutions go hand-in-hand, supported successively by discussions around intuitive visions on the one hand and by Spot Experiments on the other. Other directions of research could have brought about other valuable metaphors. But the goal of a research project is to find one solution that works well enough. There is no need, time or budget to investigate all the possible solutions and therefore no guarantee that the one that "reticulates" first is the best. However it is one of the many solutions that matches the expectations of the project team as formulated in the early intention of enhancing socialisation and the feeling of the place by creating a memory of the building

distance) into "open visualisation" (actively involving users in the participative construction processes of the scenarios).

The Spot Experiments propose an approach of rapid but sufficiently realistic simulations based on "easy prototyping" (focusing on both meaningful and easy investigations) and involving "friendly users" (who help explore the project field in a constructive way).

For the purpose of the demonstration, the methodological approaches of Scenario co-design and Spot Experiments were clearly separated. In practice, the combination of both helps to involve users in the co-production of progressively more realistic simulations towards final prototypes. In particular, the videotaping of users involved in Spot Experiments may produce very interesting material for visualising scenarios of interaction and vice-versa, the strategic conversation triggered by Scenario Co-design suggests important quick experimentation, which can be applied to help the project move forward.

References

Evans S, Burns A, Barrett R 2002 *Empathic design tutor*. Bedfordshire, UK: Cranfield University Press

Garrett JJ 2002 *The elements of user experience*. IN: New Riders

Godet M 1985 *Prospective et planification stratégique*. Paris: Economica

Grandjean E Kroemer KHE 1999 *Fitting the task to the human*. London: Taylor & Francis

Halen C, Vezzoli C, Wimmer R 2005 *Methodology for product service system innovation, how to develop clean, clever and competitive strategies in companies*. Koninklijke Van Gorcum BV

Hirschman AO 1970 *Exit, voice, and loyalty: responses to decline in firms, organizations, and states*. Cambridge, MA: Harvard University Press

Jégou F, Joore P 2004 *Food delivery solutions, cases of solution oriented Partnership*. Bedfordshire, UK: Cranfield University Press

Jégou F, Liberman J 2003 Participative scenario building. In: Manzini E, Jégou F, *Sustainable everyday, scenarios of urban life*, pp 246–255, Milan: Edizione Ambiente

Jégou F, Manzini E, Meroni A 2004 Desing plan, a design toolbox to facilitate solution oriented partnership. In: Manzini E, Collina L, Evans S (eds) *Solution oriented partnership, how to design industrialized sustainable solutions* pp 108–119, Bedfordshire, UK: Cranfield University Press

Kahn H, Mann I 1957 *Techniques of system analysis*. Memorandum.

Manzini E, Jégou F 2003 *Sustainable everyday, scenarios of urban life*. Milan: Edizione Ambiente

Manzini E, Jégou F 2004 Design degli scenari. In: BertolaP, ManziniE(eds) *Design Multiverso, Appunti di fenomenologia del design*, pp 177–195, Milan: Edizione Polidesign

Manzini E, Collina L, Evans S 2004 *Solution oriented partnership, how to design industrialized sustainable solutions*. Bedfordshire, UK: Cranfield University Press

Marzano S 1996 *Vision of the future*. Eindhoven: Philips Design

Norman DA 2004 *Emotional design*. Milan: Apogeo

Sangiorgi D 2005 Worksheet 17 – interaction table. In: Halen C, Vezzoli C, Wimmer R (eds) *Methodology for product service system innovation, how to develop clean, clever and competitive strategies in companies* vol 122, pp 133–134; vol 157, pp 159–161. Koninklijke Van Gorcum BV

Snyder C 2003 *Paper prototyping: the fast and easy way to design and refine user interfaces*. CA: Morgan Kaufmann

Chapter 7
Ubiquitous Working Environments

Carl Gustaf Jansson

Abstract This chapter presents the Ubiquitous Working Environments, a vision for the work environments of the future and how this vision is manifested in current experimental environments and projects at KTH. Building upon the Ubiquitous Computing paradigm, our research targets environments, which support collaborating mobile workers in a seamless way, providing work support anywhere and anytime. In our design work so far, we have been particularly interested in the following three design aspects: First, context aware, proactive, and adaptive services; second, ad hoc configuration and synchronization of available resources, including both devices and services; third, new ways of sharing and using resources in a work environment. The systems we design comprise both devices, services, and their interfaces.

7.1 Introduction

This chapter presents the Ubiquitous Working Environments, a vision for the work environments of the future and how this vision is manifested in current experimental environments and projects at KTH. The term "work" should be taken in a broad sense, as the technology we develop will also support activities that are not strictly considered as work, like learning situations and meetings in general, which can occur in any circumstances.

The concept of Ubiquitous working environments unifies technologies that support co-located work as well as multi-location and mobile teams of workers. One kind of technological focus is intelligent, adaptive, and self-configuring services, which relies on context information and user models. Another kind is the coordination

C.G. Jansson (✉)
Royal Institute of Technology (KTH), School for Information
and Communication Technology, Sweden
e-mail: calle@dsv.su.se

S. Lahlou (ed.), *Designing User Friendly Augmented Work Environments: From Meeting Rooms to Digital Collaborative Spaces,* Computer Supported Cooperative Work, DOI 10.1007/978-1-84800-098-8_7, © Springer-Verlag London Limited 2009

Fig. 7.1 Interactive work environments around the world

strategies for events in interactive environments and the flexible use of multiple modes of interaction.

This work is very much dependent on a network of institutions around the world sharing the same interest in interactive work environments. The network is called RUFAE and coordinated by EDF in Paris (Fig. 7.1).

The character of the research has been strongly influenced by the interdisciplinary character of the "Knowledge and Communication Engineering Laboratory" (K2LAB), combining competence in cognitive science, human computer interaction, computer supported cooperative work, artificial intelligence, as well as software engineering for distributed and mobile systems.

Also important has been the affiliation with the Centre for Wireless Systems at KTH (Wireless@KTH – funded by Ericsson and the Telia Sonera) and the geographical position in Kista (a Stockholm suburb), the site for hundreds of Swedish telecom and IT companies.

7.2   The Ubiquitous Computing Paradigm

This research is positioned within the Ubiquitous Computing paradigm, in contrast to what we choose to term the Personal Computer computing paradigm (Weiser 2001). In contrast to focusing on individual users interacting with singular computing and communication devices, we envision collaborating humans acting in environments with diverse computing and communication potentials.

This new computing paradigm has been given many other names as well: post PC computing, pervasive computing, ambient intelligence, the disappearing computer, the invisible computer, etc. (Satyanarayanan 2001). The EU IST Advisory Group (ISTAG) did in 2000 define the concept of "ambient intelligence" by the following phrase: "The convergence of three key-technologies, ubiquitous computing, ubiquitous communication, and intelligent user-friendly interfaces, which embodies, a laid-back mode of dialogue with integrated service infrastructures in which ones everyday surroundings become the interface." In this text, we will stick to the concept of "Ubiquitous Computing."

The Ubiquitous Computing paradigm implies a number of changes: First, a development towards fine-grained and embedded devices. Computing and communication devices will gradually dissolve into smaller pieces. A traditional PC would in a first step dissolve into a main computer unit and several input and output units, all wirelessly connected. The different parts may exist freely or embedded in the environment. Traditional artifacts such as furniture, cloths, interior design elements, and accessories will be immersed by interactive elements. Gradually we will also see a multitude of new hybrid artifacts with original designs.

Second, the paradigm implies a development towards interaction with devices and modalities in a more parallel fashion. Truly multi-modal interaction means parallel use of many input/output devices and interpretation/generation procedures that can handle the mappings between information units and complex media combinations. Simultaneous interaction will also be facilitated by a more frequent sharing of resources in a space.

Typically interaction in this kind of environment will involve a large set of modalities to choose from for input and output. Subtle changes of light or sound, a slight vibration of the chair, or changes in color of the lightning in the room may convey relevant information. Dependent upon the situation, sound and touch may be a better way of conveying information than vision. Dynamic blends of visual, audio, tactile and haptic interfaces have to be considered. Gesture recognition is another challenging area.

A consequence of dissolved artifacts, multiple modalities, and parallelism is that interaction will be more human-to-human like and partly subconscious. There will not be so sharp boundaries between what is physical and virtual. It should be as easy to interact with virtual objects as with real, physical objects. This should work in two ways, both by augmenting physical things with information (augmented reality) and by giving physical thing and their handling, a direct interpretation in a virtual world (tangibles). Important interactive steps could be performed by simple operations on everyday objects in the space (Ishii and Ullmer 1997).

7.3 Objectives

This research targets the design of interactive environments for collaborative work in mobile scenarios. Mobile users sometimes work individually, but more typically in collaboration. Collaboration is traditionally co-located but increasingly so distributed in space and time (Lahlou 1999). Distributed work can take the form of either subsets of teams working in a few different locations, single individuals connecting to co-located teams or totally dispersed teams.

Co-located work sessions may be either planned or spontaneously occurring when users meet accidentally. Mobile users want to experience as stable working conditions as possible when moving between different work environments, but utilizing the possibilities of each environment in a flexible way. Moving in and out of a work environment should be handled as gracefully as possible.

Building upon the Ubiquitous Computing paradigm, as described earlier, our research targets Ubiquitous Working Environments, that is, environments that support collaborating mobile workers in a seamless way, providing work support anywhere and anytime.

For co-located work sessions, the three important issues are the arrivals or departures of single individuals to and from ongoing co-located collaborative work sessions, the synchronization of parallel personal communication tasks and co-located work sessions, as well as ad hoc solutions for spontaneous collaborative work sessions (distributed or co-located). For distributed work sessions, the two issues are the connection of single distributed individuals to co-located collaborative work sessions and the effective linkage of multiple distributed co-located work sessions.

The work has originally been pursued along two lines: On the one hand, the design of interactive work environments for co-located work (Streitz et al. 2005) and, on the other hand, the design of software mechanisms for ad hoc collaboration among mobile workers. Ultimately, our ambition is to design truly dynamically configured interactive workspaces, through which a team of workers can experience a seamless situation of work, no matter where they work in the world or whether they are dispersed or not, taking a maximal advantage of the context they happen to be in.

In our design work, we have been particularly interested in the following three design aspects: First, context aware, proactive, and adaptive services; second, ad hoc configuration and synchronization of available resources, including both devices and services; third, new ways of sharing and using resources in a work environment. Specific design considerations for these aspects will be described in the next section. The systems we design comprise both devices, services, and their interfaces.

7.4 Design Considerations

7.4.1 Context Awareness, Proactive, and Adaptive Functionality

Users will have no chance to control the multitude of elements in Ubiquitous Computing environments, with the implication that such environments must be inherently adaptive at least on some level. It is important that most aspects of the environment is possible to control by software as a basis for adaptive mechanisms. This includes the behavior of services, computing devices, light and other interior design elements such as curtains.

Adaptive functionality in general and more specifically personalization to certain individuals' and groups' needs must be based on adequate observations, models, and feedback and action mechanisms. There is a grey zone between adaptive behavior and a more general proactive behavior, by which we mean that a system or environment can take its own initiatives based on the agenda of its own and inferences from contextual knowledge.

Most of the mechanisms to handle and communicate contextual knowledge and to create relevant feedback to modify the behavior are shared for both proactive and adaptive systems. Adaptive and proactive functionality can be achieved either by simple semi-automatic mechanisms or sophisticated reasoning based on artificial intelligence techniques. Examples of the latter are techniques for interpretation, diagnosis, planning, configuration, and reflection.

An important special case of personalization is the persistence of the state of an interactive environment over several work sessions. Each group has different preferences and needs and it is important for the work environment collaboration, the state of services, and the organizational context. Sensor technology is needed in the sense that a system of sensors is needed to be able to detect physical aspects of the workspace.

Is somebody entering the space? Who is entering the space? Who leaves his chair? Who approaches the wall display? Do people communicate or do they focus on individual activities, etc. These are all measurements of locations and movements and sounds within the space. Of course, all these observations only make sense in the context of an at least minimal model of the work process in the room in terms of which they can be interpreted. The feasibility of interpretations is also dependent on adequate models. Good models are even more important for other kind of contextual knowledge, such as general knowledge about the users and groups involved, the tasks being performed, and the events occurring during the work process.

To sum up this aspect, an interactive environment needs mechanisms for observing contextual knowledge of different kinds, models for interpreting these observations, to store those preferences, recognize a group, and give users back a personalized environment the next time they enter. The environment could also save its states with a certain frequency, so that it can be easily re-instantiated. In that way user can retrace to an earlier point in the work process, an interactive space should have such a persistence functionality, so that the users can feel almost that they have the room for themselves, and that they can leave all their material spread out as they like between work sessions.

A prerequisite for adaptive systems is the availability of contextual knowledge, which includes knowledge about the physical situation, the users, the task, and the state of mechanisms for communicating contextual knowledge among elements in the environment. All these form the basis for desired, adaptive, personalized, and pro-active behavior.

7.4.2 Ad Hoc Configuration and Synchronization of Resources

Ubiquitous computing environments are complex environments with a multitude of elements, devices, as well as services. Furthermore, elements are typically entering and leaving such environments in a dynamic fashion. Environments of such complexity, in which elements have to be manually configured and where devices and services are un-synchronized, will have a low probability of being accepted by their users.

In our view, devices and services must be standardized at least to the level that when they enter an environment, they get recognized (discovered) and integrated in the local system in an ad hoc fashion. Configurations typically have to be semi-automatic, in the sense that the users must be provided with flexible ways of influence the details of the configurations. Mechanisms on many system levels are needed to realize such a scheme, including wireless protocols, low and high level software, and applications.

Wireless connection of devices is an important feature in the establishment of interactive work environments. There exist many options of radio communications today to achieve a satisfactory wireless connection for each single link in such complex systems. However, it is still a challenge to arrange the whole layered system needed. We need to create wireless systems spanning buildings, sections of buildings, corridors, rooms, sections of rooms, bodies, etc., with a precise coverage over the specific physical regions we are interested in and with overlaying communications in the same space.

Being in an environment, resources must synchronize their behavior in such a way that the users perceive a consistent pervasive system. Synchronization presupposes software control of all devices and an architecture for coordinated distributed behavior. How much centralized control imposed and the exact mechanisms to achieve it is a detailed design decision. The predominating design paradigm today is a multiagent system paradigm. Using this paradigm, in the extreme case, every artificial action in an environment is the net result of a negotiation among all software agents controlling the present resources, devices, as well as services.

Maybe less obvious but none the less important is the dynamic configuration and synchronization of services. Open sets of services have to be handled with a provision of private, web-based, public, or situation-specific services on an equal basis. Services could either be actively routed to or retrieved from the current work environment. Mechanisms for flexible composition, interoperation, and synchronization of services must be provided.

To sum up this aspect, an interactive work environment needs mechanisms for the configuration and synchronization of resources, devices, as well as services. When resources enter or leave an environment, integration and configuration must be predominately automatic, with possibilities for users to influence and adjust the specific set-up. Being in an environment, resources must synchronize their behavior in such a way that the users perceive a consistent pervasive system.

7.4.3   New Ways of Sharing and Using Resources

As have been emphasized for the first two categories of design considerations, the complexity of interactive work environments realized by ubiquitous computing environments can be mastered if adequate mechanisms are provided for adaptation based on contextual information as well as synchronizing the behavior of devices and services by configuring elements of the system in semi-automatic ways. These two phenomena provide the technological basis for a more methodologically oriented aspect, which has to do with the sharing and reuse of available resources in an interactive workspace.

Traditionally, specific resources, devices, and services, available in a certain situation, have well defined purposes and roles. Either they are associated statically internally or with specific subtasks, individuals, or sub-groups. Examples are plenty: interactive devices such as keyboards or mice are dedicated to specific work areas, in turn controlled by specific computers. Laptops, phones, or pocket computers are typically strictly personal and used only by their owners.

The most obvious aspect to change is the static configuration of particular resources. It is obviously desirable that interaction devices should be possible to be utilized freely in conjunction with all computers and associated work areas. To be able to move computational entities freely between work areas and computers is also an obvious goal. More challenging, due to the permanence of old habits, is the change towards blurred boundaries between what is private and what is public.

The normal case has been to use personal devices for private tasks and public devices for common tasks in a particular work environment.

We envision that future work environments to a larger extent will contain public devices that are free to be used for a diversity of private and public tasks more or less temporarily. An example of such a change is that a mobile user coming into an interactive work environment can augment the work on a pocket PC by using an available wireless keyboard and a wall-display.

Both the above changes do change the character of the interaction, basically interactive devices and work areas are used exactly in the traditional way, even though the utilization of available resources are better. A more fundamental change would be to design new patterns of interaction on the available resources. We are specifically interested in exploring the tradeoffs between interaction in focus and in the periphery. An obvious example is how we process the text on street signs, which we ignore most of the time but which appears out from the background when we need it.

To sum up this discussion, an interactive work environment is more effectively utilized if available resources can be shared and reused much more flexibly than what is traditionally possible. On one hand, static links between interactive devices, work areas, and computers can be broken. On the other hand, the borders between what is private and what is public can be blurred. Finally, resources can be used in untraditional ways for purposes not yet conceived of.

7.5 An Experimental Environment: The iLounge

7.5.1 General Features

The iLounge is a prototype of an interactive workspace, established at the KTH Kista Campus. It is designed and built by the author's research group, with support from the architects Gullström Architects AB. The intention of this interactive space is to offer an environment that supports collaborative work, especially collaborative design work.

Apart from being a research environment, it has also been used for everyday work by student groups on project-oriented courses at the KTH Kista Campus. These student groups have also been used for field studies. The iLounge consists of two heart-shaped areas and a corner for audience and side activities. It is constructed as a room within a room. The two main areas are framed by curved mobile walls and curtain rails with several levels of curtains of different character, partly motor driven. Behind the curved inner wall is the "back stage" area for technicians and researchers (Fig. 7.2).

The atmosphere in the iLounge is meant to be more like a studio or a small theatre than like an office. High quality wooden floor, choice of wall fabrics and textiles in combination with flexible light setting should contribute to this effect. There are holes of varying size in the curved inner wall for additional room equipment. The holes are covered with semi-transparent plastic "bubbles," back-lit by light from optic fibers. By changing the color of the light, a subtle visual effect is achieved, which can be used, for example, for output. Light could contribute by varying in the intensity to adapt to different tasks. For example, if the focus of the meeting is on a projected media, the lightning directed on the media would be reduced, but if the focus is on a conventional whiteboard or something written on a regular paper,

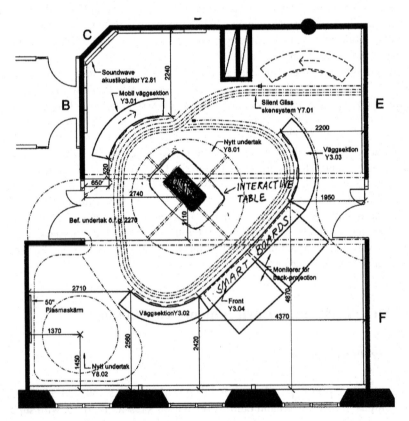

Fig. 7.2 Architects blueprint – the iLounge

Fig. 7.3 The interactive wall and the interactive table

there is a need for higher light intensity. The lightening could also contribute by affecting the atmosphere through variations in the light sources and their colors. Both lights and curtains are computer controlled (Fig. 7.3).

There is high quality audio and video equipment that serves several purposes for both input and output: recording work for user studies and other kinds of analysis, recording speech, for example, for voice recognition, loudspeakers playing background sounds and sound cues, and high quality of video communication for distributed work. A standard video conference system is used as the basis for communication between interactive rooms. This is augmented by several additional elements.

A simple scenario description is given below, which illustrates the kind of collaborative work we have initially focused on.

7.5.2 Example Scenario: Planning a Trip in the Highlands

John, Jill, Mary, and Sam have decided to use the iLounge for planning a trip in the Highlands. Sam has his material at home on his computer, while Jill arrives empty-handed. John and Mary have brought their material on their laptops and will continue to use these in the iLounge.

When the iLounge recognizes their arrival, it gets customized for the needs of this specific group, retrieving relevant patterns of work from the past. Sam can establish a workspace on one of the wireless pads that is part of the workspace and can be used as a private workspace. Jill can use the wireless pointing devices in the room to participate in the interaction.

They all sit down at the interactive table and study material on its surface display. They first start exploration by browsing maps, texts, videos, and music. By pointing and touching, items can easily be transferred and presented on any audio-visual device in the room.

They agree on a few sub-problems that have to be discussed in detail: the selections of golf courses to play, the castles to visit, the distilleries to enjoy, and how to cruise in the Hebrides by boat.

Sam moves materials relevant for the golf course Odyssey to the left part of the interactive wall and they all engage in the editing of a travel plan, taking only golf into consideration. They can interact freely and the iLounge is sensitive to moves and gestures.

The table is still used in parallel for continued information retrieval. Information items encountered here can easily be moved to any of the other work areas. Regularly during the work, snapshots of state in the iLounge are saved. These states can be later retrieved either for backtracking to an earlier point of the work or for taking up work in a later session.

When finished with this aspect, they move the golf travel schedule to the right wall display and continue with the castle tour. When they are satisfied with this schedule, they try to integrate it with the golf schedule.

The planning of the trip in the Hebrides turns out to be particularly tricky, and so John and Jill withdraw to the right interactive corner to solve this problem separately. Mary and Sam continue to plan the trip to the distilleries.

Finally, they integrate all four fragments of the plan on the interactive wall. The solution is saved on their personal workspaces, which are automatically stored as they leave the iLounge.

7.5.3 Main Public Workspace

In the main workspace, there is an interactive wall consisting of two large, touch sensitive wall displays built into the curved inner wall. The displays are 72" back-projected Smart-Boards. When not needed, the interactive wall can be "hidden" either physically by drawing curtains or by displaying suitable wallpaper patterns and artwork.

Actors in the iLounge are able to instantly present information from their personal environments on the interactive wall and the wall will provide further possibilities for any actor to manipulate the shared information, either from his or her personal artifact, the shared artifacts in the room (table, wireless keyboard, pads, etc.) or directly on the wall. The wall will also function as a display for video and other streaming information. Examples are video conferencing and lecturing.

The wall can accommodate many different streams of interaction in parallel. Typically the wall is a live surface, where movements and changes will be the default rather than constant images. If the default behavior includes parallel action and constant changes, the appearance of new information useful to individuals and subgroups within the iLounge can occur without unnecessary intrusions on the rest of the group.

In front of the interactive wall in the iLounge is an interactive table (Rogers and Lindley 2004). The table is the size of a normal conference room table, big enough for six to eight people to sit or stand around it. It has an oval-shaped surface with an embedded 50" plasma display. On top of the plasma display is a Smart-Matisse screen, a product from Smart Technologies, making plasma screens touch sensitive. The main function of the table is seamless sharing of information. A specially developed software makes it possible to move objects like pictures across the display by touching and dragging them, just like you move a physical picture lying on a table surface (Rekimoto 1997). They can also be scaled, rotated, and moved to other displays across the room.

7.5.4   Smaller, Mixed Public and Private Work Areas

Apart from the large wall and table work areas, there are also a heterogeneous set of smaller work areas in the iLounge. Some of these are there on a more permanent basis, while others are brought into the room by the users.

The small permanent work areas should be thought of as public and stationary devices, acting as objects d'art when not interacted with. Given that they are interpreted by the people in the room as public artifacts used for more or less private purposes systematically during interactions in the room, information can be displayed on them in nonintrusive manners, as changes of content and purpose on this displays are considered as a normal phenomena in the i-space.

A natural comparison is the role of an ordinary clock on the wall in a room. By removing a "bubble" in the curved inner wall, a smaller display can be embedded into the wall. One example of this is the iClock, which shows a clock most of the time, but can also fade in text messages every now and then. With the iClock, we want to examine a service that is public, peripheral, visual, and that displays the message explicitly.

The smaller work area in the corner by the window has a more relaxed atmosphere and can be used for smaller groups discussing a sub-problem or for individual work. In this smaller area, there is a 42" Sony plasma display on the wall, a small table, and three low chairs. In a default mode, the display shows a selected painting but can be activated for both messaging, video or as a work area.

In the iLounge are available a number of tablets, or pads, wirelessly connected computers with touch sensitive screens. They are being freely available in the room and can be seen as "electronic" paper, used for taking notes during meetings instead of using, for example, laptops. Another function of the pads is that they can be used as remote controls for different kinds of interaction with applications running on other computers in the room, giving, for example, mouse or text input.

The tablet computer screens that lay flat on the table might be perceived as less intrusive then vertically positioned laptop screens. In addition, the use of public and shared artifacts might be perceived as less intrusive than private ones. The slimmer and more paper like these pads will be, the less intrusive their utilization will be perceived.

Typically users also bring their own personal equipment into the iLounge. Such personal equipment can be mobile phones, handheld computers, or laptops. It can also be commercially available kits of wearable computers. In the iLounge, there is both WLAN and Bluetooth wireless connection available. Users bringing personal computer equipment need WLAN or Bluetooth technology plus some basic iLounge-specific software on their devices to function in the room in a fully integrated manner.

7.5.5 *Interaction Devices*

Parallel multi-modal interaction is supported both by traditional input/output channels like wireless keyboards, pointing devices, and the various computer displays as well as alternative ways of interaction like tangible interactive elements (Dourish 2001). In the context of the iSpace project (see below), devices of this kind are called iStuff.

On all tables in the room, there are wireless keyboards and wireless mice available. Physically all these devices are associated with one computer and display area, but logically it is perceived differently. A specific software component allows one computer to control another computer in the room by sending keystrokes and mouse events. Using that application, you can sit at any keyboard in the iLounge and choose any display for your output.

The room is also equipped with interaction devices that will be used to control the intrusiveness level for the room ("The Knob"). The device consists of a knob placed on the table. The adjustment of the knob is readable from software services in the room and represents the user preferences regarding accepted level of intrusiveness. Personal hardware and software scale devices are also available.

We have also been experimenting with a generalized remote control ("The iWand"), a handheld laser pointer that can be pointed to any target in the room equipped with specifically designed laser targets. This device will make it possible to logically connect a keyboard to a certain display in the room by pointing at it. In the first step, only the identification of the artifact is achieved by pointing. The rest of the adjustment is made through a standardized interface on the handheld device.

The use of Tangibles in the iLounge has also been extended with a prototype mechanism for setting up the room in different desirable states. A small set of artifacts can be placed in a bowl (the "fBowl") on the table to achieve specific actions. This example of tangible interaction is built upon RFID technology.

7.5.6 Detection of Room States

A fundamental issue for achieving a context-sensitive functionality in the room is the ability to characterize and detect a set of high-level states in the room. Is somebody entering the room? Who is entering the room? Who leaves his chair? Who approaches the interactive wall? Are some people leaning on the interactive table? Do people listen or communicate or do they focus on individual activities, etc.? To be able to answer such questions in real time and with sufficient granularity, a diverse sensor technology for primary observations and interpretative techniques for aggregating and abstracting from observations is required.

We are using several technologies in parallel for the above purpose. This has several reasons. For most cases, it will be enough to know which people are in the room, but in some situations it is interesting to position people with finer granularity. It might, for example, be interesting to know if somebody is performing a presentation by the white-board or if the person is sitting by the table. Another aspect is whether the positioning should be automatic or require some sort of conscious action from the user. An automatic positioning might be practical, but it raises a number of privacy issues. Some positioning tasks may need physical observations, while others can be solved using a combination of different system information pieces. We will also provide an easy way for guests and other people who are unknown to the system to be identified and positioned, for example, to be solved by providing temporary guest devices.

The particular sensor technologies used in our early experiments are RFID tags and readers, Mica Motes, Ibuttons, Tracking of sounds, as well as WLAN and Bluetooth technology. RFID tags are used both for identification and positioning purposes. MICA Motes are used both to create a sensor network and to add on specific sensors to measure levels of light, sound-level, motion, temperature, moisture, etc. WLAN and Blue-tooth technology (cards and base-stations) are used for positioning purposes. Tracking of sound is used for positioning purposes. Ibuttons (Dallas semiconductors) are used for identification purposes. These devices contain a programmable memory that can contain a reference to a person. They provide fine granularity and requires explicit actions from the users.

7.5.7 Software Platforms and Services

The iLounge is supported by a middleware platform for the controlling of events in the interactive space. It includes many different functionalities, all with the aim to support application development for this kind of environment.

The key components of this software were developed at Stanford University, but adapted and in certain respects extended at KTH for the purposes of the iLounge. We will refer to this software broadly as iROS (iRoom Operating System) (Johanson et al. 1993). The borderlines between core iROS components and applications built on top of these are somewhat blurred. However, a core element is a data structure for synchronization of events in an interactive space (the Event Heap).

Apart from the central coordination mechanisms, iROS contains a cluster of software components that supports easy configuration of devices of services, information sharing (Multibrowse), and shared interactions of a touching and pointing nature (PointRight, iStuff. iWand): on the one hand, components for easy and ad hoc integration and removal of new devices and services (public as well as personal) in an interactive environment. Closely related to these are software that supports the coupling and coordination of devices. An example of this is the dynamic rescheduling of interactive devices (wireless keyboards and mice) to computers and work areas in the interactive space. Finally, support for movement of documents and applications across work areas and computers. This includes traditional cut and pastes, web browsing, and other computations.

An important extension to iROS is a set of mechanisms for saving, retrieving, editing, and reusing states of the interactive space (WorkspaceNavigator). Another extension is the software used in conjunction with tangible devices to enhance easy set up of an interactive space with personalized characteristics (buttons, panel, Magic bowl + tokens, knob, tags, etc). A complement to these techniques is the retrieval and editing of saved states (see workspace navigator above). Finally, some software components support the linkage of multiple interactive spaces (Distributed Event Heap, enhanced video conferencing, Voice over IP).

The middleware developed for this kind of interactive space (with iROS as the kernel) has eventually been commercialized with the name Teamspace by the small start up company Tidebreak. The design objectives for the Teamspace software apart from the original objectives were affordability, replicability, ease of deployment, intuitive installation, stand alone operation, self-initiated error recovery, and cross platform availability. The software is not limited to static tailored interactive spaces, but can be used for dynamic constellations of hardware components. It supports computer-based teamwork for teams with >3 members and can coordinate large displays (the public desktop) + private laptops.

7.6 Methodology

Our methodology comprises many different elements such as scenario work, theoretical analysis, interaction design, software prototypes, hardware prototypes, and user studies.

The scenario work has captured many different kinds of collaborative work scenarios, for example, collaborative learning. The theoretical analysis has been based on the perspectives from distributed cognition and activity theory. Interaction design involves the use of participatory design, design patterns, and a technical focus on tangible interfaces.

Software prototypes were developed iteratively and interleaved with user studies. Hardware prototypes have been developed as part of an exploratory processes based on both the scenario work and the user studies.

User studies have been based on particular instances of work scenarios, interactive environments, and prototypes. The tasks, durations, and populations for these studies vary from realistic tasks to artificial tasks, from intense short studies to month long periods, and from inexperienced to experienced users.

The development of our technology and its applications has evolved as two streams of activities: on the one hand, the development and utilization of physically co-located interactive spaces with possibilities for distributed work through enhanced connection to other similar spaces; on the other hand, the development of mechanisms for context-sensitive and ad hoc functionality in interactive work environments. Projects within these two areas are described below.

7.7   Projects on Design and Use of Co-located Interactive Spaces

7.7.1   The iSpace Project

Much of the basic development of the iLounge as described above has been part of project called iSpace funded by the Swedish Wallenberg Foundation and performed in cooperation with the Computer Science department at Stanford University. The goals for this project has been to study how new forms of group-oriented human-computer interaction technologies can improve performance of learning communities engaged in sustained project-driven collaborative activity. The goal has also been to develop appropriate technologies and study the subsequent evolution of collaboration patterns in an international network of connected, augmented learning environments, or "iSpaces" (Jansson 2005; Sundholm 2006).

By focusing on the interaction-rich domain of project-based design courses, the project has developed a body of research that carefully evaluates the impact of new technology tools in ongoing activity and provides actionable data on their value in educational contexts (Sundholm et al. 2004a, b; Sundholm 2007).

On a more specific level, the goal has been to effectively integrate new technology into the physical learning environment and to test and improve existing and new physical environments for their suitability for collaborative project-based learning scenarios. The performance implications associated with particular design aspects of an iSpace was also studied. Another issue was how to support persistence (capturing knowledge and experiences) in an interactive space and across interactive spaces. Tightly coupled to this is how teams can be enabled to reconfigure an iSpace with a minimum off effort and to restore a captured state of a work environment and to adapt it to the current type of activity.

A third group of research questions was concerned with the design of next-generation interfaces appropriate for group activities in team environments.

This included the design, implementation, and evaluation of new, multimodal input and output devices and interaction metaphors, such as gesture systems and large displays (Crone and Sundholm 2003; Crone 2006; Mattsson 2007).

The project involved an extensive evaluation in the form of field studies in higher education settings both at KTH and Stanford. Study student teams worked on real project-based design assignments on both sites. The evaluations resulted in proposals for redesigns and extensions of iSpace functionality.

Finally, an important part of the project comprised the development of middleware platforms necessary for coordinating events in the interactive spaces (see above).

7.7.2   The Fasade Project

The work in the iSpace project was followed up in a project called *Fasade*, which explored the appropriate balance between reactivity and pro-activity for a particular service/set of services within a ubiquitous work environment?

In this project, we augmented several existing services in such an environment in the direction of pro-activity (i.e., components that takes own initiatives within the work process). Software agent technology was used to realize the necessary communication and synchronization of all software components. The primary application area was the support for collaborative design teams.

Initially pseudo-pro-activity was explored in the sense of adaptive or indirectly reactive services. By augmenting context modeling and use of sensor equipment in particular situations, we created a functionality of services with clearly proactive characteristics. However, the behavior was still largely due to responsiveness based on enhanced context sensitivity. Prototypes were evaluated for a meeting management application.

This was followed up by design of more truly proactive services in the sense of having a dynamic goal-based behavior strongly grounded in the particular task and situation at hand (Werle et al. 2001). Furthermore, communication and synchronization of proactive services was studied. Pro-activity was explored in a limited scale that influence service behavior to some point, but not drastically changes the collaborative work situation.

The projects developed theoretical framework for studying heterogeneous situations where humans and proactive artificial components collaborate termed "Hybrid social spaces." Specific research questions included the following: What is the appropriate balance between reactivity and pro-activity for a particular service? How does the manifestation of the proactive service influence the users' perception of its functionality? What aspects of service functionality trigger a shift between perceiving a service as a tool or as a social actor? How do we perceive pro-activity of easy distinguishable individual services in contrast to the room as a whole?

7.7.3 The Weblabs Project

The Weblabs project was an EU funded project, with the purpose to enhance science education in secondary school by technological means. The focus was on support for collaboration and simulation. Within that project, the KTH team did some experiments that to some extent contributed to the classroom of the future. Kids used both the iLounge and a dynamic set up in an ordinary room to set up a simulation collaboratively through tangible means. The dynamic set up consisted of a carpet on the floor where the kids configured tangible elements. The configuration was memorized using RFID technology and transferred to the computerized simulation model, which eventually could be run on an available big or small screen (Fernaeus and Tholander 2005, 2006; Tholander and Fernaeus 2006).

7.8 Projects on Context-Aware and Ad Hoc Functionality

7.8.1 The FEEL Project

Our work on context-aware and ad hoc functionality in a Ubiquitous Work environment was initiated in a project called *FEEL*, which started in 2001 (Espinoza et al. 2007). It was funded by the EU IST Disappearing Computer Program and performed together with SICS and University of Southampton. The goal was to deal with the problem of the intrusiveness of today's mobile communication technology and how to enhance work in Ubiquitous Working environments by introducing the idea of nonintrusive communication services.

The background of this project was the conflict between collaborative activities in a local physical and social context and parallel individual communication tasks. The aim was to contribute to the restoration of a number of the desired properties of traditional co-located communication technology-free work environments.

Intrusiveness is caused by at least four typical phenomena, which has influenced current technology: First, focus-demanding and clearly distinguishable artifacts like phones or PCs explicitly and directly mediate communication in a context free fashion.

Secondly, the functionalities of services are traditionally based upon the assumption that communication is a deterministic flow of passive information, which, for example, does not include information of the participants' current context. Services do not communicate on a profound level

The switch between contexts introduces a high cognitive load, as each distributed context typically has its own system of characteristic objects and rules.

The FEEL project delivered newly gained knowledge about the management of intrusiveness in technology intensive environments and situations. The knowledge was gained by analyzing the existence and characteristics of intrusiveness, designing methods, and mechanisms to manage intrusiveness, implementing technological solutions to manage intrusiveness, and by testing the solutions with users.

The approach was based upon a combination of the utilization of a richer set of information channels for interaction (Kilander and Lönnqvist 2002) and the enforcement of synchronized service and artifact behavior (Jonsson 2002; Werle and Jansson 2002).

The main results included an analysis of the characteristics and causes of intrusiveness, service-based software to manage intrusiveness in common technology intensive scenarios.

The results also comprised a software package for performing agent-based negotiation based upon the notion of argumentation with fine grained per-message intrusiveness management as well as a software platform for service oriented computing (S-view) (Espinoza 2003).

7.8.2   The ACAS Project

The work in the FEEL project has been followed up and extended in a project called ACAS, which started in October 2002. The acronym stands for Adaptive and Context-Aware Services. The project was funded by the Swedish Foundation for Strategic Research (SSF) and performed in the context of the Centre for Wireless Systems at KTH and in collaboration with Ericsson Research.

The long-term objectives of ACAS are to achieve seamless functionality of services for collaborating mobile users in heterogeneous scenarios primarily by designing for adaptive and context-aware utilization of devices, services, and communication infrastructures in such scenarios.

The ACAS project targets both how to support the navigation of users to adequate work environments with appropriate services and also to route services to situations where they are potentially needed. Both the technical solutions as well as possible business models are of importance.

In the first of the two work packages (context aware user interaction) was addressed how groups of mobile users can collaborate using dynamic configurations of devices and services. Configurations and functionality of configured system depend upon contextual knowledge. Contextual knowledge utilized includes knowledge about available devices, services, tasks, physical situation as well as personal and group characteristics. Contextual knowledge is modeled and communicated in a decentralized fashion (Li et al. 2004; Jonsson 2007). The ACAS service architecture provides a network for the publication, aggregation, and dissemination of group state information. Applications running in the users' PCs provide a view of each member and the member's relation to the group.

In the second work package (context-aware service delivery), the objective was the creation of affordable support for adaptive and automatic (re)configuration of local and global infrastructure, facilitating the interaction of end-users with their services in heterogeneous networks in an opportunistic and co-operative manner.

7.9   Lessons Learned

In this section, we summarize a number of observations from the described projects. The success of this technology will ultimately depend on how accessible and easy to use it is. To have a special remote room where skilled technicians are required on every instance of use will obviously block the scale up of the technology. When we used subsets of the technology in our day to day meeting rooms and coffee rooms, this proved to be most successful.

Our attempts to use tangible interfaces (like a knob, cards or a bowl with tokens) as simplified means to start, reconfigure, and tailor the spaces to particular needs proved to be very successful.

Light weight technological solutions that can be instantiated in virtually any room are the way forward. The experiences with the Teamspace technology are very promising in this respect.

Very important is also the openness of the system, in the sense that devices and services can be added and removed in an ad hoc fashion without disturbing the functionality of the whole system.

Using the rooms for teamwork, letting the technology make most aspects of the collaborative process very explicit, had a positive effect on the role-play in the teams, in the sense that the balance between dominant and less outspoken team members did level out.

Related to that, the shift in balance from pure communication to actual work within the sessions in the spaces also had a positive effect on the role play. Silent but productive team members gained in importance.

The combination of two large screens and personal laptops proved most useful. Even if we still believe in the role of interactive tables and more specialized displays, we have not been their usefulness empirically. A disclaimer here is that our implementations for these devices may not have been optimal.

Apart from the well known observation that high quality sound is a prerequisite for distance communication, we have not been able to explore the usefulness of sound and speech technology in our interactive spaces.

Adaptive functionality is still a challenge for interactive spaces as well as for personal devices/services. Complex technical support systems will need adaptivity, but the balance between user and system control is very delicate.

Adaptivity needs context information, and apart from physical measurements that can be done automatically, it is still a challenge to which degree users are willing to provide information about the selves, both for practical and privacy reasons.

As the experiences of interactive spaces are very new to most people, it is a challenge to perform empirical studies on advancement of the technology. An example of this was our attempts to study the functionality of the Workspace navigator, the tool for logging, editing, and re-instantiating room states. Analytically this approach was very promising but we were not able to produce empirical evidence of its benefits.

Finally using the new technological solutions for your own daily work and communication is a great strategy. Our regular communication with Stanford and our distance meetings within the RUFAE network showed that.

7.10   Concluding Remarks

The vision of Ubiquitous Work Environments is to create truly dynamically configured interactive workspaces, through which a team of workers can experience a seamless situation of work, no matter where they work in the world or whether they are dispersed or not, taking a maximal advantage of the context they happen to be in.

Today, we have experience only from fragments of this scenario. We have experience of the design of powerful but still relatively static interactive workspaces as exemplified by the iLounge. Such environments provide flexible and media rich environments for collaborative work.

The distributed aspect is covered in the sense that interactive workspaces can be coupled and the traditional video communication is completed with additional synchronizations of the two spaces.

We also have experience of the mobile and distributed aspects in the sense of context-aware and adaptive mobile services.

Although the present versions of our technology has the potential to facilitate intuitive communication and interaction in familiar collaborative work situations and in individual mobile and ad hoc work situations, the long term ambition of Ubiquitous Work Environments is to flexibly recreate these conditions in mobile collaborative work situations at remote places or in dynamic team constellations.

Acknowledgments The work has been made possible due to the efforts of postdoctoral researchers: Fredrik Kilander and Harko Verhagen, and PhD students: Peter Lönnqvist, Martin Jonsson, Johan Matsson, Li Wei, Maria Crone, Hillevi Sundholm, and Patrik Werle.

The most important international partner has been the Computer Science Department at Stanford University, represented by professor Terry Winograd, professor Armando Fox, Andrew Milne, Brad Johanson, Arna Ionescu, Lawrence Neely, Andy Szybalski, Wendy Lee, Clara Shih, and Jan Borchers, Stanford (now at Aachen University).

The work described has been made possible due to the generous grants from Alice and Knut Wallenberg Foundation, The Swedish Foundation for Strategic Research (SSF), VINNOVA and the EU IST 5th framework program.

Special thanks to Dr. Saadi Lahlou at EDF for initiating and running the RUFAE network among international institutions interested in this field.

References

Croné M (2006) Interactive Workspaces as Support for Collaborative Work. Licentiate thesis, Stockholm University

Croné M, Sundholm H (2003) Evaluating a Ubiquitous Service Environment for Collaborative Work. In Proceedings of the Eighth European Conference on Computer Supported Cooperative Work (CSCW 2003), Helsinki, Finland

Dourish P (2001) Where the Action Is: The Foundations Of Embodied Interaction, Cambridge, MIT

Espinoza F (2003) Towards Individual Service Provisioning. In Proceedings of International Conference on Intelligent User Interfaces (IUI 2003), pp. 239–241, Canada, ACM Press

Espinoza F, De Roure D, Hamfors O, Hinz L, Holmberg J, Jansson C-G, Jennings N, Luck M, Lönnqvist P, Ramchurn G, Sandin A, Thompson M, Bylund M (2007) Intrusiveness Management for Focused, Efficient, and Enjoyable Activities. In: Streitz N, Kameas A, Mavrommati I (eds) The Disappearing Computer, LNCS, vol 4500, pp. 143–157

Fernaeus Y, Tholander J (2005) Looking at the Computer but Doing it on Land: Children's Interactions in a Tangible Programming Space. In Proceedings of HCI2005, Edinburgh, p. 3–18

Fernaeus Y, Tholander J (2006) Finding Design Qualities in a Tangible Programming Space. In Proceedings of CHI2006, pp. 447–456

Ishii H, Ullmer B (1997) Tangible Bits: Towards Seamless Interfaces Between People, Bits and Atoms. In Proceedings of CHI'97, pp. 234–241

Johanson B, Winograd T, Fox A (1993) Interactive Workspaces. IEEE Computer 36:4, 99–103

Jansson E (2005) Working Together when Being Apart – An Analysis of Distributed Collaborative Work through ICT from an Organizational and Psychosocial Perspective, PhD Thesis, Stockholm University

Jonsson M (2002) Context Shadow: An Infrastructure for Context Aware Computing. In Proceedings of the Workshop on Artificial Intelligence in Mobile Systems (AIMS), in conjunction with ECAI 2002, Lyon, France

Jonsson M (2007) Sensing and Making Sense, PhD Thesis, KTH

Kilander F, Lönnqvist P (2002) A Whisper in the Woods – An Ambient Soundscape for Peripheral Awareness of Remote Processes. In Proceedings of ICAD 2002, Kyoto, Japan

Lahlou S (1999) Observing Cognitive Work in Offices. In: Streitz N, Siegel J, Hartkopf V, Konomi S (eds) Cooperative Buildings. Integrating Information, Organizations and Architecture. Heidelberg, Springer, Lecture Notes in Computer Science, vol 1670, pp. 150–163

Li W, Jonsson M, Kilander F, Jansson CG (2004) Building Infrastructure Support for Ubiquitous Context-Aware Systems, ISPA 2004, pp. 509–518

Mattsson J (2007) Pointing, Placing, Touching – Physical Manipulation and Coordination Techniques for Interactive Meeting Spaces. PhD Thesis, KTH

Rekimoto J (1997) Pick-and-Drop: A Direct Manipulation Technique for Multiple Computer Environments, ACM Symposium on User Interface Software and Technology, AB, Canada, pp. 31–39

Rogers Y, Lindley S (2004) Collaborating Around Vertical and Horizontal Displays: Which Way is Best? Interacting with Computers, 16, 1133–1152

Satyanarayanan M (2001) Pervasive Computing: Vision and Challenges, IEEE Personal Communications, August

Streitz A, Röcker C, Prante T, van Alphen D, Stenzel R Magerkurth C (2005) Designing Smart Artifacts for Smart Environments. In: IEEE Computer, March, pp. 41–49

Sundholm H (2006) To Share or Not to Share – Distributed Collaboration in Interactive Workspaces. In: Hassanaly P, Herrmann T, Kunau G, Zacklad M (eds) Cooperative Systems Design: Seamless Integration of Artifacts and Conversations – Enhanced Concepts of Infrastruction for Communication. Amsterdam, IOS Press, pp. 270–285

Sundholm H (2007) Spaces within Spaces – The Construction of a Collaborative Reality, PhD thesis, Stockholm University

Sundholm H, Artman H, Ramberg R (2004a) Backdoor Creativity: Collaborative Creativity in Technology Supported Teams. In: Darses F, Dieng R, Simone C, Zacklad M (eds) Cooperative Systems Design: Scenario-Based Design of Collaborative Systems. Amsterdam, IOS press, pp. 99–114

Sundholm H, Ramberg R, Artman H (2004b) Learning Conceptual Design: Activities with Electronic Whiteboards. In: Eriksen MA, Malmborg L, Nilsen J (eds) CADE2004 Web Proceedings of Computers in Art and Design Education Conference, Denmark, Copenhagen Business School

Tholander T, Fernaeus Y (2006) Multimodal Interaction in Children's Programming with Tangible Artifacts, In Proceedings of ICLS 2006

Weiser M (1991) The Computer for the 21st Century, Scientific American, September, pp. 94–104

Werle P, Kilander F, Jonsson M, Lönnqvist P, Jansson CG (2001) A Ubiquitous Service Environment with Active Documents for Teamwork Support, In Proceedings of Ubicomp 2001, Atlanta, GA
Werle P, Jansson CG (2002) Achieving Non-intrusive Notifications in a Ubiquitous Service Environment, In Proceedings of RVK 2002, Stockholm, Sweden

Chapter 8
Psychological Methods for the Study of Augmented Environments

Valery N. Nosulenko and Elena S. Samoylenko

Abstract In this chapter, some psychological perspectives to study activities in Augmented Environments are outlined. Main concepts related to theories of activity are discussed namely, subjects' goals and motives as well as tools used during its realization. It is argued that knowledge about the structure of the users' activity facilitates elaborates the corresponding techniques of its recording and analysis. An overview of the so called "perceived quality" approach is given and the questions about what is perceived by individual (group) as the actor of digitized environment as well as about how to study the perceived quality of such environments are discussed. Several examples of results obtained using this approach are presented.

8.1 Introduction

We give here a brief description of a number of Russian Psychological approaches used in studying human activity in complex technical systems. Research in the Laboratory of Design for Cognition enables us to adapt the methodology to studies of augmented environment, AE (Lahlou et al. 2002, 2007; Lahlou and Nosulenko 2005), which also stimulated creation of similar projects in Russia.

How can we analyze and design human activities in AE, considering that its components are distributed over space and time? Classic ethnographic observation is not well suited to the analysis of such settings (see also Hutchins and Hollan, Chap. 9). We approach this issue in the context of activity theory (Rubinstein 1922, 1957; Leont'ev 1975), which gives a systematic framework for the analysis of distinctive properties, and of the content and structure of the activity. Practical implementation of this theory in the so called anthropocentric approach adopted by Russian engineering psychology and ergonomics (Lomov 1966, 1977) is briefly outlined as well. Also, a number of ideas developed by Russian psychologists

V.N. Nosulenko (✉)
Institute of Psychology, Russian Academy of Sciences,
13, Yaroslavskaya str., 129366, Moscow, Russia
e-mail: valery.nosulenlo@gmail.com

S. Lahlou (ed.), *Designing User Friendly Augmented Work Environments: From Meeting Rooms to Digital Collaborative Spaces,* Computer Supported Cooperative Work, DOI 10.1007/978-1-84800-098-8_8, © Springer-Verlag London Limited 2009

regarding the concept of mental image are presented. We introduce the "perceived quality" approach which is a practical synthesis of the theoretical contributions of Russian psychology to the problems of activity and mental images. In this connection, the techniques and procedures we elaborated for defining subjective evaluations of relevance of different objects situated in AEs as activity mediators are described.

Our analysis aims at giving a simple and usable description of the qualities of those mediators as perceived by people working in such an environment and the same is presented, even though their global perception is complex. In the course of this analysis, we focus on "perceived qualities" of the mediators and the actual context of their use, as well as the perceivers' goals related to mediated activity. We discuss the advantages and limitations of the methodology, illustrated by empirical investigations.

8.2 The Concept of Activity in the Framework of Augmented Reality

Theories of activity, mainly the ones created by Rubinstein (1922, 1957) and Leont'ev (1975) propose the conceptual means for the analysis of activities in general, and those (this was the focus of the psychology of engineering, cf. infra) taking place in complex environments mediated by technology. These theories may be useful in developing psychologically adapted work spaces and associated tools. More precisely a number of ideas elaborated in the theories of activity addressing its psychological nature are of direct interest for "activity design" in AEs, digital spaces, and service science.

According to Rubinstein, who introduced the notion of "subject-oriented activity", an activity is always done by a subject, that is, by a human being (vs. by an animal or a machine) having his individual needs to be satisfied: the subject's personality (individual cognitive style, personal motives and history, etc.) has influence on the activity. Conversely, activity is experience that shapes the subject. In the course of transforming the context, a human both manifests his/her personality and it is being "formed" as well (Nosulenko and Rabardel 2007, p. 140).

An activity is an interaction between a subject and an object; it is necessarily object-oriented and has a specific content.

Human actions are considered to be goal directed. Activity even when realized in cognition and transformation of external world, is social by its nature and is inscribed into human relations. By this we mean that everything a person does has a certain social effect: through influence on objects (i.e., through activity) a person acts upon people.

The specificity of Rubinstein's concept of activity is manifest in the way he describes the nature of the relation between internal and external realities in the *determinism principle* (Rubinstein 1957). Any external (manifest, observable) phenomenon is considered to be more or less mediated by internal conditions. "Internal conditions" are all those hereditary and genetic heritage, psychological characteristics, and life experience and, generally speaking, the whole personality of a person, that already exist at the moment of a new external influence. External phenomena (whether perceptions, or motor actions) are objectively mediated and caused by the "objective" neuronal machine which a human is. Subjective reflections of objects (how people perceive objects) exist *objectively* as internal states: neural arrangement activation thresholds, etc.; and these states have been constructed through the life experience of the subject, and they form as a global system, i.e., the subjects' personality. Since all these internal states are an objective reality, they can be instigated with scientific techniques. Subjective reflection of reality can be investigated either through direct objective record of physiological states, or through human subjective reports about thoughts, emotions and perceptions.

As for the structure of activity, its main components are represented by motives, goals, actions and operations (ways of realization of actions) (Leont'ev 1975; Rubinstein 1957). According to Rubinstein, the integrity of activity manifests itself primarily in the system of the subject's goals and their underlying motives. At different stages of activity, the general activity-related motives and goals generate local, specific motives and goals, which characterize the actions.

For example, a person having a general motive to improve the quality of his well being puts in a purpose to find a new good job. Consequently, the person aims his whole activity at the realization of this goal. As soon as a new job is obtained the person is induced by a local motive to get a good salary. This motive in same way pushes him towards the realization of the goal to increase his labor productivity. Fulfillment of the later goal presupposes, for example, improving knowledge in informatics and as a result obtaining a new computer, taking corresponding courses, etc. Thus, all of these local goals are subordinated to the initial general motive to improve the quality of well being.

Rubinstein's conception of activity structure is somewhat different from the one proposed by Leont'ev (1975). The later one, while considering the same activity components, strictly refers the motive to the whole activity, goals to actions and operations to concrete situations, in a strict hierarchical manner. Moreover, Leont'ev interprets the motive as a material or ideal object of need rather than as a psychic phenomenon (experiencing some specific need, e.g., hunger or desire for social recognition).

The subject-oriented theory of activity (Abulkhanova 2007; Rubinstein 1922, 1957) defined the "anthropocentric" approach. This approach differs from the modern "human centered" approach in that while the latter focuses on the human subject and on their experience, the anthropocentric approach takes the perspective of the user, in a first person manner, not only for perception, but for the whole activity including motives and goals. Lomov (1977) adopted this approach in Russian engineering psychology and ergonomics, in response and opposition to the technocentric approach in the analysis of "Man-Technology" systems. The latter was, according to Lomov, based on a principle of simplification that reduces the importance of human activity in the system design orientation.

The anthropocentric approach considers an individual as the core rather than a simple element of a "Man-technology" system. The approach postulates that individuals organize the system's global operation towards the achievement of their own set goals. The approach considers man-technology relationship as the one between "the working subject" and "the work tool." In fact, in the framework of the anthropocentric approach, the goal-directed activity of the human operator is considered to be the basic systemic process. It is man who provides flexibility of the system's operation. He determines tasks, performing actions, as well as evaluation of their result. Thus, the technical systems cannot be considered to have the same importance as the man because they are only the tools, means, used by a man to realize his actions and to obtain information upon these actions.

The anthropocentric approach was implemented in practice in the design of various human operators' activities in complex socio-technical systems (e.g., aerospace), while their analysis was integrated into the overall process of the development of the system (Lomov 1977). In other words, evaluation of the activity was explicitly a part of the design project and cycle. This approach was novel at that time; it turned out to be similar to the principles adopted in the user-oriented approach or participation design, elaborated later on (Ehn 1992; Kyng and Mathiassen 1997; Norman and Draper 1986, etc.).

The analysis of the operator's activity structure and dynamics as well as the study of the mechanisms of its psychic regulation are of special value in the design of the human operator's activity. The main element of such a design process is the description of psychological constituents of human activity in the technical system. Such a description should anticipate the different variants of realization of actions and evaluate the way the proposed interfaces ensure an anticipation of the system's functioning by an operator. This approach is robust because it is founded on what is stable, the goals, and adopts an opportunistic and realist view similar to the strategy of the operator, who makes her best efforts to reach the goal with whatever resources are available in the conditions given, whether they are optimal and meeting specification; or minimal.

A specific objective of the design process is to define the "zones" of activity which need "creative decisions." The design also addresses the training scheme of the personnel: for activity planning skills, self-control skills as well as skills of using personal reserves in order to create the special adequate behavior in unpredictable situations (incidents). The conception of technical tools (interfaces, control, and communication systems, etc.) is incorporated into the working out of the psychological design of the operator's activity. Here, designers and engineers are considered to be inside rather than outside of the whole system being under elaboration.

Thus, activity theories provide methodology for investigating "man and environment" interactions. In this sense, the primary role is attributed to interrelations existing between activity components. In the context of analyzing activity the components being evaluated are as following:

- The individual or collective subject/s of activity
- The environment objects and systems an activity is directed at
- The motives or needs that induce activity
- The goals – conscious representations of future result to be reached
- The aims – intermediate stages in reaching the goal

- The actions and operations (motor and/or cognitive) carried out by the subjects in order to reach the goals
- The tools used to transform the external environment

As for the modes of investigation of these components, some of them like actions or operations can be observed and recorded (e.g., opening the door, typing a password) while others, like motives or goals can be revealed and characterized only by means of techniques developed to analyze and evaluate subjective representations.

The analysis of activity structure and the mechanisms of its regulation were widely used in ergonomics and engineering psychology (Barabanshikov 2007; Nardi 1996; Nosulenko et al. 2005; Nosulenko and Rabardel 1998). Let us see how this type of analysis can be developed for the study of human activity in AEs.

The notion of activity briefly described earlier is useful for answering the question of how we should, in practice, investigate the man-environment interaction in this case. In AEs, individual or collective activities involve objects and tools which are not so easy to identify because they are digitized, and often symbolic; so it is difficult to determine with mere behavioral observation what is mobilized by the subject at a given point. In the non-augmented environment, the object of activity is identifiable by an external observer; and localized in space and time. For example, a person carries out an activity with an object like a car which is localized here and now as a more or less stable element of the external world. In this case, it is easy to identify and measure the types of operations carried out with the object, to trace its movement in space, that is to record some of the externally observable parameters of activity. Verbal reports of the subjects of this activity can be also analyzed in order to identify their motives and goals and to refer them to externally observed parameters of activity.

Thus, it seems to be possible to give a psychological description of a practical activity when solving the following research goals:

1. To identify the physical object and its transformations as well as precise operations carried out with this object
2. To reveal "internal" components of activity at the different moments of its realization
3. To trace relationships between externally observable parameters of activity and its internal components

This given process of analysis turns out not so easy to apply when activity takes place in AE. A first problem is that the objects of such an environment are in some way physically "delocalized" in space and time (Lahlou and Nosulenko 2005; Lahlou et al. 2007; Nosulenko 2007, 2008). For example, a workflow, or a video-conferencing system, a database, are somewhat delocalized and appear only through some aspects during some activity with their interface. The "object" is in fact much wider in extension than the local part manipulated by the user. Therefore "what the object is," what is relevant for activity, is not really its actual affordances (if even such a notion was specifiable), but rather the mental model which the user has of the object in the local perspective of her present goals.

Moreover, a growing part of the digital system's resources is used to produce an "intuitive" user and technology interaction. In this case, the system and its elements might become "invisible" for a researcher (and for the user as well). For example, when an individual A is connecting with his partner B by means of an information network, it becomes rather difficult to identify and record objectively those elements and states of this network which are related to observable operations of the individual A. This problem refers to localization both in space and in time: the network is "living with its own life" which is not always reflected in the subjective representations of its user and is not always accessible for external research observation.

It is possible to record concrete operations that an individual A is performing: e.g., he detects the presence of his partner B in the network (the icon referring to individual B is activated in the chat window) and calls him for discussion of the joint project, supposing that at this moment his partner is staying at his work place. However, it is only in the course of communication that A discovers that the partner is indeed connected (hence the icon of presence in the chat interface), but physically far away from his office and doesn't have access to the documents to be discussed. Thus, it turns out to be difficult for the researcher to grasp the whole set of internal and external components of activity due to the fact that the system is physically distributed in space. As a result, modeling an activity taking place in augmented reality becomes complicated.

This is especially problematic when the goal of analysis is, precisely, to make a better system. This is where it becomes crucial to base the analysis on the activity and tasks, and not on the present state of the system. Activity then becomes the outline against which interaction with the objects is evaluated, as to whether this interaction is efficient and comfortable. It is not the interaction with the devices per se which is evaluated, but how fluidly this interaction allows the subject to progress towards his goals, compared with other alternatives.

For example, in one study on PDAs and networks we did in 2001, a PDA with high bandwidth wireless capacity (802.11b Wifi enabled) was judged more comfortable, easy, etc. for Internet browsing, but less "useful" than another PDA which only had a very slow bandwidth through mobile phone connection, although the latter was judged less comfortable, slow, etc.

This paradox can be simply explained through the activity theory: which system actually helped fulfill users' goals better? At the time (2001) Wifi was very scarce and in practice users could only access it through their home or office access points. In these contexts, they also had their own PC which had a larger screen, keyboard, and better interface than the Wifi PDA. So this one was indeed "useless" in that context. On the other hand, the mediocre PDA with phone connection could save the day when the user was away "on the road" because it enabled the subjects to collect email, even if at a slow speed and at the cost of a painful process (Nosulenko and Samoylenko 2001; Lahlou et al. 2009).

Description of the relevant elements for an activity oriented analysis can be obtained in cooperation with the individual, e.g., by Talking out loud protocols, by asking her the goals and sub-goals of her activity during self confrontations with recordings of the activity, and evaluations about the quality of support provided by the environment for this activity. Specific techniques of debrief have been set up for this purpose, which will be illustrated in Sect. 3.

The problem of "delocalization" in space and time is crucial for the digital environment since it is often created primarily, to be used in communication and joint activity of people who are distributed in space and time. Therefore special attention must be paid to the components of joint activity, and first and foremost to the joint goal – the representation of future result to be reached by the "collective subjects" of this activity (Lomov 1984).

In sum, activity taking place in AE has peculiarities. It needs to be analyzed with methods giving access to both internal and external to its components. One of the possible ways of such an analysis is proposed in the framework of the 'perceived quality approach'.

8.3   Perceived Quality Approach

The perceived quality approach is a practical framework useful to understand, and to a certain extent measure, how subjects perceive and evaluate objects as means for reaching certain goals of activity. We can use this framework to analyze the practical activities taking place in real world contexts, and to identify those elements of the environment which are considered by individuals to be the most valuable in the course of realization of their aims. The approach is also adequate to analyze joint activity with the emphasis on its main component, the joint goal, which is essentially a representation of the future result that a group of individuals (collective subjects) seeks to reach.

The perceived quality approach is based on some ideas developed in the theory of mental image, elaborated by a number of Russian scholars. This theory contains important concepts about the role of subjective images in the regulation of an activity (Lomov 1984; Nosulenko et al. 2005; Zavalova et al. 1986). Formation of a mental image is considered to be an intentional process; and its dynamics determined by the aims to be realized in the course of the activity. *It is the concrete aim that defines the value attributed to a certain object's property represented in the user's mental image.* This is not difficult to understand: an office chair with five small wheels will be of good quality for seating in front of a computer, but of poor quality as a vehicle to go from one building to another in the campus; conversely, a bicycle will be of poor quality as a seat, but of good quality as a vehicle for the same goal of transport on campus. It is therefore surprising that such a truism is so often forgotten in user research; where engineers often evaluate the devices and systems per se instead of in the perspective of the actual context of the activity.

According to Oshanin (1973) the aim determines: (1) the object's characteristics that are most significant for the realization of action; (2) the form and consequence of the representation in the mental image of the object's different elements as well as evaluation of their level of significance in the whole structure of the image. It is the aim that determines the way information is chosen, systematized and further used during the performance of an action. The ideas about the role of the aim in the formation of a mental image as well as the elements of the theory of activity serve as the theoretical basis for the perceived quality approach.

The expression "perceived quality" is widely used. It almost replaced the term "quality" in the vocabulary used by some specialists engaged in the evaluation of the characteristics of products and services proposed to end users. According to Giordano (2006), the term "perceived quality" is primarily attributed to the marketing domain and is defined as a set of sensory impressions and those qualities that attract and fascinate at first glance, that are interpreted by a client as a premise of quality and a guarantee of getting satisfaction during its use. The expression is used in a similar sense in the majority of studies aimed at the analysis client satisfaction (Deschamp and Nayak 1996; Gale 1994; Hill et al. 2001; Horovitz 1987). However, although the word "perceived" is widely used in those studies, the problem of perception itself is not the point of real interest. The word "perceived" seems to be added to stress the crucial role of the clients in the final evaluation, and the importance of specific studies addressing this issue when marketing product. This seems logical, but is not enough to understand the real nature of perceived quality.

We attribute a different meaning to the notion of perceived quality; we use it in the perspective of activity: goal directed interaction of individuals with their external environment. In this perspective, the perceived quality of objects will focus on the set of their characteristics which are the most significant for reaching the goals at hand.

Let's take an example. Subject A willing to "communicate information to his co-worker B", investigates the tools available in his environment to reach this goal (mobile telephone, computer etc...). He notices that his computer is not connected to the network and as a result, uses his mobile phone. The perceived quality of the chosen tool is its capacity to establish a quick connection with another person and to ensure immediate voice reactions to the information given. The telephone's size, color and other features of its design do not have a high value for this kind of activity. However, in reaching some other types of goals, like, for example, "to display a certain image about oneself, or status to other people," the telephone's fashion design, or brand, might turn out to be crucial.

The perceived quality approach proposes an analysis based on the general idea that it is not smart to define a priori a set of so called "objective" parameters of the object or the system under study (size, form, speed, etc.). *The characteristics of the system actually significant for the subject are identified in the process of evaluating the perceived quality* and this makes it possible to determine the structure of the system, what the problem is and how it could be improved.

Let's discuss this idea in more details.

Most classical paradigms of investigation are based on:

- Initial identification of the object or system
- Measurement of their objective parameters (e.g., intensity, color, size)
- Analysis of how these objects or systems are subjectively perceived/liked

Thus, a researcher begins with creating a "physical model" of the investigated object and tries to reveal the relationships that might exist between its features and their perceptions (for example, between the level of sound intensity and subjectively evaluated level of its loudness). This approach is fruitful for pure laboratory experiments aimed at revealing the cause and effect relationships between independent (e.g., intensity operationalized by a researcher) and dependent (e.g., subjective evaluations of loudness) variables.

However, sometimes it turns out to be difficult to reveal a direct relationship between certain parameters of a complex object and its subjective perception and evaluation as a whole. The real life situations are hardly inscribed into the classical experimental design with strict operationalization of dependent and independent variables. It is difficult to enumerate in advance the whole set of parameters that a subject is going to perceive in an object or a system involved in his activity. Besides, the relationship of the parameters to perceived quality may be indirect, and mediated by other parameters or situations. It particularly refers to AE, where most parts of a system are connected and many functions are distributed.

In contrast, the perceived quality approach begins with identifying the aspects of the object or a system that are subjectively valuable for a certain individual in the course of the given activity. The strategy is to elaborate and empirically prove a number of hypotheses concerning those of its parameters that constitute a core of its perceived quality. It assumes that these aspects will be included into their perceived quality, and sets up a measurement system based on them as they appear in open ended individual evaluations. (e.g., "useful", "fast," "clear," "comfortable," "difficult"). What physical (or cultural) aspects of the artifact construct these subjective characteristics will appear only in the course of a careful examination of the activity. And it is by confronting these evaluations with moments of actual activity and their description by activity theory that this will happen. For example, we shall discover for which subgoal or operation the artifact produces an impression of clarity or slowness in use. And it will then become obvious what affordances are at stake. This is where, once again, activity theory brings a crucial contribution to efficient design by uncovering a functional basis to subjective perception.

Perceived quality is different in its approach to subjective evaluation in that it takes seriously the way the user expresses the quality: when a subject declares that "comfortable" is a dimension relevant for her evaluation, the analyst does not consider that the subject would use "comfortableness" as a clumsy and imprecise way to express the "real" issue which is a matter of physical characteristics. He takes the judgment at face value, and accepts that "comfortability" is actually one of the perceived dimensions through which the subject considers the object. His efforts are to understand in what steps of activity the interaction with the object in the course of activity does construct this perception. The step by step analysis of real activity, in collaboration with the subject, will show at which point the subject says "this" is (un) comfortable. From the comparison of the goals at this critical point and what actually happens the analyst will understand in functional terms as to what creates (dis) comfort.

A key method to make analysis easy is to use a comparison process, where a subject is asked to compare several objects (or situations) related to the same activity.

In this case, peculiarities of interaction with the objects can be easily matched with the differences in evaluations.

A practical perspective of the proposed approach concerns a simultaneous analysis of the object's or system's perceived qualities that are formed, on the one hand, in a user and, on the other hand, in a designer. The discrepancies between these perceived qualities are determined by different initial goals. For a designer, the initial goal is to create a product that a potential user would wish to buy. Designer's perceived quality is generally described in terms of objectively measured parameters of a product (technical, physical, etc.). But the user does not normally buy "technical parameters." The user's goal is to satisfy his personal needs in the best way. Such a discrepancy in the goals is expressed in different "languages" in which the object's descriptions are made. The designer's (developer's) perceived quality of the object represents a "physical model" of the object or system. The user's perceived quality is based on a variety of perceptual characteristics and subjective estimations. He perceives the object as a "perceptual model" and describes it in terms of perception and subjective assessment (Fig. 8.1).

The research's task is to "translate" the user's language of perceived quality (his "perceptual model") into the language used by a designer in the course of the creation of the object ("physical model"). Mainly, from the analysis of these two perceived qualities of the same object that exists in a user and in a designer, a tendency of "hiding" a system's important elements from a user might be revealed. For example, if the proposed function of "identification of a user in the network" as designed by the designer is not represented in the system's perceived quality that exists in a user (that is the user is unaware about it) a question about possible consequences of this fact, namely, the problem of privacy, appears.

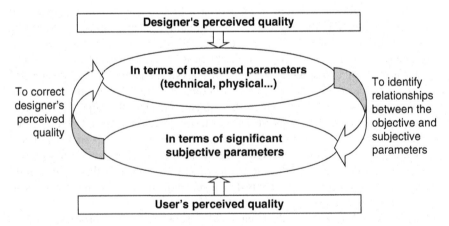

Fig. 8.1 Relations between the object's perceived qualities formed in a user and in a designer

8.3.1 Cultural Differences

The objects and complex systems having the same perceptual core refer to the same categories that are organized on the basis of their subjective perception by people dealing with them in the course of their individual or joint activity. For example, an information network would be perceived as being different from a set of computers connected if in the course of using it an individual is able to reveal its functional or operational meaning (for example, as a means of distribution of goals between members of joint activity). The network's perceptual core would be related rather to its use with this purpose and not as mere a sum of individual computers' functions.

8.3.2 Halo Effects

It should be mentioned that the "traces" referring to peculiarities of both the environment and the human activity itself are represented in the perceived quality. For example, an individual performing an activity she doesn't like will tend to attribute bad quality to the objects of this activity.

An individual perceives and evaluates his own actions and operations; as a result the components of activity become the components of the perceived quality. That is, environment is perceived both in its object-related qualities, and operational qualities (Nosulenko 2007; Nosulenko and Samoylenko 2001). This issue is important from the methodological point of view: revealing the structural components of human activity (its goals, tasks and operations) is a necessary aspect of investigating perceived quality for this reason also (which are the liked/dislikes subgoals). Thus, the specificity of our approach is in its systemic analysis of observed activity along the following lines:

- Analysis in terms of *activity*: making explicit its components and which objects of the world it is directed at
- Analysis of *subjective experience* related to this activity: what an individual thinks about the various elements of the activity (goals, subgoals, objects, operations...) and how he describes them in his own words
- Connecting the elements of activity to the subjective experience, and understanding which aspects of activity actually construct the experience
- Finally, redesigning the activity (by finding another preferred path of subgoals, changing the affordances of objects, etc.) in order to produce a better final overall perceived quality

To analyze subjective experience, the analysis of verbal data constitutes an important moment in our approach. We consider the verbal data obtained from free verbalizations as being representative for reflecting on perceived qualities (Nosulenko and Samoylenko 1977, 2001; Samoylenko 1986). The method of analysis of free verbalizations we have developed is based on the quantitative representation of the discovered regularities thus providing opportunity to construct "verbal portraits" of the objects studies (Nosulenko 2007; Nosulenko and Samoylenko 2001). The method of "verbal portrait" makes it possible to establish significant characteristics that determine estimation and preference in human judgments as well as the "weight" of each of them.

The verbatim are obtained by asking the subjects to describe their activity as they perform it, usually by comparing the present situation with another (comparing two or more systems successively for the same activity, or comparing the "new" system with what their usual practice is, etc.)

To sum up: research in perceived quality is aimed primarily at identification of subjectively significant features of an object or system and these features constitute a certain stable core, specific for a certain human population. Identification of such a "core" help to reveal socio-cultural aspects of perceived quality, and then to determine the characteristics depending on the tasks of the activity, professional and everyday life experience of individual, his education, etc. In a certain way, this approach is a procedure for "measuring" characteristics of an image, reflecting reality and regulating the subject's activity. Comparison of verbal data with information collected by objective methods results in determination of parameters of the device/systems that are most significant for the user, and produce the perceived quality in the process of use. This kind of data processing of comparative data may be used to show how the characteristics of an object the designers develop may be improved to meet the expectations of the users.

8.4   Examples of Practical Application

The main idea of our analysis is to identify the elements of digital environment and of human activity that are integrated in the "perceived quality" of such an environment. A number of empirical examples of analyses are presented below.

8.4.1   Analysis of Perceived Quality of a Personal Digital Assistant as a Tool of Professional Activity

To illustrate the perceived quality approach, a brief review of a few results obtained in the study of activity using a personal digital assistant (PDA) is given. A detailed analysis of this study is presented elsewhere (Lahlou et al. 2002; Lahlou and Nosulenko 2005).

The purpose of the study was to determine the peculiarities of the use of different PDAs in conditions of AE, as well as to identify the problems which users faced when fulfilling different professional goals. Two versions of PDA and one portable personal computer were compared during their actual use by participants for whom they were daily tools of professional activity. The study encompassed both individual activity (e.g., search for information in Internet), and joint activity (conference planning, information exchange on a joint project and notes during a conversation, etc.).

Each participant compared the devices when fulfilling the following goals:

1. To plan a meeting with a partner;
2. To find an address in the device's personal contact database;
3. To add new information to the address book;
4. To check up a mail-box, to compile and send a message to a certain addressee;
5. To find an address of a certain shop, using the Internet.

The analysis was aimed at identifying concrete tasks and operations the user executes to reach these goals with the help of each of the three devices. Simultaneously, subjective evaluations of the devices and their functions were recorded, as well as participants' comments on their own actions and operations, with a talking-out-loud protocol (Nosulenko and Samoylenko 1997, 2001).

Verbalizations obtained during participants' comments on their activity were coded with respect to their reference to the main components of the activity. Participants were requested both to describe the perceived quality of a certain device, and to comment on their on-going actions and operations. The activities and verbalizations as well as the state of screens of the devices tested were recorded by a digital video camera.

The data obtained in the study were processed for analysis of the perceived quality of the devices in the following directions:

- Identification of users' knowledge and experience in dealing with the evaluated device; in order to understand what helps users to anticipate their own operations and the system's responses.
- Identification of the qualities of the device (or of its components or of operations) which the user considers most important in each task.
- Definition of the axes characterizing similarities and differences between the compared devices and revealing the users' preferences for a certain device for a task.

In the course of the analysis, relations between the data received in external (video) observation and the data received from the participants' verbalizations were investigated. The statistical analysis of the video data included calculations of frequency of specific operations carried out in the course of a certain task, and identification of their sequences and length. Analysis of verbalizations was aimed at creating the so called "verbal portraits" of the devices, in general and for specific functions. Each verbal portrait is a profile of the evaluations of the device (in general, of only a specific function) on all the axes of evaluation. The peculiarities of the corresponding method of verbal data analysis are presented elsewhere (Nosulenko and Samoylenko 1997, 2001; Nosulenko 2007; Samoylenko 1986).

Here are several empirical illustrations. In the course of the study, a comparison was made between the set of operations explicitly planned in advance by the participants and those actually done in the task to "send an electronic message" using the device 'Palm Pilot IV', with which they were fluent (their 2 year experience of daily use).

Before test, we asked the subjects to describe precisely what they were going to do. The sequence of planned operations they gave turned out to be very precise: enter main menu, start program, open "new," enter mail address, put in subject matter, etc. The users considered that they thoroughly knew the way to solve the task.

However, the comparison with what they actually did showed that a considerable number of actual operations had not been foreseen: realization of those operations took 58% of the total time of execution of the task.

In practice, the user had to deal with some problems he had not anticipated. For example, the supposedly routine operation of entering the name of the addressee took an unexpectedly long time and elicited several additional operations. Because of the unexpected reactions of the system, this simple operation (i.e., automated routine sequence) transformed into a special task (i.e., consciously monitored sequence of actions): "enter e-mail address." Analysis revealed that the problem of entering the address in one of the devices (Palm Pilot IV) was connected primarily with the fact that the subject had used another device (I-Paq) for several months just before the test, and more or less lost the operation of entering the @ sign in Graffiti language. Indeed, with the I-Paq, the graphic conventions are closer to "normal" handwriting. When the subject attempted to use his I-Paq-bound skill when working with the Palma, it failed; and the subject took some time to identify correctly the nature of the problem and elaborated an alternative strategy. The verbal portraits of the two devices compared for the operation "writing" demonstrate the differences between the two devices (Fig. 8.2): Palm is perceived less "easy" for writing. The detailed analysis reveals

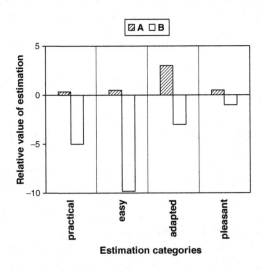

Fig. 8.2 Verbal portraits of the operations realized using the devices Palm Pilot ("A") and I-Paq ("B") as related to the text writing task (Lahlou et al. 2002). Positive direction of values means that, in the framework of a corresponding category, the majority of participants positively evaluated the device (for example, each participant evaluated the device "A" as an adapted one three times on the average). Negative values correspond to participants' negative attitude to a given device (each participant evaluated the device "B" as not adapted one 2, 9 times on the average)

exactly the reasons of this difference. If, per se, the Graffiti language used for Palm may be easier, the fact that subjects continuously use another convention (normal handwriting) makes the actions of entering data on the Palm less easy in actual life conditions than writing on the I-Paq which uses conventions closer to natural handwriting.

Here we see how our protocol uses the analysis of discrepancies between what is "foreseen" and what is really done as a way to find those moments in using the device that are problematic. This can be used as a general strategy.

Other examples demonstrate verbal portraits of the two devices used by a group of participants when performing two different tasks. On the Fig. 8.3a, the perceived quality of operations manifested in receiving, preparation and sending massages (task "mail") are shown. On the Fig. 8.3b, verbal portraits characterizing the perceived quality of two devices connected with the search of information and retrieval from the Internet (task "web") are given.

Such an analysis of perceived quality makes it possible to differentiate between those components which refer to "material" qualities of an object (general appearance, form, information representation, etc.) and those ones which refer to perception of operations carried out in the course of realization of this device. In some cases, as for example, in the "text writing" task, perception of operations fulfilled (e.g., "practical," "easy" "adapted" and "pleasant" operations of writing) stands on the first plan in the whole perceived quality of an object and as a result defines its evaluations. In other cases, as for example, in the "web" task, evaluation of information represented on the screen of the device becomes the leading one ("practical," "quick," "pleasant," "good quality," and "adapted" presentation of information). Such a presentation of data clarifies the areas where the use of a specific device is most efficient. As a result, a feed-back from the user of the device to the designer is ensured. (c.f. Fig. 8.1).

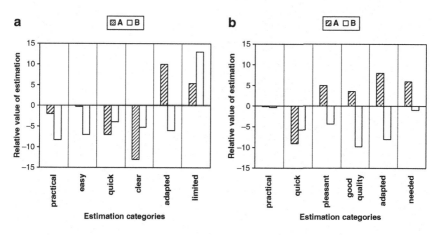

Fig. 8.3 Verbal portraits of the devices "A" and "B" in (**a**) task "mail" and (**b**) task "web" (Lahlou et al. 2002)

As we have mentioned above, the perceived quality approach presupposes an analysis of differences in subjective representations of the device that exist in the designer and in the user. This analysis should be carried out at the stage of designing the device. The examples presented below refer to the failure that took place in designing of the system when its perceived quality as existing in its users was not sufficiently taken into consideration.

8.4.2 The "HelloWall" in Two Different Contexts of Users' Tasks

The use of the system of artifacts by visitors participating in a big social event ("Printemps de la Recherche") was the object of analysis.[1] The new artifact called the "HelloWall" (interactive screen) was supposed by its developers to animate the general context of this event and to promote participant interaction. The HelloWall is an example of unobtrusive technology presenting abstract information via an ambient art-like display (Fig. 8.4). It shows by means of corresponding patterns presented on its display the current "mood" and people's presence, that is, a general atmosphere existing in the social space.

Fig. 8.4 The installation of the "HelloWall" near the entrance of a social event space (the failure in its use)

---

[1] Ambient Agoras (IST/Disappearing Computer Initiative contract No IST-2000–25134). Cf. Streitz et al. 2007.

This study was based on the ethnomethodological paradigm that presupposed a detailed observation of visitor's behavior in a natural setting of the social event. The main idea of evaluation concerned both specific features of the given artifact and its social functions. The artifact was predicted to have a special communicative function: facilitating exchange between participants of the "Printemps de la Recherche" with their ideas about what is happening there. This function was considered by designers to be a very important one.

However, according to the analysis of activities carried out by visitors of the "Printemps de la Recherche" as well as according to their subjective evaluations of the HelloWall, the communicative function didn't play an important role in the participants' "perceived qualities" of this artifact. The failure in use of this artifact was shown: participants didn't appreciate it. The artifact's functions which were expected to be very important by its designers were not revealed in perceived qualities existing in participants. The reason of that failure might be explained by insufficient analysis of needs and goals of participants of the given social event at the preliminary stage of designing of this system. It seems to be typical for the cases of designing new technologies when it is the device rather than its use for an activity which is the main point of interest.

These conclusions were supported by the results of another study where the same artifact was used to support distributed joint activity. The HelloWall screens were installed in two working spaces: IPSI (Darmstadt, Germany) and Laboratory of Design for Cognition (LDC EDF R&D, Clamart, France). In the course of the study, the two laboratories were fulfilling one and the same task – preparation of report on the European project. Two HelloWalls were introduced into a united communicative system that also had another tools of interaction (videoconference, e-mail, telephone, etc.).

On the screens, the patterns constructed in advance could be presented. The patterns were supposed to help: (1) to get information about the presence of remote partners (visualization of personal symbols of participants), (2) to show the degree of presence of members of a corresponding laboratory, (3) to ask the partners for a video conference by means of the so called "Request Pattern" (each team possessed the Request button (used), and (4) to reflect the general mood that exists in the partner laboratory (Fig. 8.5).

General atmosphere and mood that existed in labs were evaluated by research workers themselves: each team possessed a 3-buttons unit to communicate a local mood to distant team members. By means of this device, each participant introduced into the system his (her) evaluations of mood choosing between "bad," "average" and "good" (Fig. 8.6). The mean value of all individual evaluations served as the basis for automatic presentation of the pattern representing the general mood existing in this or that lab. Thus, a possibility of exchange of information concerning general mood taking place in collaborating labs was ensured.

Information about presence and activities of researchers was generalized by the system on the basis of data received from electronic detectors, as well as from video images given by OffSat cameras (displacements of researchers, etc.). Observation of the process of the HelloWall usage lead to a conclusion that information

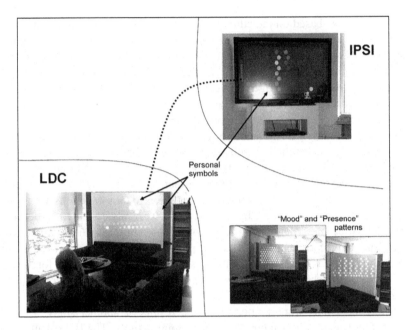

Fig. 8.5 The installation of the "HelloWall" to support distributed joint activity (the relative success in its use)

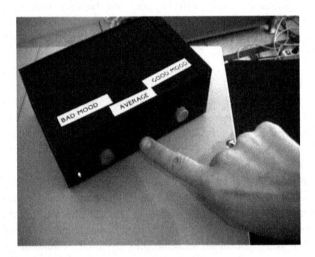

Fig. 8.6 A device used to communicate the level of mood

represented on the screens was useful for fulfilling joint activity. Information about presence and activities of the lab's members played a positive role: the higher the level of presence identified by the system, the more was the communications initiated by their partner lab.

According to the OffSat video recordings, participants spent considerable amount of their working time near the HelloWall. They tried to identify symbols of their partners whom they wanted to enter into a contact with, as well as the local mood and presence at the remote lab. A cause and effect relationship was identified between the information represented on the HelloWall and attempts of connection through a videoconference.

An analysis of questionnaires filled by participants in the course of 12 days showed that their general impression from using the HelloWall was positive. This was explained by a possibility to know about the general atmosphere of what was happening in another lab. This possibility was considered to be extremely important for the establishment good relationships between the labs and for facilitating mutual communications. The HelloWall made the labs' members feel less isolated.

Thus, we may confirm that the real functional use of the HelloWall was determined by the presence of concrete tasks. In the first situation ("Printemps de la Recherche" social event), this artifact itself didn't attract special attention since it was not inscribed into the set of tasks of the participants of the social event. In the second situation, the same device helped to stimulate communication between remote participants of joint distributed activity. Thus, the device found itself useful for solving joint goals by people actively using it in the course of interaction.

8.4.3 The Perceived Quality as Related to the Goals of Activity

What an individual perceives in an object depends upon what he is going to do with it. Here is an example referring to the use of another artifact (called the "Videomaton") representing information about the given social event for its participants (Fig. 8.7). The large screen represented the video clips which participants were able to choose for viewing. The clips contained brief interviews with people visiting the social event. The interviews were taken by the "video-journalist," transformed into clips and stocked into the system in real time.

According to the designers, the artifact which was included into the social context was to help the visitors to effectively use the space, to localize subjectively important objects, to identify interesting people and learn their point of view on what was happening there and chose the information worthy of interest. The system had to integrate information distributed in space and time as well as to present it to the visitors. An attractive form of this device and the content of its clips were supposed to promote interaction between the visitors and animate the general context of the social event.

In other words, the artifact was conceived to help visitors to create subjective representations about what was happening (perceived quality of the event).

We supposed that the visitors' goals would have an impact on the perceived quality of the artifact.

Fig. 8.7 The installation of the "Videomaton" in context of social event

In the course of the study, an analysis of comments given by participants when using this device was carried out. As a result, several groups of visitors were identified on the basis of their goals for visiting the social event.

- The first group of visitors had the only goal "to walk through" the pleasant environment.
- The second group of visitors had the goal "to meet colleagues," who were present in the context of this social event.
- The third group of participants had a precise goal directly related to the goal of the scientific social event, that is, "to visit stands."
- The forth group of participants were interested in the content of the event and had a goal "to ask for information."

A comparison of perceived qualities of the given artifact that were specific for different groups of participants was made. Comments given by those visitors who more or less used the Videomaton (491 individuals) were analyzed. In the course of the analysis, 225 verbal units referring to Videomaton's social functions were extracted from the whole set of verbal data. In the most of cases, these functions related to the informational capacities of this artifact. The following main groups of judgments were revealed.

- *Information access facility*, containing such utterances as: "gives additional information," "gives a panorama of what's going on," "concentrates information," "gives a possibility to learn a lot of new information," "it's an informational wall," "gives a possibility to learn different points of view", etc.

- *Facilitation of identification of personal points of view*, containing the utterances referring to those kinds of information presented in the video clips that refer to different personal points of view on the ongoing events. Here are several examples of the utterances: *these are personal comments, it's good to understand the points of view of other people on what's going on, you have a possibility to see somebody's attitude, it shows personal impressions, it gives a possibility to personally meet a colleague, I see those people whom I know*, etc.
- *Facilitation of Social perception*, containing the utterances referring to the Videomaton's role in the representation of the general social context, of the social interaction and communication that took place at the "Printemps de la Recherche." Here are several examples of the utterances: *it gives a possibility to meet a lot of people at once, it's a means of real life communication, here, we are together, it's a real interaction, I have a possibility to see my acquaintances*, etc.
- *Facilitation of spatial organization of information*, containing the utterances referring to the advantages given by the Videomaton for the spatial organization of information represented at the Y building. Here are several examples of the utterances: *it helps to avoid unnecessary transitions, it helps to see how the stands are located in space, it's interesting to see the spatial picture of the events, you see at once where you need to go*, etc.
- *Facilitation of time organization*, containing the utterances referring to information that gives a possibility to visitors to effectively distribute their time in the course of their visit. Here are several examples of the utterances: *it gives more time for communication, it helps to gain time, we have a possibility to see everybody at once, there is a possibility to make a search in time, we can see what happens at what time moment*, etc.
- *Usefulness for social events' organization*, containing the utterances referring to Videomaton's usefulness as an effective means of organization of large social events. Here are several examples of the utterances: *it's useful for large congresses, it can be successfully used for the organization of large scale events*, etc.
- *Event's tracing*, containing the utterances referring to the Videomaton as a means that could be used by people to retrieve information concerning the events that have taken place some time ago as well as to subjectively represent the events' time sequences. Here are several examples of the utterances: *it's useful to understand what has happened, it gives a possibility to reconstruct the sequences of events, I can learn what has happened yesterday, it helps to retrieve from memory the most interesting information*, etc.
- *Presence effect insurance* contains the utterances about people's satisfaction with a possibility of co-presence with the ongoing events given by the Videomaton. Here are several examples of the utterances: *I am a part of the whole range of events taking place at the Printemps de la Recherche, I have a feeling to be everywhere, «all different events are taking place just close to me*, etc.
- *General Mood expression*, containing the utterances referring to the function of the Videomaton to represent the general emotional atmosphere taking place at

the social event. Here are several examples of the utterances: *you can feel the mood of people, I see that everybody is satisfied*, etc.

First of all, frequencies of appearance of these different categories of judgments referring to the artifact social functions were calculated.

The percentage of the different categories of judgments for four different goals of visit significantly varied. On Fig. 8.8, only the most significant categories of judgments representing in sum more than 90% of the whole set of judgments produced by the visitors of each group are represented.

As Fig. 8.8 shows, not more than 3 categories of judgments used to the evaluate social functions of the artifact were identified. Only for the goal "to ask for information" four categories of evaluative judgments were revealed. Depending on the goal of activity, different categories of judgments were most frequently used. For example, the judgments belonging to the category "Information access facility" were most often used by visitors who have come to get information. People who have come with the principal goal to meet colleagues judged the artifact from the point of view of the possibilities given by it to facilitate social perception. For both groups of visitors, the function of facilitation of personal identification was important. People having the goal to visit the stands attributed a special importance to the function that helps to orient oneself in the space organization of the stands. People who didn't have a special goal of visit ("To walk through") preferred to give judgments concerning the usefulness of the artifact for social events.

A more detailed analysis of these results is presented elsewhere (Lahlou et al. 2007; Nosulenko et al. 2003; Nosulenko 2008).

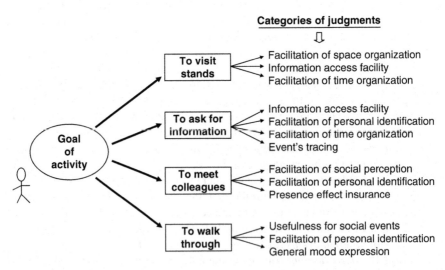

Fig. 8.8 Significant categories of judgments concerning artifact's social functions as related to the goals of visit

8.5 Conclusion

One of the issues discussed in this chapter concerns the question about "what" is perceived by individuals and groups being the actors of AE as well as "how" to interpret a set of its valuable components – its perceived qualities – in order to explain peculiarities of human activity taking place in the AE.

These questions turn out to be particularly important for the study of digital environment where distribution in space and time of the objects and subjects of activity take place. The approach of "perceived quality" proposes a concrete way of scientific analysis of these questions and can have different perspectives of investigation. Knowledge about main components of activity and content of mental images formed in individuals gives the valuable points of departure for revealing those parameters that are needed for comparison. The goals and intentions of people being in the digital environment represent the functional core for unifying different types of data obtained in different types of studies.

References

Abulkhanova KA (2007) Le sujet de l'activité ou la théorie de l'activité selon S.L. Rubinstein. In: Nosulenko V, Rabardel P (eds) Rubinstein aujourd'hui. Nouvelles figures de l'activité humaine. Octarès – Maison des Sciences de l'Homme, Toulouse – Paris, pp 83–128

Barabanchtchikov VA (2007) La question de l'activité dans la psychologie russe. In: Nosulenko V, Rabardel P (eds) Rubinstein aujourd'hui. Nouvelles figures de l'activité humaine. Octarès – Maison des Sciences de l'Homme, Toulouse – Paris, pp 41–82

Deschamp J-P, Nayak PR (1996) Les maîtres de l'innovation totale. Paris: Editions d'Organisation

Ehn P (1992) Scandinavian Design: On Participation and Skill. In: Adler PS, Winograd TA (eds) Usability: Turning technologies into tools. New York: Oxford University Press, pp 96–132

Gale BT (1994) Creating quality and service that customer can see. New York: The Free Press

Giordano J-L (2006) L'approche qualité perçue. Paris: Editions d'Organisation

Hill N, Self B, Roche G (2001) Customer satisfaction measurement for ISO 9000:2000. Oxford: Butterworth Heinemann

Horovitz J (1987) La qualité de service. A la conquête du client. Paris: InterEditions

Kyng M, Mathiassen L (1997) Computers and design in context. Cambridge, MA: MIT

Lahlou S, Nosulenko V (2005) Eksperimental'naya real'nost': sistemnaya paradigma izutchenia i konstruirovania raschirennykh sred' (Experimental reality: systems paradigm of study and design of augmented environment). In: Barabanshikov V. (ed) Ideya sistemnosti v sovremennoi psikhologii (Systems ideas in contemporary psychology), Moscow: Institute of Psychology, Russian Academy of Sciences: pp 433–468

Lahlou S, Nosulenko V, Samoylenko E (2002) Un cadre méthodologique pour le design des environnements augmentés. Social Science Information Sur Les Sciences Sociales 41(4): 471–530

Lahlou S, Nosulenko V, Samoylenko E (2007) 'Sredsva obshchenia s kontekste individual';noi i sovmestnoi deyatel'nosti' (Communication tools in context of individual and joint activity) In: Barabanshikov V, Samoylenko E (eds) Obshchenie i poznanie (Communication and cognition), Moscow: Institute of Psychology, Russian Academy of Sciences. pp 407–434

Leont'ev AN (1975) Activité, conscience, personnalité. Moscow: Editions du Progrès

Lomov BF (1966) Tchelovek i tekhnika (man and technology). Moscow: Sovetskoe radio (Soviet Radio)

Lomov BF (1977) O putiakh postroenia injenernoi psikhologii (Perspectives of construction of engineering psychology). In: Lomov BF, Rubakhin VF, Venda VF (eds) Injenernaia psikhologia (Engineering Psychology), Moscow: Nauka (Science), pp 31–54

Lomov BF (1984) Teoria i metodologia psikhologii (Theory and methodology of psychology). Moscow: Nauka (Science)

Nardi BA (1996) Context and consciousness: activity theory and human-computer interaction. Cambridge: MIT

Norman DA, Draper S (1986) User centred system design: New perspectives in Human Computer Interaction. Hillsdale, NJ: Lawrence Erlbaum Associates

Nosulenko V (1986) A system approach to the study of auditory perception. *Soviet Journal of Psychology* 7(5): 555–565

Nosulenko V (1989) The psychophysics of a complex signals: problems and perspectives. *Soviet Psychology* 17(1): 62–78

Nosulenko V (2007) Psikhofizika vospriatia estestvennoj sredy. Problema vosprinimaemogo katchestva (Psychophysics of perception of natural environment. A problem of perceived quality). Moscow: Institute of Psychology, Russian Academy of Sciences

Nosulenko V (2008) Mesurer les activités numérisées par leur qualité perçue. *Information Sur Les Sciences Sociales, Numéro Spéciale: Technologies Cognitives* 47(3): 391–417

Nosulenko V, Rabardel P (1998) Ergonomie, psychologie et travail dans les pays de l'ex-URSS. (Historicité et spécificité du développement). In: Dessaigne MF, Gaillard I (eds) Des évolutions en ergonomie... Octarès, Toulouse, pp 13–28

Nosulenko V, Rabardel P (eds) (2007) Rubinstein aujourd'hui. Nouvelles figures de l'activité humaine. Toulouse & Paris: Octarès & Editions de la Maison des Sciences de l'Homme

Nosulenko V, Samoylenko E (1997) Approche systémique de l'analyse des verbalisations dans le cadre de l'étude des processus perceptifs et cognitifs. *Information sur les Sciences Sociales* 36(2): 223–261

Nosulenko V, Samoylenko E (2001) Évaluation de la qualité perçue des produits et services: approche interdisciplinaire. *International journal of design and innovation research* 2(2): 35–60

Nosulenko V, Samoylenko E, Welinski P (2003) Hello Wall and Videomaton user experience. observation and evaluation. In: Ambient agoras: dynamic information clouds in a hybrid world. Darmstadt: IST. pp 203–279

Nosulenko V, Barabanshikov VA, Brushlinsky A, Rabardel P (2005) Man-technology interaction: some of the Russian approaches. *Theoretical Issues in Ergonomics Science* 6(5): 359–383

Oshanin DA (1973) Predmetnoe dejstvie i operativnyj obraz (Object related action and operative image). Unpublished Thesis, Moscow: Institute of psychology, USSR Academy of pedagogical sciences

Rubinstein SL (1922) Printsip tvorcheskoi samodeyatel'nosti (Principle of creative activity) *Uchenye zapiski Vysshei shkoly g. Odessy* (Scientific reports of high school of Odessa), 2: 148 – 54. (French version: Rubinstein SL (2007) In: Nosulenko V, Rabardel P (eds) Rubinstein aujourd'hui. Nouvelles figures de l'activité humaine, Toulouse & Paris: Octarès & Editions de la Maison des Sciences de l'Homme), pp 129–40

Rubinstein SL (1957) Bytie i soznanie (The being and consciens). Moscow: USSR Academy of Sciences

Samoylenko E (1986) Operatsiya sravneniya pri reshenii kognitivno-kommunikativnykh zadach (Operation of comparison in cognitive-communicative tasks). Unpublished Thesis, Moscow: Institute of psychology, USSR Academy of Sciences

Streitz N, Prante T, Röcker C, van Alphen D, Stenzel R, Magerkurth C, Lahlou S, Nosulenko V, Jégou F, Sonder F, Plewe D (2007) Smart artefacts as affordances for awareness in distributed teams. In: Streitz N, Kameas A, Mavrommati I (eds) the disappearing computer. Lecture notes in computer science, vol 4500. Heidelberg: Springer, pp 3–29

Zavalova ND, Lomov BF, Ponomarenko VA (1986) Obraz v sisteme psykhitcheskoj regulyatsii deyatel'nosti (The image in the system of mental regulation of the activity). Moscow: Nauka (Science)

Chapter 9
Opportunities and Challenges for Augmented Environments: A Distributed Cognition Perspective

James D. Hollan and Edwin L. Hutchins

Abstract Currently a new generation of inexpensive digital recording devices and storage facilities is revolutionizing data collection in behavioral science, extending it into situations that have not been typically accessible and enabling the examination of the fine details of action captured in meaningful settings. The ability to record and share such data has not only created a critical moment in the practice and scope of behavioral research but also presents unprecedented opportunities and challenges for the design of future augmented environments. In this chapter, we discuss these challenges and argue that fully capitalizing on the associated opportunities requires theoretical and methodological frameworks to effectively analyze data that capture the richness of real-world human activity. We sample five recent research projects from our laboratory chosen to exemplify a distributed cognition perspective and highlight opportunities and challenges relevant to the design and evaluation of augmented environments.

9.1 Introduction

There is currently a shift in cognitive science toward a view of cognition as a property of systems that are larger than isolated individuals. This extends the reach of cognition to encompass interactions between people as well as interactions with resources in the environment. As a consequence, the human body and material world take on central rather than peripheral roles. As Andy Clark put it, "To thus take the body and the world seriously is to invite an emergentist perspective on many key phenomena – to see adaptive success as inhering as much in complex interactions among body, world, and brain as in the inner processes bounded by the skin and skull." (Clark 1997) This new perspective is emerging from the fields of

J.D. Hollan (✉)
Department of Cognitive Science, Distributed Cognition and Human-Computer
Interaction Lab, University of California, San Diego, CA, USA
e-mail: hollan@cogsci.ucsd.edu

S. Lahlou (ed.), *Designing User Friendly Augmented Work Environments: From Meeting Rooms to Digital Collaborative Spaces,* Computer Supported Cooperative Work, DOI 10.1007/978-1-84800-098-8_9, © Springer-Verlag London Limited 2009

distributed cognition (Hutchins 1995a, b; Goodwin 2000; Hollan et al. 2000), embodied interaction (Clark 1997; Nunez 1996; Dourish 2001), and dynamical cognition (Port and van Gelder 1995; Thelen and Smith 1994).

Our research group at UCSD is dedicated to developing the theoretical and methodological foundations engendered by adopting this broader view of cognition and interaction and understanding how it can support the design of effective computer-mediated environments. Research in our lab ranges across cognitive science. We are particularly interested in understanding interactions among people and technology. Our work combines ethnographic observation and controlled experimentation to support theoretically informed design of digital work materials and collaborative work environments. Members of our lab are united in the belief that distributed cognition is a particularly fertile framework for designing and evaluating augmented environments and digital artifacts. A central image for us is workplaces in which people pursue their goals in collaboration with the elements of the social and material world. Our core research efforts are directed at understanding such environments: what we really do in them, how we coordinate our activity in them, and what role technology should play in them.

Currently a new generation of inexpensive digital recording devices and storage facilities is revolutionizing data collection in behavioral science, extending it into situations that have not been typically accessible and enabling the examination of the fine details of action captured in meaningful settings. Researchers from many disciplines are beginning to take advantage of increasingly inexpensive digital video and storage facilities to assemble extensive data collections of human activity captured in real-world settings. The ability to record and share such data has not only created a critical moment in the practice and scope of behavioral research but also presents unprecedented challenges and opportunities for the design of future augmented environments.

In this chapter, we discuss these challenges and argue that to fully capitalize on the associated opportunities three main issues must be addressed: (1) developing the theoretical and methodological frameworks required to effectively analyze rich real-world behavioral data, (2) reducing the huge time investments currently required for analysis and (3) understanding how to visualize and coordinate analyses focused at different scales so as to profit fully from the complementary perspectives of multiple disciplines. We first discuss the underlying behavioral challenge and then briefly introduce distributed cognition, the theoretical foundation for our work, and cognitive ethnography, the methodological approach we are developing. We then focus on examples (projects) from our lab to exemplify the approaches we are taking for capturing and analyzing data from real-world settings. We end the chapter with a set of lessons for the design of augmented environments.

9.2   A Challenge for Behavioral Science

What conditions can facilitate rapid advances and breakthroughs in behavioral science to rival those seen in the biological and physical sciences in the past century?

The emergence of cognitive science and the converging view across multiple disciplines that human behavior is a complex dynamic interaction among biological, cognitive, linguistic, social, and cultural processes are important first steps. While empirical and theoretical work is rapidly advancing at the biological end of this continuum, understanding such a complex system also necessitates data that capture the richness of the real-world human activity and analytic frameworks that can exploit that richness. This is important because to understand the dynamics of human and social activity, we must first understand the full context of those activities and this can only be accomplished by recording and analyzing data of real-world behavior. While such data are certainly needed, mere data cannot be the whole answer, since many researchers already feel that they are drowning in data. Data without appropriate theoretical and analytical frameworks do not lead to scientific advances.

Fortunately the revolution in digital technology can be coupled with exciting recent developments in cognitive theory. While these developments also heighten the importance of understanding the nature of real-world activities, they are in addition beginning to provide an analytic framework for understanding how cognition is embedded in concrete contexts of human activity. As described earlier, cognition is increasingly viewed as a process that extends beyond the skin and skull of the individual (Pea 1993; Hutchins 1995a, b; Cole 1996; Nardi 1996; Hollan et al. 2000; Clark 2003; Rogoff 2003). This shift in framing the unit of analysis for cognition introduces a host of previously overlooked cognitive phenomena to be documented, studied and understood.

Rich new digital data sources coupled with this shift in theory promise to advance the understanding of the links between what is in the mind, and what the mind is in. For example, just as widespread availability of audio tape recording supported the development of conversational analysis (Goodwin and Heritage 1990; Hutchby and Wooffitt 1998; Prevignano and Thibault 2003) and the ethnography of speaking (Gumperz and Hymes 1986; Bauman and Sherzer 1989), the advent of inexpensive digital video is starting to have a fundamental impact on cognitive science. The ability to record, view, and re-view the fine details of action in meaningful settings has made it possible to examine the phenomena at the core of embodied (Varela et al. 1991; Brooks 1991; Thelen and Smith 1994; Clark 1997; Lakoff and Johnson 1999), situation (Suchman 1987; Lave 1988; Brown et al. 1989; Chaiklin and Lave 1996; Clancy 1997) and distributed cognition (Hutchins 1995a, b; Clark 2001). The rise of studies in gesture in the past decade was also made possible by these technological changes and it is now transforming fields such as linguistics (McNeill 2005) and education (Goldin-Meadow 2003).

Sensor technologies starting to be deployed in augmented environments and new computational algorithms promise to further extend this transformation by enabling automatic recognition, tracking, and summarization of the meaningful components of the audio-video data (Zhao et al. 2003; Jones and Jones 2004). Thus, changes in theory give us new phenomena to see and provide new relevance to things already seen. Developments in digital technology create potential for new tools with which to see those things (Hollan et al. 1997; Card et al. 1999). Understanding these changes and developments are central to advances in behavioral science and these advances in turn provide a scientific foundation for the design of augmented environments.

9.3 Distributed Cognition

Distributed cognition promises to be a fertile theoretical framework for exploring the dynamics of human activity and for providing a foundation for design of augmented environments. It extends conceptions of cognitive processes beyond individual interaction and challenges key implicit presuppositions of current views. Like any cognitive theory, distributed cognition seeks to understand the organization of cognitive systems. And like most of cognitive science, it takes cognitive processes to be those that are involved in memory, decision making, inference, reasoning, learning, and so on. What distinguishes distributed cognition from other approaches is the commitment to two related theoretical principles.

The first of these principles concerns the boundaries of the unit of analysis for cognition. In every area of science, the choices made concerning the boundaries of the unit of analysis have important implications. Boundaries are often a matter of tradition in a field. In distributed cognition, one expects to find a system of systems that can dynamically configure itself to bring sub-systems into coordination to accomplish various functions. A cognitive process is delimited by the functional relationships among the elements that participate in it, rather than by the spatial co-location of the elements. Sometimes the traditionally assumed boundaries of the individual are exactly right. For other phenomena, however, these boundaries are not right because they either span too much or too little. Distributed cognition looks for cognitive processes wherever they may occur and does that looking on the basis of the functional relationships of elements that participate together in the process. A process is not cognitive simply because it happens in a brain, nor is a process non-cognitive simply because it happens in the interactions among many brains. For example, we have found it productive to consider small socio-technical systems such as the bridge of a ship (Hutchins 1995a, b), an airline cockpit (Hutchins 1995a, b; Hutchins and Klausen 1996), and as we discuss later, an automobile, a law office, and an augmented environment to assist interaction between deaf patients and physicians, as the unit of analysis.

The second principle concerns the range of mechanisms that may be assumed to participate in the cognitive processes. Whereas psychology looks for cognitive events in neural events inside individual actors, distributed cognition looks for a broader class of cognitive events and does not expect all such events to be encompassed by the skin or skull of an individual. For example, an examination of memory processes in an airline cockpit shows that memory involves a rich interaction between internal processes, the manipulation of objects, and the traffic in representations among the pilots. A complete theory of individual memory by itself is insufficient to understand how this memory system works. And a complete theory of internal cognitive functioning by itself is insufficient to understand the dynamics of human activity in augmented environments.

9.3.1   Distributed Cognition and Human Activity

When one applies these principles to the observation of human activity *in the wild*, at least three interesting kinds of distribution of cognitive process become apparent: (1) Cognitive processes may be distributed across the members of a social group. Tracking these processes produces insights about the dynamics of the social processes. (2) Cognitive processes may be distributed in the sense that the operation of the cognitive system involves coordination between internal and external (material or environmental) structure. Tracking these processes produces insights about the dynamics of agent/environment relations and is particularly relevant for understanding and designing augmented environments. (3) Processes may be distributed through time in such a way that the products of earlier events can transform the nature of later events. Tracking these processes produces insights about the dynamics of social and cultural systems on longer timescales. The effects of these distributions of process are extremely important to an understanding of human cognitive accomplishments as products of human social dynamics and as a basis for building effective augmented environments.

9.3.2   Embodied Cognition

Distributed cognition theory embraces the movement in cognitive science toward a conception of embodied cognition. From this perspective, the organization of mind – both in development and in operation – is an emergent property of interactions among internal and external resources. In this view, the human body and the material world take on central rather than peripheral roles. For the understanding of human social dynamics, this means that elements of the social and material environment are more than simply stimuli for a disembodied cognitive system. Social and material patterns become elements of the cognitive system itself. This theoretical perspective promises an intellectual basis for a paradigm shift in thinking about human social dynamics and the design of augmented environments; one that takes material and social structures to be elements of cognitive systems and views on-going activity as a continually renegotiated emergent product of interaction.

9.3.3   Cognition and Culture

With the much more intimate relation between mind and environment that is provided by distributed cognition theory, comes the possibility of seeing new kinds of relations between culture and cognition. Hutchins treats this at length in his book, *Cognition in the Wild* (Hutchins 1995a, b). These new relations appear when we address the functional specifications for human cognition. What is a mind really used for? How are thinking tasks really done in the everyday world?

Permitting the boundary of the unit of analysis to move out beyond the skin situates the individual as an element in a complex cultural environment. In doing this, we find that cognition is no longer isolated from culture or separate from it. Where cognitive science traditionally views culture as a body of content on which the cognitive processes of individual persons operate, in the distributed cognition perspective, culture, in the form of a history of material artifacts and social practices, shapes the dynamics of the cognitive systems that transcend the boundaries of individual persons.

A central idea in distributed cognition is the notion of intelligence as an emergent property of interactions. This idea is reinforced by the connectionist challenge to traditional models of cognitive processing, and we have developed connectionist models of the emergence of structure in the interactions among networks in a community of networks. Connectionism, however, says nothing about the marginalization of the body and world. So to the idea of emergence, we add the idea that persons are embedded in complex environments that can be seen as active resources for learning, problem solving and reasoning. Culture is a process that accumulates partial solutions to frequently encountered problems. We live with the residue of previous activity and that is both enabling and constraining. Both culture and biology work this way and this fundamental fact gives life and mind a dynamic signature that is not seen in strictly physical systems (Thompson 2007). The intellectual tools that culture provides enable us to accomplish things that we could not do without them. At the same time, though they may blind us to other ways of thinking and make some things seem impossible, culture is a process that involves the interactions of mental structure, material structure, and social structure.

Distributed cognition returns culture, context, and history, to the picture of cognition. But these things cannot be added on to the existing model of cognitive processes without modifying the old model. That is, the new view of culturally embedded cognition requires that we remake our model of the individual mind in ways that incorporate social, cultural, and environmental structures as well as the wider ecologies of activity systems and processes involved in meaningful human activity.

Similarly, data about real-world activity becomes essential to evaluating models of cognition and ethnography, the fine-grained examination of real-world behavior, and plays an increasingly crucial role. The methods of participant observation and analysis of audio and video recordings are the stock in trade of the ethnographer. These methods build up representation of activity systems in real-world contexts. They address questions such as "What are people really doing?," "What are they trying to do?," "What reasons do they give themselves and each other for doing what they do?"

9.4 Cognitive Ethnography

As a basis for work in our laboratory we are developing a method that we call *cognitive ethnography*. The goal of cognitive ethnography is an improved functional specification for the human cognitive system. Cognitive psychology has traditions of testing hypotheses within particular research paradigms, but the relevance of these hypotheses to the activities that people actually engage in is largely unknown (Neisser 1982). Concerns about the ecological validity of experiments have fostered attempts to assess the relationship between experimental tasks and real-world tasks (Cole 1996). Yet, there is no way to address this relationship in the absence of a careful study of real-world cognition.

Historically, cognitive ethnography has fallen between the borders of the traditional disciplines of psychology, anthropology, sociology, communication, and linguistics. While each of these fields has an interest in either cognition or ethno graphy, until very recently ethnographic studies of cognition have been rare. The most significant initiative in this domain came in the 1960s and 70s when cognitive anthropology emerged as a distinct subfield. But there the theoretical framework of the studies was a sort of information processing psychology that saw cognition as a disembodied process (D'Andrade 1995). Because of these theoretical roots, ethnographic studies of cognition in this tradition ignored everyday activity (Werner and Schoepfle 1987).

A primary goal of cognitive ethnography is to better understand everyday activity.

Fine-grained examination of real-world behavior provides evidence counter to two traditional divides. First, an examination of cognition situated in interactions with the social and material world narrows the gap between thought and action. Doing is a kind of thinking and thinking is doing. Perception and action turn out to be more closely related than had previously been thought (Clark 2001; Noë 2003). Second, real-world activity always has an affective component. Cognition and emotion are more closely linked than has traditionally been assumed. The examination of real-world activity can reveal the nature of this linkage (Goodwin and Goodwin 2001). These considerations create a demand for ethnographic studies that focus on cognitive processes as they are enacted in naturally situated activity. We call this cognitive ethnography.

The theoretical emphasis from distributed cognition is reflected in a methodological focus on events. Since the dynamic cognitive properties of systems that are larger than an individual play out in the activity of the people in them, a cognitive ethnography must be an event-centered ethnography. We are interested not only in what people know, but in how they go about using what they know, to do what they do.

It is important to note that cognitive ethnography is not any single data collection or analysis technique. Rather it brings together many specific techniques, some of which have been developed and refined in other disciplines (e.g., interviewing, surveys, participant observation, video and audio recording). Which specific technique is applied depends on the nature of the setting and the questions being investigated. Because of the prominence of events and activity in distributed cognition theory, we give special attention to video and audio recording of events.

As alluded to earlier, a new generation of inexpensive digital recording devices and storage facilities is revolutionizing data collection in behavioral science, extending it into situations that have not typically been accessible and enabling examination of the fine details of action captured in meaningful settings. The ability to record and share such data has not only created a critical moment in the practice and scope of behavioral research but also presents unprecedented opportunities and challenges for the design of future augmented environments. In the next section, we briefly discuss examples of research projects attempting to meet these challenges and exploit opportunities presented by new technological facilities.

9.5 Examples of Research Projects: Lessons for Designing Augmented Environments

Here we sample five recent research projects from our laboratory. Each was chosen to exemplify a distributed cognition perspective and highlight opportunities and challenges relevant to the design of augmented environments. The first project demonstrates the richness of activity that can be captured by augmenting an automobile with ten cameras and discusses the opportunity for computer-vision techniques to assist the analysis of the video data. The second describes projects capturing histories of workstation activity and the analysis challenge the finding of patterns in this rich data. The third highlights the challenges and opportunities of using data from high-fidelity flight simulators to help to understand the complex socio-technical system of commercial aviation. The fourth describes the challenge of designing a multimodal augmented environment to assist communication between deaf patients and non-signing physicians. The fifth describes opportunities associated with creating paper and audio augmented digital documents.

9.5.1 Video Capture of Driving Activity: The Opportunity of Computer Vision to Reduce the Cost of Analysis

Computer vision techniques have advanced in capabilities and reliability to the point that they promise to be highly useful tools for aiding analysis of video data. To characterize this potential we describe recent experience automatically annotating video recordings of driving activities. The goal of this project is to understand the cognitive ecology of driving as the basis for designing instrumentation and controls to augment and improve driver safety (McCall et al. 2004; Boer et al. 2005). In order to ground design in real driving behavior, our lab in collaboration with Mohan Trivedi's Computer Vision and Robotics Research Lab instrumented an automobile to record multiple video streams and time-stamped readings of instruments and controls. This included video from a head-band 3rd-Eye camera we developed and from an array of other cameras (see Fig. 9.1) positioned to capture views from within and around the car, as well as of the driver's face and feet. Timeline-based representations were particularly useful for assisting with analysis of video of this rich activity data and for associating data from multiple instruments. Figure 9.2 depicts graphs of selected car parameters coordinated by time and linked to GPS-derived freeway locations.

Fig. 9.1 *Top*: Head-band "3rd Eye" camera (*left and middle*) and view from it (*right*). *Bottom*: Example views from selected other cameras (composite on *left*, omniview in *center*, and rear view on *left*)

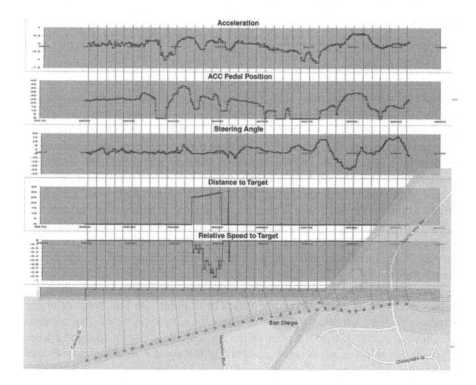

Fig. 9.2 Results from an analysis tool we developed to allow analysts to graph selected car parameters. This can include results from automated video analyses and can be linked by time or to GPS-derived freeway locations

We are encouraged by our success in automatically annotating this video data to aid analysis. For example, we developed code to compute the lateral angular velocity of the head from the 3rd-Eye camera video. This allows identification of even small head position adjustments as well as glances to the rear view mirror, glances to the left or right side mirror, and large over-the-shoulder head movements. By thresholding the amplitude of recorded audio we indexed times when someone was speaking in the car. Foot motion and lateral foot position were extracted from a "Foot-Cam" video using a simple detection algorithm. In combination with recordings of brake pedal pressure this easily enables determining, for example, when drivers move their foot to the brake in preparation for braking. We also developed a code to determine where the hands were positioned on the steering wheel and to automatically compute lateral position of the car as a basis for detecting lane changes. It is important to note that unlike most work in computer vision, annotating video to aid analysis does not typically require real-time processing. Offline processing is usually sufficient.

This work has led to an on-going effort in our lab to build an Ethnographers Workbench that integrates a variety of computer-vision and other facilities to assist annotation and analysis of video data. While we do not have space to review all the vision-based techniques we see as promising for automatic annotation, we briefly mention two examples: object recognition and face and emotion detection.

9.5.1.1 Object Recognition

It would be a boon to digital video analysis if the computer could automatically label all (or even most) frames or segments of a video in which a particular object is present. For example, if analysts are interested in activities involving interaction with specific objects, they might want to view only those segments of video that involve those objects. One very promising candidate technique uses distinctive invariant features extracted from training images as a basis for matching different images of an object. An important aspect of the Scale Invariant Feature Transform (SIFT) technique (Lowe 2004) is that it generates large numbers of features that densely cover the image over the full range of scales and locations. The features are invariant to image scale and rotation, and provide robust matching across a substantial range of affine distortions, additions of noise, and changes in viewpoint and illumination.

Since this algorithm is probabilistic, we can allow the user to modify the algorithm's threshold depending upon the task. For example, the threshold for object detection could be set at a low value in which virtually every frame that contains the object is detected, with the price of having some false alarms (flagged frames in which the object is not actually present). In this case, a small amount of user intervention would be required in order to cull the false alarms from the true detections. On the other hand, the object detection threshold could be set at a high value so there would be virtually no false alarms (every flagged frame is a true detection), with the price that in some frames the object would be present but not detected.

Depending upon the analysis task (finding every instance vs. finding a collection of representative instances), one or the other threshold (or somewhere in between) might be appropriate.

9.5.1.2 Face and Emotion Detection

There are myriad ways in which computerized face detection and face tracking could enable new types of analyses with huge potential gain and minimal time commitment on the part of the analyst. Current face detection algorithms (Viola and Jones 2002) could be employed to annotate the video so that appropriate video segments could be located quickly and accurately. One example of the state of the art in current research is work by Tim Marks, one of our recent Ph.D. students, and colleagues to automatically annotate a video with the subjects' emotions, as determined by their facial expressions (Marks et al. 2004). Computerized analysis of facial expression can be done with existing technology on the frontal views of faces. To analyze facial expressions from non-frontal views of a person's face, sophisticated 3D tracking algorithms such as G-flow (Marks et al. 2004) can be used to find the 3D pose of the face and the 3D locations of key points on the face from 2D video of the subject. By fitting the 3D locations of these key points to a database of laser scans of human heads (Blanz and Vetter 1999), we can synthetically rotate the face from any viewpoint to a frontal view, from which the emotion of the subject can be determined using a facial expression analysis system.

9.5.2 Activity Trails: Challenge of Finding Patterns in Workstation Activity Histories

There is a long history and a recent resurgence of interest in recording personal activity. Personal storage of all one's media throughout a lifetime has been desired and discussed since at least 1945, when Vannevar Bush published *As We May Think* (Bush 1945), positing the Memex, a device in which an individual stores all their books, records, and communications, and which is mechanized so that it may be consulted with exceeding speed and flexibility. His vision was astonishingly broad for the time, including full-text search, annotations, hyperlinks, virtually unlimited storage and even stereo cameras mounted on eyeglasses.

Today, storage, sensor, and computing technology have progressed to the point of making a Memex-like device feasible and even affordable. Indeed, we can now look beyond Memex at new augmented environment possibilities. In particular, while media capture has typically been sparse throughout a lifetime, we can now consider continuous archival and retrieval of all media relating to personal experiences. For example, the MyLifeBits project (Gemmell et al. 2006) at Microsoft Research is recording a lifetime store of information about the life of Gordon Bell. This includes not only video but the capture of a lifetime's worth of articles, letters, photos, and presentations as well as phone calls, emails, and other activities. This and related projects are documented in the recent series of ACM CARPE workshops on capture, archiving, and retrieval of personal experiences.

Hollan has long been interested in visualizing activity histories. In early work on ReadWear and EditWear (Hill et al. 1992), he and his colleagues modified an editor to collect detailed histories of people editing text or code and made those histories available in the scrollbar of the editor in ways to inform subsequent activity. Over the last few years lab members have conducted a series of pilot projects collecting workstation activity of users. In one effort, Etienne Pelaprat built facilities to record a low-level operating system call activity on a workstation and then explored parsing that low-level activity record into higher level activity descriptions. The motivation was to have recording facilities that did not require modification to any applications participants used in their normal workstation activity.

Gaston Cangiano is currently building a system, Activity Trails (Cangiano and Hollan 2009), to unobtrusively capture histories of all user activity on the desktop. The tool has very low memory overhead and employs low level system calls so that there is no performance impact noticeable to users. The tool records a bitmap snapshot of the desktop at regular intervals, as well as XML output containing all information about input devices, windows and applications (including titles and content for selected applications). Studies in cognitive ethnography often suffer from uneven sampling so that it is impossible to know how representative any particular event is of overall behavior patterns. By collecting a complete record, Activity Trails supports the creation of frequency distributions for the various categories of observed events.

ActivityTrails also has the capability to playback summaries for given times or dates. A screenshot of the design is shown in Fig. 9.3. The playback area at the bottom allows users to scroll back and forward in time. The thumbnails on top represent individual episodes. The time elapsed between each episode varies depending on the results from parsing the recordings. One goal is to provide an episodic view in which thumbnails index landmarks or natural breakpoints in user activity.

There is considerable evidence that people organize their memory for activities around landmarks (Robinson 1986; Tulving 2002; Shum 1994; Huttenlocher and Prohaska 1997). The challenge is to develop a parsing algorithm to detect breakpoints in activity that match what people report as the boundaries of their activities. We have been capturing workstation activity from workers in a law office and from undergraduate students. To obtain subjects' views of workstation activities we have had them explain what they were doing as they watch screen recordings of their past activities. We are testing how well parsing algorithms we have been developing can match the activity boundaries that participants mention. While results are still preliminary, we are encouraged by the ability for cross-correlations of mouse, window, and keyboard activity to determine boundaries. The fact that people develop stable windowing styles for different types of activities is a nice example of how cognitive activity is distributed through time. Stable windowing practices facilitate the allocation of attention in subsequent activity, thus reducing cognitive workload.

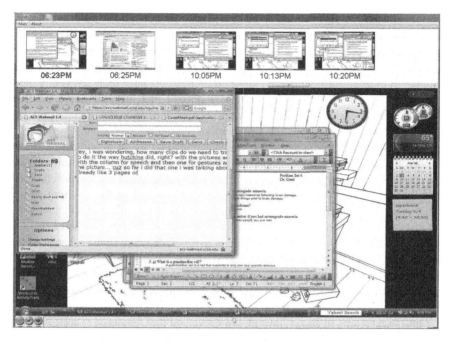

Fig. 9.3 Episodic view of past activity – summaries: each thumbnail in the *top* portion of the window represents a short activity

9.5.3   Commercial Aviation: Challenge and Opportunities of Understanding a Complex Socio-Technical System

Under a multi-year agreement with the Boeing Commercial Airplane Group, Hutchins has negotiated access to training activities at a number of airlines outside the US (Security provisions enacted in the wake of the 9/11 terrorist attacks have made work with US airlines impossible). Boeing's interests lie in specific applications and interventions concerning training, operating procedures, and flight deck design in the next generation of airline flight decks. Hutchins has already collected video data in Japan, New Zealand, Australia, and Mexico. In addition to collecting data in simulators located at the training centers of non-US airlines, the project also collects data in simulators located at the Alteon/Boeing training center in Seattle.

These data provide an absolutely unique look at complex, highly structured, expert activity in a setting that is spatially, temporally and institutionally constrained. The activities recorded in high-fidelity flight simulators, a most interesting augmented environment, are complex. They involve the production of multimodal acts of meaning making that are embedded in social and material context. The script-like structure of the phases of flight and of flight deck procedures provides a common framework with respect to which of the activities of different pilots and even different populations of pilots can be compared. This attribute of the activity also makes it a good early choice for exploration with timeline representations because there are recognizable shifts in activity structure in successive phases of flight. By the time they are in training for commercial air operations, pilots have high levels of expertise. Studying expert real-world skills is important, but difficult to do because analysts must have considerable expertise themselves in order to interpret the significance of the presence (or absence) of particular behaviors. Fortunately, Hutchins' years of experience as a jet-rated pilot and as an aviation researcher provide the necessary analytic expertise. The spatial and temporal constraints on activity in the flight deck make data collection tractable in the sense that recording equipment can be installed in fixed locations, or attached to the clothing of the participants, and the activities to be recorded are sure to take place in an anticipated amount of time (usually about 2 h). The institutional constraints guarantee that the data recordings will be rich in observable activity (little down time) because of the high cost of operating the simulator. Finally, as was the case with our instrumented car, it is possible to acquire a rich digital data stream from the simulator itself. Time synching simulator data to the observational data provides a documentary richness that is simply not possible in most activities.

Our observations in Japan have already revealed that language practices in the Japanese airline flight deck can be seen as adaptations to a complex mix of exogenous constraints. Institutions, such as regulatory agencies, adapt to the constraints of global operations when setting the rules that govern airline operations; the decision that air traffic control communications shall be conducted in English, for example. Airlines adapt to the regulatory environment, the marketplace, the characteristics of their workforce and the nature of the technology when setting training and operational policies. Pilots adapt to the residues of the adaptive behaviors of institutions in constructing meaningful courses of action in flight (Hutchins et al. 2006).

Commercial aviation is a complex socio-technical system that has developed most rapidly in North America and Europe. Because we are working with non-US airlines, we are also able to examine how other cultures integrate the practices of commercial aviation into their particular cultural and cognitive ecology (Nomura et al. 2006). This is a unique perspective on the globalization of one of the most complex socio-technical systems in today's world. Dramatic changes in the demographics of the global population of commercial airline pilots are currently underway. For example, the mean age of pilots worldwide is rapidly decreasing as aviation expands in Asia and Latin America.

The data collected in the Alteon/Boeing training center is especially interesting because it involves American flight instructors working with pilots from other nations. These data permit us to examine the dynamics of a special case of intercultural learning. Airline pilots everywhere share certain elements of professional culture, but in intercultural training, professional culture becomes a resource for overcoming the boundaries of national culture. They permit us to see the contextual grounding of intercultural communication and learning (Hutchins et al. 2006).

9.5.4 A Multimodal Augmented Environment: The Challenge of Supporting Medical Conversations Between Deaf and Hearing Individuals

Loss of hearing is a common problem that can result from noise, aging, disease, and heredity. Approximately 28 million Americans have significant hearing loss, and of that group, almost six million are profoundly deaf. A primary form of communication within the United States deaf community is American Sign Language. It is estimated to be the fourth most commonly used US language. While ASL is widely used in the US, no one form of sign language is universal. It is important to note that ASL is not just a visual form of English; it is a different language with its own unique grammatical and syntactical structure.

ASL interpreters play a central role in enabling face-to-face communication between many deaf and hearing individuals. For the deaf population fluent in ASL, communicating through an interpreter is an optimal choice for many scenarios. Interpreters, however, are expensive and not always available. Furthermore, though interpreters are bound by a confidentiality agreement, the presence of a third person in a highly private conversation may reduce a deaf person's comfort and inhibit their willingness to speak candidly.

While other viable communication tools for the deaf community exist, in our lab Anne Marie Piper and Hollan have been exploring tabletop displays with speech recognition to facilitate medical conversations between deaf and hearing individuals (Piper and Hollan 2008). Consultations with physicians often involve discussion of visuals such as medical records, charts, and scan images. Interactive tabletop displays are an effective tool for presenting visual information to multiple people at once without necessarily designating one person as the owner of the visual. Taking notes while meeting with a physician is problematic for deaf individuals because it requires simultaneously attending to the doctor's facial expressions, the interpreter's visual representation of speech, and notes on paper. A tabletop display allows all the active participants to maintain face-to-face contact while viewing a representation of the conversation in a central location. The Shared Sound Interface Piper and Hollan designed incorporates keyboard input by the patient and speech input by the doctor, allowing the physician to speak and gesture as they discuss medical details and visuals with the patient. SSI leverages the affordances of multimodal tabletop displays to create an augmented environment to enhance communication between a doctor and a patient, potentially transforming a challenging situation into a constructive and collaborative experience (Fig. 9.4).

SSI uses a MERL DiamondTouch table (Dietz and Leigh 2001) and the DiamondSpin toolkit (Shen et al. 2004). The DiamondTouch table is a multi-user, multi-touch top projected tabletop display. Users sit on conductive pads that enable the system to uniquely identify where each user is touching the surface. SSI enables conversational input through standard keyboard entry and a headset microphone. The audio captured from the microphone is fed into a speech recognition engine (currently this is Microsoft Windows' default recognizer, but the application easily

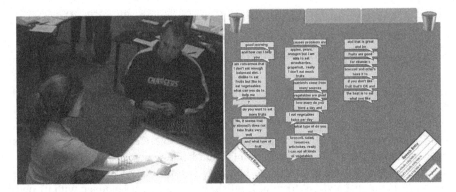

Fig. 9.4 Doctor (*left person*) and patient (*right person*) point together as they discuss part of a medical visual (*left*). A screen shot of the shared speech interface application (*right*) shows that speech bubbles from a doctor and patient consultation persist on the display and are available for manipulation and later reference

adapts to any off-the-shelf recognizer). SSI uses the Java Speech API and CloudGarden software to interface with the speech recognition engine and send converted speech-to-text into the main application running on the DiamondTouch table.

To evaluate the SSI system Piper and Hollan conducted a laboratory study with eight deaf participants who were born deaf or became deaf before the age of one. All participants were fluent in ASL and proficient at reading and writing in English. Each deaf participant conversed with a medical doctor and a professionally trained ASL interpreter about a sample medical issue. Overall, participants indicated that digital tables are a promising medium for facilitating medical conversations. Survey data indicated that the application was good for private conversations and enabled independence.

There were several key differences in communication between the Digital Table condition and a condition in which an ASL interpreter was present. The Digital Table condition allowed for asynchrony in communication, whereas the interpreter acted as a broker of conversation and thus encouraged synchronous interactions. Conversation in the Interpreter condition was the fastest and allowed a greater number of turn taking exchanges. Equitable participation levels were observed in the two conditions, the doctor and patient each contributed to about half of the conversation.

In the Digital Table condition, non-verbal and gestural communication played an important role in augmenting speech and ensuring successful communication. The co-located, face-to-face nature of the digital table allowed participants to provide feedback to their partner about their state of understanding through deictic gesture (e.g., pointing), gaze sharing, and head nodding. There were also differences in how patients attended to the doctor when the interpreter was present. Deaf participants looked at the doctor when they signed but then shifted their gaze to the interpreter when the doctor began speaking. In the Digital Table condition, participants typically looked at the doctor when she was speaking and then looked down at the display.

From the perspective of augmented environments, it is important to note that the digital table transformed the ephemeral nature of speech into a tangible and persistent form, thereby creating affordances that are not available in traditional conversation. For example, there were interesting behaviors with the speech bubbles because of their form. When a phrase was added to the display that referred to a previous utterance, the "owner" of the speech bubble often moved the new phrase close to the previous utterance. In conversation, the speaker must help listeners understand a reference to a previous utterance through context and explicit referencing. The digital table allowed users to reference previous conversation by placing new speech near an existing speech bubble. Similarly, the doctor and patient used the tail of the speech bubble as a pointing mechanism. That is, participants strategically placed speech bubbles around the display so that the tail of the speech bubble pointed to part of a background visual. The persistent nature of speech with the digital table allowed participants to review their conversation. Both the doctor and patients looked back over their previous conversation. The doctor said "it was good to look back at what I had covered with that particular patient," and explained that "it would be helpful because it is not uncommon in medicine to have very similar conversations with different patients throughout the day."

This work exemplifies the importance of adopting a unit of analysis that spans across the doctor and patient as well as their speech, gestures, and interactions with the digital table. Understanding the functional relationships among these elements is fundamental to designing an effective augmented environment.

9.5.5   Paper and Audio Augmented Digital Documents: Opportunities from Bridging the Paper-Digital Divide

Paper persists as an integral component of virtually all environments and tasks because it provides ease of use unmatched by digital alternatives. Paper documents are light to carry, easy to annotate, rapid to navigate, flexible to manipulate, and robust to use in varied environments. Interactions with paper documents create rich webs of annotation, cross reference, and spatial organization. Unfortunately, the resulting webs are confined to the physical world of paper and, as they accumulate, become increasingly difficult to store, search, and access. XLibris (Schilit et al. 1998) and similar systems address these difficulties by simulating paper with tablet PCs. While this approach is promising, it suffers not only from limitations of current tablet computers (e.g., limited screen space) but also from loss of invaluable paper affordances.

For the last several years, Hollan has been collaborating with Francois Guimbretière and others on the design of PapierCraft a gesture-based command system that allows users to manipulate digital documents using paper printouts as proxies (Liao et al. 2008). Using an Anoto digital pen (Anoto 2008), users can draw command gestures on paper to tag a paragraph, email a selected area, copy selections to a notepad, or create links to related documents. Upon pen synchronization, PapierCraft executes the commands and presents the results in a digital document viewer. Users can then search the tagged information and navigate the web of annotated digital documents resulting from interactions with the paper proxies. PapierCraft also supports real time interactions across mix-media, for example, letting users copy information from paper to a Tablet PC screen.

Recently we have started to explore a new Anoto-based technology that supports the integration of audio. The Livescribe Pulse pen (Livescribe 2008) functions like earlier digital pens but also provides the ability to capture and play audio. For example, during a meeting one can record what is being said while taking notes on paper. Subsequently, touching a section of one's paper notes allows one to hear what was being said at the time that section of notes was being written. This technology enables a variety of interesting opportunities to augment environments.

One opportunity we are pursuing is to incorporate Livescribe pens into the Ethnographer's Workbench we are designing. For an ethnographer, the ability to easily capture audio and index into it via associated paper notes changes the relations between listening and writing in powerful ways. The content of written notes can shift from recording speech to coding and other sorts of meta-data representations of the recorded event. We also are exploring the ability to create special data notebooks that provide the ability to flexibly annotate sections of notes by touching categories printed on the pages. Recently, we initiated the design of such a notebook for a research team studying synchrony of behavior between a Beluga whale and her new calf. The ability to automatically record the temporal aspects of the data is particularly valuable. Similarly, timestamps can be used to link paper and audio notes with camera images or video. The ButterflyNet system (Yeh and Klemmer 2005), designed to support field biologists is an interesting example.

9.5.6 Lessons for Designing Augmented Environments

A rapidly evolving technology landscape and recent advances in cognitive theory make this an exciting time for the design of augmented environments. We see great potential for exploiting new facilities to record the fine details of action captured in meaningful settings as a basis for better understanding of the dynamics of human behavior and thus providing a solid foundation for designing augmented work-places in which people can pursue their goals in collaboration with the elements of the social and material world.

In this chapter we have briefly described what we see as the major challenge for behavioral science: developing the requisite theoretical and methodological frameworks to effectively analyze data that capture the richness of real-world human activity. We then discussed selected recent projects in our laboratory in which we are attempting to further develop distributed cognition and cognitive ethnography. We conclude by characterizing lessons our work has for designing and evaluating augmented environments:

1. There is currently a tremendous opportunity to exploit computer vision techniques to automatically annotate video data and thus assist analysis and evaluation. Today the high labor cost of analyzing rich activity data leads to haphazard and incomplete analyses or, all too commonly, to no analysis at all of much of the data. Even dataset navigation is cumbersome. Data records are chosen for analysis because of recording quality, interesting phenomena, and interaction density – producing a haphazard sampling of the recorded set. Good researchers have a nose for good data, but also have a tendency to focus on small segments of the record that contain "interesting" behavior, analyze them intensively, and then move on to the next project. When analysis is so costly, few analyses can be done – so datasets are severely underutilized – and researchers come to have a large investment in the chosen data segments. Since each analysis may appear as an isolated case study, it can be difficult to know how common the observed phenomena may be. Larger patterns and contradictory cases can easily go unnoticed. Well-known human confirmation biases can affect the quality of the science when each analysis requires so much effort. Thus, one promising research strategy is to develop and assemble tools and practices to increase speed and improve analysis. Here we argue that computer vision techniques can be employed to automatically annotate video data and help to manage and coordinate data analysis.

2. Since so much of peoples' activity currently takes place while using computers, there is an unprecedented opportunity to capture and study this activity. This enables not only examination of detailed activity histories to better understand the dynamics of cognition but also can serve as the basis for summaries of those activities to help people to reestablish previous contexts and find needed information. Augmenting environments to encapsulate histories of activity and provide visualizations of it is an important research direction. We see it being useful for augmented environments like we described (workstations, driving, flight simulators, and multimodal interfaces) as well as for the increasing range of ubiquitous computing environments currently being developed.

3. *Tools to help capture, visualize, and analyze activity data are fundamental to advancing research.* We argue that integrated capture, analysis, and visualization facilities such as we are designing can increase speed, improve, and help coordinate analyses focused at different scales so as to profit from the complementary perspectives of multiple disciplines. For example, the Ethnographer's Workbench we are building incorporates paper and audio augmented digital notebooks with facilities to support multiscale visualization and analysis of video and other time-based data. A significant scientific challenge for all disciplines is how to represent data so as to make important patterns visible. In the behavioral sciences, researchers transcribe and code data in a wide variety of ways, creating new re-representations of the original events. Currently the coordination of multiple re-representations with the original data is typically done by hand, or not at all. Since this re-representation process – including all sorts of transcription, coding system development and implementation, and re-description – is what allows us to do scientific work, even small improvements in automating coding, transcription, or coordination of representations can be crucially important. Recent developments

in behavioral science theory create special challenges in this regard. Increasingly theories are concerned with patterns that can emerge from the interactions of many dynamically linked elements. Such interactive patterns may be invisible to approaches that decompose behavior into the more or less independent components created by historical distinctions among behavioral science disciplines. This is why multidisciplinary behavioral science is necessary. But tools that match this multidisciplinary vision are also needed.

The richly multimodal nature of real-world human activity makes analysis difficult. A common strategy has been to focus on a single aspect of behavior or a single modality of behavior, and to look for patterns there. However, the causal factors that explain the patterns seen in any one modality may lie in the patterns of other modalities. In fact, recent work suggests that activity unfolds in a complex system of mutual causality. Analysis may still be based on decomposition of the activity, as long as there is a way to put the pieces back together again. That is, as long as there is a way to visualize the relations among the many components of multimodal activity.

The structure of the existing academic disciplines attests to the fact that human behavior can be productively described at many levels of integration. Neuroscientists describe regularities at a finer scale than psychologists, who describe phenomena at a finer scale than linguists, who in turn tend to describe behavior at a finer scale than anthropologists. A deep understanding of the nature of human behavior demands not only description on multiple levels, but integration among the descriptions.

As behavior unfolds in time, describable patterns that take place on the scale of milliseconds are located in the context of other describable patterns that display regularities on the scale of seconds. Those patterns in turn are typically embedded in culturally meaningful activities whose structure is described on the scale of minutes or hours. Patterns at larger time scales are created by and form the context for patterns at shorter time scales. Visualizing and reasoning about such nested temporal relations requires representations that allow coordination of analyses across multiple scales.

References

Anoto (2008) http://www.anoto.com
Bauman R, Sherzer J (1989) Explorations in the ethnography of speaking. Cambridge University Press, Cambridge
Blanz V, Vetter T (1999) A morphable model for the synthesis of 3D faces. In: SIGGRAPH 99 Proceedings, pp 187–194
Boer E, Forster D, Joyce C, Fastrez P, Haue JB, Garvey E, Choski M, Mogilner T, Hollan J (2005) Bridging ethnography and engineering through the graphical language of petri nets. In: Measuring Behavior; 5th International Conference on Methods and Techniques in Behavioral Science Research, Wageningen, The Netherlands
Brooks R (1991) Intelligence without representation. Artificial Intelligence Journal 47: 139–159
Brown JS, Collins A, Duguid P (1989) Situated cognition and the culture of learning. Educational Researcher 18(1): 32–42
Bush V (1945) As we may think. The Atlantic Monthly 101–108

Cangiano G, Hollan J (2009) Capturing and restoring the context of everyday work: a case study of a law office. In: Proceedings of HCI International. In press.

Card S, Mackinlay J, Shneiderman B (1999) Readings in information visualization: using vision to think. Morgan Kaufmann Publishers, California

Chaiklin S, Lave J (1996) Understanding practice: perspectives on activity and context. Cambridge University Press, Cambridge

Clancy WJ (1997) Situated cognition: on human knowledge and computer representations. Cambridge University Press, Cambridge

Clark A (1997) Being there: putting brain, body and world together again. MIT, Cambridge

Clark A (2001) Mindware: an introduction to the philosophy of cognitive science. Oxford University Press, New York

Clark A (2003) Natural-born cyborgs: minds, technologies and the future of human intelligence. Oxford University Press, New York

Cole M (1996) Cultural psychology: a once and future discipline. Belknap Press, Massachusetts

D'Andrade RG (1995) The development of cognitive anthropology. Cambridge University Press, New York

Dietz P, Leigh D (2001) DiamondTouch: a multi-user touch technology. In: Proceedings of the 14th Annual Symposium on User Interface Software and Technology. ACM, New York, pp 219–226

Dourish P (2001) Where the action is: the foundations of embodied interaction. MIT, Cambridge

Gemmell J, Bell G, Lueder R (2006) MyLifeBits: a personal database for everything. In: Communications of the ACM. ACM, New York, pp 88–95

Goldin-Meadow S (2003) Hearing gesture: how our hands help us think. Belknap Press, Cambridge

Goodwin C (2000) Gesture, aphasia, and interaction. In: McNeill D (ed) Language and gesture: window into thought and action. Cambridge University Press, Cambridge

Goodwin C, Goodwin M (2001) Emotion within situated activity. In: Duranti A (ed) Linguistic anthropology: a reader. Blackwell, Massachusetts, pp 239–257

Goodwin C, Heritage J (1990) Conversation analysis. Annual Review of Anthropology 19: 283–307

Gumperz JJ, Hymes D (1986) Directions in sociolinguistics. Blackwell, Oxford

Hill W, Hollan J, Wroblewski D, McCandless T (1992) Edit wear and read wear. In: Proceedings of the SIGCHI Conference on Human Factors in Computing Systems. ACM, New York, p 3–9

Hollan JD, Bederson BB, Helfman J (1997) Information visualization. In: Landauer TK, Prabhu P, Helander MG (eds) The handbook of human computer interaction (Chap. 2). Elsevier Press, Amsterdam, pp 33–48)

Hollan J, Hutchins E, Kirsh D (2000) Distributed cognition: Toward a new theoretical foundation for human-computer interaction research. In: ACM Transactions on Human-Computer Interaction. TOCHI '00. ACM, New York, pp 174–196

Hutchby I, Wooffitt R (1998) Conversation analysis: principles, practices and applications. Polity Press, Cambridge

Hutchins E (1995a) Cognition in the wild. MIT, Cambridge

Hutchins E (1995b) How a cockpit remembers its speed. Cognitive Science: A Multidisciplinary Journal 19. 265–288

Hutchins E, Klausen T (1996) Distributed cognition in an airline cockpit. In: Engestrom Y, Middleton D (eds) Cognition and Communication at work. Cambridge University Press, New York, pp 15–34

Hutchins E, Nomura S, Holder B (2006) The uses of paper in commercial airline flight operations. In: Proceedings of the 2006 20th Anniversary Conference on Computer Supported Cooperative Work. ACM, New York, pp 249–258

Huttenlocher J, Prohaska V (1997) Reconstructing the times of past events. In: Stein N, Orenstein P, Tversky B, Brainerd C (eds) Memory for everyday and emotional events. Lawrence Erlbaum, New Jersey

Jones V, Jones M (2004) Robust real-time face detection. International Journal of Computer Vision 57(2): 137–154

Lakoff G, Johnson M (1999) Philosophy in the flesh: the embodied and its challenge to western thought. Basic Books, New York

Lave J (1988) Cognition in practice. Cambridge University Press, Cambridge

Liao C, Guimbretière F, Hinckley K, Hollan J (2008) Papiercraft: a gesture-based command system for interactive paper. In: ACM Transactions on Computer-Human Interaction. ACM, New York, pp 1–27

Livescribe (2008) http://www.livescribe.com

Lowe D (2004) Distinctive image features from scale-invariant keypoints. In: International Journal Computer Vision. Springer Netherlands, pp 91–110

Marks T, Hershey J, Roddey C, Movellan J (2004) 3D tracking of morphable objects using conditionally gaussiean nonlinear filters. IEEE Conference Computer Vision and Pattern Recognition 12: 190

McCall JB, Achler O, Trivedi M, Fastrez P, Forster D, Haue J, Hollan J, Boer E (2004) A collaborative approach for human-centered driver assistance systems. Proceedings of the 7th IEEE Conference on Intelligent Transportation Systems 3: 663–667

McNeill D (2005) Gesture and thought. University of Chicago Press, Chicago

Nardi B (1996) Context and consciousness: activity theory and human-computer interaction. MIT, Cambridge

Neisser E (1982) Memory observed: remembering in natural contexts. WH Freeman, San Francisco

Noë A (2003) Action in perception. MIT, Cambridge, MA

Nomura S, Hutchins E, Holder B (2006) The uses of paper in commercial airline flight operations. In: Proceedings of Computer Supported Cooperative Work 2006 (CSCW 2006), pp 249–258

Nunez R (1996) Could the future taste purple? Reclaiming mind, body, and cognition. In: Nunez R, Freeman WJ (eds) Reclaiming cognition: the primacy of action, intention and emotion. Imprint Academic, Thorverton

Pea RD (1993) Practices of distributed intelligence and designs for education. In: Salomon G (ed) Distributed cognitions. Cambridge University Press, Cambridge

Piper A, Hollan J (2008) Supporting medical conversations between deaf and hearing individuals with tabletop displays. In: Proceeding of Computer Supported Cooperative Work 2008 (CSCW 2008), ACM, New York, pp 147–156

Port R, van Gelder T (1995) Mind as motion: explorations in the dynamics of cognition. MIT, Cambridge, MA

Prevignano CL, Thibault PJ (2003) Discussing conversation analysis: the work of Emanuel A. Schegloff. John Benjamins Publishing Company, Amsterdam

Robinson J (1986) Temporal reference systems and autobiographical memory. In: Rubing D (ed) Autobiographical memory. Cambridge University Press, Cambridge, pp 159–188

Rogoff B (2003) The cultural nature of human development. Oxford University Press, New York

Schilit B, Golovchinsky G, Price M (1998) Beyond paper: supporting active reading with free form digital ink annotations. In: Proceedings of the SIGCHI Conference on Human Factors in Computing Systems. ACM, New York, pp 249–256

Shen C, Vernier F, Forlines C, Ringel M (2004) DiamondSpin: an extensible toolkit for around-the-table interaction. In: Proceedings of the SIGCHI Conference on Human Factors in Computing Systems. ACM, New York, pp 167–174

Shum M (1994) The role of temporal landmarks in autobiographical memory processes. Psychology Bulletin 124: 423–442

Suchman LA (1987) Plans and situated actions: the problem of human-machine communication. Cambridge Press, Cambridge

Thelen E, Smith LB (1994) A dynamic systems approach to the development of cognition and action. Bradford Books, Cambridge

Thompson E (2007) Mind in life. Harvard University Press, Cambridge, MA

Tulving E (2002). Episodic memory: from mind to brain. In: Annual Review of Psychology. Annual Reviews

Varela FJ, Thomson E, Rosch E (1991) The embodied mind: cognitive science and human experience. MIT, London

Viola P, Jones M (2002) Fast and robust classification using asymmetric adaboost and a detector cascade. In: Advances in Neural Information Processing System. MIT Press,14:1311–1318

Werner O, Schoepfle GM (1987) Systematic fieldwork. Sage, California

Yeh R, Klemmer S (2005) ButterflyNet: mobile capture and access for biologists. In: Conference Supplement to UIST 2005: ACM Symposium on User Interface Software and Technology. ACM, New York

Zhao W, Chellappa R, Phillips PJ, Rosenfield A (2003) Face recognition: A literature survey. In: ACM computing surveys. ACM, New York, pp 399–458

Chapter 10
The Aachen Media Space: Design Patterns for Augmented Work Environments

Jan Borchers

Abstract *Design Patterns* are a format to capture the knowledge about successful solutions to recurring design problems in a uniform, interconnected, and easily understood way. The format originated in urban architecture, but has made its way into software engineering and Human-Computer Interaction (HCI). This makes them an ideal format to provide guidelines for the design of Augmented Environments (AEs), which requires a highly interdisciplinary team to collaborate.

The author, who published the original book on HCI design patterns, has worked on AEs since 1995. He has captured his experience in designing such environments within the patterns presented here. The chapter first introduces the design pattern format, gives practical tips for reading and writing design patterns, and presents the AE from which the patterns in this chapter were distilled. The main part of this chapter then consists of the collection of design patterns for AEs. These patterns provide practical guidance on how to create an AE, with a focus on architectural, interior design, software infrastructure, and user interface considerations. The chapter includes 19 such patterns connected into a network, as well as suggestions for additional patterns.

10.1 Augmented Environments: A Highly Interdisciplinary Endeavor

Designing user-friendly Augmented Environments (AEs) requires expert input from many disciplines: architects for the overall space design; furniture designers for the physical "stuff" in the room; hardware integrators for the interactive devices; software engineers for the OS, middleware, and applications; HCI experts for designing the users' experience with the interactive technology; psychologists

J. Borchers (✉)
RWTH Aachen University, Aachen, Germany
e-mail: borchers@cs.rwth-aachen.de

S. Lahlou (ed.), *Designing User Friendly Augmented Work Environments: From Meeting Rooms to Digital Collaborative Spaces,* Computer Supported Cooperative Work,
DOI 10.1007/978-1-84800-098-8_6, © Springer-Verlag London Limited 2009

for judging the cognitive impact of the space; and social scientists to support specific activities and work patterns in the environment. Other interactive products usually require only a subset of these disciplines, but AEs are unique, in that they demand the joined expertise of physical and virtual environments, of physical space design and interaction design, to arrive at successful solutions.

10.2   Why Design Patterns?

This chapter will review and summarize design recommendations for such spaces pulled from all of the above disciplines. It will use a particular format for these recommendations, called *Design Patterns*. This is no coincidence: this format is, one might argue, almost destined to be used in this case. The reason is that design patterns, just like AEs, have developed at the crossroads of traditional architecture and HCI.

The idea of pattern languages was originally conceived by architect Christopher Alexander. Each pattern of his large collection (Alexander et al. 1977) captured a successful solution to a recurring problem in urban architecture, from ideal sizes for working neighborhoods, to the right layout of a street cafe front, down to details such as the distribution of seating areas in a single room. Each pattern carried a descriptive name and described its problem, solution, examples, and connections to other patterns on several pages of text and images in a uniform, highly structured format, making it easy for the reader to pick up these design recommendations. The connections to other patterns formed a graph called a pattern *language*. The theory behind pattern languages was laid out in Alexander (1979), and a sample project using them in Alexander et al. (1988).

Alexander actually wrote his patterns not for professional architects, but for the inhabitants, or users(!), of a building or neighborhood to create an interdisciplinary *vocabulary* that would allow them to express their interests and preferences in the design process in a user-centered way. This idea implements well-known results from psychological research about *verbal recoding*: "When there is a story or an argument or an idea that we want to remember [...], we make a verbal description of the event and then remember our verbalization" (Miller 1956). The idea can be recalled when its short name is remembered.

Around 1987 (Beck and Cunningham 1987), software engineering picked up and quickly adopted the pattern format, though not quite the larger ideas behind it. The *Gang of Four* book on patterns in software engineering (Gamma et al. 1995), became one of the most widely known programming titles, but unlike Alexander's, its patterns were not readable by nonexperts or users, and they did not adopt Alexander's inherent goal of creating more human-friendly environments, as he pointed out in Alexander (1996). Nevertheless, annual Pattern Languages of Programming (PLoP) conferences have continued to refine the otherwise successful concept of patterns in software engineering.

The "true heir" to the design patterns idea is arguably HCI, not software engineering. Both architecture (in the physical world of buildings) and HCI (in the virtual world of user interfaces) deal with the task of making these environments as humane to use as possible. Software engineering, on the other hand, is concerned with the construction of robust underpinnings and structures for this user experience – much in the way structural engineering complements the work of the architect.

Surprisingly, Alexander's ideas were referenced as early as 1986 by several seminal HCI books (Norman and Draper 1986; Norman 1988, p. 229; Apple Computer 1992). Still, it was not until the late 1990s that the concept was explored more rigorously in HCI (Barfield et al. 1994; Bayle et al. 1998; Granlund and Lafrenière 1999; Borchers 2000b, 2000c; Borchers et al. 2000). In 2001, the author published the first book on HCI design patterns (Borchers 2001). Since then, several successful titles have followed (van Duyne et al. 2006; Tidwell 2005).

So far, the most thorough review of Alexander's work and its implications for HCI can be found in (Borchers 2001). Dearden and Finlay (2006) compare recent HCI design pattern collections.

10.3   The Pattern Format

The design patterns in this chapter are arranged such that they deal with design decisions in the rough order that they are faced when planning an AE.

Each pattern is presented as several pages of illustrated text, using a very uniform structure and layout with the following components, closely following Alexander's original form (Alexander 1977, p. x). To better see how this structure maps onto the actual patterns, each component includes the corresponding text from the first pattern in the language.

Name: A meaningful, concise name identifies the pattern and serves to build a vocabulary for design discussion. The first pattern, for example, is called 500 SQUARE FEET. Following Alexander's example (Alexander 1979) like most pattern books and collections do, pattern names are always written in lowercase small caps in this language.

Ranking: This indicates the validity of the pattern, that is, in how far the author believes this pattern is an exclusive option to solve the problem described. One star (*) means that it is probably only one of many options; two stars (**) suggest that this is likely among the best of only few options to address the problem, while three stars (***) indicate that any problem of the described kind will likely include an example of this pattern in its solution. The first pattern, for example, is ranked with two stars (**).

Picture: This gives a "sensitizing" and easily understood example of the pattern applied to quickly help newcomers to get a feel for what the pattern is about, and to set the mood for the remainder of the pattern. The first pattern has an image of the Aachen Media Space, for example, to illustrate the space requirements that pattern talks about.

Context: This is a single paragraph that explains which earlier patterns the present pattern helps to implement. It gives the designer an idea of when, at which stage of the design process, to consider this pattern. The context references back to "higher-level" patterns in the language – in our case this means patterns that the designer should have looked at before the current one.

Together with the references, the context constitutes the edges of the pattern language graph, while the patterns themselves are the nodes of the graph. Generally, context and references are forward and backward versions of the same link, although exceptions to this rule are sometimes made if it appears didactically useful; after all, the language is designed for humans, not computers, and so satisfying precise graph conditions does not constitute a value by itself in this case.

In our example, the pattern context says that "you are just beginning to plan your AE, wondering where in your building to locate it and how big it should be."

After the context, the "introductory" part of the pattern is complete, and the "core" part of the pattern begins. This is indicated by three diamonds (♦ ♦ ♦).

Problem: A short problem statement starts this core part by summarizing which problem this pattern addresses. As design is always a tradeoff, the statement is often worded in the form of competing "forces" or design tradeoffs. In our example, that statement is the following: "**The bigger the AE, the more flexibly it can be used; but space in most institutions is severely limited**." The problem statement is always printed in *boldface*, because together with the solution (also in boldface), it is the core message of each pattern. If you want to quickly skim a pattern language, you can usually just read the problem and solution statements, and you should have a good idea of what the patterns are about (if the language was written well).

Examples: This is usually the longest section in a pattern. It expands upon the problem statement, and provides examples of existing solutions to it, or other empirical or theoretical background information. It is the "rationale" explaining why the solution provided next is sound. It also often introduces additional recommendations that usually only come "on second thought" – or after the experience of having tried to solve this problem in one or more concrete projects.

Solution: The solution is the single most important pattern component, generalizing the examples into a clear, but generic set of instructions that can be applied in varying situations. If you only read one sentence of each pattern, read this one. It is also printed in **boldface**. Our example pattern suggests: **Reserve a space of at least around 500 square feet for your AE. That size will support typical meeting activities for groups of up to 15 people**.

Diagram: While the initial photo gave a concrete example to set the scene and was the visual equivalent of the "Examples" section, the *diagram* describes the solution and its constituents graphically in a simple, memorable sketch; abstracting from the details, it is the visual equivalent of the solution statement. When going back through a pattern language you read earlier, the diagrams, due to their visual, iconic nature, should help you to very quickly recognize each pattern again while browsing – faster than by reading any text. Our sample pattern has a simple rectangular floor plan sketch with the words "500 SQUARE FEET" written into it, reminiscent of what you would find in the floor plan of a building.

This completes the core part of each pattern, as indicated by three more diamonds (♦ ♦ ♦).

References: Finally, the *references* point you to subsequent patterns that can be used to implement or flesh out the present pattern further. They are not to be confused with scientific references (citations) to other works. They are like annotated forward links to smaller-scale patterns that come later in the design process; the "context" links are the corresponding backlinks. You can check this: generally, all patterns that 500 SQUARE FEET (1) refers to in its references, and only those, will have a link back to this pattern in their context. Our sample pattern has a fairly long reference section:

> "Once the required size is determined, you should consider the right location for your AE – WINDOW SPACE (2). The space that the room takes up can be used much more efficiently if its furniture supports multiple usage scenarios – FLEXIBLE FURNITURE (4) and by making mounts for unforeseen technology to be added later available under the ceiling – CEILING GRID (5) and floor – RAISED FLOOR (6). The size of your room also determines how big your group displays have to be to be readable from anywhere in the room – MEDIA BOARDS (7). If you plan to include noisy equipment or rear-projected wall displays, consider adding a shell around the room for that technology – ROOM SHELL (12)."

10.4   Pattern Reading and Writing Tips

Much of the advice in these patterns will sound quite trivial to an expert from the respective traditional profession – "of course people want daylight in their environment," any architect will say, for example, about the pattern WINDOW SPACE (2). The point of this collection is to make people from outside each respective profession aware of these rules as well in the interdisciplinary way that patterns were originally intended to be used. AEs are a new field that requires interdisciplinary exchange across traditional professional boundaries. Each of us has a lot of basics to learn in this process.

With AEs being a fairly young field, many patterns are still really only *proto-patterns*, with only one or a few examples drawn from the working experience of the author, as well as other members of the RUFAE network, who authored other chapters in this book.

When using the patterns in the language to apply them to your own design of an AE for research or deployment, keep in mind the above tips about skimming problems and solution, and finding patterns again by diagram. It is also important to understand that patterns are not cookbook recipes: Usually, you will still have to make a creative design decision; the patterns just help you to think about the right questions at the right time, and to avoid overlooking important design implications.

After applying these patterns, or maybe based on your existing experience in the field, you may feel that the patterns need amendments, corrections, additional examples, etc. This is the best way to use this language: let it evolve, personalize it with your own examples from projects you and your colleagues know, change or drop some patterns, and add others.

The author has guided students in writing their own patterns in a semester-long class dedicated to HCI design patterns for several years (Borchers 2002), and while reading patterns is very easy (that is what they were designed to support), writing patterns is much more difficult to learn to do well. Some tips to keep in mind:

- *Make sure to get the abstraction level right.* General "golden rules" such as PROVIDE FEEDBACK are very useful to analyze existing designs and explain problems, but as design guidance they are too generic. A good test is whether the pattern provides some *constructive* guidance as to what to do in the specific context. On the other hand, if patterns become too concrete (AVOID COMBOBOXES UNDER WINDOWS XP), it becomes harder to apply to different interfaces, and becomes outdated as quickly as the toolkit it refers to. One test that may help is to see if the pattern can apply to interfaces of different modalities – not just GUIs, but also voice or gesture interfaces.
- *Get the granularity right.* Often an initial pattern idea may draw in more and more additional advice about the topic until it becomes too large for a single pattern. A good limit is 2–4 book pages. Beyond that, consider drawing out different aspects of the solution you are proposing, and turning them into a connected, hierarchical set of individual patterns.
- *Pay attention to the problem statement.* The problem statement often seems harder to write than the solution statement! That is because the problem statement forces you to really think about when your solution is applicable – and when it is not. If you have a hard time coming up with a good problem statement, you may have a one-size-fits-all solution that is not refined enough yet. Similar caveats apply to the context: it also helps you to consider when, or even if, the pattern is useful.
- HCI Design Patterns aim to capture tried solutions to recurring design problems in interactive systems. As such, they have been shown to help especially newcomers to quickly get up to speed in a new interaction design area. They are less effective to improve the work of seasoned professionals, because those experts already know most of what the pattern language suggests. Use this language, or your own, especially to communicate with customers, others outside your own discipline, and to get new team members up to speed – much more quickly than by having them look at all the projects your company did over the last 20 years.

10.5   About the Group

To understand what kind of experience the following patterns represent, it is important to know from which background they are coming – what projects have led to this list of patterns, and what were the environments that have been constructed to serve as testbed for the validity of these guidelines.

The author has worked on technology-augmented collaborative work environments since 1995, when he contributed to the conceptual design and setup of the *Conference/Classroom of the Future* (Mühlhäuser et al. 1996) in the *Ars Electronica Center* in Linz, Austria. Subsequently, as acting assistant professor at Stanford University in Terry Winograd's Interactivity Lab, he worked on the *Stanford Interactive Workspaces Project* and its *iRoom* environment, in particular contributing to some of its cross-platform middleware applications, and initiating the *iStuff* project to support rapid physical prototyping of post-desktop interaction techniques. He was also involved in the *iSpaces* project that coordinated and exchanged interactive workspace technologies between Stanford University and KTH Stockholm in Sweden, where the *iLounge* was constructed, and that moved iRoom technology into experimental classrooms in Stanford's Wallenberg Hall building.

When joining the CS faculty at RWTH Aachen University to establish a new chair in Media Computing and HCI in 2003, the experience from these projects led to his design of the *Aachen Media Space* that aimed to improve on many aspects of the previous spaces, in particular their flexibility, appropriateness for long-term use, and ability to seamlessly handle audiovisual media in addition to more traditional document types. The design of this space was heavily influenced by his continued involvement with the *RUFAE* research network, in particular through Saadi Lahlou's and Volker Hartkopf's work on highly flexible workspace designs.

The present pattern language therefore reflects the accumulated experience from these projects, and takes most of its concrete examples from the Aachen Media Space as the latest generation of these environments that the author has created, and is continuing to develop, with his team. However, the Aachen Media Space is far from finished. It is a work in progress, but it serves three purposes:

- As a melting pot and testbed to install our own prototypes and new systems to support post-desktop group work on multiple media
- As an everyday meeting room our group actually uses on a daily basis
- As a demonstration and presentation environment to visitors interested in our work on augmented environments

Thus, using it as an example for the patterns in this language is simply based on observations what has worked well so far.

The language focuses on the patterns the author considers most central. Obviously, there were many more candidates for patterns that did not make it into this language because of space considerations. Some candidates were the following:

Mobile Walls: Larger environments can benefit greatly in their flexibility from walls that can be moved around by a single person (but consider their weaker noise blocking qualities).

Tackable Surfaces: Hanging up good old paper is still necessary, even in a hightech environment. Some wall materials will suffer when even the tiniest scrap of sticky tape is applied; avoid them.

Tiling Tables: Tables with wheels really begin to shine if their surfaces can be folded upright to stow them against a wall with little wasted space. Check their robustness though.

Autonomous Seats: Some augmented environments, like the Spaces in Wallenberg Hall, feature chairs that have built-in power supplies and/or networking access. This makes them less mobile, but more convenient.

Wired and Wireless Access: Naturally, any AE will offer WiFi access. But wired connectivity has its place, especially when working with large digital media files, streaming video presentations, and for similar tasks.

Presentation Wall: Sometimes there is the need for something larger than a mobile Media Board, but not as fancy (and immobile) as an interactive wall. A projection screen mounted on a stand or on a wall, with an ultra-short-throw projector on a table in front of it, will usually do fine. This only concerns larger spaces where people cannot read the Media Boards across the room anymore.

Printing and Scanning: Scanning in an analog document that someone brought to the meeting is often a convenient feature if it is fast, fluid, and seamless. A fast feeder scanner or a mounted digital still camera, serving all files up for the AE to access, is a great addition. Printing documents, on the other hand, is usually better done on a networked printer in an adjacent room to avoid the noise and disturbance.

Cross-Platform Support: The AE needs to handle the machines of regulars and visitors well independent of their operating system. Ensure access to the basic features such as file sharing for anyone coming to the environment with a minimum of hassle.

Recovery-Oriented Computing: The middleware used in the AE should support graceful degradation and self-healing when individual components – even a central server – fail to be reachable. Stanford's iROS and its commercial successor TeamSpot are examples of such infrastructures.

Legacy Software Support: Even an advanced AE will face the challenge of visitors "just wanting to show their PowerPoint slides" in everyday use. So make sure your system, as advanced as it may be, does not sacrifice compatibility to widely used software. Not only will this save you from problems with visitors, but also, by supporting standard software and adding to its features through scripting and plug-in architectures, you will benefit from their continued evolution and development, instead of having to keep up with those trends through upgrades of your own.

15 People Max.: This is a recommendation on the maximum group size using your AE. Not only will larger groups present problems in managing them effectively, but they will also require a larger space, and in turn larger displays to be readable from a distance, and the social protocols (see the pattern) tend to break down due to anonymity.

Full-Time Technician: Not a design pattern, more a process recommendation. Experience from several different rooms, at different institutions, even countries, and over quite a few years, has confirmed that such a high-tech environment will quickly fall apart if there is not at least the equivalent of one full-time technician who feels that an always-ready, always-working AE and related technology (videoconferencing unit, Media Boards, etc.) is their pride and responsibility (possibly along with maintaining the remaining infrastructure of the group owning the space). Keep this in mind when budgeting.

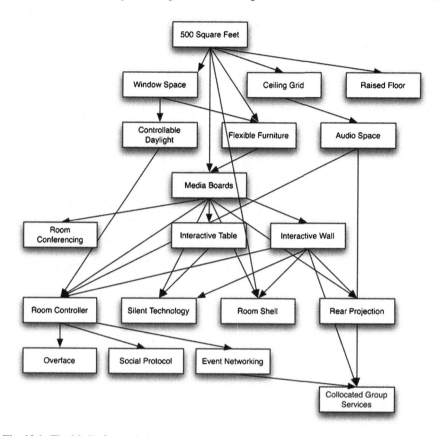

Fig. 10.1 The Media Space design pattern language

10.6   The Pattern Language

1   **500** *SQUARE FEET* ******

Fig. 10.2 The Aachen Media
Space in use

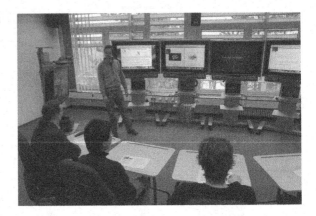

...you are just beginning to plan your Augmented Environment (AE), wondering
where in your building to locate it and how big it should be.

◆ ◆ ◆

**The bigger the AE, the more flexibly it can be used; but space in most
institutions is severely limited**.

Sometimes an entire floor, department, or even building is being redesigned from
scratch, and there is enough commitment and funding to turn the entire space into
an AE (see Hartkopf's chapter on floor designs at CMU). But in most cases, the
augmentation is limited to a common space such as a meeting room or a semi-
public area that all members of a team can use. The deciding factor for its size is
the type of activities it should support. A typical meeting-room-sized space is the most
common format; it supports one collaborative activity at the same time. To support
multiple collaborative activities at the same time will require a much larger space to
avoid distractive acoustic interference between the groups.

This also means that such a room can typically support teams of around five
full-time members, with roughly another ten infrequent visitors who come to some of
the meetings. The tasks envisioned for spaces of this size include internal presentations,
brainstorming and group discussions, administrative meetings, and hosting external
visitors and their presentations, and presenting demonstrations to them.

The Stanford iRoom has 20'3" × 17'10" = 360 ft² of usable main room area, plus
another 210 ft² occupied by rear-projection displays on two sides, for a total of 570
ft² (including the technology hidden behind walls). It also has an adjacent developer
area with workstations covering another 250 ft². The KTH iLounge has a similar
size. The Aachen Media Space is 8 by 6 m or 517 ft². Our latest Media Spaces
for the HumTec center at RWTH Aachen University are more varied, and will

accommodate activities of smaller and larger groups: 7 by 4.6 m, 9.4 by 4 m, and 5.8 by 14 m, or 350, 400, and 870 ft².

Therefore,

Reserve a space of at least around 500 square feet for your Augmented Environment. That size will support typical meeting activities for groups of up to 15 people.

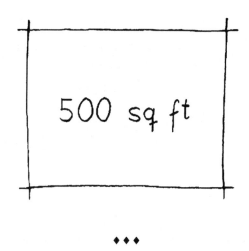

♦ ♦ ♦

Once the required size is determined, you should consider the right location for your AE – WINDOW SPACE (2). The space that the room takes up can be used much more efficiently if its furniture supports multiple usage scenarios – FLEXIBLE FURNITURE (4) and by making mounts for unforeseen technology to be added later available under the ceiling – CEILING GRID (5) and floor – RAISED FLOOR (6). The size of your room also determines how big your group displays have to be to be readable from anywhere in the room – MEDIA BOARDS (7). If you plan to include noisy equipment or rear-projected wall displays, consider adding a shell around the room for that technology – ROOM SHELL (12). ...

2   *WINDOW SPACE* ***

Fig. 10.3 Daylight entering
the Aachen Media Space

...you have determined the size of your AE – 500 SQUARE FEET (1), and are wondering where to put it in your building.

◆ ◆ ◆

**An AE is often added to an existing building or department, and the
remaining available space is often unattractive with no daylight; but humans
do not enjoy being in a space without daylight for long, especially for the
creative activities that are supposed to happen in the AE.**

When the Stanford iRoom was planned, the only location with enough contiguous
space left for it was in the basement, so it was installed there. But when prolonged
meetings where held there, participants frequently expressed an urge to leave the
space and continue outdoors in daylight. The space seemed fine for solitary, concentrated work in which one became largely oblivious to one's surroundings, but for
the social activities for which it was designed, a more humane environment with
daylight turned out to be important.

Similar observations were made with users of the Classroom of the Future at the
Ars Electronica Center in Linz, Austria (AEC). Short-term visitors had no problems
with its artificially lit interior, but people staying for more than an hour would
frequently report slight discomfort.

As a result, the location of the Aachen Media Space was chosen such that one
entire wall was a window front, allowing lots of daylight to enter. The users of this
space have not reported any of the adverse symptoms observed in the other spaces.
The EDF space in Paris also features more frequent windows.

Therefore,

**Make sure your AE has as much access to daylight as possible, ideally
directly through windows, or at least indirectly via indoor glass panes and
ceiling lights.**

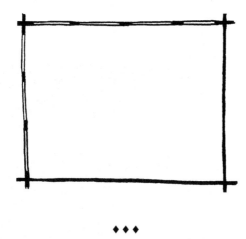

♦ ♦ ♦

Unlimited daylight can make it hard for people to work with the technology in the space, so make sure to make its intensity adjustable – CONTROLLABLE DAYLIGHT (3). Some setups will work best with daylight coming from a different direction than others, so keep your interior setup moveable – FLEXIBLE FURNITURE (4). ...

3   *CONTROLLABLE DAYLIGHT* ***

Fig. 10.4 Half-closed blinds
in the Aachen Media Space

...you have found a space that provides daylight – WINDOW SPACE (2), but are wondering what kind of blinds may be necessary.

◆ ◆ ◆

Daylight is essential for humans to feel comfortable in a space for prolonged periods of time. Yet, some displays may seem to require low-light conditions to work best.

When projection technology was just becoming affordable for office use, its light output was often insufficient to work in daylight conditions. This has changed, and most projectors and screens actually work well even with indirect daylight on them. There is hardly any need for darkening a room for projection, unless the projector is underpowered for its projection surface (700 ANSI lumen per square meter is a good rule-of-thumb for projectors).

The Aachen Media Space has a whole window front on one of its sides, and it has light, electrically controlled vertical blinds that can be opened, closed, and turned to shield the room from direct sunlight, while still letting in some daylight.

The environment at EDF is located in a room with an extensive glass front. Much of that front is shielded from daylight using heavy shutters to allow projection screens to be read easily. But there are easy ways to open those shutters from within the room, and an additional area high up below the ceiling can be opened to daylight as well.

The Media Space at KTH Library in Stockholm also features large overhead daylight windows, but it is equipped with drapery that can be remotely controlled from a central room controller to automatically open or close, depending on the usage scenario selected.

Therefore,

Equip your daylight windows with easily adjustable blinds. You should be able to close and open them fully in 10 s. They should allow at least three

different settings with different daylight levels. When closed, they should leave the room inside light through their own color. Avoid black drapes.

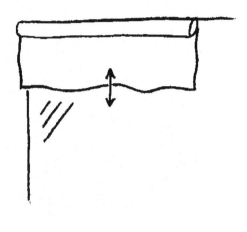

♦ ♦ ♦

You may want to consider making the blinds electrically controllable and integrating them into the room control interface – ROOM CONTROLLER (15). But make sure that they close and open quickly: if you have to wait for 2 min before they have opened fully, nobody will bother using them much. This can be difficult with electrically controlled systems. ...

4   *FLEXIBLE FURNITURE* **

Fig. 10.5 Moving a wall in
the Augmented Environment
at EDF in Paris

...you have determined the general size and location of your space – 500 SQUARE
FEET (1), WINDOW SPACE (2), and are beginning to think about how the room should
be equipped with furniture.

◆ ◆ ◆

**An AE will be used for a variety of different tasks; however, these tasks all
require different furniture configurations to be supported as well as possible**.

Activities that the Aachen Media Space, for example, has been used for include
internal and external research talks and presentations, brainstorming sessions,
group meetings to discuss progress and to plan next steps on a project, discussion
rounds with a mix of 5–10 student or faculty members, two-way and multipoint
video conferences with one or multiple participants at both the local and remote end
or ends, and technology demonstrations of current research projects to internal or
external audiences. The other AEs built by RUFAE members have mostly seen a
similar breadth of activities.

Almost every single one of the above tasks, however, requires a different spatial
arrangement of chairs, tables, displays, and other technology for optimal support.
The RUFAE environments have addressed this need to varying degrees and in
different ways.

The Stanford iRoom contains a large central table that includes rear-projection,
but is not moveable. Three fixed SMART Boards are built into one of its walls, and
a fourth, 10-Megapixel display wall into an adjacent wall. The result of this
arrangement was that it supported small group discussions quite well, but it was
difficult to use the room for presentations, as the table in the middle did not leave
enough room for additional people to sit in front of it towards the wall displays. It
also created a boundary that people were unlikely to cross in order to engage in

interaction with a wall display in collaborative work sessions (Gill and Borchers 2003). The KTH iLounge followed a similar design , with an immobile large table in the middle of the room and a display integrated into one wall.

The spaces at EDF, CMU, and Aachen were designed to be more flexible. Their furniture can be moved and even folded away easily. Everything is on wheels and easy to move by one person alone; in Aachen, this extends not only to tables and chairs, but even the wall displays – MEDIA BOARDS (7). EDF even has a larger space with moveable walls, which can be pushed around by one person, yet provide perfect visual and decent sound shielding.

The Aachen Media Space often looks a mess after a meeting, because tables and chair are all over the place. However, they are placed that way because when people came in for the activity, they grabbed a chair and a one-person table and wheeled them to where they wanted – which hardly ever leads to a straight, perfectly aligned square or similar formation. Before representative events, one of our staff members goes in and arranges the room to fit that event as well as possible in advance – which is easy because he can move everything alone and without effort.

The one-person rule is critical: not only should a table have wheels, but one person, male or female, with more or less physical strength, has to be able to move each piece of furniture with one hand, ideally even stow and unfold tables, because the other hand is often holding a laptop or notepad as he or she comes in. Anything that does not fulfill that criterion, from our experience, will not be moved around most of the time even when it would be beneficial to the task at hand.

Tables that cannot just be wheeled around but also folded up and stowed away easily will be somewhat less sturdy than their inflexible counterparts. So expect to pay significantly more for the "mobile" version of your furniture, in order to get something that is built as sturdy as you need it – tables to lean or even sit on, for example. Good mechanics make the difference here. A clunky folding mechanism that gets stuck frequently will never get used and therefore will be a waste of your money.

For the Aachen space, the most helpful question to ask in each step of the design and furniture was, "will this nail down any spatial aspect, the location, or orientation of any activity in the room?" When the answer was "yes," we looked instead for a more flexible solution. In general, anything that would get fixed to a wall or ceiling or would be too heavy to move easily was a candidate for improvement. Because of that rule, we have not even installed a fixed projector and screen in the room, and have instead opted for moveable large screens – MEDIA BOARDS (7).

Similar ideas about flexible furniture were used by the author in an earlier project merging future conference and classrooms (Mühlhäuser et al. 1996).

Therefore,

Try not to bolt down any aspect of the room's spatial furniture and technology arrangement. Put as much of your furniture in your AE on wheels, or make it otherwise easily moveable by a single person: Chairs, tables, even displays, and other equipment. Make tables fold and stow in a corner easily, saving space when not in use.

♦ ♦ ♦

Putting group displays on wheels as well is a good idea – MEDIA BOARDS (7). ...

5   *CEILING GRID* **

Fig. 10.6 The Aachen Media
Space ceiling

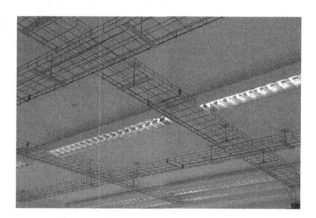

…you have decided about the general size of the space – 500 SQUARE FEET (1), and
are now wondering where to run the cables that the room requires.

♦ ♦ ♦

**AEs require a lot of cables to interconnect the technology in the room.
But running cables across the floor is hazardous. Also, new small devices like
additional switches, power adapters, microphones, cameras, or other sensors
are often introduced into an AE after the fact, but there is no easy way to mount
them anywhere**.

The Aachen Media Space features a 3-ft ceiling grid of open "cable trays" made
from strong wire mesh. It has served to hold the initial audio cables for the speakers
in the room – AUDIO SPACE (14), as well as additional optical and copper network
cables, media converters, switches, power adapters, a wireless router, and other
parts introduced to the environment as technology progresses. Having this easily
accessible structure under the ceiling makes it much more likely that new technologies are installed promptly, without requiring any construction work or drilling
holes. It also helps to get technology off the floor, reducing tripping hazards and
extending the life span of cables. All the time, this grid usually remains unnoticed by
people using the room, making the technology hide from their conscience.

The space at EDF features a similar grid.

Therefore,

**Put a wire mesh grid under the ceiling of your AE, at about a 3-ft raster, to
have a quick way to attach or hold cables and small devices installed in the room**.

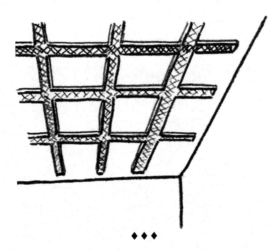

♦ ♦ ♦

The grid is a good place to hold, for example, cables for room speakers – AUDIO SPACE (14) …

6   RAISED FLOOR *

Fig. 10.7 An open floor panel in the
Aachen Media Space. The entire panel
including the floorbox can be moved

...you have decided on the overall size of your room – 500 SQUARE FEET (1), and are
wondering where to put the cabling, switches, and related technology infrastructure.

◆ ◆ ◆

**Users in an AE want access to power and networking where they sit.
Floorboxes are a natural choice for this. But in a flexible space, people end up
moving their chairs and desks into many different spatial arrangements. Even
with wireless networking, users will usually still want access to power for
their laptop or other personal devices, especially when presenting or in longer
sessions.**

An elegant solution to this problem is a raised floor. The EDF lab features a
reconfigurable raised floor with tiles that can be taken out completely. Most major
cabling is done in the raised floor. The Stanford iRoom uses a similar arrangement,
although it is less accessible due to the immobile furniture.

The Aachen Media Space also features a raised floor, and here the tiles are not
only removable, but the tiles with floorboxes in them can actually be disconnected
completely, allowing users to even move the floorboxes around, for example, to cluster
power and fast networking access points in a corner of a room to set up a cluster of
computers or neighboring displays. The connections providing power and networking

to the floorboxes are numerous, long, and flexible enough to be moved elsewhere in the room before being reconnected to the floorbox at the new position.

Floorboxes, even when they are completely flush with the ground as in the Media Space, always constitute a tripping hazard when cables protrude from them. However, with moveable floorboxes, this risk can be reduced: the floorboxes will end up spread out across the Media Space floor in an arrangement that best fits its current typical layout. For example, we have moved one floorbox each directly beneath where we typically have our Media Boards, thus moving their power connection out of the way.

The floorboxes ideally contain main power and Ethernet ports. They can also have rolled-up Ethernet cables inside to save users from having to find these elsewhere. Or, if the users have fairly homogeneous technology (as is the case in the Media Space), power adapters for the standard laptop brand (Apple in our case) can be put right into each floorbox, simplifying the most frequent access needs even further.

Note that you will have to work with your institution's safety department to ensure that fire safety regulations are being followed (you may need to install separate smoke or heat detectors in the floor), and that electrical safety standards are met if floorboxes are unpluggable.

Therefore,

Raise your floor by about 1 ft (30 cm), and put power and networking cables/switches into the raised floor. Provide power and network outlets at floorboxes, at least one at every 5 ft (1.5 m) in each direction, and make them moveable to accommodate future spatial configuration needs. Make the floorboxes deep enough to be able to include network cables and power adapters inside the floor boxes.

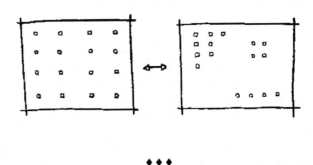

♦ ♦ ♦

This is a basic pattern with no further references within this language.

7 *MEDIA BOARDS* *

Fig. 10.8 A media board in the Aachen Media Space

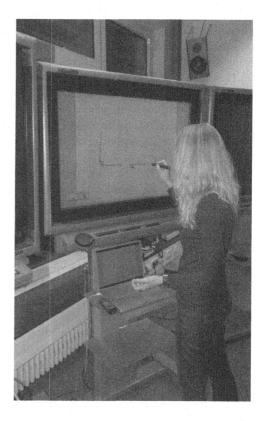

…you have determined the basic furniture to be put into your AE, and decided to make it as flexible as possible – FLEXIBLE FURNITURE (4). You are now thinking about the right display technology to go with this design.

♦ ♦ ♦

Any computer-supported group activity greatly benefits from large, shared display surfaces that can also be sketched upon and interacted with. However, projectors and projection screens are noisy and hard to move around quickly.

Groups need group displays. We have all huddled over a laptop with others, or squinted at it from across the table at some point to see what someone is trying to show us, and it is not a very productive spatial arrangement.

The most frequent solution to this problem is using projectors. They are cheap, can project large images (if they have strong lamps and short-throw lenses), are easy to carry around, and can project on a white wall, if necessary. However, projectors have a few drawbacks: First, they invariably include a fan that will create background noise in the room unless shielded from the users. Second, even though they are quick to move, setting them up and aligning them for good projection takes time, breaking the flow of a meeting. Third, when portable, the projection is usually from the front, and the presenter will often have to look into the lens and cast a shadow. Projecting from the rear solves that problem, but this only works where there is a special rear-projection screen surface installed, takes up space behind the screen, and provides only narrower viewing angles. Finally, projectors usually require a cooldown time before being disconnected from power, further slowing down any quick reconfigurations.

The Aachen Media Space instead features four moveable, interactive 40-in. displays. We called them *Media Boards* because they serve to interact with different media types: they let users project and interact with on-screen presentations, a web browser, other desktop applications, or special whiteboarding software. Each is constructed from an LCD screen with a touch-sensitive SMART Board overlay that lets users use their fingers or passive plastic pens to point and write on the board. The board is mounted on a mobile four-wheel stand that balances the weight of the screen to prevent the board from toppling over when it is being moved. A laptop is placed on a separate shelf under the display, providing a keyboard when needed, and (thanks to its battery) allowing the board to be moved around with power disconnected without having to reboot the computer. A second shelf can be attached to hold, for example, a portable video conferencing unit. The display can be adjusted in its height to serve different purposes, such as presentations (at standing height) and video conferences (at sitting height). Local speakers are mounted on the outer ends above the display. Thanks to wireless networking and a power strip and cable mounting grid at the back of the stand, the only cable going away from the display into the ground is a single power cord. Separate ethernet, DVI, VGA and audio cables are rolled up at the back of the stand to quickly connect other sources such as a visitor's laptop or demo machine when needed.

Plasma displays are less suitable for use in Media Boards than LCD screens, because they are heavier, typically require integrated fans for cooling – SILENT TECHNOLOGY (13), they suffer from burn-in problems with static content (unlike LCDs) and brightness loss over time, and their higher contrast is not crucial for the typical work tasks and lighting conditions in AEs.

Therefore,

Provide mobile LCD screens at least 40 in. in diameter, complete with a hooked-up laptop and optional connections for external sources, with speakers, and on a stand that can be wheeled around and is height-adjustable, with a single power cord to plug-in for use.

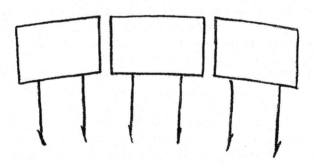

◆ ◆ ◆

As display technology advances, equipping entire walls and even whole rooms wall-to-wall with INTERACTIVE DISPLAY surfaces INTERACTIVE WALL (8) is gradually becoming affordable. But even in such environments, moveable displays are useful, as any area in the room (not just along the walls) can be picked to display and interact with information. The flexibility rule suggests providing display space *as a commodity*, easily made available wherever it is needed at the moment. Note that without a heavy counterweight, it is impossible not to have the stand reach out beyond the front of the screen. One thing to keep in mind, then, when choosing a stand is that people will want to walk up to the display to use it, and so its feet should not get into the way. Also, the displays may need to be pushed together as closely as possible for certain multi-screen scenarios. If the screens are to be tilted slightly towards each other when standing beside each other, then make sure that the wheels and sides of the display stand do not get in the way to do so at the required angle. Feet that can be turned towards the inside or outside can help to minimize the impact of this for different scenarios. The 40-in. size of the existing Media Boards in Aachen is sufficient for small group interaction, although it can sometimes be taxing to view smaller details in presentations on them from all across the room. Affordable LCD screen sizes are continuing to increase, however, and 60-in. screens will be more than sufficient for a typical-size augmented meeting room – 500 SQUARE FEET (1).

As with all technology, ensure that your boards do not create distracting noise through fans or transformers – SILENT TECHNOLOGY (13). If you need to consider projectors, choose a rear projection setup – REAR PROJECTION (11). You may be able to address space requirements and remaining noise problems of this arrangement better if you put it behind interior room walls – ROOM SHELL (12). A height-adjustable media board will work well for room-scale videoconferencing – ROOM CONFERENCING (10).

For some tasks, a horizontal display may be better suited, especially in addition to wall displays – INTERACTIVE TABLE (9). The Media Boards should be controllable from a web page and dedicated mobile device in the room – ROOM CONTROLLER (15). ...

8 *INTERACTIVE WALL* *

Fig. 10.9 The DynaWall® by
Norbert Streitz' group

...you are deciding on the display technology to put into the AE. You are either
planning to turn all walls into display surfaces, or you know that the AE will have
only a few, clearly defined, constant tasks. Or maybe you need a resolution higher
than what mobile displays can provide. Because of this, you have decided to look
into a static installation of display technology instead of, or in addition to, using
movable interactive group displays – media boards (7).

♦ ♦ ♦

**Groups need group displays to work with digital data, and complex
information requires lots of screen real estate; however, standard displays
come in small sizes and low resolution**

Large interactive walls have a big benefit over smaller, mobile displays, in that
they can display more context and detail at the same time. Walls also are more
appropriate than tables for many tasks as they provide a common, easy-to-read
vertical perspective on the contents for all users in a collaborative group, whereas
tables will need to provide special mechanisms to reorient content for different
users around the table – INTERACTIVE TABLE (9).

The Darmstadt IPSI environment featured one of the earliest interactive walls,
the *DynaWall®* (Streitz et al. 1999), made up from three rear-projected large touch
screens built side-by-side into a wall. The Stanford iRoom featured a very similar
setup, using three SMART Boards. It was augmented by a fourth, large 10-mega-
pixel display made from 4 × 3 standard projectors hooked up to a rendering cluster
(Guimbretière et al. 2001), with software focusing on brainstorming activities.
The three-display iRoom design was subsequently adopted in the design of the
Wallenberg Hall interactive learning spaces at Stanford. The iLounge at KTH and
the EDF space in Paris also have one wall with a large built-in projection which is
usually where presentations are being shown. More recent interactive wall work

from the IPSI group includes the *InfoRiver* and *Hello.Wall* (Streitz et al. 2005) that also focus on informal group communication.

There is not much use for a gigantic screen (beyond around 40 inches) in a meeting room unless its resolution also goes well beyond 1,024 × 768. Some large displays feature high resolution already; another option is to tile smaller standard displays together into a large, smooth surface. Aim for very small seams between tiles for visual continuity in this case. A good target resolution is at least 60 dpi, which is close to the 72 dpi of traditional desktop monitors.

Making such surfaces interactive usually required attaching an external sensor system (such as an eBeam® or Mimio® system) to the display, which then sensed touch via special pens. Alternatively, touchscreens such as SMART Boards can be tiled, with the advantage of supporting bare finger input. More recently, infrared light has been used successfully to accurately detect multiple-finger touch on rear-projected surfaces (Han 2005) and on flat LCD screens (Hodges et al. 2007), opening up the potential for more natural interaction gestures.

Therefore,

Include a wall-size display in your AE. Make it rear-projected or use LCD screens. If budget allows, aim for a pixel resolution of at least 60 dpi, if necessary by tiling multiple smaller displays with as small seems as possible. Make the surface interactive with at least 1 mm resolution to allow for touch input and sketching, if possible with multi-touch support.

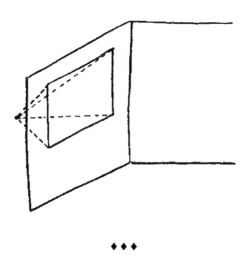

◆ ◆ ◆

Middleware can link independent displays together to effectively provide a larger, contiguous display to the user – COLLOCATED GROUP SERVICES (18). This software can help to integrate multiple small mounted screens into an interactive wall or to combine mobile displays into one. Like the Media Boards, the Interactive Wall should be controllable from a web page and a dedicated mobile device in the room – ROOM CONTROLLER (15). If projectors must be used, consider projecting from behind the wall – REAR PROJECTION (11) and/or putting the wall technology into a space behind the room's interior wall – ROOM SHELL (12). ...

9 *INTERACTIVE TABLE* **

Fig. 10.10 The multitouch
table, designed by David
Holman from the author's
Media Computing Group, in
use at a research exhibition

...you have decided on your vertical display space - media boards (7), but are
considering the need for horizontal display surfaces as well.

◆ ◆ ◆

**Some activities, such as collaborative photo sorting and analysis, are best
done by a group around a table. However, traditional laptop or wall displays
do not lend themselves well to this situation**

Streitz et al. created a touch-sensitive table as part of their *Roomware®* research
and product development. (Streitz et al. 1999). The Stanford iRoom included a
table, but it was immobile, with its rear-projection built into the raised floor.
The KTH iLounge also featured a fixed table in the middle of the room.

More recently, the author's Media Computing Group has built multitouch-sensitive
tables that use rear projection and afford more natural interactions with multiple
fingers and hands. This technology has been used, for example, in a multitouch
table exhibit for a Dutch children's museum. Microsoft's *Surface* project builds
on these ideas to create a commercially viable multitouch table.

The big caveat with tables is their inherent orientation. Reading text together is
much harder around a table than on a shared wall display. The direct interaction
with artifacts that would also be shuffled around on a real table, however (such
as photos), is a big plus, especially if the table is multitouch-enabled (single-touch
inhibits the natural parallelism and overlap of collaborative human activity).
Toolkits such as DiamondSpin (Shen et al. 2004) allow for easier development of
rotation-enabled interfaces.

The second issue with tables is their immobility. Heavy technology such as a large,
possibly stationary rear projection system should be avoided. Small projectors or
LCD screens are a better choice to keep the table moveable.

Therefore,

Consider adding an interactive group table to your room, especially if you are interested in this topic for research purposes. Choose a design that remains mobile and that is supported through software libraries to develop and run the somewhat idiosyncratic UIs required for it.

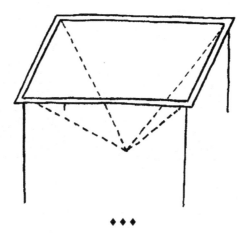

♦ ♦ ♦

Table users are very close to the table, in order to reach its surface. Because of this, it is important that the table does not create unnecessary noise, for example, through fans in its rear projector or the connected computer – silent technology (13). ...

10   *ROOM CONFERENCING* **

Fig. 10.11 Users in
front of a Polycom
videoconferencing unit

…you are putting together the list of services and technologies to put into your AE –
MEDIA BOARDS (7), and are thinking about video conferencing connectivity to the
outside world.

♦ ♦ ♦

**Today, video conferencing is used regularly to avoid having to fly people
around the globe. However, users often report inadequate audio and video quality,
and an overall unsatisfying experience when using simple videoconferencing
solutions**

It is vital to distinguish between two groups of systems. They both provide a
live audio/video link between two sites, but their intended use is fundamentally
different:

Personal or Desktop Videoconferencing Systems: These are typically software solutions that use the processing power, display, and speakers of a desktop or laptop
computer with an attached camera and microphone (or a headset). They often
even support application or document sharing across the video link. Examples
include Apple's iChat A/V that comes free with their operating system, or Polycom's
PVX® software. They are designed to capture *one person's* audio and video input
well. This is their important limitation: as soon as a group of people in one place
tries to use these systems, they begin to break down due to lower video resolution,
insufficient room characteristics of microphones, and limited echo cancellation.

Room Videoconferencing Systems: Their optical camera quality, video resolution
(moving to HD as of this writing) and compression technology, microphone design,
echo cancellation, and audio processing (all done in hardware) are designed to
handle multiple speakers in the same room on the system's end. They feature locally

and remotely controllable cameras, multiple microphones, and web streaming interfaces for additional passive participants. Prices for high-end systems lie in the $10k range. A current example is Polycom's VSX® 7000 system.

Getting a desktop system for budget reasons when a room system would have been needed is a certain recipe for failure when trying to use the technology constructively.

For best eye contact, lower the screen showing the remote participants so that their eyes on-screen are at eye level of the local participants (around 4 ft high), and mount the video camera directly above the upper edge of the screen. If the system provides a picture-in-picture feedback view of its own local camera image, enable it to allow participants to notice when they are off-screen, for example. Place that view at the top center of the screen if possible, immediately under the camera.

If frequent collaborators are already known, then the system should be chosen to be compatible with existing technology on the other end. The camera should always be as close as possible to the top of the screen for best mutual eye contact. The Media Board or other screen should be lowered so that participants see eye-to-eye.

Therefore,

Provide a portable but high-end room videoconferencing system of adequate quality for the size of your AE. Put it on top of a MediaBoard screen lowered to sitting eye height, so it can be moved easily.

This is a basic pattern with no further references within this language.

11 *REAR PROJECTION* **

Fig. 10.12 SMART Board with rear projection (Image copyright 2001–2008 SMART Technologies ULC. All rights reserved.)

...you are planning the outfitting of your AE with displays – media boards (7), interactive wall (8), and are wondering whether to use front or rear projection for your projector-based setups.

♦ ♦ ♦

Projectors, even short-throw systems, need a certain distance from the screen. However, in an AE, users should be able to interact with displays by touching them, in which case they are directly in front of the display and in the projector's path, casting shadows just where they are working.
Many systems have recognized this problem and opted for rear projection, such as our conducting exhibits (Borchers et al. 2004), even when the user is not directly touching the display. The reason is that rear projection reaches higher display contrast than front projection, improving the visual quality of the interface.

With interactive surfaces, many solutions such a SMART Technologies' rear-projection SMART Boards opt for rear projection to avoid shadows on the surface. If there is no space for rear projection, an ultra-short-throw front projection (projection distance to projection width <<1) can be used.

A more elegant solution may be using an LCD screen, as it does not bring the depth requirements with it (or noise problems) that rear projection has. Therefore, rear projection is usually chosen when relatively low resolution but a large projection area is needed.

Rear projection does not mean that the projection needs to be mounted on a fixed wall, as the movable SMART Boards demonstrate. In any case, the rear-projection housing may serve to shield some of the projector's noise.

Therefore,

If projectors must be used in an AE, use rear projection for shadow-free operation, better contrast, and somewhat less noise.

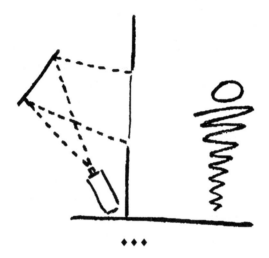

♦ ♦ ♦

This is a basic pattern with no further references within this language.

12   ROOM SHELL

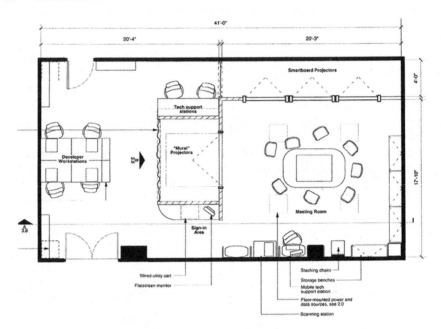

Fig. 10.13 Layout of the Stanford iRoom. Note the shell spaces for rear-projection technology along the top and left sides of the main room

…you have decided on the size of your interior space – 500 SQUARE FEET (1), and on what display technologies you intend to provide – MEDIA BOARDS (7), INTER-ACTIVE WALL (8). You are now wondering where to put the extra technology required.

◆ ◆ ◆

AEs require additional computers, amplifiers, and similar technology that normal workspaces do not feature in the same amount. However, there is usually not enough space to put that technology into the room itself, and it may constitute a noise problem; on the other hand, the technology has to be close to the room because of cable length limitations and the need to access the technology when problems arise.

This conflict was addressed in the Stanford iRoom by putting an entire shell around two sides of the room. That shell was deep enough to house rear projected screens, and even opened up towards a developer space on one side.

The KTH iLounge used a similar approach, putting much of its technology behind a rounded inner "cocoon" that was used by the participants as meeting space.

The raised floor in the Aachen Media Space can be seen as a shell, but its design without projectors and noisy technology removed the need for such a shell, which in turn left more space for the actual room itself.

At UCSD's Distributed Cognition and Human-Computer Interaction Lab, a space adjacent to their meeting environment both houses the rear projection and provides additional storage space for technology.

At EDF France's LDC space in Paris, the raised floor also serves as a shell providing space for various infrastructure technologies. It is also air-conditioned, with adjustable floor outlets, providing the flexibility that moveable walls and furniture require.

Therefore,

If rear-projected screens are needed inside the walls, or noisy technology needs to be stowed away while still being accessible, and your AE does not become too small by this, consider closing off a secondary space, about 4 ft deep, around one or more of the walls of your AE.

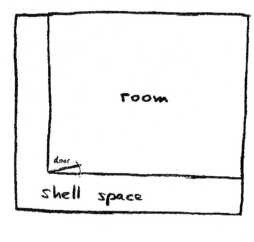

♦ ♦ ♦

This is a basic pattern with no further references within this language.

13 *SILENT TECHNOLOGY* **

Fig. 10.14 A computer fan

...you have decided on your overall devices to put into your AE, such as displays – MEDIA BOARDS (7), INTERACTIVE WALL (8), INTERACTIVE TABLE (9) – and are selecting particular models and technologies

◆ ◆ ◆

Background noise elevates stress levels and is detrimental to users' health, ability to concentrate, and productivity. However, AEs require a lot of technology to be integrated into the space that users work in.

Desktop computers and towers, projectors, plasma displays, external hard drives, and many other devices today contain fans for cooling or otherwise produce noticeable noise levels. Even these low noise levels have been shown to introduce stress to people in the environment.

To avoid these factors, selecting the right technologies is the most helpful step. For example, unlike projectors, LCD screens are silent because they have no fans. Laptops, unlike desktop or tower computers, will run without their fans spinning up for most of the time, and can easily master most tasks in AEs today.

Even within a given technology, there are sometimes huge differences in noise levels between competing products. It pays to check for the dB level ratings. And especially hard drives can develop whining noises with age, so exchange them after 2–3 years.

The equipment in the Aachen Media Space, for example, was selected to contain not a single constantly running fan, mostly by choosing LCD screens over projectors and laptops over stationary machines.

Therefore,

Keep the noise level added by the technology to a minimum, by avoiding equipment with constantly running cooling fans, drives, or other noisy mechanics.

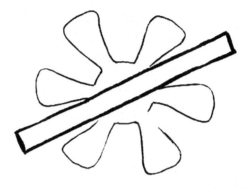

♦ ♦ ♦

If noisy equipment is unavoidable, consider shielding it inside larger encasing, or behind a wall – room shell (12). Of course, the original position of the room would have to support a quiet environment to begin with – window space (2). Also have an eye (or rather ear) on any air-conditioning system in the room. ...

14   *AUDIO SPACE* *

Fig. 10.15 One of the eight speakers around the Aachen Media Space

...you have settled on the furniture and display equipment – MEDIA BOARDS (7), INTERACTIVE WALL (8), and are now thinking about the audio side of your setup.

◆ ◆ ◆

Laptops and stationary machines will often need to play back audio for the participants in the room, but running audio cables across the room is an unsatisfying solution.

An early part of the software development going into the Aachen Media Space was the *AudioSpace* software, originally developed for Mac OS X 10.3 by Stefan Werner in a co-advised diploma thesis (Werner 2005). It consisted of two parts: you installed a client-side driver on your laptop that would let you choose a new virtual audio output to direct your audio to driver would not play back your audio, but instead package it up and send it via a TCP network connection to the AudioSpace server application. The server would unpack the data and play it back via its local audio interface, typically connected to the PA system in the room you are in. The result: Anybody in the room could play audio using the room audio system, from their laptops, without any audio cabling to the laptops required.

Other software exists that allows for a similar wireless audio link. The downside, in all cases, is of course that software needs to be installed on each machine that wishes to participate; but the advantage of cable-free access to room audio is quite significant.

Therefore,

Make software available for machines in the AE to wirelessly send their audio output to a room audio system.

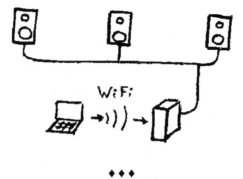

♦ ♦ ♦

This functionality could be wrapped into the general software required to connect to the room infrastructure – collocated group services (18), and control could be offered via a mobile device – room controller (15). ...

15 ROOM CONTROLLER **

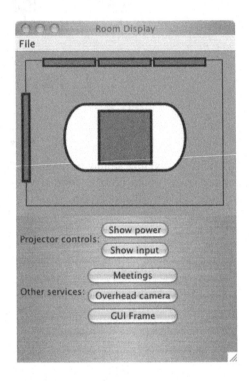

Fig. 10.16 The UI for a tablet- or PDA-size room controller, showing a room layout with lights, projectors, etc., to control the Stanford iRoom

…you have settled on the interactive technology to be installed in the AE – CONTROLLABLE DAYLIGHT (3), MEDIA BOARDS (7), INTERACTIVE WALL (8), INTERACTIVE TABLE (9), AUDIO SPACE (14). Now you need to design a way for users of the room to control the technology.

♦ ♦ ♦

Technology added to a work environment often dictates its own, proprietary user interface through its physical design, and is usually only controllable locally at the device, or through a single physical remote control. However, users think in different, more space- and task-oriented ways when trying to operate this technology, and want to operate it wherever they are in the room.

In the Stanford iRoom, three projectors, a high-resolution projection wall, a rear-projected table, and multiple ceiling lights had to be operated to get the room into a particular state. To achieve this from anywhere in the room, their proprietary control interfaces were adapted to a TCP-based protocol, and a graphical user interface showing all devices in a simplified floorplan of the room was generated as an interactive web page. Any browser could open that page, and it was adaptable to displays of different form factors (such as mobile devices), but it was also displayed on a dedicated wireless tablet PC that was always available in the room. This allowed users to grab the device or have it passed to them when they wished to change something, with everybody else realizing what was going on.

Therefore,

Make sure your devices are controllable via a standard, open protocol such as serial or TCP/IP communication. Provide a graphical spatial floor map that shows where your interactive devices are situated in the AE, and that lets the user operate the devices from this map. Create the floor map from a service description so that it can be adapted to different display sizes and UI form factors, and so that it can dynamically change as new devices become available. Make the map displayable on any browser, but also provide a dedicated mobile touch display in the room that always shows this map.

♦ ♦ ♦

The room controller requires the room technology to be accessible via the network – EVENT NETWORKING (17). It can be a good representation for the unified interface to the room and its services – OVERFACE (19). Its usage, as with all other technology in the environment, should not get into the way – SOCIAL PROTOCOL (16). …

16   *SOCIAL PROTOCOL* ***

Fig. 10.17 Passing on a mouse for a group display

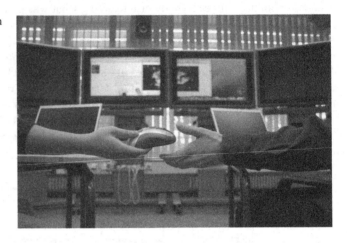

...you have picked your hardware to control the room and its services – ROOM CON-TROLLER (15), and now need to decide how the technology is operated by the users.

◆ ◆ ◆

Interactive technology likes to be told when something happens or when it is supposed to do something. But people easily forget that extra step, especially when in the middle of a high-energy brainstorming session.

A research video by MIT once showed a group of researchers having a meeting around the table, and the room was "listening in" on the conversation going on. Whenever a certain point was reached, such as deciding to add a new item to the agenda or delegating a task to a member in the room, everybody had to shut up, and the moderator would speak the corresponding commands for the computer to keep up with what was going on. It was the worst group support interface imaginable.

Good group support software follows what is going on in the room as good as it can, trying to detect from a variety of sensors, models, and other input what the current activity and actors are, and then takes initiative on a simple, reliable level to help the actors, without presuming to understand more than it can.

Computer scientists will argue that deriving this information from sensor values is not reliable, and so the computer needs clear commands in order not to do something wrong. This is perfectly true in distributed settings with low bandwidth for human communication: if user A decides to pass control over the shared mouse cursor to remote user B in a shared application, he usually has to click a button to do so.

In a collocated setting of an AE, an enormous advantage comes to the help of the system: social protocol. The people in the room can see and hear each other. If one person is controlling the mouse cursor using their laptop, and someone else wants to take over with their own laptop, they will just say so. The computer does not need to understand this verbal command, nor does he need to lock the cursor for everybody else, but one user at a time: It can simply accept cursor movement from everybody in the room; if there's a conflict of concurrent access, the users will quickly and easily notice and resolve it among themselves. This approach, on the other hand, saves the users having to send explicit messages each time they wish to pass control of that cursor to someone else, making the interaction much more fluid.

Examples include the design of the interaction for the iRoom's remote cursor control that allows "mouse fights" to occur, simply always using the last coordinate received, or its iClipboard feature that lets people cut and paste in a single shared clipboard for the room.

Winograd et al., in their chapter elsewhere in this book, reflect on this concept by suggesting room infrastructure in which "...users and social conventions in an environment take responsibility for actions, and the system infrastructure is responsible for providing a fluid means to execute those actions."

Therefore,

Do not put unnecessary protocols into place that are aimed at avoiding overlapping access to technology, if that collision can be easily noticed and fixed by the users through social interaction. If a user issues a social protocol act, such as passing a wireless mouse to someone else, never require an additional repetitive step from the user to tell the room what he just did for everyone else to clearly see.

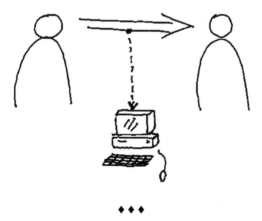

♦ ♦ ♦

This is a basic pattern with no further references within this language.

17 *EVENT NETWORKING* **

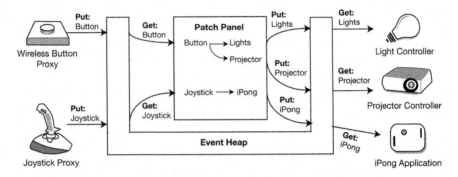

Fig. 10.18 The flow of events from input devices and applications, through a central networked event management (EventHeap) and mapping (PatchPanel) service, to the appropriate output applications and devices

…you have installed your hardware and made OS choices. Now it is time to think about the middleware to let your users collaborate fluidly in the AE.

◆ ◆ ◆

It is easy to link computers over a data network and send data using application-specific protocols. However, in an AE, the machines, operating systems, and applications must exchange information about events occurring on them in a more general and useful way.

One of the key principles in any operating system that supports interactive applications is *event processing* – button clicks on a mouse are passed via drivers into system-wide queues, where they are ordered, prioritized, and then distributed to their target application, typically depending on which application has the input focus at the moment. This mechanism has been highly optimized in modern operating systems to ensure immediate feedback and continuous control for the user.

AEs require a similar mechanism, but now at the level of communication across multiple computers and operating systems. This means that everything needs to be internet-controllable, from devices such as projectors, speakers, and lamps, to applications such as presentation and brainstorming apps. For example, the Stanford iRoom and KTH iLounge were equipped with projectors that could be turned on and off via web-based interfaces. Scripting interfaces for applications such as PowerPoint were used to provide remote control of presentations.

The standard will most likely be a TCP/IP-based protocol, usually via a web interface. But it can also be another technology such as Bluetooth, or a mix of these. The important thing is that all components in the room support being set up and controlled via events.

Therefore,

Provide each technology component in your AE with a control interface using an open networking standard.

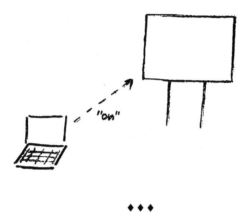

♦ ♦ ♦

Once devices and applications can be controlled via events, you can create services based on that infrastructure – COLLOCATED GROUP SERVICES (18) …

18 *COLLOCATED GROUP SERVICES* **

Fig. 10.19 Users collaborating in a TeamSpot?. (Image copyright 2004–2008, TideBreak™, Inc.
All rights reserved.)

...you have found a way to send information about events between your room
components in a meaningful and practical way – EVENT NETWORKING (17), and
prepared the room to share media between participants – INTERACTIVE WALL (8),
AUDIO SPACE (14). Now you need to decide on what services to build on top of this
infrastructure.

◆ ◆ ◆

**Today's operating systems and applications make working alone quite
effective, but in an AE the group will want to work on information together,
with frequent exchanges of digital information between the participants – and
this is badly supported in today's standalone systems.**
The Stanford Interactive Workspaces project tackled this problem by developing
a robust, fault-tolerant middleware that built on the concept of the Event Heap, a
tuplespace with publish-subscribe semantics (see Borchers et al. 2002 or Winograd's
chapter for details). It allowed applications to send or subscribe to particular events,
enabling applications, devices, and services to talk to each other. Its loose coupling
allowed individual components to disconnect without disrupting the remaining
network.
On top of this, the software provided easy ways for room users to move their
mouse cursor from their own laptop up to a shared screen in the room, with keyboard
input following along. The package also enabled quick and easy sharing of URLs
and arbitrary files or text and graphics clippings between people in the room that had
the client software installed. An important principle of these tools promoted in part by
the author was the use of core features such as copying and pasting between computers
without having to remember any new commands or keyboard shortcuts, instead
simply using the existing commands and shortcuts for the expanded functionality.

The software was successful enough to be turned into a commercial product, *TeamSpot*, based on the same principles, that has since added screen sharing, full cross-platform support, and many additional features and improvements to the mix.

Since then, other software packages have developed similar ideas, though usually not as comprehensive. One example is DropCopy (http://10base-t.com/software/macintosh/dropcopy.html) for quick sharing of files between Macs and iPhones.

Therefore,

Provide seamless means for users of your AE to move files, text snippets, graphics and other media, URLs, and entire screen contents around the room to other personal laptops or shared displays.

♦ ♦ ♦

This is a basic pattern with no further references within this language.

19 OVERFACE **

Fig. 10.20 In the i-LAND®
environment, windows are
crossing screens and machines,
and users work with a
seamless interface
(Streitz et al. 2001)

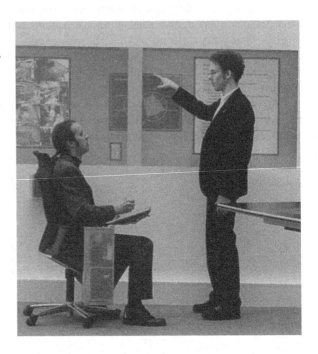

...you have chosen what devices and services to make available in your AE, and are trying to come up with a good user interface representation to control everything – ROOM CONTROLLER (15).

♦ ♦ ♦

People working in an AE tend to think of the environment and its computing services as a single, coherent entity. However, today's Personal Computers and their operating systems and applications are designed around a single-person interaction model.

The iRoom provided a web-based interface to control the entire room, and allowed for task-centered actions such as "make the room ready for a meeting" to be set up as commands, which would have turned on lights and projectors, launched certain applications, and brought up appropriate work documents and web pages.

At one point, we created a "Start the Room" button using our iStuff toolkit (Borchers et al. 2002) that could simply be tacked to a wall near the entrance and would complete this setup procedure when pressed.

Therefore,

Give the user the illusion that he is interacting with a single, coherent user interface, not with an assortment of individual systems with different rules, metaphors, and conceptual models.

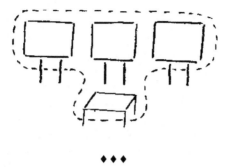

♦ ♦ ♦

This is a basic pattern with no further references within this language.

10.7   About the Author

Jan Borchers is a professor of computer science and head of the Media Computing Group at RWTH Aachen University in Germany. With his group, he explores human–computer interaction beyond the desktop, from interactive workspaces and ubiquitous computing environments, to audio and video streams, to mobile and wearable devices. He has been involved in the research and design of interactive workspaces since 1995, including the Classroom of the Future project for the Ars Electronica Center in Linz, Austria (Mühlhäuser et al. 1996), the Stanford Interactive Workspaces (iRoom) project (Borchers et al. 2002) and its middleware software later commercialized as *TeamSpot* (see also the chapter by Johanson et al.), the interactive workspaces at Stanford's Wallenberg Hall and the iLounge at KTH (see also the chapter by Jansson), and lately the Aachen Media Space (Borchers 2006) at RWTH Aachen University, the author's present institution, as well as three similar spaces for *HumTec*, an interdisciplinary research center on humans and technology at the same university. See http://hci.rwth-aachen.de.

Acknowledgments The author would like to thank the members of the RUFAE team for the many shared projects, discussions, and demonstrations that led to this pattern language, and Thorsten Karrer, Yvonne Jansen, and the other members of the Media Computing Group for their support in formatting and collecting many of the photographs in this language. This work was funded in part by the German B-IT Foundation and by the German Government through its UMIC Excellence Cluster for Ultra-High Speed Mobile Information and Communication at RWTH Aachen University.

References

Alexander C. *The Timeless Way of Building*. Oxford University Press, Oxford, 1979.
Alexander C. *Keynote Speech, OOPSLA'96 11th Annual ACM Conference on Object-Oriented Programming Systems, Languages and Applications* (6–10 October 1996, San Jose, California), 1996 (Conference video).
Alexander C, Ishikawa S, Silverstein M, Jacobson M, Fiksdahl-King I, and Angel S. *A Pattern Language: Towns, Buildings, Construction*. Oxford University Press, Oxford, 1977.
Alexander C, Silverstein M, Angel S, Ishikawa S, and Abrams D. *The Oregon Experiment*. Oxford University Press, Oxford, 1988.
Apple Computer. *Macintosh Human Interface Guidelines*. Addison-Wesley, Reading, MA, 1992.
Bayle E, Bellamy R, Casaday G, Erickson T, Fincher S, Grinter B, Gross B, Lehder D, Marmolin H, Moore B, Potts C, Skousen G, and Thomas J. Putting it all together: Towards a pattern language for interaction design. *SIGCHI Bulletin*, 30(1):17–23, 1998.
Beck K and Cunningham W. Using pattern languages for object-oriented programs. Technical Report CR-87-43, Tektronix, Inc., 17 September 1987. Presented at the *OOPSLA'87* workshop on Specification and Design for Object-Oriented Programming, 1987.
Borchers JO, Griffiths RN, Pemberton L, and Stork A. Pattern languages for interaction design: Building momentum. Workshop at CHI 2000 (The Hague, Netherlands, 2–3 April 2000), 2000.
Borchers J, Lee E, Samminger W, and Mühlhäuser M. Personal Orchestra: A real-time audio/video system for interactive conducting. *ACM Multimedia Systems Journal Special Issue on Multimedia Software Engineering* 9(5):458–465, 2004.

Borchers J. *A Pattern Approach to Interaction Design.* Wiley Series in Software Design Patterns. John Wiley & Sons, Chichester, UK, 2001.

Borchers JO. CHI meets PLoP: An interaction patterns workshop (at ChiliPLoP'99 Conf. on Pattern Languages for Programming, Wickenburg, AZ, 16–19 March 1999). *SIGCHI Bulletin,* 32(1): 9–12, 2000b.

Borchers JO. Interaction design patterns: Twelve theses. Position paper for the workshop *Pattern Languages for Interaction Design: Building Momentum,* CHI 2000 (The Hague, Netherlands, 2–3 April 2000), 2000c.

Borchers J. Teaching HCI patterns: Experience from two university courses. In *Position Paper for the HCI Patterns Workshop at the CHI 2002 International Conference on Human Factors and Computing Systems.* ACM, April 2002.

Borchers J. The Aachen Media Space: Multiple displays in collaborative interactive environments. In *CHI 2006: Workshop "Information Visualization and Interaction Techniques for Collaboration across Multiple Displays",* Montreal, Canada, April 2006.

Borchers J, Ringel M, Tyler J, and Fox A. Stanford interactive workspaces: A framework for physical and graphical user interface prototyping. *IEEE Wireless Communications* 9(6):64–69, 2002.

Barfield L, van Burgsteden W, Lanfermeijer R, Mulder B, Ossewold J, Rijken D, and Wegner P. Interaction design at the Utrecht School of the Arts. *SIGCHI Bulletin* 26(3):49–79, 1994.

Dearden A and Finlay JE. Patterns in HCI: A critical review. *Human-Computer Interaction Journal* 21(1):49–102, 2006.

Gill SP and Borchers J. Knowledge in co-action: social intelligence in collaborative design activity. *AI and Society Journal of Human-Centred Systems and Machine Intelligence* 17: 322–339, 2003.

Gamma E, Helm R, Johnson R, and Vlissides J. *Design Patterns: Elements of Reusable Object-Oriented Software.* Addison-Wesley, Reading, MA, 1995.

Granlund A and Lafrenière D. A pattern-supported approach to the user interface design process. Workshop Report, *UPA'99 Usability Professionals' Association Conf.* (Scottsdale, AZ, 29 June–2 July 1999), http://www.gespro.com/lafrenid/Workshop_Report.pdf, 1999.

Guimbretière F, Stone M, and Winograd T. Fluid interaction with high-resolution wall-size displays. In *UIST'01: Proceedings of the 14th Annual ACM Symposium on User Interface Software and Technology,* pp 21–30, ACM, New York, 2001.

Han JY. Low-cost multi-touch sensing through frustrated total internal reflection. In *UIST'05: Proceedings of the 18th Annual ACM Symposium on User Interface Software and Technology,* pp 115–118, ACM, New York, 2005.

Hodges S, Izadi S, Butler A, Rrustemi A, and Buxton B. Thinsight: Versatile multi-touch sensing for thin form-factor displays. In *UIST'07: Proceedings of the 20th Annual ACM Symposium on User Interface Software and Technology,* pp 259–268, ACM, New York, 2007.

Mühlhäuser M, Borchers J, Falkowski C, and Manske K. The conference/classroom of the future: An interdisciplinary approach. In *Proceedings of the IFIP Conference on the International Office of the Future: Design Options and Solution Strategies,* pp 219–235, Tucson, Arizona, 1996. Chapman & Hall, London.

Miller GA. The magical number Seven, plus or minus two: Some limits on our capacity for processing information. *The Psychological Review* 63:81–97, 1956. http://www.well.com/user/smalin/miller.html

Norman DA and Draper SW. *User-Centered System Design: New Perspectives on Human-Computer Interaction.* Lawrence Erlbaum Associates, Hillsdale, NJ, 1986.

Norman DA. *The Psychology of Everyday Things.* Basic Books, New York, 1988.

Streitz NA, Geißler J, Holmer T, Konomi S, Müller-Tomfelde C, Reischl W, Rexroth P, Seitz P, and Steinmetz R. i-land: An interactive landscape for creativity and innovation. In *CHI'99: Proceedings of the SIGCHI Conference on Human Factors in Computing Systems,* pp 120–127, New York, NY, USA, 1999. ACM, New York.

Streitz N, Magerkurth C, Prante T, and Röcker C. From information design to experience design: Smart artefacts and the disappearing computer. *Interactions* 12(4):21–25, 2005.

Streitz N, Tandler P, Müller-Tomfelde C, Konomi S. Roomware: Towards the next generation of human-computer interaction based on an integrated design of real and virtual worlds. In: J. Carroll (Ed.): *Human-Computer Interaction in the New Millenium*, Addison-Wesley, Reading, MA, 2001. pp. 553–578.

Shen C, Vernier FD, Forlines C, and Ringel M. Diamondspin: An extensible toolkit for around-the-table interaction. In *CHI'04: Proceedings of the SIGCHI Conference on Human Factors in Computing Systems*, pp 167–174, New York, NY, USA, 2004. ACM, New York.

Tidwell J. *Designing Interfaces: Patterns for Effective Interaction Design*. O'Reilly, Sebastopol, CA, 2005.

van Duyne K, Landay JA, and Hong JI. *The Design of Sites: Patterns for Creating Winning Web Sites*, 2 edn. Prentice-Hall, Englewood Cliffs, NJ, 2006.

Werner S. An algorithm for audio skew compensation in low latency environments. In *Proceedings of the ICMC 2005 International Conference on Computer Music*, San Francisco, CA, 2005. International Computer Music Association (ICMA).

Index

A

Aachen Media Space, 24, 25, 261–310
Abuse (es), 27, 131
Access keys, 8
Action (s), 124, 167
Activity-based design, 121, 122
Activity-orientedness, 26–27
Activity path, 125, 126, 129
Activity theory, 11, 20, 27, 204, 213, 218, 221
Activity Trails, 247–249
Adaptability, 12, 14, 20, 26, 68, 70, 78, 84
Adaptive and context-aware services (ACAS),
     20, 208
Advanced Building Systems Integration
     Consortium (ABSIC), 67, 84
Affordances, 65–67
Agentic, 7
Alexander, C., 24, 262, 263
Ambient Agoras, 145, 155, 177, 179–181,
     183, 185–188
Ambient intelligence, 4
Amenities, 13, 65, 66, 81, 140, 144
Annotation (s), 16, 53, 87, 90, 92, 93, 246,
     247, 253
Anoto, 253, 254
Antenna, 121, 148–150, 152
Anthropocentric approach, 213, 215, 216
Application Ensembles, 46
Architecture, 2–6, 11–15, 17, 26, 28, 35, 42, 64,
     83, 87, 88, 94, 98, 104–106, 108, 133,
     135, 163, 179, 196, 208, 261, 262, 268
Ars Electronica, 266, 272, 310
ASL, 251, 252
Attali, 19
Attention, 27, 31, 32, 41, 42, 52, 53, 55, 59,
     67, 84, 88, 92, 109, 110, 114, 123, 128,
     149, 219, 231, 243, 248, 266
Audio space pattern, 298
Augmented reality, 17, 144, 193, 214, 218
Authentication, 5, 15, 87, 98, 107, 108, 150

Automobile, 23, 240, 244
Aziz, A., 13, 63–84, 155

B

Back, M., 6, 15, 87–111, 114, 120, 155, 161
Ballagas, R., 42, 50, 109, 141, 149, 155
Barehands, 38
Beaconing, 48
Best practice, 129
Bicycle, 127, 219
Biometrics, 15, 98, 131
Blinds, 145, 274, 275
BlueBoard, 43
Bluetooth, 202, 203, 304
Borchers, J., 3, 11, 24, 135, 155, 261–310
Boundary, 35, 53, 242, 276
Boundary Principle, 12, 35, 45
Bounded rationality, 114
Budget, 115, 121, 171, 183, 188, 287, 291
Bugs, 45, 146
Building as Power Plant (BAPP), 83–84
Building Investment Decision Support Tool
     (BIDS), 14, 75–76, 80
Bush, V., 247
ButterflyNet, 254
Button, 15, 37, 43, 50, 83, 88, 95–97, 99–103,
     107, 109, 110, 121, 148, 150, 153, 188,
     204, 229, 302, 304, 308

C

Cabling, 25, 69, 73, 281, 298
Calendar, 91, 92
Cancellation, 9, 290
Capture, 3, 9, 17, 23, 24, 36, 39, 53, 59, 88,
     91, 110, 119, 125, 127, 142, 143, 172,
     204, 205, 238, 239, 243–245, 247, 248,
     251, 254, 255, 262, 266, 290
Carbon dioxide (CO_2), 69, 119

Card reader, 98
Carnegie Mellon, 3, 11, 13, 16, 25, 68, 78, 83, 84, 135
CARPE, 248
Ceiling, 17, 43, 49, 73, 74, 115, 129, 135, 137, 140, 144, 145, 265, 271, 272, 274, 277, 279, 300
Ceiling grid pattern, 115, 135, 137, 140, 265, 271, 279–280
Center for building performance and diagnostics (CBPD), 13, 14, 75, 77, 82–84, 135
Center for integrated facilities engineering (CIFE), 36, 51–52
Chair, 82, 97, 130, 144, 146, 147, 193, 195, 201, 203, 219, 267, 276, 277, 281
Charrette, 136–137
Churn, 13, 75, 80
Circulation, 13, 65–67, 82, 133
Clark, 237–239, 243
Clients, 3, 7–9, 17, 40, 44–48, 50, 57, 66, 82, 103, 110, 152, 220, 298, 306
Cockpits, 23, 240
Codes, 4, 5, 8, 40, 43, 44, 47, 50, 52, 66, 99, 104, 105, 132, 225, 246, 248, 255
Coffee machine, 126, 133
Cognitive attractor, 3, 11, 17, 21, 27, 28, 114, 122, 126–128, 130
Cognitive ethnography, 11, 23, 24, 27, 238, 242–244, 248, 254
Cognitive overflow syndrome (COS), 116–118, 126
Cognitive theories, 56, 239, 240, 254
Cognitive worker, 113–119
Cognitive workload, 248
Collaboration, 11–14, 17, 19, 20, 22, 36, 39–41, 55–57, 64–65, 67, 68, 77, 79–82, 122, 127, 129, 143, 186, 193–195, 205, 207, 208, 221, 238, 244, 254
Collaborative place, 13, 65
Collocated group services pattern, 287, 299, 305–309
Co-location, 35, 55, 240
Comfort, 1, 2, 6, 13–15, 25, 56, 64, 67, 68, 74, 79, 83, 84, 114, 118, 119, 129, 135, 140, 144, 147, 218, 221, 251, 272, 274
Commercial-off-the-shelf (COTS), 11, 26, 34, 124
Comparison, 22, 201, 221, 224–226, 232, 235
Computer Supported Collective Work, 1
Computer vision, 244–246, 255
Conference room, 4, 12, 15–16, 19, 35, 38, 87–111, 122, 139, 144, 151, 181, 201

Confidentiality, 92, 251
Confusion, 52
Connectivity, 1, 5, 19, 20, 64, 68, 74, 76, 144, 152–154, 268, 290
Console, 15, 16, 88, 97–99, 102–104, 107, 108
ConsoleUI, 88, 98, 99, 102–104, 110
Context-Aware Computing, 1
Contextual knowledge, 20, 195
Continuous design, 26–28, 115
Contrast, 11, 21, 129, 136, 151, 192, 206, 221, 284, 292, 293
Controllable daylight pattern, 274–278
Controlled projection, 163, 187
Controls, 2, 35, 69, 88, 116, 161, 194, 216, 244, 274
Convener, 132, 133
Cooling, 70, 72, 73, 83, 84, 284, 296, 297
Cost, 1, 9, 15, 18, 75, 79, 80, 116, 119, 121, 124, 128, 129, 146, 147, 152, 178, 218, 244–246, 250, 255
Counter-reference, 146
Coupling, 128, 130, 204, 306
Creativity, 67, 68, 145, 147, 160, 185
Crossroads, 13, 65–67, 262
Cubicle, 67
Customization, 72, 88

D
DataHeap, 45–47, 49
Deaf, 24, 240, 244, 251–253
Debrief, 94, 124, 126, 219
Decommissioning, 71
Decoupling to make system more flexible, 46
Designers, 2, 3, 7, 14, 15, 18, 23, 24, 27, 28, 39, 41, 43, 53, 57, 75, 123, 124, 128, 130, 132–134, 137, 143, 160, 174, 181, 216, 224, 229, 231, 261
Designing, 2–4, 10, 11, 15–16, 22, 24–26, 28, 32, 87–111, 113, 116, 119, 124, 126, 132, 134, 168, 179, 207, 208, 223, 228, 229, 238, 241, 244, 253–255, 261
Design patterns, 11, 18, 24–25, 204, 261–310
Desktop, 25, 33, 42, 49–50, 52, 73, 120, 127, 133, 152, 154, 204, 248, 267, 284, 287, 290, 296, 310
Determinism principle, 214
Diamond Touch, 36, 41, 251, 252
Digital ethnography, 17, 22, 114, 140–143, 153
Digital table, 252, 253
Digitization, 113–116, 153
Disappearing computing, 1, 7, 29
Dispersion, 2, 193, 194, 210

Displays, 8, 32, 66, 88, 122, 170, 197, 228, 251, 265
Dissemination, 4, 114, 208
Distractions, 41, 81
Distributed cognition, 3, 11, 21–24, 27, 130, 204, 237–256, 295
Document, 47, 55, 80, 89–92, 104, 106, 107, 118, 124, 129, 137, 154, 181, 204, 218, 239, 244, 248, 250, 253–254, 267, 268, 290, 308
DOME, 4, 17, 114, 150, 153
Dourish, P., 202, 238
DumbleTag, 121, 149, 150
Dynamism, 11, 33

E
eBeam, 37, 58, 287
EditWear, 248
Education, 20, 36, 40, 206, 207, 224, 239
Electricité de France (EDF), 3, 11, 16, 17, 19, 21, 25, 113, 114, 140, 144, 149, 151, 154, 167, 192, 229, 272, 274, 276–278, 281, 286, 295
Electronic place (EP), 13, 65, 76, 78
email, 17, 90–92, 115, 116, 118, 125, 127, 130, 218, 248, 253
Embodied cognition, 241
Emergence, 239, 242
Emergent effects, 4, 6
Enclave, 115, 138–140
Engineering, 21, 36, 40, 51, 63, 67–69, 75, 77, 84, 98, 130, 131, 192, 213–215, 217, 262, 263
Entheasy, 124
Envelope, 70, 71, 115, 135, 137
Environmental sustainability, 14, 69
Ergonomics, 19, 69, 80, 213, 215, 217
Errors, 52, 56, 103, 104, 129, 183, 186, 204
Ethnographers Workbench, 246
Ethnographic studies, 16, 243
Ethnography, 11, 17, 22–24, 27, 114, 140–144, 153, 238, 242–244, 248, 254
European Disappearing Computer Privacy Design Guidelines, 7
Evaluation, 3, 11, 18, 21, 22, 26, 27, 53, 69, 79, 82, 119, 124, 134, 178, 206, 214, 216, 218–222, 225, 227, 229, 255
Event Heap, 12, 42, 44–46, 48, 50–52, 57, 58, 203, 204, 304, 306
Event logging, 23
Event networking pattern, 304
Event sink, 52
Event source, 52
Event space, 228

Executive, 15–16, 76, 87–111, 114, 118, 143, 146, 149
Experimental reality, 12, 16–17, 113–154
Externalities, 26, 28, 131

F
Face, 2, 5, 7, 8, 11, 33, 93, 98, 109, 143, 145, 221, 243, 246, 247, 268
Face detection, 247
Face-to-face, 89–90, 127, 251, 252
Facility manager, 3, 13, 25, 131, 137
Failure, 9, 11, 12, 14, 33, 34, 44–46, 71, 98, 121, 124, 128, 132, 143, 146, 147, 150, 182, 228, 229, 291
False alarms, 246
Fasade, 20, 206
Feedback, 90, 97, 98, 110, 111, 122, 149, 152, 160, 167, 173, 178, 185, 194, 195, 252, 266, 291, 304
FEEL, 20, 207–208
Fingerprint, 98, 107
Flash, 16, 102–104
Flexibility, 12–14, 25, 70, 78, 84, 99, 135, 136, 143, 160, 166, 216, 247, 267, 285, 295
Flexible furniture pattern, 276
Floor, 37, 38, 48, 69, 73–75, 82, 136, 137, 139, 140, 144, 148, 181, 198, 207, 264, 265, 270, 271, 279, 281, 282, 288, 294, 295, 301
Floorplan, 20, 138, 139, 300
FlowMenu, 37, 41, 52, 53, 58
Fluid interaction, 32–33, 36, 40–43, 52, 124
Folding table, 144, 147
Foundation Maison des Sciences de l'Homme, 155
Fox, A., 11, 31–58, 88
Fraunhofer-IPSI, 3, 25
Friendly user, 19, 144, 183–185, 189
Fuji-Xerox Palo Alto Laboratory, 15
Furniture, 1, 17, 68, 72, 74, 129, 135, 136, 139, 144–148, 164, 168, 181, 193, 261, 265, 271, 273, 276, 277, 281, 283, 295, 298

G
GATEP, 139
Gestalt, 126
Gibson, J.J., 130
Goal, 2, 4, 7, 8, 14, 20–22, 24, 26–28, 34, 36, 52, 68–69, 78–79, 81–84, 88, 98, 99, 110, 119, 123, 124, 143, 184, 185, 188, 197, 205–207, 214–225, 229, 231–235, 238, 242–244, 248, 254, 262

Goodwin, C., 238, 239, 243
GPS, 244, 245
Granularity, 203, 266
Graphic user interface (GUI), 49, 53, 121
Grid, 54, 71–74, 115, 135, 137, 140, 265, 271,
      279, 280, 284
Gridboard, 120, 133, 149, 151–154
GroupBoard, 36
GSA, 78, 79, 82

H
Halo effect, 132, 223–224
Haptics, 1
Hartkopf, V., 3, 12–14, 16, 25, 63–84, 137,
      267, 270
Health, 65, 66, 68, 69, 72, 79–84, 296
HelloWall, 228–231
Heterogeneity, 4–6, 11, 33, 44
Hollan, J.D., 6, 10, 22, 130, 213, 237–256
Horikiri, K., 6, 15
Hutchins, 6, 10, 22, 23, 130, 133, 142, 213,
      237–256
HVAC, 14, 64, 68, 70–72, 137

I
iClock, 201
Identification, 8, 9, 149, 185, 202, 203, 220,
      222, 224, 225, 233, 234, 246
iDog, 42
iLounge, 35, 43, 149, 197–205, 207,
      210, 267, 270, 277, 286, 288,
      294, 304, 310
Immersion, 63
Inagaki, M., 15
Indexing, 122, 142
Individual Place, 67, 76
Information Technology Enabled
      Sustainability Testbed (ITEST), 83
Informed consent, 143
Infrared, 140, 287
Infrastructure, 2, 11–14, 16, 25, 32–35, 39,
      42–51, 56–58, 64, 68, 69, 71–75, 78, 83,
      91, 135–137, 140, 144, 150, 170, 193,
      208, 268, 281, 295, 299, 303, 305, 306
Institution, 2, 16, 17, 25, 27, 28, 32, 57, 114,
      119, 120, 128, 130, 131, 134, 192, 249,
      250, 264, 268, 270, 282, 310
Integration, 2, 12, 14, 20, 32–35, 37, 41, 45,
      58, 64, 67–69, 79, 80, 82–84, 99, 196,
      204, 254, 256
Intelligent Workplace (IW), 13, 14, 25, 64,
      67–71, 74, 77–78, 82–84

Intelligent Workplace Energy Supply System
      (IWESS), 83–84
Interaction design, 12, 20, 32, 42, 57, 131,
      204, 262, 266
Interactive mural, 12, 37–40, 52, 53, 58
Interactive table pattern, 288
Interactive wall, 199–201, 203, 268, 285–287,
      292, 294, 296, 298, 300, 306
Interactive wall pattern, 286
Interactive workspace, 11–12, 31–58, 194,
      197, 210, 266, 267, 306, 310
InterfaceCrafter, 42, 47, 49, 50, 58
Internal conditions, 21, 214
Interview, 16, 89, 91, 92, 123, 140, 162, 166,
      171, 177, 231, 243
iPong, 43
iRoom, 11, 25, 35, 37–40, 42, 43, 47, 48, 54,
      55, 57, 58, 203, 266, 267, 271, 272,
      276, 281, 286, 288, 294, 300, 303, 304,
      308, 310
iRoom Operating System (iROS), 11–13, 32,
      34–36, 40, 42–48, 50, 53, 57–59, 203,
      204, 268
iSpace, 19, 40, 45, 50, 58–59, 202,
      205–206, 267
iStuff, 40, 42, 43, 50–51, 58, 121, 149, 202,
      204, 267, 308
iTable, 36, 38, 39, 41, 51, 58
iWall, 56, 58
iWand, 202, 204
IW Intelligent Workplace, 13, 14, 25, 64,
      67–71, 74, 77–78, 82–84

J
Jansson, C.G., 5, 19, 120, 191–210, 310
Jégou, F., 7, 10, 12, 16–19, 135, 144,
      159–189
Johanson, B., 11, 31–58, 203, 310

K
K1, 13, 16, 114, 115, 132, 134–138,
      140, 149, 153
Keyboard, 5, 41, 48, 127, 133, 145, 147, 149,
      152, 197, 200, 202, 204, 218, 248, 251,
      284, 306
Kirsh, D., 155
K2LAB, 192
K1 testbed, 16, 132, 134
KTH, 3, 11, 19, 20, 25, 35, 40, 43, 149, 191,
      192, 197, 198, 203, 206–208, 267, 270,
      274, 277, 286, 288, 294, 304, 310
Kumo, 25, 90

L

Laboratory of Design for Cognition (LDC),
  16, 19, 21, 25, 114, 115, 118, 125, 132,
  142, 154, 229, 295
Lack of time, 115, 116
Lahlou, S., 1–29, 113–154, 193, 213, 217,
  218, 224, 226, 227, 234
Laptop, 25, 32, 33, 36–39, 41, 42, 48, 50,
  55–58, 89, 90, 98, 103, 105, 197, 199,
  201, 202, 204, 209, 277, 282–284, 288,
  290, 296–298, 302, 303, 306, 307
Lata, 28, 126, 128
Lave, J., 239
Layers, 2–4, 13, 17, 47, 107, 108, 131, 132,
  136, 144–146
Layers of ownership, 63
Leadership, 13, 65, 66, 91
Leont'ev, A.N., 213–215
Life cycle, 14, 69, 71, 74, 124
Lifelogging, 140
Lighting, 14, 69–72, 74, 83, 84, 111, 137, 144,
  145, 151, 187, 188, 284
Livescribe, 254
Living laboratories, 2, 64, 67–71, 82,
  83, 115
Lobby, 65, 66
Location of data, 8
Loftness, V., 11–13, 25, 63–84, 135
Lomov, B.F., 21, 131, 213, 215, 216, 219
Loss of time, 75
Lounge, 132, 133, 139, 144, 145, 148

M

Magic Bowl, 43, 204
Maintenance, 2–5, 114, 115, 118–121, 124,
  147, 150
Management, 4, 11, 14, 33, 41, 51, 53, 57, 64,
  69–71, 79, 82, 89, 91, 109, 116,
  131–133, 152, 154, 161, 162, 174,
  206–208, 304
Mattsson, J., 149, 155, 206
Media boards pattern, 283
Mediating structure, 17, 23, 28, 133
Meeting place, 13, 65, 67, 76
Meeting room, 2, 4–6, 11, 15, 17, 65, 66, 82,
  88, 91–93, 109, 114, 119, 122,
  131–134, 137, 139, 140, 144–153, 168,
  181, 209, 267, 270, 285, 287
Meeting types, 16, 93
Memex, 247
Mental model, 8, 120, 133, 152, 217
Metrics, 64
Misuse, 27, 131

Mobile, 16, 20, 23, 25, 32, 39, 76, 103,
  109–110, 124, 144–148, 191–194, 197,
  198, 202, 207, 208, 210, 218, 220, 267,
  268, 277, 281, 284–289, 299–301, 310
Mobile Walls, 25, 198, 267
Mock-up, 18, 124, 165, 168, 172, 178, 181
Modular, 13, 14, 45, 46, 69–71, 73, 74, 137,
  176–177
Modular restartability, 46, 47
Moisture, 203
Mother room, 12, 17, 27, 134, 144, 153, 154
Motives, 2, 20, 21, 27, 121, 124, 214–217
Mouse, 20, 37, 48, 133, 147, 152, 202, 248,
  302–306
Multibrowse, 42, 47, 49, 55, 56, 58, 204
Multimodal, 20, 50, 122, 124, 206, 244, 249,
  251–253, 255, 256
Multiplicities, 11, 34, 35

N

Nardi, B.A., 20, 217, 239
National Environmental Assessment Toolkit
  (NEAT), 82
Never-endingness, 4–5, 12, 17, 26–28, 119,
  134, 144, 153, 154
Node, 13, 14, 53, 54, 72–74, 152, 264
Noise, 25, 151, 246, 251, 267, 268, 283, 285,
  289, 293, 294, 296, 297
Nomadic, 5, 139, 143, 154
Nomura, S., 155, 250
Norman, D.A., 21, 159, 216, 263
Nosulenko, V., 3, 11, 12, 17, 20, 21, 23, 119,
  130, 213–235
NO_x, 69

O

Oblivion, 10
Observation, 10, 15–17, 24, 35, 88, 89, 91–93,
  114–116, 123, 124, 134, 140–144, 153,
  159, 160, 165, 175, 178, 183, 184, 186,
  187, 194, 195, 203, 209, 213, 217, 218,
  225, 229, 238, 241–243, 250, 267, 272
Obsolescence, 14, 70–74
OECD privacy guidelines, 10
OffSat, 17, 115, 129, 140–142, 229, 231
Openness, 4, 5, 8, 19, 27, 209
Open space, 138, 140
Operation, 4, 5, 7–9, 15, 16, 22, 23, 47, 48,
  70–71, 83, 101, 106, 118, 121, 132,
  134, 139, 147, 149, 204, 215, 216, 221,
  226, 241, 293
Organizational flexibility, 14, 78, 84

Oshanin, D.A., 219
Overface, 12, 14, 15, 26, 33, 42, 47, 58, 301
Overface pattern, 308
Overheads, 43, 47, 56, 105, 114, 118, 119,
     143, 248, 274
Overload, 10, 116, 127, 157
Override, 149

P

Panoramic, 142
Paper, 12, 24, 28, 43, 52, 84, 89–94, 97, 115,
     116, 124, 146, 154, 169, 178, 182, 198,
     201, 202, 244, 251, 253–255, 267
PapierCraft, 253, 254
Partitions, 34, 136, 137, 139
PatchPanel, 50–51, 58, 304
Patterns, 3, 11, 18, 24–25, 126, 128–130,
     135, 149, 161, 181, 187, 197, 200,
     204, 205, 228, 229, 241, 244, 247–249,
     255, 256, 261–310
Payback, 75
Payment, 8, 120, 121
Pen, 32, 37, 41, 42, 47, 52, 53, 147, 253, 254
Perceived quality, 21, 22, 25, 27, 134, 214,
     219–229, 231–235
Personal Aura, 167
Personal digital assistant (PDA), 15, 33, 37,
     42, 50, 97, 98, 125, 167, 218, 224, 300
Pervasive computing, 1, 192
Phenomenological tunnel, 17, 123, 124
Physical token, 122
Physicians, 24, 240, 244, 251
Piper, A., 251, 252
Plasma, 25, 36, 201, 284, 296
Plug-and-play, 14, 70, 72, 78, 104
PointRight, 42, 47–48, 54, 55, 58, 204
Politecnico di Milano, 11, 17
Portapres, 140
PostBrainstorm, 37, 41, 52–53, 58
Power outlet, 148
Prante, T., 155
Prescribed behavior, 7
Presentation, 6, 17, 21, 23, 38, 41, 45, 47, 89,
     90, 92–94, 97, 99–102, 107–110,
     118–120, 126–131, 137, 141, 147, 150,
     153, 163, 167, 168, 177, 181, 203,
     216–219, 223, 227–229, 231, 233, 240,
     242, 244, 248, 250, 251, 254–256, 267,
     268, 270, 276, 284–286, 301, 304, 308
Presentation wall, 268
Privacy, 4, 6–10, 29, 67, 72, 81, 110, 120, 122,
     135, 143, 174, 175, 188, 203, 209, 222
Privacy dilemma, 7

Privacy razor, 7–9
Privacy reduction, 8
Proactive services, 20, 206
Productivity, 14, 64, 68, 74–84, 215, 296
Product-service system, 159–163, 167, 169,
     172, 173, 175, 176, 179–183, 186–188
Profile, 8, 92, 98, 225
Project Impro, 174–176
Projector, 37–39, 42, 48, 88, 89, 98, 105–107,
     109, 147, 268, 274, 277, 283–289,
     292–294, 296, 297, 300, 304, 308
Project place (PP), 13, 65, 67, 76, 77
Project room, 65, 82
Project space, 33, 36, 40, 82, 115, 132, 133,
     136, 138, 139, 144
Prototyping, 11, 12, 20, 27, 33, 34, 42, 50,
     124, 160, 181–184, 189, 267
Psychology, 21, 27, 28, 130, 131, 213–215,
     217, 240, 242, 243

Q

Quality, 2, 14, 18, 20–22, 25, 27, 42, 64, 67,
     69, 71, 72, 74, 79, 82, 123, 129, 134,
     136, 143, 144, 146, 151, 178, 198, 199,
     209, 214, 215, 218–225, 227, 228,
     231–235, 255, 290–292

R

Rabardel, P., 214, 217
Raised floor pattern, 281
RAO, 17, 114, 119, 132–135, 139–141,
     144–153
ReadWear, 248
Realism, 18, 26–28
Rear projection pattern, 292
Reboot, 11, 104, 150, 284
Reception, 47, 65, 66, 118
Reciprocity, 10
Recovery, 11, 34, 110, 204, 268
Redboard, 40, 58
Redundancy, 70
Rekimoto, J., 42, 201
Remote, 36, 41, 53–55, 57–59, 88, 90, 98,
     105, 107, 108, 137, 140, 145, 147–150,
     165, 171, 175, 176, 186, 201, 202, 209,
     210, 229, 231, 274, 276, 291, 300,
     302–304
Representation, 6, 17, 21, 23, 45, 110,
     118–120, 126–128, 130, 131, 137,
     163, 181, 216–219, 223, 227, 228,
     231, 233, 240, 242, 244, 250, 251,
     254–256, 301, 308

Research on User-Friendly Augmented
    Environments (RUFAE), 2, 3, 16, 17,
    25, 141, 149, 155, 199, 209, 210, 265,
    267, 276, 310
Resistance, 130
Retention, 66, 75, 82
Return on investment (ROI), 14, 115, 154
RFID, 4, 15, 20, 43, 98, 107, 108, 140,
    148–150, 202, 203, 207
Robustness, 11, 58, 267
Röcker, C., 155
Roomba, 148
Room conferencing pattern, 290
Room controller, 48–50, 274, 275, 285, 287,
    299–302, 308
Room controller pattern, 300
Room shell pattern, 294
Rubinstein, S.L., 21, 213–215
Russian activity theory (RAT), 20–22
RWTH, 3, 11, 267, 270, 310

S
Samoylenko, E., 17, 20, 21, 23, 119, 130,
    213–235
Sandbox, 153
Satisficing, 27
Scalability, 146, 150, 151
Scanner, 40, 43, 65, 268
Scenario, 11, 16, 18–20, 27, 50, 79, 80, 88,
    94–98, 160–177, 187, 189, 193,
    199–200, 204, 205, 208, 210, 251, 265,
    271, 274, 285
Scenario Co-design, 18, 160–177, 187, 189
Schedule, 73, 94, 106, 108, 119, 149, 173, 200
Screen, 15, 25, 37, 38, 43, 48, 49, 52, 53, 55,
    56, 58, 59, 76, 88, 89, 98–104, 107,
    109, 120, 121, 124, 127, 129, 130, 133,
    140, 141, 145, 147–149, 151–153, 165,
    170, 171, 201, 202, 207, 209, 218, 225,
    227–231, 248, 252–254, 268, 274, 277,
    283–288, 291–297, 306–308
Screen capture, 3, 23
Script, 104, 107, 128, 249
Secretary, 132
Self-configuration, 20
Self confrontation, 123, 218
Semantic Rubicon, 4, 12, 14, 28, 35, 131
SenseCam, 140
Sensing, 4, 19, 83, 110, 146
Serendipity, 76
Service pubs, 13, 65
ServiceTag, 120, 140, 148–150, 152, 154
Shadowing, 123

Sidetrack, 17, 125, 128
SIFT, 246
Silent technology pattern, 296
Simplicity, 10, 43, 47, 88, 152
Situated, 123, 140, 187, 214, 243, 301
SMART, 6, 15, 38, 39, 276, 284, 286, 287,
    292, 293
SmartBoard, 53, 88, 105
SmartPresenter, 59
SO_2, 69
Social conventions, 12, 35–36, 303
Social networking, 65–67, 81
Social place, 67, 76
Social protocol pattern, 302
Solar heating, 70
Sound, 20, 38, 88, 118, 123, 136, 139, 142,
    151, 193, 195, 199, 203, 209, 221, 251,
    264, 265, 277
Speech bubble, 252, 253
Sponsor, 14, 40, 118, 154
Spot Experiment, 18, 160, 182, 183
500 square feet pattern, 263–265, 270–272,
    276, 279, 281, 285, 294
SSI, 251, 252
Stackable, 144, 146
Stairs, 66
Stakeholder, 3, 7, 10, 11, 13, 14, 25, 123,
    130–132, 137, 161, 162, 167, 169
Stanford, 3, 11, 12, 19, 25, 32, 35–37, 40, 41,
    55, 57, 142, 203, 205, 206, 209,
    266–268, 270, 272, 276, 281, 286, 288,
    294, 300, 304, 310
Stanford Interactive Workspaces Project,
    11–12, 31–58, 266, 306
Story-board, 38, 166, 167, 169, 170, 173,
    179, 186
Strategic Design Scenarios, 17, 170, 171
Streitz, N., 3, 42, 64, 88, 194, 286–288, 308
SubCam, 3, 17, 23, 27, 114, 119, 122–130,
    134, 140, 143, 153
Subfilms, 123, 124
Subgoal, 21, 22, 221, 223
Suchman, L.A., 7, 239
Sustainability, 10, 14, 17, 69, 83, 170, 176
Synchronization, 195–196
System response, 16, 109, 128, 149, 181, 225

T
TabEc, 146, 147
Table, 33, 36, 38, 39, 41, 43, 52, 54, 56, 58,
    94, 97, 139, 149, 170, 176, 199–203,
    251–253, 268, 276, 277, 283, 285, 286,
    288, 289, 296, 300, 302

Tablet, 43, 97, 98, 103, 104, 146, 147, 201, 202, 253, 254, 300, 301
Tabletop control, 15
Tackable surfaces, 267
Tag, 5, 121, 132, 148–150, 152, 203, 204, 253
Tasks, 4, 12, 14, 21, 22, 32, 33, 35, 36, 47, 55, 56, 66, 72, 76, 79, 81, 90, 91, 94–100, 104, 107, 109, 116, 125, 133, 134, 194, 195, 197, 198, 203, 205–208, 216, 218, 222–231, 241, 243, 246, 247, 253, 263, 268, 270, 276, 277, 284–286, 296, 300, 302, 308
Team, 11, 13–18, 21, 27, 35, 36, 38, 40, 41, 56, 57, 64, 67, 76, 77, 79–83, 89, 123, 134, 137, 153, 154, 159, 160, 162, 164–167, 170–188, 191, 193, 194, 204–207, 209, 210, 229, 254, 266, 267, 270
Teamspace, 35, 36, 40, 55–56, 59, 204, 209
Technological adaptability, 14, 68–69, 78
Teleconferencing, 35, 55, 88
Temperature, 72, 203
Testbed, 12, 16, 17, 31, 83, 84, 114, 132, 134, 138, 266, 267
Third-party, 9
Tidebreak, 40, 57, 204, 306
Tiling tables, 267
Time, 2, 32, 66, 89, 114, 160, 193, 213, 238, 265
To-do list, 116
Toilets, 133, 139, 140, 144, 148, 149
Token, 9, 43, 108, 109, 120, 122, 132, 150, 204, 209
Touch-screen display, 56
Tracking, 20, 37, 203, 239, 241, 247
Transaction, 6, 8, 9, 47
Transportation, 119
Triple determination framework, 114, 130–133
Triple determination system, 131
Troubadour, 149
Trust, 9, 16, 99, 107, 108, 111, 135, 143, 146, 154
Tunneling, 127
Tuplespace, 44, 306
Typed drag-and-drop, 53

U

Ubiquitous computing, 1, 4, 12, 19, 28, 32, 34, 35, 42, 45, 192–196, 255, 310
Ubiquitous working environments, 19–20, 191–210

UCSD, 23, 25, 142, 238, 295
Usability, 5, 17, 19, 40, 88, 122, 125, 153
Usable smart environments (USE), 15, 88, 89, 94, 97–99, 103, 104, 109–111
User-centred approach, 159, 160, 173, 178
User experience, 11, 12, 20, 32, 181, 263
User-friendly, 2, 20, 28, 135, 183, 193, 261
Users, 1, 32, 69, 88, 114, 159, 191, 215, 246, 261
User studies, 12, 20, 23, 53, 55, 99, 199, 204, 205

V

Ventilation, 14, 70, 71, 73, 83, 137, 144, 151
Verbal description, 22, 262
Verbal portrait, 22, 224–227
Verbal recoding, 262
Videoconference, 2, 3, 19, 99, 102, 107, 133, 135, 139–141, 145, 148, 149, 151, 152, 229, 231
Videomaton, 231–233
VideoSketching, 18, 163–165, 174, 175
Video trolley, 148
Viral diffusion, 153
Virtual Auditorium, 39, 53–55, 59
Volatility Principle, 45

W

Wall, 33, 38–40, 42, 54, 56, 58, 69, 74, 136, 146, 187, 188, 195, 197–201, 203, 232, 265, 267, 268, 271, 272, 276, 277, 283, 285–288, 292–294, 296–298, 300, 306, 308
Waste, 69–71, 118, 182, 267, 277
Wearable, 17, 32, 123, 202, 310
WebDiver, 142
Weblabs, 20, 207
Wheel, 127, 139, 144, 219, 246, 267, 277, 278, 284, 285
Whiteboards, 15, 37, 43, 66, 88, 89, 92, 93, 98, 105–107, 145–147, 198, 203, 284
White collar, 113, 116, 117
Window space pattern, 272
Winograd, T., 3, 4, 11, 14, 19, 28, 31–59, 131, 266, 303, 306
Wireless, 33, 38–40, 48, 50, 89, 140, 148, 192, 193, 196, 197, 200–202, 204, 208, 218, 268, 279, 281, 284, 298, 301, 303

Wizard, 4, 15, 27, 88, 115, 132, 133, 148, 150
Wizard of Oz, 19, 124, 183
W2K bug, 118
Workflow, 88–91, 93, 94, 122, 126, 127, 154, 217
WorkspaceNavigator, 36, 39, 40, 53, 204
Workstation, 14, 23, 33, 37, 54, 69, 72–74, 118–120, 140, 150, 244, 247–249, 255, 270

X
Xerox, 1, 15, 16, 65, 143

Z
Zavalova, 219
Zero, 45, 55, 84, 106, 119–122, 152
Zero list, 17, 119, 122, 152, 154
ZoomScape, 41, 52–53